Creative Home Schooling for Gifted Children: A Resource Guide

Lisa Rivero

Creative Home Schooling for Gifted Children: A Resource Guide

Cover Design: ATG Productions
Interior Design/Layout: The Printed Page

Published by Great Potential Press, Inc.
(formerly Gifted Psychology Press, Inc.)
P.O. Box 5057
Scottsdale, AZ 85261
www.giftedbooks.com

ISBN: 0-910707-48-0

06   05   04   03   02   6   5   4   3   2   1

Library of Congress Cataloging-in-Publication Data
Rivero, Lisa
    Creative home schooling for gifted children: a resource guide / Lisa Rivero
       p. cm.
    Includes bibliographical references (p.) and indexes.
    ISBN 0-910707-48-0
       1. Gifted children--Education--United States. 2. Home schooling--United States. 3.
Educational acceleration. I. Title

LC3993.2 .R58 2002
371.95--dc21

2002019166

Dedicated to the gifted and creative men in my life:
Harley,
Vincent and Paul,
Al, with all my love, and
Albert, my greatest teacher.

And in memory of Alice.

Acknowledgments

The heart and soul of this book are the parents and children who willingly and generously shared their experiences, concerns, and advice about what it's like for gifted children to learn at home. They offer invaluable examples of what education can be if we open our minds to new possibilities.

Several people read the manuscript and offered ideas and advice that improved the book immeasurably. I would particularly like to thank Kathi Kearney, Kathleen Kustusch, and Laura Wynia for their careful readings and thoughtful comments.

I am honored to have been able to work with Jim Webb and everyone at Great Potential Press who believed in the importance of this topic, and I owe a particular debt to my editor, Janet Gore, whose vision for this book and whose magic with words taught me more about writing than I ever learned in a classroom. My appreciation as well goes to Jen Ault Rosso for her careful proof reading and to Alicia Fox and Lynn Gudhus for their assistance in planning the publicity and marketing.

Finally, I am very grateful to all of my teachers and informal mentors, both in and outside of the classroom, and to my parents, who gave my brothers and me the room we needed to find our own paths. And most of all, I thank my family, without whose support, patience, and love this book would have never been written.

Preface

This September day could have been like any other. The leaves show sudden splashes of brilliant red and orange and will soon begin to fall. The morning air is just cold enough to remind us of winter, yet the brief afternoon warmth carries lingering memories of summer. We are on the cusp between seasons, preparing for inevitable change.

Yet this September is unlike any other we've known. As I finish this book, I'm acutely aware that readers will view this particular month with an extraordinary perspective. The aftermath of September 11, 2001, is new and raw. Terrorists used four hijacked planes to claim the lives of thousands of people from dozens of countries, destroying the World Trade Center in New York City and part of the Pentagon in Washington, DC, and *everything* feels changed. As a world, we must grapple with new questions and understanding. It will not be easy. In this age of electronic information, parents face unique challenges in helping children find understanding and truth without overwhelming them with graphic images of violence and hatred.

Our son is also on a cusp, in that sometimes-awkward transition between having been a child and getting ready to be a man. Like all other children, he is struggling to make sense of a new world reality—a reality he finds neither comfortable nor welcome. To my surprise, however, and in part due to what we've learned through home schooling, he already has the courage and life skills to search for questions that have no quick or easy answers.

Our immediate response as a family to this tragedy has been to learn more, not just by relying on television news, but by asking questions and by searching for different perspectives and deeper understanding. We've suspended much of our previously scheduled curriculum to read about the Middle East and New York City. We've discussed the human achievement of the World Trade Center, the emotional attachment that human beings feel for special pieces of architecture, and the number of countries who lost citizens. We've talked about how we take for granted our police force, fire fighters, and rescue workers.

The recent tragedies bring home to us why we home school. We home school, in the words of Annemarie Roeper, to educate for life rather than simply to educate for success. Not until recently, however, did I begin to understand the full scope and significance of that idea.

Even before the tragedy, our son had begun to move from the summer of Asimov to the autumn of World Religions, showing a great interest in the religious histories and sacred texts of different cultures. We trust his innate drive and ability to learn, even—and especially—when the subject matter is outside the usual notions of what constitutes a K-12 education. His growing interest in and willingness to ask life's big questions is helping him deal with the recent events with compassion and courage, with the understanding that sometimes there are more questions than answers.

When we met with our home school support group this week—the first meeting of the new "school" year—I was nearly overwhelmed with emotion as I watched the children discard their troubles for games of tag and capture the flag. Our group—a mixture of ages, cultures, and faiths, including Christians, Jews, and Muslims—is a welcome normalcy in an otherwise troubled time, and I appreciated as never before the acceptance and openness of the families who came together as one that day.

I began to understand on a new level. We don't learn about architecture or read great books or study world countries in order "to home school." We home school so that we're free to learn about life in its unpredictable complexity. We home school to ask questions and to seek answers for ourselves, to put ourselves in another's place, to begin to forge new connections and relationships for a new global community, to do our small part as citizens of the world.

Our son has often asked what his generation will be called, having heard about the Baby Boomers, the Me Generation, and Generation X. I told him yesterday that perhaps his generation will be Generation Hope, a fresh generation of compassionate young people who know no boundaries or borders, who will use their creativity to find new solutions, who will work and live together rather than push one another apart.

My hope is that we will each do what we can to ensure that all children, with their unique and individual gifts and talents, with all their creativity and sensitivity—whether they learn at home or in schools—will be educated for life and all that life brings.

—LMR, September 19, 2001

Foreword

Homeschooling gifted children poses two great challenges for parents, namely 1) we weren't homeschooled ourselves; and 2) many of us are probably less gifted than our children, or at least feel that way. So we are cast adrift on a journey with neither compass nor map; sometimes it feels like there is a small being from another planet in the boat!

Giftedness, whether of the intellectual or other varieties, exists on a continuum like most other human characteristics. But the reality that it presents itself on a continuum should not be a reason to call its existence into question. To say, as some are wont to do, that 'all children are gifted' makes no more sense than saying that 'all children are disabled'.

But what is true is that all children are *gifts*, and individual and unique ones. To deny this or to act as if this isn't so is irresponsible, and remains irresponsible even if it is the guiding principle behind public education in our country. We might labor to change this principle, and we must, but our kids can't wait, and we are casting off.

Because she and her husband have occupied their own little boat with her son, Lisa Rivero shares the great secret of homeschooling the gifted child, and this is to let him or her steer. One quickly learns anyway that you can't really choose otherwise, for his hand is stuck to the tiller, and he is guided by the light of his own stars. You, dear parents, whether you like it or not, are just along for the ride. What comes through clearly in Lisa Rivero's eloquent writing is that one does not homeschool a gifted child; one homeschools *with* a gifted child.

Creative Home Schooling for Gifted Children is a guidebook to the sights, sounds, and experiences that will enrich your journey. It will at once reassure anxious parents that you are not alone in this voyage, and it will provide you with tools for thinking creatively about what it means to take primary responsibility for your gifted child's education. Her "Questions for Reflection" help provide an orientation to the undertaking, as do extended quotations reflecting what other parents and homeschoolers have learned along the way. Comprehensive reading lists related to both homeschooling and gifted children, an excellent section on learning styles, and attention to the questions parents most frequently ask—all make *Creative Home Schooling for Gifted Children* an indispensable resource.

As my own journey with two gifted (but very different and unique) children draws to its conclusion, Creative Home Schooling for Gifted Children reminds me how much I'd like to do it again!

David H. Albert
Author, *And the Skylark Sings with Me: Adventures in Homeschooling and Community-Based Education*, and columnist, *Home Education Magazine*

Contents

List of Tables

Introduction

[W]e learn by chess the habit of not being discouraged by present bad appearances in the state of our affairs, the habit of hoping for a favorable change, and that of persevering in the search of resources.

—Benjamin Franklin, *Morals of Chess*

I often take my work with me while our home schooled son is engaged in outside activities such as ice skating lessons, open gym time, or community classes for children at a local university. He particularly enjoys a weekend chess gathering at a bookstore, facilitated by an enthusiastic instructor known to the children simply as David. The gathering is informal—usually about a dozen children ranging in ages from five to 12. To make the most of my time alone, a rare commodity for home school parents, I sit at the café on the sidelines with my writing and a cup of coffee.

Usually, I don't work much at the café. As is the case with many home school families who have discovered the secrets of learning, I find what is going on in real life around me far more instructive and valuable than the work I had planned to do.

I notice the way David manages the action, greeting each child with a smile as he or she arrives. "Glad to see you!" he says, putting an easy hand on the child's shoulder. "So, ready to play chess?" For the first half hour or so, the children play in pairs with no clocks or close supervision. David deftly and subtly suggests partners based on ability level and personalities. After a game, if the combination of players isn't right, the children usually move on to a new partner. When they find a match that "clicks," they often play game after game together, talking and laughing and competing. Sometimes David asks a child whether he or she won or lost a particular game. If the child says she lost, he says, "That's okay. What did you learn?"

After about 30 minutes, David sets up a demonstration game on an easel. He lets the children know that he wants to show them something and that they can return to their games later. Most of the children leave their games and watch, but a few remain playing quietly and are not disturbed. David begins with a brief history of the game and players, then starts the moves, asking the children for input, predictions, and reasons for moves. Children bounce in their chairs with excitement over strategies or jump to their feet when they can "see" what move will happen next. At the end of the demonstration, David comments upon the elegance of the game and the beauty of the skill involved rather than on who won or lost. As the children return to their own games, he mingles among them, answering questions and offering suggestions, simply sharing his love of the game with the children.

I am continually struck by the children's love of learning in this setting, their willingness to take risks, their easy competitiveness and lack of anxiety. I never see David treat them as school pupils. I never hear him use a tone of voice that suggests an authoritarian position. The children respond in kind, choosing to come back week after week, responding to his natural authority as someone who knows more about the game than they, and most of the time showing respect for him and other players. David is pleasant with the parents but reserves his focus for the children. If a parent talks about chess in a way that places too much emphasis on achievement or progress or winning, he offers a gentle reminder: "It has to be fun."

Occasionally, another parent comes over to my table to say hello. I feel an unspoken kinship with these parents and their children who choose to spend Sunday afternoons playing chess. These children are all intense, creative, sensitive, self-determined. Sometimes they ask about our son's age or grade as a way to make conversation, and I'm taken aback by the question. It seems out of place in this setting and in our home schooling life in general, but it reminds me that for many people, a child's age and grade still define who the child is. One of the wonders of home schooling, as in this chess gathering, is that age, grade, and previous school history simply do not matter. We are all free to learn, to explore, and to play according to our own abilities and interests. We are not measured by age or grade. Without these constraints, our life education can now be truly individuated. We can come home to our innate joy of learning.

The Decision to Home School

We didn't always home school. Our son enjoyed a child-centered preschool, followed by kindergarten and part of first grade at our local public school, where he was in a weekly pull-out program for gifted students. In the middle of first grade, he switched to a small private school for gifted learners, which he attended for one and one-half years, and where he made some invaluable and continuing friendships.

In each educational setting, he experienced many of the successes, failures, and challenges familiar to other intense, sensitive learners and their families. His kindergarten teachers were enthusiastic about teaching young children and responsive to his social and emotional needs. When a school-wide assembly proved to be too much stimulation for his sensitive ears and eyes, a teacher's aid kindly asked if he'd like to help her get the classroom ready during the assembly time. She later told me that he talked more in that half hour alone with her in the classroom than he had all year. When he stood in front of his classmates at age four to make an impassioned plea for unconditional acceptance after the class read the book *Rainbow Fish*, his teacher understood and accepted his heightened sensitivity and sense of justice. He didn't seem to mind that so little of the academic work was challenging; he continued to learn other things on his own, at his own initiative, at home.

By first grade, his teacher told us at the first parent conference that in spite of having entered kindergarten one year early, he knew everything she planned to teach that year, so her goals for him were strictly social-emotional. We soon learned that this meant trying to cure his perfectionism and to curb his intense emotional reactions. Like many gifted children, he was "out of sync" with his classmates—behaving his age but far ahead of others in intellectual and conceptual thought and performance. At the same time, his strong emotions often caused him to appear even younger than he was. He began to fear having his name written on the blackboard for misbehavior, even though this disciplinary act never happened to him. He also began think of school as a place to show what he already knew rather than as a place to explore new knowledge. As months went on, we saw his love of learning slowly but surely fade until it was nearly gone. We didn't see our sensitive, gifted son headed on a path of joyful learning.

Second grade at the small, private school posed a different problem. Like many gifted, creative learners, our son can be simultaneously an introverted learner and an extraverted socializer. David Willings (1980), in *The Creatively Gifted: Recognizing and Developing the Creative Potential*, calls this personality the "introverted swashbuckler," a type often misunderstood by peers and teachers. Introverted swashbucklers are self-reliant at young ages, and their dual preference for solitude and society makes them seem inconsistent to the children and adults around them. Such children may have difficulty focusing in a classroom setting and much prefer to have their socialization separate from intense learning experiences. Because our son's classmates, also highly gifted, were equally intense, he was exhausted by the daily interaction and became moody and angry. He had difficulty concentrating on learning in such a high-stimulus environment. Every day he said he'd had a "bad day" at school, but would offer no further details. By the time he came home, he was emotionally and physically drained. By the end of second grade, he seemed at an impasse, neither thriving nor happy most of the time, getting through each day but without a sense of wholeness or purpose.

The option to home school grew in our minds slowly. Both my husband and I had been involved extensively in formal education as students and later as teachers; so, at least academically, the traditional education system had worked for us. I was a technical writing instructor at an engineering college and had just begun to work with gifted elementary school students in the classroom. My husband, a professor of Eighteenth Century British Literature and director of a university honors program, had been a *summa cum laude* Ivy League graduate and a Fulbright scholar.

Of course, from the vantage point of our present adulthood, we tried to forget the excruciating boredom we had once experienced in the classroom, the nagging feeling of being different but not knowing why, the fear of making a mistake or of not living up to one's potential, and most of all, the long days spent waiting for the last bell to ring so we could run home to our favorite books, hobbies, and projects. In my case, I remember spending hours pretending to be the characters from books; being enchanted by the world of *Star Trek* in my middle school years but knowing no other child who liked science fiction; keeping an extensive scrapbook of newspaper clippings from my favorite professional football team; and writing stories in bed, using a flashlight, in the glorious privacy of late night hours. I attended a small, rural elementary school on the Rosebud Sioux Reservation in South Dakota with only two other children in my grade, and I felt inexplicably different from the other dozen or so children in the school. No one else seemed to think or feel as I did. By the time I was ready to move on to the county-wide public high school, I was spending most of my time learning how to conform so I could fit in better. I remember almost nothing of what I learned in school during that time, even though my grades were good and I was valedictorian of my high school class. I entered college on a scholarship with almost no study skills, ashamed to admit that I hadn't a clue how to study for a test or take lecture notes. Not until graduate school did I begin to feel comfortable with myself as an independent, self-directed learner. Looking back, I felt as though most of my prime years of formal schooling had been wasted.

But that is the real world, isn't it? Aren't such difficulties not only necessary but somehow good for us—even character building? If we had managed to live through it, couldn't our son, too?

We decided we wanted something better for our son.

Coming Home

As a result, during the spring months of our son's second-grade year, we stepped out of our comfort zones and opened our minds to alternatives to traditional education. Although we still hadn't decided definitely to home school, we started the process of planning (and deciding) by taking the advice of David Guterson (1992)—award-winning novelist, home school parent, and author of *Family Matters: Why Homeschooling Makes Sense*—to examine our own expectations and goals. We agreed that we were not interested in achievement for achievement's sake. We agreed that the true end of education is neither the best school nor the highest honors—though some students measure success by those milestones on their way—but that excellent education exhibits a joyful and purposeful integration of life and work and learning. Such an education would allow children to find work they love, which might or might not be in the area of their highest potential. Such an education would also help children to know and to be themselves just as they are, with all of their magnificent quirks and passions and insights and ideas, and to find their own place in the world.

We knew from our reading and our own experience that children with traits of the exceptionality known as giftedness think and experience life differently from many other children and therefore need an education carefully tailored to their unique learning styles and interests. Such an education must take into account their abilities to question and think in abstract patterns as well as their complex personalities, fears, joys, and true love of learning. We therefore spent a good deal of time getting to know our son better, paying attention to how he learns best, and noting when his threshold for stimulation was optimal. We knew that our son's intensity means he prefers not to separate learning into times and subjects, and that, perhaps due to his perfectionistic tendencies, formal evaluation seems to interfere with his learning process. We were also aware of his extreme sensitivity. We had watched him react with strong emotions to events and crises in the books he reads or hears. At age three, when he first heard the story of Peter Rabbit's father being eaten in a pie, he burst into tears of sadness. When he saw his preschool teacher act out a scene from the children's book *Caps for Sale*, where a peddler yells at some mischievous chimps, he became inexplicably fearful and upset. We also noticed how he naturally seeks patterns and order and relationships in nearly everything he experiences, and how he finds "busy work" meaningless. We wanted to provide him with an education that could help him realize his sensitivity, idealism, work ethic, and perfectionism as strengths rather than as handicaps or burdens.

Finally, we had to face the toughest questions every parent considering home schooling has to face: "Are we capable of doing this?" "Can we teach our son what he needs to know to succeed?" "How will we meet his social and emotional needs?" "What are they exactly, anyway?" We knew that we had provided an educational environment before he went to school that allowed him to learn freely and joyfully and according to his needs, so we must have been doing something right back then.

So rather than focus on teaching, we began to focus on learning. "Can we adequately help our son to learn?" "Can we help him rediscover how to learn and recover his joy of learning?" "What will his social and emotional needs be when a classroom of age peers is no longer a consideration?"

Once we allowed ourselves to consider seriously the *possibility* of home schooling, the decision was easy and relatively quick. The difficulty was only at the start, when we knew we would be diverging from the well-trodden path of public and private school education. By having a child who was gifted, we were already a minority in the broader community of parents. By home schooling, would we be isolating ourselves even further? Would we find enough support and information? Like so many other parents who seek information on which to make schooling decisions, we studied books, magazines, and Internet resources, and we talked to other parents and teachers in an attempt to understand our son's educational needs and options. We soon discovered that although a "significant percentage" of the estimated 500,000 to 1.2 million children who learn at home are gifted (Ensign, 1997), few written resources exist specifically for parents who are considering home schooling their gifted children.

Most advice for parents about education for gifted children focuses on how to navigate public school programs and services. The advice for parents who home school either skips the issue of giftedness altogether or treats the term "gifted" as a label designed mostly for ambitious parents (Dobson, 1998). A parent may thus be left with the belief that: (1) learning at home is not a wise choice for gifted students, or (2) giftedness ceases to exist as soon as one enters the home schooling realm. Nevertheless, we continued our search for information and insight.

A writer by profession and an avid reader by compulsion, I soon found myself delving into issues of education, home schooling, and giftedness beyond what is presented in the popular press. I became acquainted with several home schooling families in our local area and, through the Internet, across the U.S. and Canada. The more I learned, studied, and listened, the more I became convinced that for many families of precocious and intense learners, home schooling is an educational path that can provide the intellectual, social, and emotional support necessary for a fulfilling life. I found that theoretical research about the needs of gifted children and the practical experiences of home schooling families converge in many areas. Here are examples.

- Whereas gifted children are often uneven in their academic and emotional development, home schooling offers an environment in which grade levels don't matter and in which a child can learn at several different levels simultaneously.

- Whereas gifted children's high levels of sensitivity and perfectionism require understanding of caring adults for discussion, guidance, and support, home schooling gives families the opportunity to research and address specific social and emotional needs of children in a loving and accepting atmosphere.

- Whereas gifted children tend to think in new, divergent, and creative ways and often have a strong internal drive, home schooling offers the chance to integrate meaningful self-direction into the child's education. In addition, home schooling can support rather than limit divergent thinking.

- Whereas gifted children have complex social needs and often need several different sets of peer groups in order to meet those needs, home schooling allows and in fact encourages children to socialize with a variety of groups and ages.

Our deliberations and conclusions—which form the heart of this book—brought us to the inevitable conclusion that home schooling was not only possible, but was the optimal educational option for our family. Once we came to that realization, we knew that we would be doing our son a disservice by providing him with anything less. When we mentioned the idea of home schooling to him, he was more than willing to give it a try, especially after we assured him that we would do everything possible to ensure that he could still see his school friends regularly. A change in my writing schedule allowed me to do all of my work from home; we purchased a couple of extra bookcases for our son's room and were on our way.

Since that beginning, we have watched our son grow emotionally, socially, and intellectually. To say he is happier misses the point somewhat, though he is certainly happier. What seems more important is that he is finding himself and discovering who he wants to be. Many of the inherent characteristics and concomitant struggles of giftedness such as perfectionism, intensity, and sensitivity are still there, but facing them and understanding them is certainly easier. At the same time, many of the struggles—such as being out of sync with traditional grade levels or not being able to capitalize on individual learning styles and preferences—have dropped away.

Deciding to home school has been the most important, the most natural, and the most rewarding educational decision our family has ever made. At no other time in his schooling has our son been more comfortable with himself, more willing to take intellectual risks, or more self-directed in his learning. Home schooling has made us better parents, him a better student, and all of us a happier family.

One of the publicly voiced concerns about home schooling is that it isolates children from society. We have experienced the opposite. Home schooling has broadened, rather than limited, our child's social opportunities and participation in the world in which he lives. A typical week for us includes a home school gym time or group meeting with children of all ages, an afternoon playing and socializing with a core group of friends ages five to 13, bowling after school with former classroom friends, participating in a book discussion group with other home schooled children ages nine to 12, learning with age peers in a Saturday College for Kids program, and of course, playing chess at a bookstore with other children on Sunday afternoon. Our son knows the people who work at the post office, bank, library, grocery store, and other local places of business. He is comfortable being with people of all ages, from preschoolers to older adults, and he has a healthy mixture of close friends and acquaintances,

This book is not about our journey. As I did my research, I gradually began to put together the kinds of resources that I wish I'd had when we started. I decided to write the kind of home schooling book I wish I'd had—one that is informed by the research and scholarship of gifted education and home schooling advocates as well as by the wisdom of other families of home schooled gifted learners who agreed to be interviewed and to share their experiences. You'll meet these families in Chapter 1 and throughout the book. Their experiences and examples offer refreshing alternatives to the stereotype of home school parents who pull their children from school only to push them to go higher and faster or to hide them from the rest of the world. You'll meet parents who seek to discover what learning is all about. Sometimes this means scrambling to keep up with their children's young, quick, creative minds!

This summer has been for us the summer of Asimov. As I work on this introduction on a stormy afternoon, our nine-year-old son has been sorting through his collection of Isaac Asimov novels, essays, and short story collections. With my library books and notes scattered in front of me, I sit at the dining room table as brief snatches of bright summer sunshine steal their way through the window between low rumbles of thunder and approaching Midwest rain showers. Our son kneels comfortably on the living room floor just a few feet away, surrounded by his own library books, science fiction magazines, and notes. Today he is putting together a chronological list of Asimov's short stories, and he has begun to compile a comprehensive guide to which short story anthologies contain which stories. He hums while he works, and every so often, he talks about what he's doing or asks a question. Sometimes he shows me a sample of his work, which was not assigned and is considered part of his free time.

Although on this day I work for only an hour or two, he busily stays with his project most of the day, from about 11:00 a.m. until suppertime. He stops his activity for lunch, to make the salads for supper, and to fold and put away his freshly laundered clothes. After supper, we will probably spend time together as a family reading or talking or watching a movie.

Today could as well be any day of the week when weather prevents us from being outdoors and when we have few outside appointments or activities. Some of our days involve a wide range of subjects, such as watching history documentaries or doing science experiments or studying math. Other days may involve more social interaction or group activities, such as weekly get-togethers with a small group of home schooled children who are equally precocious, intense, and sensitive.

I don't know how long we'll home school, but I do know that for now, home schooling is allowing our son to become comfortable with himself as a learner and a person. I have nothing against public or private schools; I have the highest respect for professional teachers, but the school system as it presently exists is not a good fit for our child. We know home schooling is working, not because of test scores, although our son tests well, but because for the first time in years, he is fitting this description of the appropriately challenged and well-nurtured gifted boy (Kerr & Cohn, 2001).

O He is learning that there are ideas worth falling in love with.

O He is alive to this world and full of the kind of self-esteem that results from real work done well.

O He achieves for the pleasure of achieving, rather than for the fulfillment of external standards, and he is becoming more inner-directed.

O His family supports and understands his intensity.

O He has friendships with both boys and girls.

O He is not shamed for the expression of emotion and is encouraged in his kindness.

O He has a strong sense of self and an emotional resilience.

We are grateful. Home schooling is certainly not for everyone, but for us and for thousands of other families, home schooling offers a respite from sometimes inappropriate education, or in some cases, a long-term or near-permanent alternative to formal education. It is my hope that other families can realize the sense of joy and wholeness home schooling can bring, including reduced stress and the freedom to learn according to the child's need. I hope that this book will serve as a source of support, inspiration, and information for other parents who are considering home schooling a child who is intense, creative, and wonderfully complex.

Pros and Cons of the Word "Gifted"

Parents of gifted children face unique challenges that are seldom discussed or taken seriously by other parents or school personnel. While parents should not become preoccupied with a child's potential nor should they organize the entire family around the gifted child,[1] it is extremely beneficial for parents to be aware of: (1) why their children seem different, and (2) that the difference is real and necessitates unique parenting and educational approaches. I cannot adequately describe the relief I felt when I finally met other parents who, like me, were accused of being pushy when their young children taught themselves to read before school age, or who felt helpless as they watched their child's extreme and painful sensitivity, or who struggled to keep up with the reasoning powers of a six-year-old asking a question a minute.

The temptation for parents whose children are in school is to take advantage of every service for gifted students that is offered to them, even though some gifted

---

1   National Association for Gifted Children: www.nagc.org/CounGuide/family.html.

and talented programming does not serve every gifted student positively. On the other hand, parents whose children learn at home may feel pressure never to let the word "gifted" enter their thoughts, or if it does, to encase it in quotation marks and declare that in the home school setting, every child's gifts flourish, which of course, on one level, is true.

While it may be in vogue (or politically correct) to scoff at any distinction between gifted and more average learners, any parent who has lived with a gifted child knows that gifted children do experience life differently and that efforts to make them fit in with the crowd only serve to reinforce the child's suspicion that "something is wrong with me." When gifted children experience emotional difficulties, the cause is usually *not* their inherent giftedness alone, but the interplay between their gifted traits and the environment (Webb, 2000a), so the more that parents understand the unique needs and challenges of gifted children, the better equipped they are to offer an environment that promotes healthy social and emotional development.

Part of the problem is one of nomenclature. The word "gifted" is ambiguous at best and understandably elicits envy and even hostility, especially if people equate gifted with special or "better." All children are special. All children have talents. Certainly gifted children are not "better" or more valuable than any other children. They are *as* valuable as other children, however, and thus deserve an education that meets their needs.

I debated with myself whether to use a different word for this book so as not to confuse or offend some readers, but the terms that make the most sense to me— "intense learners" and "overexcitable learners"—do not have similar connotations for other readers. "Talented" is the preferred word among many educational professionals these days, but it does not adequately describe the gifted child's true nature and makes me think of talent shows with scrubbed, smiling faces and big blue ribbons—a not entirely benign misrepresentation. Perhaps the word gifted does not adequately describe these enigmatic children either, but other phrases such as "more able learners," "high ability children," "intellectually talented children," and "highly intelligent childr_____ ____ __ better and are certainly less graceful from a writer's standpoint. So_____ _____ _____ _____ __ describe learners wh_____ ___ _____ _____ ___ their learning.

It's interesti___ ___ _____ ____ __ is similarly prob_____ ___ __ _____ and, my person__ _____ _____ of the alterna____ _____ _____ ences for ho_____ ___ _____ _____ decision t_____ ___ ___ ___ chooling"_____ ____ __ ___ would h____ ____ ____

___ ____ ___ and the____ ___ ___ __ book, since th_____ ___ ____ fort and biases. Thu___ ___ ____ perhaps precisely because of __ a homogeneous group. One gifted child may be obviously above grade level in most or all subjects while another, (like Thomas Edison), struggles to learn to read at age seven. One gifted child may be reflective in thought, giving the impression of being "slow," while another may be impulsive, making her seem flighty. A gifted child may be physically strong or stereotypically bookish or "nerdy." There are as many unique forms of *The Gifted Child* as there are children within any group.

Words like "smart" and "bright" are often used to describe gifted children, but there is a difference between the smart child and the gifted child. Children who are smart or bright are generally satisfied to learn the knowledge of others, to answer questions, and to have good ideas. Children who are gifted are seldom satisfied to know the right answer. They are driven to go farther, to develop and uncover new knowledge. They ask endless questions. They have unusual, even outrageous ideas. Smart or bright children can be very easy to teach. Gifted children rarely are easy to teach. That is not to say that smart children do not deserve an individualized education, but they have different academic, social, and emotional needs from the gifted child.

In many ways, the child who is very smart but *not* gifted is at an advantage, since he or she is probably in the range of what Leta Hollingworth (1942) called "optimal intelligence"—bright enough to succeed at almost any profession but not so different from most people as to prevent the child from fitting in easily or being able to lead. What sets the gifted child apart from her bright classmates are the following traits: *intensity* and *insight*; *self-determination* and an *unrelenting drive* to learn about the world; *divergent thinking*; *perfectionism*; and *sensitivity*. Other lists suggest even more traits Whatever list one prefers, usually a combination of some of these traits are intricately and magically woven into one complete and complex child who may or may not achieve—now or later—according to the world's timetable or standards.

Parents who believe their child is smart but not gifted can still benefit greatly from this book, however, because all children have the potential to develop their creativity and to learn in more divergent and self-directed ways. Many of the resources, principles, and strategies used in gifted education have been found to benefit all students. Strategies such as individual pacing, open-ended questioning, and using different points of view—all foundations of gifted education programming—can be offered by home school parents, who have the flexibility to do so for any and all children, regardless of assessment results or labels.

If the experiences, descriptions, and resources in the following pages are helpful to your child and family, even if your child has not been formally identified as gifted, or if you simply wish to avoid the term, please don't let terminology stand in the way. Because programming for gifted is often one of the few ways that children can receive an enriched, individualized education in schools, it should come as no surprise that many parents want their children to qualify for such programs. But a home-based education permits any child to receive an education tailored to the child's unique needs without having to fit the child into a label or a category. If your child has not been tested by the school but you strongly suspect he or she is an especially gifted learner, you may just be right. Parents have been found to be more effective than teachers in recognizing and identifying young gifted children (Gross, 1993).

Additional information about traits and behaviors of gifted children can be found in various sources, some of which include: *Growing Up Gifted: Developing the*

Potential of Children at Home and at School, sixth edition, by Barbara Clark (2002); *Guiding the Gifted Child: A Practical Source for Parents and Teachers,* by James T. Webb, Elizabeth Meckstroth, and Stephanie Tolan (1982); *Helping Gifted Children Soar: A Practical Guide for Parents and Teachers,* by Carol A. Strip (2000); *Teaching Young Gifted Children in the Regular Classroom: Identifying, Nurturing and Challenging Ages 4-9,* by Joan Franklin Smutny, Sally Yahnke Walker, and Elizabeth Meckstroth (1997); and *In the Mind's Eye: Visual Thinkers, Gifted People with Dyslexia and Other Learning Difficulties, Computer Images and the Ironies of Creativity,* by Thomas G. West (1997).

How the Book Is Organized

The book is written in three sections, and each section explores a different part of the home schooling path. Readers should feel free to turn to the section that pertains most to them. While some readers may benefit from reading the book sequentially from start to finish, others will use it more as a trusted reference to be consulted for specific concerns and needs as they arise.

Part I, At Home with Gifted Children, shows how giftedness affects the choice to home school and how being gifted shapes a child's personality, behavior, and education. Part I describes learning traits common to gifted children. This section also explores ways parents can manage the dual roles of parent and teacher and still address social and emotional needs. It examines family dynamics associated with giftedness, and it synthesizes recent expert advice on working and living with sensitive, creative, and sometimes overexcitable children. It introduces the idea of keeping a Home School Journal as a way to sort through and put into practice ideas and suggestions. Questions for Reflection are included at the end of each chapter.

Part II, Creating Your Home School Approach, explains the importance of self-directed learning, including how to integrate self-directed learning with common home education approaches. It outlines gifted education and creativity research and the implications for home schooling. It covers curriculum options and costs. This section also describes the Big Ideas for Big Thinkers Unit Study approach and offers examples of self-directed, interdisciplinary unit studies for Big Ideas Units.

Part III, Your Home School Toolbox, discusses what curriculum materials are available and how to obtain them, how to keep records, and special issues such as gifted teens and highly or profoundly gifted children. This section also contains an annotated compilation of curriculum resources as well as testing information for home schooling needs.

If you have one of the following specific questions or concerns about home schooling, here's where to look for answers right away:

Throughout the book, all of the examples and quotes from home school parents and children are from families who agreed to participate in written or e-mail interviews for this project. To protect their privacy, names have been changed, except for Luke and Olivia, who requested that their real names be used.

Part 1

At Home
With Gifted Children

The Decision

*If you are going to keep your children out of schools,
you had better decide what an education means
because no one else is going to do it for you.*

—David Guterson,
Family Matters: Why Homeschooling Makes Sense

So, you want to learn more about home schooling. You probably have a lot of questions. Can children learn effectively at home? What are the benefits of home schooling versus traditional school? How will home schooled children make friends? How can parents best facilitate a child's education at home?

If you are considering home schooling an especially gifted and creative child, you may have even more questions. What is giftedness? What is creativity? In what ways do gifted students learn differently? How do they experience the world around them? How is home schooling different for children who are gifted and creative, if at all? What exactly is involved in schooling a bright, intense, sensitive child at home? If you've ever asked yourself these questions, this book is written for you. Whether or not you decide to home school, this book will help you understand the kind of learning environment needed for bright, intense learners and will perhaps help you work with your child's school or teacher to provide that learning environment.

Sometimes children have been identified as gifted by the school system but do not experience joyful learning, the kind of learning you remember from pre-kindergarten days. Sometimes gifted and talented programs, enrichment opportunities, and grade acceleration, while beneficial for many students, are simply not the best choices for all gifted children.

Perhaps your child does not meet all the criteria for the school's gifted program, but you know in your heart that she is a creative thinker who would benefit from more challenging or open-ended activities. It may be that hours of rote learning leave her frustrated or withdrawn, and you see her steadily losing her love for learning.

Maybe your school does not acknowledge giftedness. "We believe *all* children are gifted," school officials sometimes say. Unfortunately, this kind of statement usually means that the gifted child's unique social and emotional needs—and even intellectual needs—will most likely be unrecognized, overlooked, and certainly misunderstood. Maybe you are already home schooling but suspect that your child is different from other home schooled children you know. He's more intense. He resists standard curriculum packages, or he gets frustrated and anxious if his work isn't perfect. Perhaps his skills and achievement levels are uneven. He asks difficult questions about complex issues. Certified gifted or not, children who are sensitive, intense learners do require a modified curriculum and a specialized approach, whether they learn in school or at home. Here is what three parents say about why they home school.

Why Home School?

> *I knew my son would never be able to sit still in a classroom. He would have been labeled ADD right from the start and would therefore be seen as a problem. I also knew that we wanted to control, as a family, what he was exposed to and what value system he would receive. A third factor was that we realized he could never fit in at school because of his advanced abilities in math, reading, and other areas. Finally, his overall asynchronous development would have prevented any ordinary school or teacher from dealing adequately with him.*
>
> —Barbara, home school parent

Families choose to home school for a variety of reasons. Some value the extra time available for family and community. Others appreciate how home schooling can provide a truly individualized education. And some families with highly gifted children find that their children's emotional and intellectual needs are so different from the norm that home schooling is necessary for the child to thrive educationally. Reasons for home schooling a gifted child usually fall within four broad categories: (1) Intellectual Needs, (2) Social and Emotional Needs, (3) Self-Actualization, and (4) The Last Resort. Examples follow.

> *My greatest joy as a home school parent is seeing my son regain his self-confidence. Our family is so much more peaceful now. We home school in order to provide a self-paced education in an environment that is warm and nurturing and designed with children's individual learning styles in mind.*
>
> —Claudia, home school parent

> *There are many reasons we home school, including:*
>
> - *the ability to go at our children's pace.*
> - *freedom to travel.*
> - *more time together as a family.*
> - *avoiding schedule-related conflicts.*
> - *freeing our children from the massive time waste involved in traditional schooling.*
> - *better socialization.*
>
> —Claudia, home school parent

A Tradition of Home Schooling

Learning outside of school is an educational tradition with a long and impressive history in the United States, whether the children were taught by one or both parents, tutored, or mostly self-taught. Benjamin Franklin's formal education ended at age eight, but through self-directed studies, he mastered several languages and published his first essay at age 16. Abraham Lincoln's formal education was very limited; he taught himself by voracious reading and by seeking the tutelage of mentors. Susan B. Anthony, who could read at age three, was educated mostly at home. Florence Nightingale was taught entirely at home, mostly by her father (Dobson, 2000).

Thomas Edison's mother taught him at home after he had spent just a few months in school and where his teacher thought him "addled." Michael Faraday never attended school and was mostly self-taught. Anthropologist Mary Leakey received most of her early education by traveling through Europe with her father. Her later experience with formal schooling was quite short-lived. Expelled from two schools, she continued her education at home with tutors. Mystery writer Agatha Christie taught herself to read at age five and was taught at home until high school (Dobson, 2000).

In an interview for *Gifted Children Monthly*, Andrew Wyeth said that he was tutored at home until age 18, although school officials disapproved and couldn't understand why he couldn't be like "any average child having an education." How did some of these well-known individuals feel about learning at home? Wyeth said that rather than feeling isolated, he knew he was different and thus cherished his time alone (Baum, 1986). Famous photographer Ansel Adams, who received most of his education outside of school, said that learning at home allowed him to retain and develop his natural curiosity and internal spark.

The precedent for education outside of school is clear, both in the sciences and the arts. In *Homeschoolers' Success Stories*, Linda Dobson (2000) discusses many more notable "home schooled" children, including writer Willa Cather, violinist Yehudi Menuhin, statesman Patrick Henry, and Supreme Court Chief Justice John

Marshall. Accounts such as these remind parents that learning does not have to occur in school for a person to realize full human potential. With the passage of time, many parents stop thinking of home schooling as the least harmful educational choice for their child and instead come to embrace home schooling as the best of all possible learning environments for their entire family.

> *I went from a person who never considered home schooling, actually knew nothing about it, to someone who will be doing it for years to come. I think most parents will go out of their way to do whatever they can do to help their child when the child obviously needs something different from what they can get at school. Some parents are able to advocate successfully within the school system. In our case, that was not possible, so we home school.*
>
> —Casey, home school parent

> *My 13-year-old daughter had been in a public school for four years, then a private school for gifted learners for two years. When we chose to leave, there really was no other place that seemed able or willing to meet her needs as a gifted learner. She also expressed a desire not to return to a traditional school at that time. After reading as much as possible in a short time about home schooling, we decided to give it a try.*
>
> *Now, after a year and a half, I still choose home schooling, because it has worked out to be the best option for our children. My son became "school age" as his sister came home for school; he has home schooled ever since.*
>
> —Kathleen, home school parent

Intellectual Needs

Intellectual or academic needs are cited by many families as a primary reason for home schooling. Sometimes this is related to the child's unusual ability or intense desire to learn. In other cases, parents cite the schools' inadequacy in meeting the intellectual needs of their children. Jon and Alisha first considered home schooling after their five-year-old son scored far beyond their expectations on an IQ test required for entrance to a private school.

> *We don't believe that a public or private school would provide sufficient curriculum accommodations for our profoundly gifted young son. Home schooling is also his own choice. We offered him several educational options, and he chose home schooling without hesitation.*
>
> —Jon and Alisha, home school parents

Monica, who has been home schooling her daughters, ages nine and 10, for two years, writes that she has learned that the "public school way is not necessarily the best way for a child to learn."

> I wish that we had considered the possibility of home schooling earlier. I assumed that the school would do everything possible to challenge my child and that school was the place where all learning occurred. I expected the school to accommodate a gifted child, and I was shocked when they would not.
>
> We chose home schooling after our oldest went to public school for kindergarten and first grade, and then to private school for second and third. She began to hate school. I was a substitute teacher in the private school, and I saw first hand how much time was wasted during the day. We tried to get accommodations for our daughter, but nothing promising ever came about. I did not know how to be assertive about what she needed because I didn't know what was best.
>
> If I had known that home schooling would be so wonderful for my kids, I would not have bothered with searching so long for the perfect school.
>
> —Monica, home school parent

Most parents sympathize with the demands and constraints of classroom teachers who often lack the resources and training to understand or serve the needs of gifted children.

> We're home schooling because I can provide a better environment for my sons, ages six and three, to learn and explore than if they were in school. They have more freedom to pursue their interests. They go on many more fieldtrips. They have more time to read and play. They have less busywork, less time wasted standing in lines, less time spent on crowd control activities. Home schooling improves their quality of life.
>
> I have nothing against our local public school. The principal and teachers are caring and dedicated, and they provide a good education for most children.
>
> —Stacy, home school parent

> *We home school because we understand that the average teacher doesn't have eight hours a day to devote to the individual needs of a child. She has to follow the curriculum given to her, and she has very little time to devote to individual needs and interests. Our daughter can run through a grade level in any typical curriculum at breakneck speed and get little out of it. Although it was allowing her to advance to the next level of curriculum, this approach didn't give her what she needs. She needs to think and analyze, to ask why and how, and to be able to find out the answer even if it takes a day of research or experimentation. Home schooling is the only way we can accommodate her in this way.*
>
> —Colleen, home school parent

Some children learn a staggering amount of information on their own at great speed. It is not uncommon for a highly gifted child to test several levels above grade level in a few or several subjects, even though the child has never encountered the material in a classroom (Hollingworth, 1942; Rogers, 2002). How is this possible? The child has a great memory for details and naturally makes connections between old knowledge and new information. Anything the child hears, sees, or encounters—whether on television, from a museum visit, or through leisure reading—becomes a part of the child's knowledge. For such children, a lock-step, grade-based curriculum actually holds them back from learning.

Many gifted children not only learn faster than their age peers, but also learn differently. They need less drill, or prefer to learn independently, or learn best visually or through a holistic, whole-to-parts curriculum. Juliann, a parent of three, found that teaching these different learning styles at home is easier.

> *I've taught other home schooled children, both individually and in co-op classes. Gifted children are much quicker and more curious, but home schooled children in general find it easy to offer feedback to adults, and that's refreshing. It's easier to teach a given concept, subject, or skill to gifted children simply because they can absorb the basics so quickly and allow you to move on to the "fun stuff," like experimentation and application and discussion. With other children, you have to be careful not to assume understanding.*
>
> *On the other hand, gifted children can be considered difficult, in that it is necessary to have a far wider range of resources at one's fingertips. A week's lesson plan can easily be shot in an hour, and you've got to keep going. Or you may find that you need to approach the subject from several different angles to get that "click" that the gifted child craves. Searching for that groove can slow your progress, so you've got to be flexible and keep your bag of tricks handy. Once the "ah-ha" moment happens, you are back to learning at the speed of light. Gifted children are very honest about what they do and don't understand.*
>
> *Gifted children appreciate and marvel at the connections between the traditionally separate branches of pedagogy. Last week, a home school mother asked our home school skating group, "Is anybody else studying (state) history this year?" My children would wither and die if forced to study one, sole, isolated piece of history for an entire year. They enjoy looking at the combinations, the relationships between mankind's progress in science and literature, exploration and philosophy. Gifted children tend to see the BIG picture and prefer to learn using the big picture.*
>
> —Juliann, home school parent

Gifted learners have complex intellectual needs. Joyce Van Tassel-Baska (1997), Director of the Center for Gifted Education at the College of William and Mary, recommends curriculum that:

○ *Tailors subjects and content of study to the advanced content knowledge of the student.* If a child already knows how to read fluently at age seven and has an extensive knowledge base of facts about transportation, for example, the child's curriculum should not rely on early readers or basic study of cars and trains. Instead, the curriculum should incorporate books and articles at the child's higher reading level and a more advanced level of study that presupposes basic knowledge, such as transportation systems or modern technological innovations in transportation.

○ *Offers higher order thinking and processing activities.* Young children are often insatiably curious about the world around them, but some children move quickly from wanting to amass and comprehend information (lower level thinking skills) to needing to think about what they learn—to *analyze* and *synthesize* different knowledge and ideas, and then *evaluate* conclusions (higher level thinking skills). Thus, a gifted middle school child studying transportation might be encouraged to analyze costs of automobiles versus public transit, then synthesize the information by using what he's learned to predict possible future directions of transportation, or evaluate the effectiveness of speed trains and debate with like-minded students who take turns presenting differing points of view.

○ *Is interdisciplinary and organized around themes that are both practical and theoretical.* If content of study is arranged around broad themes rather than strictly according to subject area and grade level, the curriculum can better address the various complex learning needs of advanced learners. Rather than offer geometry in the morning and Ancient Greek history in the afternoon, an interdisciplinary approach might incorporate both areas into "Shapes in History." The student would then learn about geometry *and* Ancient Greece (by learning about Greek mathematicians Archimedes, Pythagoras, Euclid), or geometry and architectural design of ancient civilizations. Such integrated study helps promote connections in history and humanity in a way that traditional study of separate subjects discourages. Other subjects—spelling, reading, and writing—would also be integrated. Integrated thematic learning is effective for all students, not just gifted students. It promotes long-term retention, better transfer of knowledge from one field to another, and encourages children to develop their learning potential to its fullest.

Most states have laws that require schools to differentiate curriculum for students who are gifted. Differentiated curriculum provides "learning options that meet the students' special needs for acceleration of content and greater depth, breadth, and complexity for instruction" (Strip, 2000, p. 71). Differentiation can take place in the regular classroom or in separate classrooms of gifted students or even in separate schools. The extent and quality of differentiation for gifted children in schools varies tremendously by state and school. The teacher's knowledge and training in gifted education, school policies, and funding are all factors that influence the level or extent of differentiation. Some of the more common program options (and subsequent differentiation) are as follows (Arizona Department of Education, 2001).

Level One: Enrichment activities without acceleration, academic competitions, advanced placement classes. These differentiation techniques are good for most students, but do not necessarily meet the needs of gifted students.

Level Two: Cluster grouping, pullout classes, enrichment *with* acceleration, multi-age and cross-grade grouping, ability grouping, honors classes, interdisciplinary curriculum. These options meet the needs of some, but not all, gifted students.

Level Three: Acceleration by allowing students to work at their own pace, ability grouping and honors classes, seminars on special topics, grade skipping, gifted schools, mentorships, independent study. This level of differentiation addresses the needs of moderately and highly gifted students.

Level Four: Early entrance to high school or college, summer or after-school programs offered through universities, special accelerated college programs. This level of differentiation is designed for highly and profoundly gifted children who often need "radical acceleration" or grade skipping of two or more levels over time.

One-third of the 36 families I interviewed for this book stated that their child had been in a gifted program or a school for gifted students before they decided to home school. Even if your child is currently in a school program for gifted and talented, the extent of differentiation of curriculum offered through the program may not necessarily meet a particular child's intellectual needs, especially if a child is offered only one of the above levels of differentiation. In contrast, learning at home can allow home school families of gifted students to pick and choose areas of differentiation according to their child's needs rather than having to rely on a school's particular gifted program options. Home schooled children often use options from differentiation levels two and three above by participating in home school multi-age learning groups, meeting with other gifted home schooled children for book discussion and science clubs, using an interdisciplinary curriculum and unit studies, accelerating by working at their own pace, taking community classes on topics of interest, moving past grade-level work the child already knows, finding mentors in the child's area of interest, and practicing self-directed independent study. Home school families use level four differentiation when they enroll in Talent Search programs or seek part-time or full-time early high school or college entrance for their exceptionally gifted children.

Home school parents also have the option of not using differentiation options. Not every type of gifted programming is appropriate for every gifted child. Grade acceleration, or whole grade skipping, for example, may ensure academic work at a more challenging level, but the *method* of instruction will most likely be the same—that is, designed for the average level student at all levels. Pull-out programs for gifted children can have inherent difficulties as well, by removing responsibility from classroom teachers for meeting the needs of the gifted students in their regular classrooms (Rogers, 2002).

Does this mean that school gifted programming options are ineffective? Of course not, but neither does the mere existence of a program guarantee an appropriate education for a gifted child. It depends on the expertise of the gifted teachers and the flexibility of the school's willingness to offer acceleration where needed, for example. There are many degrees, kinds, and areas of giftedness. Some children work comfortably one or two grade levels above their age peers, while others are ready for high school level work in fourth grade. Some children are particularly gifted in language and verbal expression; others exhibit strength in math and science. It is easy to see how the extreme diversity of gifted children's abilities and needs makes it hard for schools to offer an optimally designed program for each individual gifted child.

Even a classroom or school designed exclusively for gifted children is not always the answer. Daily interaction between intense and overexcitable learners can be too much stimulation for many children, especially for very introverted or reflective children. And unless the school recognizes the varying degrees and complexity of giftedness, the needs of highly gifted or highly creative children may never be recognized, understood, or accommodated.

Karen Rogers, in *Re-Forming Gifted Education: Matching the Program to the Child* (2002), recommends that parents exhaust the possibilities of tax-supported educational options in their local public school system, however, before turning to home schooling. Perhaps that is good advice, perhaps not. Only you can make that decision. One parent describes below how she tried to make both public and private school work for her son:

> *We spent a full year working and hoping to make public education work for our very asynchronous child with his uneven abilities. Meetings with teachers. Meetings with administrators. Working on gifted education committees. Establishing guidelines for a self-contained class for highly gifted. Despite the best of intentions, the clearest of guidelines, it became apparent that public education, even a self-contained gifted program, was not able to meet the needs of our "out-of-sync" child.*
>
> *So we looked at private schools. Alas, the private schools, even those boasting of being "schools for the gifted student," were not appropriate. They seemed to be one to two years accelerated in all subjects when compared with the public school. But there were significant performance expectations—papers, worksheets, projects, reports. What my son, then nine years old, needed was college level work in some subjects and below grade level work in others.*
>
> *Finally, we realized that our expectations were simply not reasonable. Our child was just too different. Home schooling has proved to be our best option.*
>
> —Sondra, home school parent

Some parents have found that their school simply cannot or will not acknowledge or accommodate the needs of highly precocious, intense, or creative learners:

> *We chose to home school in order to meet our seven-year-old son's needs, academically and emotionally. He attended one year of public school kindergarten. It quickly became apparent that our school district is just not able to handle a child who is four grade levels ahead in math and six levels ahead in reading. Our son began to withdraw and develop a negative self-image. He complained that he was "strange" and "different" from his age peers. Our school district refuses to accelerate a child in any way.*
>
> —Casey, home school parent

> *We chose home schooling for our kids mainly because school was not a good fit for my eight-year-old son. He was going to a private school for gifted children, but even there they could not challenge him or even hold his interest. He was constantly getting in trouble for attention-seeking behavior.*
>
> —Juliann, home school parent

Just as not all gifted programs are appropriate for all gifted children, neither is home schooling the best option for all gifted children. Kathi Kearney (1992), founder of the Hollingworth Center for Highly Gifted Children and a home schooling specialist, advises parents that home schooling requires commitment, time, and strong family relationships. Levels of personal commitment, capability, and passion are important factors to assess before deciding to home school. One home school parent writes that she needed a full year of research before she felt committed to home schooling, capable of home schooling, and passionate about home schooling. She says, "If a parent is still on the fence, I don't think home schooling will be successful for the family."

Parents who are unsure as to whether schools may work for their children and are considering home schooling may wish to ask themselves these questions, adapted from a *Gifted Children Monthly*[2] article, "Home Schooling: Is it right for you?" (Macmillan, 1986):

- O Does your home offer a nurturing, creative spirit where the child is free to learn?

- O Are you willing to spend hours of time in preparation, instruction, and answering questions?

- O Are you determined enough to search the community for additional resources and mentors in fields of knowledge unfamiliar to you?

---

2   *Gifted Children Monthly* is no longer in print but is available as the website www.gifted-children.com.

○ Are you capable of designing a coherent educational philosophy?

○ Are you willing to research your state's laws on home education and your district's position on parents as teachers?

Parents who cannot answer "yes" to these questions may decide that home schooling is not the answer for their family and that instead they should try to work with the schools. Two recent books, *Helping Gifted Children Soar: A Practical Guide for Parents and Teachers*, by Carol A Strip (2000), and *Re-Forming Gifted Education: Matching the Program to the Child*, by Karen Rogers (2002), offer extensive information about gifted education programs in schools, as well as much practical advice on how to work positively with schools and teachers.

Rethinking Intellectual Needs

Home schooling offers the opportunity to review and expand our notion of what constitutes appropriate academic education. When children attend public or private schools, parents often take for granted the design and the day-to-day implementation of traditional models. They assume that teacher-directed learning, short class periods, separate subjects of study, and a grade-restricted curriculum are just "the way things are." But are these educational models really the best ways to learn, or are they comfortable because they are familiar? The child schooled in the classroom is certainly affected by various educational forces—by standards and reform, by committee and curriculum—but the child has little say in that process. Instead, she is moved along on a conveyer-belt form of education.

As Annemarie Roeper noted, the current national trend is toward a curriculum-centered education rather than a child-centered education: "Children are viewed as individuals only as they relate to specific material and subject matter" (Roeper, 1995, p.136). She asserts that modern education lacks both foresight and insight.

> *We are not looking at the purposes of modern education. We have not thought about why we are doing what we are doing. We have not established a philosophy that relates to modern life. We continue to educate for the next step, the next test, the next grade, the next school. We educate in isolated fragments, and we fail to bind the fragments together into a meaningful whole* (Roeper, 1990, p. 5).

Rather than educate for life, we too often define education as preparation for college. The unfortunate result is that learning counts only when it leads directly and measurably to good grades, honor rolls, high SAT scores, scholarships, and entrance to Harvard or MIT. Because home schooling offers the opportunity to de-emphasize grades and emphasize learning, home schooled children can begin a lifelong love affair with learning that does not stop with a final report card or degree. As home schooling recognizes, intellectual needs are not a boxed, defined compartment in a child's mind or life. Education for life allows students to follow their interests beyond the constraints of a simple textbook and classroom. A home schooled child who is ready and eager to move forward in a particular subject has no artificial constraints holding him back. The concept of a more challenging education does not necessarily mean using a standard curriculum package at a higher grade level. This is perhaps the most liberating aspect of home schooling a gifted child. Many subjects in which gifted children may be interested and from which they may benefit are far beyond the idea of any grade level at all!

Consider a 10-year-old who develops a strong interest in legal issues. Grade-based curricula can provide a starting point, but the home school student can easily exceed material designed for classroom use. In the larger world of people, ideas, and resources, he can visit the county courthouse, read current material about local government, write to legislators, travel with his family to the state or national capital, interview an attorney, stage mock trials with his friends, or if his interest is strong enough, even begin to study constitutional law and Supreme Court cases through resources such as *You Decide! Applying the Bill of Rights to Real Cases* (Critical Thinking Books & Software). Public and private school systems most often assign materials and activities like these to specific grade levels or save them for occasional enrichment activities, but in home schooling, there are no limits, and such materials can be used as often as necessary.

Because learning is more than curriculum and is an integral part of being human, how we learn—and how we are prevented from learning—affects our social and emotional life as well. A parent writes of the painful struggle of her son:

Stephen was seven and in a private school for the gifted. His teacher was new to the world of gifted, but had 18 years of teaching experience and insisted, "she'd seen it all."

After the first four weeks, we met with the teacher to discuss the level of work Stephen was doing, which I maintained was a repeat of material from years past. I brought in examples of his work, and she said, "Well, that was done at home, with you over his shoulder," which was not true. When I would discuss his sinking depression, she said, "He's a typical second grader who's just pulling your chain."

In January, he took an achievement test. Despite results that placed him in ninth grade for reading and fifth grade for math, his teacher would not change a thing. She even told the educational consultant from the Gifted Development Center in Denver that nothing in her curriculum plan would be altered for Stephen.

Meanwhile, Stephen, age seven, became suicidal and would hit himself while doing countless, mindless homework sheets of simple math problems or excruciatingly low-level reading comprehension sheets. Once I found him hitting his head with his fists as he stared at his homework assignment. It was a three-sentence story about a boy riding his bike over a bed of nails. The "comprehension" questions were (1) What do you think will happen?, and (2) What makes you think so?

So here we are—home schooling! The biggest joy of home schooling for me is watching my children, particularly Stephen, blossom. They are so much more self-confident and happy, even at peace with who they are and why we do what we do. It is really a great deal of fun to participate in learning and to experience the joy of learning with my children. However, it has been quite an eye opener discovering how much I did not learn in school!

Home schooling has become so much more than a school option. It is now a way of life. No alarm clocks. Nobody else's schedule to adhere to. The kids love eating when they are hungry, not when somebody says to. Stephen used to get so frustrated

Gifted children often have unique social and emotional needs caused by their academic precocity. As this parent explains, by meeting intellectual needs in a holistic and individuated way, home schooling can take important steps toward meeting social and emotional needs at the same time.

Social and Emotional Needs

Many parents of intense, sensitive children choose home schooling due to their children's social emotional needs. Jan has home schooled her 13-year-old daughter for five and one-half years. She often wonders about social/emotional issues related to her daughter's asynchronous (uneven) development, intensity, perfectionism, finding peers and friends, and high levels of sensitivity. These concerns are familiar to many families of intense and creative learners.

Schooling at home offers opportunities to integrate social and emotional development with the child's academic education. Gifted children have unique social and emotional needs, the most obvious perhaps being asynchronous development and intensity. (Note: These and other characteristics are discussed in more detail in Chapter 2, and information on meeting social and emotional needs is presented in Chapter 3.)

Asynchronous development means the child does not develop evenly with regard to what would be considered average for his age mates or for society's expectations. Finding friends who have abilities and interests in common doesn't always come easily for gifted children. A 10-year-old who is already planning a career as a software designer and who spends much of his free time designing his own website will almost surely have a hard time finding similar age peers who relate to his level of interest. He can't necessarily be friends with adult computer buffs because they will have difficulty understanding his need to be 10.

Asynchronous development also means that the child will experience being "out of sync" in areas within herself. A seven-year-old who is able to read books designed for middle school students may be unable to print or use scissors as well as most six-year-olds. When her spelling and penmanship skills lag appreciably behind her desire and ability to express herself, she may mistakenly think she is "stupid," especially if she notices other seven-year-olds who express their thoughts easily. Another child may read silently at high levels but when asked to do oral reading, may struggle because of perfectionism, introversion, or undeveloped pronunciation skills, and thus think of himself as a "bad reader." And often, when levels of thought far outstrip years of life experience, or when motor skills needed for writing cannot keep up with the child's advanced speaking and thinking ability, the child may feel at odds within himself, unable to produce or perform consistently. Home schooling respects these discrepancies without penalty, without trying to force the square peg into the round hole. Note these parents' descriptions:

Due to my son's level of asynchronicity, I do not use a grade-based curriculum. He writes at grade level (second grade) under duress, although he can dictate a much higher level. He spells at grade level. His math skills and science knowledge are at least fifth grade. His logic skills are sixth grade. He reads easily at eighth grade. So I keep track of subjects by grade level, but that's about all.

—Donna, home school parent

I have a child who loves to learn. He has a wide variety of passions including reading, math, space, poetry, historical events, and philosophical issues. He just turned seven.

The greatest joy of home schooling has been watching my son return to being happy, outgoing, and self-confident after the negative changes we saw during his one year in school. He is no longer in an atmosphere where he is constantly comparing himself unfavorably to his age mates or to what is "normal" for a child his age. He is free to be himself again.

—Casey, home school parent

The **intensity** of gifted children also sets them apart from others socially and emotionally. *Everything* matters to gifted children; nothing seems trivial or unimportant to them. Very little is taken for granted. This intensity permeates every moment of the child's life and may be either outer- or inner-directed, extraverted or introverted. Outer-directed intensity can cause a child to appear loud and boisterous, bossy or nosy. Inner-directed intensity may cause a child to seem aloof and withdrawn, too much "in her head" or self-absorbed.

Parents often report that their child's intensity is inherently connected to strong self-determination. Gifted children *intensely* want to do things their own way—to think their own thoughts, say what's on their mind, direct their own actions, and determine their own fate. A classroom setting that offers little or no choice of subject matter or room for differing opinions can be stifling to many gifted learners. They may shut down and to refuse to cooperate, or they may find themselves routinely disciplined for expressing their strong opinions and internal drive.

Home school parents can encourage a child to recognize and use this sense of self-determination, and to see himself as inner-directed rather than stubborn or controlling. They can also accept that the gifted child *will* challenge authority, *may* have little concern for the opinions of adults, and *may* be largely unaffected by the use of rewards and punishments. Knowing how to use the child's gifted characteristics as strengths, rather than weaknesses, is a necessary part of the home schooling challenge.

A gifted child's intensity has a great impact on her relationship with the world. Parents may have to look harder for friends who understand and accept their child's intense nature. And these intense, often overexcitable children need to be aware of and accept their own extreme reactions and emotions without shame or embarrassment. Only through acceptance and understanding can they eventually be less overwhelmed by their own self-determination and intensity—their very selves. Whenever possible, gifted children should have the opportunity to learn and play with other gifted children to allow them to see these traits in others and to know that they are not alone.

Social Needs: Rethinking Socialization

Socialization is often the biggest concern for home school families. Critics of home schooling ask, "What about friends?" or "How will your children learn to get along with others?" For home school parents of children who are gifted, especially naturally introverted children who get energy from being alone, socialization becomes even more complex. Indeed, parents should rethink what is usually meant by the word socialization. Socialization is "the ability to adapt to the needs of the group," which may sound good, but can be unhealthy if children adapt or "fit in" at the expense of their own personalities or lives (Silverman, 1992). *Socialization* must be distinguished from *social development*, which, as Silverman says, is "not the pressure to adapt, but a deep, comfortable level of self-acceptance that leads to true friendship with others." Social development, then, is a part of developing one's full potential, whereas socialization—conformity for its own sake—can be detrimental to knowing and accepting one's unique abilities (Silverman, 1992).

These are issues for gifted children, whether home schooled or not, and parents should look for new ways their children can practice being themselves while still belonging or being members of a group. A classroom of 20 students, or even 10 students, may present too much stimulation for some gifted children; they simply cannot hold onto their sense of self in such a setting and still interact meaningfully with others. Instead, they may follow the direction and behaviors of whoever happens to be the strongest group member, regardless of whether those behaviors are positive. Or they may shut down and refuse to participate at all. Children like these may respond better to small, regular gatherings of three or four children until they feel comfortable with voicing their own ideas and thoughts; then they can cooperate without blindly conforming to the group. Home school parents can organize small group gatherings in homes, libraries, or parks, or through existing community organizations. When parents discover other children who share their child's interests, they can go the extra mile, often literally, to encourage and support the potential friendship. Home school parents have been known to drive some distance to provide play and group learning opportunities for their gifted children. Phone conversations and e-mail correspondence are other ways that children can nurture friendships.

The bottom line is that, unless parents severely restrict their children's social lives, home schooled children are often *more*, rather than *less*, comfortable in social situations. A recent study comparing home school students and public school students found that home school students "were generally more patient and less competitive. They tended to introduce themselves to one another more, and didn't fight as much. Home schoolers were also much more prone to exchange addresses and phone numbers" (Cloud & Morse, 2001). This description certainly sounds like the kind of social development we want in the coming generation.

Home Schooling for Full Potential

To nurture full potential, home schooling integrates and synthesizes the intellectual, social, and emotional realms by giving a child the space, time, and understanding necessary to begin the process of discovering his or her true self. We could call it "whole child" home schooling, or home schooling for the love of learning, since learning is an inherent part of being human. Here is one parent's explanation:

> *Gifted children need to understand why they think differently from others, why they are different, and how to deal with that. They need to know that it is not just okay to be who they are, but terrific! They need to be taught with love how to get along in a world that is not always prepared to deal with their divergent thinking or behavior, a world that is not really prepared for them. And they need the time to grow up enough to deal with the pain and struggles this can often bring to them, especially as young children.*
>
> —Maria, home school parent

Home schooling for full potential is neither self-serving nor isolating. Rather, it can be an ongoing, lifelong process of becoming more fully who we are and who we are meant to be, both as individuals and as members of society. Of all the reasons to home school, this is perhaps the most positive and offers the most possibilities for growth and development.

What do we mean by a child's full potential? It varies for every child, because it depends on the child's life circumstances, individual strengths and talents, personality, and the child's own interests and desires. Each of us has unique potential for what we are capable of doing and being in the future—both tomorrow, and 20 or even 60 years from now. Thus, home schooling for full potential is home schooling for self-actualization.

Sometimes we are unaware of a child's potential in a particular talent area until the child becomes an adult. Famous "late bloomers" include Michael Faraday (chemist and physicist), William Butler Yeats (British poet), and British Prime Minister Winston Churchill (West, 1997). Grandma Moses showed scant evidence of being a famous American artist before she began painting in her early seventies. While it is true that the enormous potential of *some* children is strikingly evident at an early age, still, adults have no way of predicting how the child may or may not achieve in the future. What we as teachers and parents *can* do is to lay the groundwork for the child to continue on the journey of learning.

As parents, our task is to prepare our children for a life quest of learning. We cannot make the journey for them, and it is a journey with no pre-set destination. Our children will need stamina, tools, wisdom, the ability both to direct their own course and to seek direction from others, skills to ask for help and to make decisions, and courage and self-confidence to continue when the road is rough or unknown. At some point, our children will choose their own route, take their own shortcuts, build their own bridges, and proceed at their own pace. We accompany them at the start and stay beside them only until they are ready to continue the journey on their own. We must always remember that this is *their* path, not ours.

Parents must keep in mind that realizing one's full potential, even for highly intelligent children, may not necessarily involve prestige, eminence, fame, or riches. Parents of high potential children are often tempted to project their own ambitions onto their bright child. They see the tremendous potential and can hardly help hoping the child will become a doctor or scientist or writer, perhaps a career they themselves would like to have pursued. But while a successful journey for one child may include graduate school or a lucrative career, for another child, a successful life quest may be private and consist of a rich family or spiritual life, a life of contemplation. The fact is, we parents have no way of knowing what our children's ultimate path will be or with what intensity it will be pursued. We should not pressure our children to fulfill potential any more than we should pressure them to achieve or to fit in. By being careful to follow the child's lead, parents can ensure that they place neither too little nor too much value on the role of conventional "achievement" when it comes to individual self-actualization.

Home schooling for full potential is, then, about helping the child to find and follow a life path. This book focuses on four key aspects of home-based education that emphasize the role of the child in her own education. The four key aspects are these:

1. Understanding and acceptance of self
2. Creative learning
3. Self-directed study
4. Natural extension into the community

Each of these key aspects is important in fulfilling potential for all children. For children who are particularly intense, creative, and quick learners, they are of particular significance, as we will see below.

Understanding and Acceptance of Self

Gifted adults often have a moment of realization when they know that they have, for most of their lives, adopted a false self in order to fit in or to avoid having to face who they really are. Mary-Elaine Jacobsen (1999b) writes in her book, *Liberating Everyday Genius*, that several common behaviors keep us from knowing and accepting our true selves. Some of these are: (1) indulging a false self by pretending to be who we are not, (2) denying the existence of our true gifts and talents, (3) avoiding risk or realizing potential by living a "safe" life, and (4) seeking approval from others in a way that goes against our true nature. She suggests that somewhere along the way, we learn to feel guilty about being gifted, whether or not we recognize that it is giftedness that is causing our discomfort, and we then engage in a sort of "identify theft" of who we were born to be. In middle age, many adults find that these denial and camouflaging behaviors no longer work, and gifted individuals reach a crisis point where they must finally come to terms with their potential (Jacobsen, 1999b).

Jacobsen's suggestions for adults have profound implications for gifted children. When children devote mental and physical energy toward attempting to fit in, trying to be someone they are not, and living mostly for the approving smiles of peers and adults, they have little energy left to develop creative talents and pursue passionate interests. Only after a rediscovery of self in middle age are these children able to free themselves to live according to who they are meant to be rather than who they think others want them to be. By helping our children at an early age to know and accept who they are, to feel comfortable with their gifts and talents, whatever they may be, to practice necessary risk, and not to depend solely on the approval of others, we may help gifted children to avoid later feelings of guilt and confusion that plague gifted adults. Children should be free to focus time, energy, and talents on issues and aspects of life that are important to them, regardless of whether such talents and interests are popular or widely understood by others.

One parent, with four children, ages two to eight, describes it this way:

> *Only someone who truly loves the child, someone who truly knows the child, can see the child for who he or she really is. Children are not mass market products to be churned out on an assembly line. They are individuals, with individual needs, strengths and weaknesses. By home schooling our children, we are keeping the responsibility for their moral, spiritual, and emotional development where it belongs, with those who love them most. By our example, we teach them love, compassion, and caring; we teach them what it means to be part of a team, a family; we teach life as it really is.*
>
> *Children require the freedom first to be just a child; second, to grow into the people they were meant to be, on their own timetable; third, to learn the lessons of life as they become ready; and fourth, to learn how to think.*
>
> *When a child is allowed to grow and learn at home, surrounded by the love of their family, the need to "fit in" is done away with, and they are free to break the moulds of society or to change the path of the world, one person at a time. Conforming to the "norm" is a means of ensuring that each person looks the same as the next, that no one who thinks differently will threaten the security of "tradition" or the "old school," and that those who choose mediocrity will not be made uncomfortable by others who have the ability to choose excellence.*
>
> *In short, we home school in order to give our children our love, our time, our morals, and to give them back their freedom, to be their best and to be themselves.*
>
> —Maria, home school parent

Creative Learning

Creative children are able to think in new and unusual ways that veer away from the expected, away from what has been commonly thought before. These children are *divergent thinkers* who often ask "open-ended" questions that have no single right answers. For example, "What would my life be like if I had been born in a different time or country?" or "How would the world be different if the dinosaurs had not died out?" Divergent thinkers make connections between unlikely topics and invent new, creative solutions. For example, a boy who likes both robotics and dinosaurs has decided he will build robots that unearth dinosaur bones, so that he won't have to choose between two careers. Creative, divergent thinkers often focus on novelty rather than adjust to boredom. A child may study details of her environment rather than listen to a lecture on a topic she already understands. A teacher might call this "daydreaming," but the child is finding a good use for her time. Another creative child may be the class clown. Schools and society are not always tolerant or accepting of creative, divergent thinkers who are seen as disruptive since they stray from the norm.

In teaching creative learners, we must encourage them to use their divergent thinking traits as strengths rather than as weaknesses. We must encourage them to ask questions and seek answers to those questions, no matter how disconnected those questions might seem to others; only in this way can they make connections between ideas and follow the train of their own thought. That's not to say that *all* of the child's learning must be creative or divergent, but that such learning is an *important and integral part* of the child's education.

A traditional writing curriculum that does not encourage creativity might consist of weekly sentence diagramming or five-paragraph essays on a topic of the teacher's choosing, with little opportunity for self-expression or exploration. Conversely, a writing curriculum that integrates creative learning will ask the student to write about topics of his or her own choosing, to learn grammar through humorous or open-ended activities such as Madlibs™, and to critique his or her own writing through informal writing workshops. This more flexible approach increases motivation and also prepares the student for higher education when he or she will be expected to present original ideas. Creative learning also ameliorates perfectionism because it offers practice in dealing with ambiguity. Open-ended or divergent thinking activities have no single right answer; often, there is more than one possible correct answer. In life there is often no single right answer, yet schools tend to emphasize convergent thinking, where one best answer or way of doing things is wanted.

Self-Directed Study

Gifted children are particularly driven to find ways to teach themselves *what they want and need to know*—by simply asking questions of adults who know more about the subject than they do, through reading books, or by searching the Internet. The higher the child's IQ, the more likely the child will want a significant role in planning his own education (Freeman, 1985). As many parents of gifted and creative children already know, learning by teaching themselves is the whole point.

> *Teaching gifted kids is more challenging because you don't really teach them. They like to figure it out for themselves, come to their own conclusions. And they usually teach themselves better than anyone else can teach them.*
>
> —Colleen, home school parent

> *It's my daughter who strives for excellence both in the academic sense and in her day-to-day existence. I really do just follow her lead, and I help provide her with resources.*
>
> —Ruth, home school parent

Many friends compliment my skills as a home school parent. They see where my children are and how well they are doing and give me much of the credit. What no one seems to realize is that my children are doing most of their learning by themselves. I am more of a facilitator. I keep things moving and require progress in certain subjects, but they are doing the learning. I do very little formal teaching. I spend a lot of time on the computer checking out e-mail loops that discuss curricula, good books, and resources. Then I try to bring good resources home. I do some reading aloud and some coaching in math, but I don't see myself teaching a particular subject or topic. If I do explain something, the girls seem to get it right away. I don't know if I am a good teacher or not. I see myself more as just a caring parent of two gifted girls.

—Monica, home school parent

These home school parents realize that gifted children are not only capable of learning on their own, but they also prefer self-directed learning. Some readers will be frustrated with the implied flexibility and autonomy, perhaps wanting to shout, "But surely children need some structure and guidance in order to learn! You can't expect them to teach themselves!" Well, yes—and yes. Yes, they do need *some* structure and guidance, but not necessarily the kind nor the amount usually found in formal school settings. And yes, we can expect children to teach themselves—at least much of the time.

Fulfilling one's potential often involves learning to experience the "flow" within one's own personality. People who experience flow have self-directed personalities and are not overly influenced or manipulated by outside forces. They often attend to things other people miss, have deep wells of psychic energy, and have intense interests that are very important to them and that help them to understand the world. While not always happier than other people, they "are involved in more complex activities, and they feel better about themselves as a result" (Csikszentmihalyi, 1996).

A home schooling environment that respects and values these traits will rely as little as possible on coercion in the learning process, will make room for the child's intense energy, and will allow the child to have passionate interests and pursuits of her own choosing. The learning environment for self-directed study provides a careful balance of focus on self and society, individual creativity, and community cooperation.

Natural Extension into the Community

Knowing and being one's true self does not happen in a vacuum. We know who we are in part by being with others, both with those who are like us and those who are not like us. In *Re-forming Gifted Education*, Karen Rogers (2002) suggests several ways that parents can help children both to learn to be with others and to use time alone.

○ Provide opportunities for socialization with others of like ability or interests.

- Provide opportunities for socialization with a mix of adults and children of varying abilities.
- Find ways for your child to understand his own identity and uniqueness. This means you will need to carve out large blocks of time for your child to work alone or with you on the development of his unique interests and talents.

Socialization with others of similar ability or interest can be as informal as play time at the park with other creative, intense learners, or as formal as a class for gifted youth offered through a talent search program. Socialization with a variety of ages and abilities can be encouraged through scout, church, or book discussion groups; sports programs; volunteer opportunities; home school groups; or community organizations. Time alone for self-discovery can be accomplished through one-on-one time with a parent, uninterrupted conversation on topics of the child's choice, or independent study through distance learning courses or other self-directed learning activities. A balance of time with others of varying ages and time alone is easier to achieve in a home school setting than in a classroom of same-age peers.

Rethinking Achievement

Home schooling for full potential implies a new perspective on achievement and success—to "educate for self-actualization" rather than to "educate for success" (Annemarie Roeper, 1996). Self-actualization begins with the child (as the self) and trusts that as the child finds his or her place in the world, talent development and achievement will fall into place in ways that serve the needs of the child and the community. This is a different view from beginning with norms of specific achievement standards for various ages, then testing and trusting that the child will somehow discover his or her self and purpose in life along the prescribed pathways of school grade levels.

Parents who home school for full potential view achievement as something the child chooses, not an educational standard imposed from the outside.

> *Achievement is something that's accomplished on one's own timetable. For my eight-year-old daughter, right now, achievement is learning how to play the violin. She has set a certain standard for herself and is motivated to achieve it. She practices each day and is very mindful at her violin class.*
>
> —Ruth, home school parent

> *Achievement is having my children arrive at adulthood with their selves and their spirits intact. This would include a desire to go forward and be successful in a passion of their choice.*
>
> —Jessie, home school parent

> *In our home, achievement is a personal thing. It's not measured much in terms of finishing a workbook or moving up to the next reader. I see it more in personal terms. Organizing your room can be a great achievement. Finding the answers to your own questions is a great achievement. Why can birds fly? Why do leaves turn colors in the fall? What do I want to be when I grow up? All are questions that result in a sense of achievement when we discover the answers.*
>
> *High achievement is a very personal standard; only we know how hard we have worked to achieve a particular goal. It's nice to get some outside recognition at times, but setting one's own goals and achieving those goals becomes the greatest motivator to reach higher goals and reach greater levels of achievement in the future.*
>
> —Colleen, home school parent

Colleen focuses on the questions her children ask and goals they set for themselves. No one can fulfill another person's potential, and no one can determine what another person's full potential is. For one child, home schooling for full potential can mean exposing the child to a wide array of subject areas to provide a broad knowledge base. For another, it might mean allowing the child to focus more intensely on a single interest to begin early to hone certain skills and gain specific knowledge. Still another child might need a particularly safe and understanding emotional environment in which to develop skills necessary to cope with her high levels of sensitivity. Home schooling for full potential is never pushed on a child nor over-orchestrated by the parent. Home schooling for full potential always starts and ends with the child, and it takes into account the child's individual strengths, life circumstances, and unique desires and needs.

The Last Resort

Unfortunately, home schooling for some families is a last resort because other educational options are not working, and the children are suffering.

> *It's hard for me to think of home schooling as a true choice since at the time it was the only alternative left. My daughter was in a full-time gifted program that served the upper 2% of the population. As each year went by, the gap became larger and larger between what the school had to offer and what she needed.*
>
> —Anne, home school parent

> *We began home schooling because we had no other alternative. Second grade was a disaster for our daughter, with obvious and intolerable psychological effects. A very long, dismal story. I think our pediatrician was the first to bring up the possibility of home schooling. I was reluctant since we are not religious, and the only home schoolers I knew of at that time were. I knew that the parent of one of my oboe students was home schooling one of her children, and she helped me get started.*
>
> —Jan, home school parent

Joan and Bill, parents of two daughters, describe the long and difficult journey that led to their decision to home school.

> *Our reasons for home schooling were first, health and, later, philosophical. Our oldest daughter was showing physical and emotional signs of stress related to her giftedness, and our youngest had health problems that would have seen her placed in a resource room where she would probably not be intellectually challenged.*
>
> *The oldest was having dry heaves every morning before school. She had complained about school being boring from first grade on. We had tried a variety of things to make sure the problem was neither with us nor with her general health. Her doctor found nothing wrong with her. We tried to work with the school, with less than satisfying results.*
>
> *We decided to visit the Center for Gifted Education at the University of Calgary and talked with educators there who had more experience with gifted children than we. We learned a great deal from these people, who encouraged us to work it out with the public school system if we could. During this time, we also had our daughter tested privately by a licensed psychologist, as the school had a backlog six months long. The testing included an all-around assessment, not just her intelligence. It became obvious by the end of third grade that keeping her in public school was no longer an option. Since private school was not an option for our family, we were left with home schooling.*
>
> —Joan and Bill, home school parent

If you are looking at home schooling as a last resort because nothing else works or because your child is miserable in school, remind yourself that there is no shame in home schooling. When families feel that they are not freely choosing home schooling but rather that they have no other choice, the children can easily come to feel that their giftedness is a problem and that the expenses, time, and other costs of home schooling are a sacrificial burden caused by "their problem." Children should not feel guilty for their giftedness—or for who they are born to be. Whether you choose home schooling as a last resort or because of the opportunities and advantages it offers, you will want to approach your decision systematically and thoughtfully.

Home School Journal

The decision to home school takes time and thought, and your ideas may evolve in unexpected directions. It will probably be helpful to start a home school journal to record your thoughts and questions about home schooling. You may wish to include:

- A list of books you've read and materials you've reviewed.
- A record of your family's daily learning schedule.
- Observations about your child's learning strengths and habits.
- A record of your own developing ideas about education and learning.
- Questions for later investigation.
- A list of concerns.
- A list of possible solutions.

The following questions in the Questions for Reflection section of this chapter are designed to help you with your decision to home school, or if you are already home schooling, to guide you further on your journey. They can be the basis for a written journal, or they can be simply questions for reflection, a sampling of which can be found at the end of each chapter. These questions guided our own family's decision to home school and are also the questions I asked families whose experiences are shared in this book. Choose one or two questions a day to ponder. Be aware that your responses can change as your family's needs or circumstances change.

Key Points

☑ Home schooling has a long and impressive history in the United States; many notable and successful historical people were home schooled.

☑ Many parents cite intellectual needs, social/emotional needs, and the need to fulfill personal potential as reasons for home schooling their gifted child.

☑ School gifted programs may not provide what a gifted child needs intellectually.

☑ Gifted children require an education that offers differentiation on several levels, advanced knowledge, higher level thinking skills, and an interdisciplinary approach; home schooling allows parents to offer this education.

☑ Several common traits of giftedness, such as asynchronous development, intensity, and sensitivity, mean that a gifted child has unique social and emotional needs that can be addressed through home schooling.

☑ Home schooling parents focus on social development rather than socialization.

☑ Full potential presumes that success comes as a result of the child's finding and realizing his or her own unique place in the world, understanding and acceptance of the self, and exploration of one's relationship to the community, which cannot be chosen or orchestrated by anyone else.

☑ Home schooling for full potential synthesizes ways to meet social, emotional, and intellectual needs and emphasizes creative and self-directed learning.

☑ Home schooling is often a last resort for families whose children have had unhappy or harmful experiences in school; many home school families exhaust all other available options before choosing to home school

☑ Families who come to home schooling as a last resort often find, after a period of time, that learning at home offers unanticipated advantages, such as personal freedom and renewed joy in learning.

Questions for Reflection

1. What does a good education mean to you?

2. What are your educational goals for your children?

3. What educational goals do they have for themselves?

4. What are your reasons for considering home schooling?

5. Have you chosen an approach to home schooling? Is it unschooling, classical home schooling, unit studies, or something else? What are your plans so far?

6. Do you plan to use a grade-based curriculum? Will you plan to keep track of grade levels? Why or why not?

7. What kinds of resources do you plan to use? Textbooks? Comprehensive packages? Library materials? Distance learning? Mentors? Community classes? Organizations?

8. What kinds of assessments and evaluations will you use? What are state requirements for assessment, if any?

9. What are the biggest challenges you foresee as a home school parent?

10. What are the greatest rewards and joys you foresee as a home school parent?

11. How will your child's preferred learning styles play a role in your home schooling?

12. How will you deal with special issues such as ADD, learning disabilities, or others?

13. How much do you expect home schooling to cost? What expenses do you anticipate?

14. How do you plan to deal with social and emotional development while home schooling?

15. Do you expect home schooling life to be easier or harder than classroom education, or about the same? Why or why not?

16. What questions about home schooling remain unanswered or unresolved?

17. What is your home school wish list?

There are no right or wrong answers to these questions. You might ask your children for their thoughts as well, or have them keep their own home school journal or notebook. Parents of younger children can look for the book *The Creative Journal for Children: A Guide for Parents, Teachers, and Counselors*, by Lucia Capacchione. For high school students, the book *JUMPSTART: Ideas to Move Your Mind*, by Beatrice J. Elyé is a self-discovery guidebook and journal that encourages writing as a path toward self-discovery.

To jumpstart your own thinking, here are some examples of how other home schooling families have responded to a few of the above questions.

What does a "good education" mean to you?

Lynn, home school student, age 16:

Actual knowledge, to me, doesn't make up the most important part of a good education. A good education is one that instills a love of learning and encourages you to explore the world around (and inside) you. It doesn't tell you all the answers; it tells you how to find the answers. It leads you to think for yourself and be independent.

Jo, a home school parent:

I think a good education should include certain elements. First and foremost, it should foster in the student a love of learning and a sense of the lifelong nature and the constant delight of learning. At best, it should be broad and interdisciplinary, encompassing at least a basic exposure to all of the major accepted academic areas (language arts, mathematics, sciences, and social studies) as well as exposure to all areas of the arts (visual, music, dance, drama), and some in-depth experience in at least one of the arts. It should include physical education of some sort, including understanding of the workings of the body and the importance of diet, health, and fitness.

These things should all be connected to a larger sense of morality and ethics, and an appreciation for our role as humans on the planet. A good education is incomplete if it doesn't include some connection to the community, global as well as local.

In the course of such an education, it is also hoped that the student will learn to apply herself or himself rigorously, to foster self-discipline and independence of thought and work.

Denice, home school student, age nine:

A good education means you can go as deep as you want to into a subject and not be held back by the school curriculum. I also have time to learn things like French and the Latin and Greek roots of words. It is also more flexible. Sometimes I'll spend the whole day on math and do nothing else.

Home schooling is fun because you can do things you wouldn't be able to do while in school, like horseback riding and drama class. Plus, I have more free time to just be a kid. When I was in school, my lessons (French, violin, and piano) were after-school activities. By the time I got home and did my homework, practiced, and ate dinner, it was time to go to bed.

Luke, home school student, age 13:

If you're ever swindled, then you'll know that you didn't get a good education.

What are your educational goals for your children?

Jo, home school parent:

> *To be happy. To feel a part of their community.*
>
> *To foster their intrinsic passion for learning.*
>
> *To guide the development of skills such as discipline, persistence, responsibility.*
>
> *To expose them to a broad span of curricular areas and build solid foundations in each based on work that is meaningful and productive to the child.*
>
> *To help them pursue their interests and passions to their satisfaction.*
>
> *To help them improve social skills and build relationships with others which are meaningful and fulfilling to them.*
>
> *To enhance their love of books, reading, and stories.*
>
> *To build upon other areas of pleasure such as mathematical concepts and game strategy.*
>
> *To continue to teach ethical and moral analysis and behavior.*
>
> *To foster acceptance and flexibility in dealing with a diverse range of people.*
>
> *To enhance their own sense of themselves as unique and valuable individuals.*

What educational goals do the children have for themselves?

Rosemary, home school student, age 11:

> *My short terms goal include getting a good part in my next play and getting ready for college so I can go when I'm 14. I'm working on my singing, dancing, and acting for the part I want, and I'm working on my writing and math so that I'll be ready to go to college.*
>
> *My long-term goals are becoming an actress, writing a novel (I like writing), and becoming a mom. I'm going to theatre classes, doing professional theatre, and working on my skills now. I'm working on my writing by writing short books for my little sister. As far as being a mom, I'll cross that bridge when I get there.*
>
> *I can guarantee I wouldn't know half of what I know now if I went to school!*

What questions or concerns about home schooling remain unanswered or unresolved?

Carol, home school parent:

> *My 13-year-old is at a crossroads because we need to decide if she should enter our city's academic magnet high school next year or continue to home school. There is a lot of pressure from relatives and friends for her to go to public or private high school. But I don't feel that we can make an informed decision yet until the issues are completely defined in my mind.*
>
> *How difficult will it be for us to provide her with the curriculum she will need to be admitted to whatever universities or colleges she will wish to attend? How difficult will it be for us to leap through all the bureaucratic hoops necessary for college admission on our own?*
>
> *There are so many details (for example, remembering to apply in time for the PSATs!) that I'm afraid we will miss a deadline or begin planning too late.*

Jeff, home school parent:

How adequate is our child's general education level? What specific areas need work? How will this impact our daughter's ability to continue her education in a more traditional setting should she choose to do so?

Jolene, home school parent:

I need the most help in skill areas. I need to know what skills are crucial by what level of development. For example, by what age should my child be able to construct an essay of five paragraphs with adequate punctuation, spelling, etc.? It would help me when I'm trying to sort out weak spots. When the child's reading level is through the roof, and the small motor skills are average for her age, it wreaks havoc on Language Arts when trying to evaluate or know what to expect.

Barbara, home school parent:

I wonder what the future holds as my son's knowledge base quickly surpasses mine and my husband's. Finding mentors and people who understand gifted children and who allow them to flourish is a real challenge. Sometimes I still feel that I'm not finding the right materials for him, not doing him justice because I am not his intellectual equal. I hope that I will have taught him how to find the answers for himself.

Chris, home school parent:

I find a lack of information on the social/emotional aspects of giftedness and home schooling. Asynchrony is rarely discussed outside the context of precocious preschoolers. Perhaps because my two children qualify as gifted with learning disabilities their asynchrony is more extreme than most…I don't know. It's just that this asynchrony impacts every aspect of their being and is the main reason we turned to home schooling. Just because we have the flexibility to address the various learning levels doesn't mean that the issue has disappeared.

Jon, home school parent:

My main area of concern is social development. I have read many articles where people say that home schoolers have better social skills than children who go to a public school. But coming from home school parents, this information is not very reliable.

When I look several years ahead, I can clearly see that my child will have a "cultural" gap with public-schooled children. Being an immigrant to the United States, I know that I will never be able to relate to those who grew up here in every way. I miss some based on TV shows and don't know the meaning of certain slang words. The same will probably happen to my child, because he will be outside of the public school culture.

Maybe it is a blessing in disguise, because there are many negative things about this culture. But it still concerns me that home schooling will increase my child's isolation from other children. Being profoundly gifted, my child is already very different. Home schooling adds still another dimension of difference. He is happy now to stay at home and he enjoys our home schooling, but as he grows older, he may wish for the company of other children.

What is your home school wish list?

Barbara, home school parent:

I would love a resource guide containing materials for gifted visual-spatial learners. More specifically, I'd really like to see some plans laid out on different subject areas that list materials and how one would approach the teaching or sharing of knowledge with visual-spatial learners to make it easier on everyone. I don't mind asking lots of questions and searching for materials and designing our own learning environment, but I guess I'd love to have a handy dandy notebook that says, "The guide to home schooling your highly gifted visual-spatial learner."

Li, home school parent:

I'd like museums to offer classes for home schoolers on weekdays. Trying to cram what museums currently consider extra curricular events into evenings and weekends (and fighting rush hour traffic to get there) is making me nuts. The "extra curricular" events are our curriculum. I'd like to be able to do them on weekdays and reserve Saturday and Sunday for family and recreation.

Anne, home school parent:

I would love to see:

1. A review of canned curricula as to flexibility with asynchronous issues,

2. More secular lists of books and texts available,

3. More ideas, materials for the visual-spatial learner, especially videos and documentaries, and

4. Strategies for gifted and learning disability handwriting issues, writing issues, etc.

Sondra, home school parent:

#1 on my wish list: A place to view the various curriculum resources on-line (books, software, on-line programs, etc.) all in one place, sorted by subject, ability, or grade level, and (this is key) what learning style the curriculum is best suited for. I would like the grade level compared to a set of standards (perhaps a few state standards?) rather than what the publisher says is the target age/grade. On this same site, I'd like to see independent reviews of each product or book.

Resources for Home Schooling Gifted Children

Books

Baker, Janice, Julicher, Kathleen, & Hogan, Maggie (1999). *Gifted Children at Home: A Practical Guide for Homeschooling Families*. The Gifted Group Publishing.

Rivero, Lisa (2000). *Gifted Education Comes Home*. Gifted Education Press.

Articles

Kearney, Kathi (September/October, 1992). "Homeschooling Highly Gifted Children." *Understanding Our Gifted*. p. 16.

Staehle, Dori (June 2000). "Taking a Different Path: A Mother's Reflections on Homeschooling." *Roeper Review*. pp. 270-71.

Websites

Davidson Institute's PG-Cybersource Page
www.ditd.org/pgcybersource.php (scroll down to Education: Homeschooling)

"Homeschooling Gifted Students: An Introductory Guide for Parents" by Jacque Ensign. An ERIC digest
http://ericec.org/digests/e543.html

Homeschooling the Highly Gifted (links to many articles and resources)
www.hollingworth.org/homesc.html

Internet Resources for Homeschooling Gifted Students. Compiled by Kathi Kearney, Gifted Education Consultant; Founder, The Hollingworth Center for Highly Gifted Children
www.gifteddevelopment.com/Articles/Homeschool_Int_Res.htm

Smart Kid at Home. A site created by a home school parent "to present the unfolding story of our family's home schooling journey using the eclectic educational method"
www.smartkidathome.com

TAGMAX Mailing List for Parents of Gifted Homeschoolers
www.tagfam.org

The Upside-Down School Room. Created by a home school parent, this Canadian family-based company is, in the words of the owner, "the result of my search to find workable learning materials for my two sons, one of whom is an 'upside-down' kind of learner, and the different children I tutor"
www.upsidedownschoolroom.com

At Home with Home Schoolers

Philip, Age 11

Q: How long have you home schooled?

A: I tried home schooling at the end of third grade. I went back to school in fourth grade, but halfway through the year I went back to home school, and I've been home schooling since. I would be finishing sixth grade if I were in school, but now I work at a higher level in some things.

Q: Why do you home school?

A: School really didn't fit me. The way the school was set up was not right for me. I was in a class for highly gifted students, but the teachers didn't really understand what highly gifted was. They thought gifted was just being better and faster and that you could just instantly do more work, more worksheets especially.

Q: What is a typical day for you now?

A: I get up and eat breakfast. I know I need to do spelling on the computer and do keyboarding practice, so I do this on my own. I work on my handwriting in the cursive italic book. I only do one or two pages. I do math from Singapore Math, usually with my mom. I read a lot, because I like to. I guess reading could be considered school. Sometimes I watch a video on science or another subject. Sometimes I work a lot on school work, other days only a little. Sometimes I take classes, like pottery, science, geography, and French. I take horseback riding lessons once a week and go to swim team practice twice a week. That is my physical education!

Q: Has your home schooling routine changed as you've grown older?

A: Now, if I want to know something, I find information on the Internet, or read an article in the paper, or read a book. Before, my mom had to tell me everything to do, and if I had any questions, I would just ask her. I know a whole lot more than I did three years ago. I know how to get information without my mom's help, so I'm much more independent.

Q: How would you describe yourself as a learner?

A: I learn best though visual methods. Seeing something and hearing is much better than just hearing for me.

2 Traits of Giftedness

I used to believe that all children could be "gifted" if given the proper environment. With Rosemary, I've realized that there is something more there than what my other three children have. Her knowledge seems to come from within. I feel as though what she learns from her books and our discussions just gives names to concepts that she has already figured out on her own.

She also works harder at things as though she's driven to understand whatever it is she's working on. This not only goes for academics, but also physical and artistic endeavors. For instance, she will spend hours every day drawing hands until she gets it right!

—Antonia, home school parent

Gifted children are not a homogenous group. In fact, individual gifted children may differ more widely from each other than they do from other children (Strip, 2000). Thus, there is no one perfect test for giftedness, no simple defining mark or characteristic that can be used as identification. Some gifted children may be athletic and popular. Others may be scholarly, with selected intimate friends. Some gifted children may be entranced by the world of math and numbers. Others may spend every spare moment reading or writing.

Keeping in mind the diversity of gifted and creative learners, we can find enough common traits and tendencies, however, to talk about them as a group. An individual gifted child may not have all of the following traits, but he or she will demonstrate most of these traits and behaviors (Clark, 1997; Jacobsen, 1999b; Vail, 1979; Winner, 1996):

- Precociousness, especially early language development
- Uneven development
- Intensity
- A creative nature
- High levels of sensitivity
- Complexity of thought and personality
- Perfectionism and high expectations
- Highly developed or pervasive sense of humor
- Idealism and sense of justice
- Exceptional memory
- Fascination with patterns
- Unusual ability to concentrate on topics of interest
- Strong drive and developed sense of self
- Unquenchable curiosity
- High levels of energy
- Excitability

This is a good point at which to address the question of whether all children are potentially gifted. When someone says, "All children are gifted," the speaker means that all children are special, all children have specific talents and potentials, and all children are unique. In this sense, the speaker is correct, and parents and teachers who work with children should individualize education for *all* children to allow each unique child to fulfill his or her potential.

However, some children fall far outside the usual learning framework. For example, all children are curious, but these children we call gifted are *insatiably* curious, even at 10:30 p.m. when everyone else in the house is asleep. While all children like to have things their own way sometimes, the children we call gifted seem driven to fulfill some inner agenda, even when it means they will be disciplined for their actions. All children have some areas in which they excel and others in which they struggle, but these children we call gifted *excel at levels far beyond that of their age mates.*

They often have large discrepancies between their ability to think and their ability to produce. For example, a gifted child may seem driven to take apart household appliances such as toasters, clocks, and VCRs, regardless of reprimands. A gifted child may be able to read articles in the newspaper long before parents are aware of the child's ability to do so. A gifted child may envision a complex computer program before possessing the writing or typing skills necessary to make such a program a reality. In these and other ways, the gifted learner is different from other learners, and the child's education must take these differences into account.

Most people recognize that some children are simply more intense, more sensitive, more self-motivated to follow an inner voice, more divergent in their thoughts and actions. The term "gifted" is simply a convenient way to talk about how best to identify, understand, and meet the needs of such children.

Some parents may respond, "Yes, *my* child is highly sensitive and learns extremely quickly, especially in math and science, but he isn't gifted," or "My child is creative, but her IQ test shows that she's just smart, not gifted." Don't be so sure. A "non-gifted" IQ score is not a sufficient reason to discount the possibility of a child's being a gifted learner. High levels of creativity show little correlation with high IQ scores (above 120), and some specific talent areas are not measured by widely used intelligence tests (Webb & Kleine, 1993). Also, the population of gifted children, especially exceptionally gifted children, may be twice or even three times what bell curves would indicate. These "rare" children are not as rare as was once thought (Webb & Kleine, 1993).

Parents should think carefully about the traits of giftedness listed at the beginning of the chapter, including how often, with what intensity, and to what degree their children demonstrate these traits and behaviors. If several traits are evident often or almost always, or several traits are displayed with great intensity over time, this is a good indication that a child is gifted and that special resources and education advice may benefit your child. Some of the common traits and behaviors of gifted children are worth looking at in greater detail in this chapter as they relate to home schooling:

- Precociousness and asynchronous development.
- Intensity.
- A creative nature and complexity.
- Sensitivity.

Precociousness

> *My daughter showed an early interest at age two in printing letters and reading, and at three she began asking very complicated questions endlessly. I called her my child "with the inquiring mind."*
>
> —Ruth, home school parent

Whether it is talking, reading, or addition, many gifted children learn on their own at a rate faster than predicted by normal timetables. This does not mean that all gifted children learn to read early or can add or subtract at age four, but there usually are areas in which the child is significantly ahead of other children the same age. For many children, this precociousness will be most apparent in the area of language and vocabulary. For others, it will be numbers, or spatial relationships, or inter- and intra-personal communications/skills.

Early and appropriate use of advanced vocabulary is one of the most reliable indicators of intellectual giftedness (Webb, 2000a; Whitmore, 1980). Young gifted children often speak in full, complex sentences long before their age peers and truly enjoy learning and trying out new words. Sometimes, because of perfectionism, a gifted child waits to speak until he or she is sure that what is said will be correct. Preschool-age gifted children who do not yet talk extensively will nonetheless understand the advanced language of others and often enjoy being read to from storybooks written for much older children.

Precocity does not always show itself in traditional academic areas. Some gifted children may learn to read and write later than age peers, yet they understand advanced science concepts or comprehend the multiple perspectives of historical understanding at levels far beyond those of other children. We should broaden our idea of precociousness to include areas of learning other than math or language.

Asynchronous Development

> *Home schooling a gifted child requires the parent not to have expectations about what might be appropriate for a child's age level. It requires flexibility and a realization that the child can be many different ages at once.*
>
> —Casey, home school parent

The precocity of the gifted child can lead to an inordinate (and dangerous) emphasis on early achievement and fulfillment of adult expectations. When a five-year-old uses adult vocabulary, parents and teachers may unwittingly expect adult behavior, reasoning, and impulse control from the child as well. When she behaves like the five-year-old she is, she may be viewed as less mature than her age peers. And if a 12-year-old gifted student is ready for college-level math, adults may erroneously expect him to be able to perform college-level work in other subjects as well.

In 1991, a group of parents, teachers, and educators offered a new definition of giftedness that lessens the emphasis too often placed (by both parents and teachers) on achievement. The group developed this definition:

> *Giftedness is asynchronous development in which advanced cognitive abilities and heightened intensity combine to create inner experiences and awareness that are qualitatively different from the norm. This asynchrony increases with higher intellectual capacity. The uniqueness of the gifted renders them particularly vulnerable and requires modifications in parenting, teaching and counseling in order for them to develop optimally (Columbus Group, quoted in Morelock, 1996, p. 8).*

In asynchronous development, the child's various levels and types of development—emotional, intellectual, physical, social—are literally not in sync, and the child may be several ages at once. A gifted 10-year-old may "be an adult" in conversation with teachers, "be a teenager" when choosing leisure reading material, "be a 10-year-old" while away at summer camp, and "be an eight-year-old" when playing with stuffed toys. Whereas few children fit exactly the age-based norms of development on the pediatrician's chart, the gifted child's range of discrepancy is much broader than that of others. Most six-year-olds, for example, are probably within a year or two on either side of most other children of six in terms of development, but a gifted child often is three or four years "out of sync" in one or more areas—and may show great discrepancies between reading ability, mathematical aptitude, social skills, and emotional resiliency, etc.

It is precisely this problem that helps us understand that gifted children have not only specific academic learning needs, but specific social and emotional needs as well. For example, a precocious nine-year-old boy may be curious about the causes of war and can read high school level books about World War II, but he may be not yet be ready to face the inhumanity and horrors of the Holocaust. Or he may enjoy playing computer games with teenagers at their intellectual level, but may not understand why he is teased when he cries after losing a game (Kerr & Cohn, 2001). Adults who guide the learning of these asynchronous learners, then, must work creatively to design individual curriculum and to facilitate social experiences that meet the specific academic as well as the unique social/emotional needs of such children.

Intensity

Simón was nervous, always moving.
One of his private teachers called him a "keg of dynamite."
When Simón heard that, he warned his teacher to keep away.
"I might explode," he said.

—From *A Picture Book of Simón Bolívar* by David Adler

Intensity may be the most universal yet the most overlooked characteristic of gifted children (Webb, 2000a). Vera John-Steiner writes in *Notebooks of the Mind: Explorations in Thinking* that intensity is one universal trait of gifted people and that the seeds of intensity can be found in childhood: "All the individuals I interviewed recalled some recognition of their engagement with play, with ideas, with the world, and while still very young" (John-Steiner, 1997, p. 220).

To understand better the intensity of the gifted child, a Polish psychologist, Kazimierz Dabrowski, offers the concept of *superabundance*, an idea that moves giftedness beyond the confines of academic testing. Gifted children and adults are often known for being just "too much"—for example, too sensitive, too energetic, too smart for their own good, too much in their heads, too excitable. Dabrowski found that these great levels of energy—sometimes translated as "overexcitabilities" or "superabundance"—are not a bad thing and are, in fact, necessary for many gifted individuals to realize their potential (Silverman, 1998).

Superabundance can occur in the intellectual, imaginational, emotional, psychomotor, and sensual realms. The following are examples of behaviors associated with superabundance in young children (Tucker & Hafenstein, 1997; Lind, 2000).

Intellectual Superabundance

Sample behaviors include avid reading, curiosity, asking probing questions, concentration, problem solving, theoretical thinking.

Five-year-old Joanna asks questions about everything, including how Aunt Anna's baby got into her tummy, how one religion can be the right one when so many exist, and why noses are in the middle of our faces instead of combined with our ears. She is rarely satisfied with a simplistic answer. Adults sometimes tell Joanna that curiosity killed the cat and that she shouldn't ask so many questions. Her favorite activities are reading and doing puzzles.

Imaginational Superabundance

Sample behaviors include fantasy play, animistic and imaginative thinking, daydreaming, dramatic perception, use of metaphor.

Alex spent his entire kindergarten year pretending to be a cat, complete with stretching, meowing, and purring. Now at age eight, he often spends hours in his room contentedly acting out imaginative stories with his Legos®. He insists that rocks and trees have feelings, and he apologizes to flowers before picking them. Alex feels pressure from his friends to give up childish daydreams for more accepted forms of play, such as soccer.

Emotional Superabundance

Sample behaviors include concern for others, timidity and shyness, fear and anxiety, difficulty adjusting to new environments, intensity of feeling.

Zeki, age 10, gets a stomachache whenever he hears someone speak of world hunger. He regularly donates his allowance to his local food bank. Zeki's teacher tells him that he's too young to worry about the world's problems. When he meets new people, he feels his heart pound in his chest and becomes very quiet because he is afraid of saying the wrong thing. He has packed an emergency storm and tornado kit, which he stores in the basement "just in case."

Psychomotor Superabundance

Sample behaviors include marked enthusiasm, rapid speech, surplus of energy, nervous habits, impulsive actions.

Hannah, age 12, rarely sits still. When she must sit still in a waiting room or in the car, she immediately starts a conversation with the nearest person, using her hands frequently for emphasis. Her mother says that young ladies must learn not to talk so much. Hannah's favorite activities are talking, running, horseback riding, swimming, playing the drums, and karate.

Sensual Superabundance

Sample behaviors include sensory pleasures, appreciation of sensory aspects of experiences, avoidance of over-stimulation.

Seven-year-old Todd can name the ingredients in almost any dish by their smell. He insists on choosing his own clothes, because he says that soft fabrics allow him to think better. He is strongly affected by air temperature and visual stimulation. Todd's favorite activities are helping in the garden and going to art museums. His father wants Todd to find more masculine hobbies.

As the examples above illustrate, superabundance can often cause difficulties for children. One parent describes how intensity affects his family.

Superabundance or intensity of experience for individuals who are gifted does not disappear with age, and it is one of three umbrella traits that Mary Elaine Jacobsen (1999b) finds in gifted adults (the other two being *complexity* and *drive*). Jacobsen writes that intensity can come in the forms of both excitability and sensitivity, and it can lead individuals either to push themselves to physical and emotional exhaustion or to become apathetic and anesthetized.

The goal for parents should be to help children accept and use their intensity for exhilaration and enrichment; in other words, go ahead and be full of life rather than fight or be overwhelmed by it.

Self-Determination and Drive

The word intensity comes from the verb to *intend*, which in Latin means to set out on one's course. Indeed, we see the gifted child's intensity in his sense of self-determination, wanting to direct his own life and actions. When applied to a specific domain, Ellen Winner, in her book *Gifted Children: Myths and Realities* (1996), calls it a "rage to master." Many parents can relate to Howard Rowland (1975), who writes in *No More School: An American Family's Experiment in Education*, that his son Seth was, like most children, "predisposed to learn, but unlike most, he was self-propelled." Similarly, Elizabeth Maxwell (1997) of the Gifted Development Center in Denver describes the self-determined drive of gifted and highly gifted children as hard to miss; it "arrives early and [is] thrust in the face of parents and the environment in general." James Delisle (1992) similarly explains: "These children are not passive goody-goodies. They are often difficult to be around because they want to 'run the show.' Yet this same quality also makes them most interesting and stimulating to be around."

Nell describes the internal drive of her daughter, Mia, when she was six years old.

A strong internal drive does not always result in such positive learning experiences. An intense drive to learn is often more problematic for a child than it is for adults, because so much of the child's life is controlled by adults, whether out of habit or presumably for the child's own good. Excitable adults are often given some leeway for eccentric or passionate behavior, such as forgetfulness or rapid speech. The gifted, intense, driven adult at least has some freedom in choice of career, use of time, and daily schedule. A change of job or residence can be made to provide more freedom. Self-employment can allow working at one's own pace.

The gifted child, on the other hand, may find little space or tolerance for intense emotional reactions; she may even find herself punished for superabundance behaviors, such as interrupting others or getting so excited by a new idea that she forgets to do required work or chores. And children rarely are given a choice of where to receive their education, what subjects to study, or how to spend the bulk of their hours. They must live and learn where significant adults decide they will. The pace of their learning and work is usually dictated from the outside as well.

Some gifted children find positive outlets for their intensity in extracurricular or co-curricular activities, or in some other area of high interest to them. The drive to follow one's own course sometimes finds an outlet in school underachievement. Herb Kohl (1994) writes of active "not learning" that many children engage in, where the child *chooses* not to learn, exercising perhaps the only avenue of self-determination available. By saying "no" to adult expectations, these children may be letting us know that they need more, rather than less, control over their life.

To help a child feel comfortable with his own intensity, parents can offer him space to experience intense reactions, opinions, drives, and feelings. Sometimes this requires patience and a willingness to accept some misunderstanding from other adults who expect children to be nonchalant. Gifted children are rarely nonchalant about anything! When a child talks loudly and excitedly about his ideas, insists on studying a controversial topic such as religion or genetics, or likes to speak to adults on their level rather than allowing adults to speak patronizingly, the parent can refrain from scolding the child out of a sense of embarrassment. Instead, parents can steadfastly support and accept the child's intensity and self-determination. If possible, parents should seek out other parents of intense and creative children for support, ideas, and the opportunity to socialize without feeling the need to explain or defend their child's intensity.

A Creative Nature

Self-determination can lead children to think and act in ways that diverge from the crowd. Indeed, divergent thinking is the bedrock of creativity, another important trait of gifted learners.

We all have the ability to produce novelty, to think in new ways, to forge new paths and fashion new combinations. Jane Piirto, in *Understanding Those Who Create*, concludes that creativity is "a basic human instinct to make that which is new," and therefore part of the basic nature of all human beings. It needs to be nurtured, however.

While creativity is the natural propensity of human being-ness, creativity can be either enhanced or stifled. The creative personality can be either developed or thwarted. Creativity takes certain habits of mind. Creativity is not separate from intelligence or artistry, but part of the whole (Piirto, 1998, p. 41).

What seems different about creativity in the gifted child is that creativity seems more integrated with the whole being, harder to "turn off," and more of a challenge to understand and accept. A gifted child's view of the world is often non-traditional and divergent; he sees numerous possibilities hidden to others (Webb, Meckstroth, & Tolan, 1982).

Ellen Winner (1996), author of *Gifted Children: Myths and Realities*, notes that gifted children are by definition creative. Most theories of giftedness include at least some mention of divergent thinking and creativity. But children who are highly creative may score lower than less creative peers on standardized tests and IQ tests (Betts, 1985; Webb & Kleine, 1993), perhaps because they are drawn to the unusual answer, not the "correct" one. They see novel possibilities in otherwise straightforward questions. They are the students who cannot follow step-by-step instructions without embellishment, interpretation, and revision, sometimes to the dismay and frustration of the adults around them! Yet this sort of creativity and "thinking outside the box," the chance to explore new ideas as well as learn old ones, has the potential to give us inventions of the future, new ways of solving world problems, innovative works of literature and art, and new interpretations of history and philosophy.

Regrettably, these children are also likely to be diagnosed with ADD (Attention Deficit Disorder) or ADHD (Attention Deficit Hyperactivity Disorder). Some recent popular books (e.g., *Driven to Distraction* and *The Edison Trait*) have argued that creativity is "impulsivity gone right" (Hallowell & Ratey, 1995). That is, the ADHD characteristics in a bright person often result in creative leaps.

Generally, when children are allowed to learn creatively, we unlock powerful and amazing learning potential.

Complexity

Evan's parents just cannot figure him out. At home, the eight-year-old is generally quiet and thoughtful. He spends hours alone in his room reading detective comics and sorting through his various collections of stamps, rocks, postcards, and science fiction magazines. But when he plays with other children, he takes on a different personality. He becomes talkative and impulsive, the proverbial life of the party. Evan enjoys his friends, but after two or three days of socializing, he becomes moody and asks to stay home for awhile. His parents can't decide if he needs more socializing or less, if he is introverted or extraverted.

Creativity adds a dimension of complexity to a child's personality because, while creative thinking requires a certain degree of solitude, highly creative people also crave occasional social interaction and communication (Csikszentmihalyi, 1996; Piirto, 1998; Willings, 1980). The blurring of the distinction between intro-version and extroversion is just one way in which gifted and creative people are complex. Mihaly Csikszentmihalyi (1996) believes that highly creative people display several "dimensions of complexity." Highly creative people can be simultaneously:

- Energetic and restful
- Intelligent and naïve
- Playful and disciplined
- Fanciful and reality-based
- Humble and proud
- Masculine and feminine
- Rebellious and conservative
- Passionate and objective
- Suffering and blissful
- Introverted and extraverted

People with dimensions of complexity can experience each extreme with the same intensity and without internal conflict (Csikszentmihalyi, 1996). This complexity might show itself in a child wise beyond her years in matters of history and social concerns (intelligent) but who lacks "street smarts" in safely traveling about her own neighborhood (naïve), or when a child insists at a very young age that he *knows* Santa Claus isn't real (reality-based) but at a later age believes that stuffed animals have feelings (imaginative, fanciful).

The lesson for home school parents may be to make the home environment *both/and* rather than *either/or*. Both playfulness *and* hard work are appropriate for different times and circumstances, and sometimes at the same time. Both joy *and* sadness are justified reactions to events. Both rebelliousness *and* cooperation are a part of the human condition.

Gifted and creative people are often complex in terms of learning style as well as in personality. Gifted children often learn best when two or even three modes are combined—auditory (learning by hearing), visual (learning by seeing), and kinesthetic (learning by doing). These children may seem to learn without effort and are often able to switch easily from one mode to another, depending on the task involved. As they grow older, the children may need help in knowing how to control and manage their choice of learning mode (Barbe, 1985). In addition, many highly gifted children possess both visual-spatial and auditory-sequential learning styles (Silverman, 1998). For parents of these children, it is not enough to understand one learning style. Parents and teachers should be ready to support two or three learning styles, which means having more knowledge and more resources and letting the child explore various subjects using several approaches rather than a single approach.

For example, Tanya is an avid, self-taught reader who can easily follow directions and has a highly developed sense of language. Assuming she is an auditory-sequential learner, her parents usually buy curriculum materials that contain little or no visual presentation. They use textbooks and discussion for introduction of new material. But one day when Tanya is visiting a friend, she begins to play with some math fraction rods and is quickly able do fraction work two grade levels above her current math textbook. Have her parents misunderstood her learning style? What kind of curriculum materials does she require?

Like many gifted and creative learners, Tanya probably needs a variety of materials that will allow her to approach a subject from many angles. Her parents can continue to use the math textbook but can alternate with visual-spatial materials or math manipulatives. Or they can allow her a choice of ways in which to study a specific subject or skill, such as asking her whether she'd like to practice multiplication facts by using flashcards, reciting them orally or writing them on the sidewalk with colored chalk.

Sensitivity

Being able to see, hear, feel, and experience aspects of life that most people miss is a necessary part of creative production (Dixon, 1983). Sometimes the child's awareness is directed toward that which is outside; sometimes it is directed within. A highly sensitive child will likely notice a slight temperature change in a room, the first hint of green in spring grass, or the first signs of coming down with a cold.

High levels of sensitivity may be what drives intellectual giftedness; they allow the child to pick up on vast amounts of input from his environment (Freeman, 1985). When a child easily notices the details and sensory stimuli around him, he will, as a result, "know" more than less sensitive children.

Of course, heightened sensitivity can also cause much discomfort for children as they feel every twinge of growth inside an adolescent body or notice the slightest frown of displeasure on the faces of beloved adults. But we can help our children view sensitivity holistically, not simply as a negative trait. While they may suffer empathetically when they witness unfairness and cruelty, they may also experience profound joy in the presence of beauty and kindness. While they might need to be more selective than other children in their choices of reading materials and television and movies, they may also experience profound aesthetic pleasure in literature and art. Such appreciation of beauty can be a lifelong source of comfort and inspiration. A problem develops only when the world doesn't know how to deal with a child's high level of sensitivity and the child becomes ashamed of, or confused by, her own sensitive nature. Gabor Maté, author of *Scattered*, reminds us that sensitivity itself is not the problem.

> *The existence of sensitive people is an advantage for humankind because it is a group that best expresses humanity's creative urges and needs. Through their instinctual responses the world is best interpreted. Under normal circumstances, they are artists or artisans, seekers, inventors, shamans, poets, prophets* (Maté, 1999. p. 62).

Maté argues that hypersensitivity is an inborn temperament that requires a special style of parenting. Rather than regard sensitive children as "difficult," he suggests that parents look to their sensitive children for clues as to what needs to be changed in the family environment: "If we wanted to know how we were doing as individuals or as a couple, we needed only check the facial expressions and emotional responses of our daughter. What was recorded there did not always reassure us" (Maté, 1999, p. 61).

Parents and teachers can support and nurture highly sensitive children by accepting *all* of a child's feelings, even when those feelings seem over the top or not in accordance with the feelings of others. Children can be helped to know that they indeed may feel and notice more of their environment than other people, and that's okay. They can learn how to arrange their environment when necessary to better tolerate stimulation. They can adjust the volume on the TV, pay attention to the amount of visual detail that feels comfortable in their rooms, and they can also learn that other people usually don't "make faces" or say things just to drive them crazy, but that their own unusual ability to pick up on nuances and details may sometimes cause them to misinterpret others' actions and intentions.

Parents can point out how sensitivity is a valuable human trait that leads to great art and music, humanitarian actions, and in smaller but equally valuable ways, to acts of kindness, deep friendships, and the ability to empathize with others so as to offer an understanding ear or other assistance. Bibliotherapy, the use of books to better understand ourselves and to deal with concerns, is also very useful for coming to appreciate sensitivity. For example, the young adult book, *Ordinary Miracles*, by Stephanie Tolan, is the story of a sensitive and thoughtful eighth-grade boy who experiences deep and conflicting feelings about his father, his role in his family, and his friendship with a stranger who happens to be a Nobel-prize winner. Other ideas for good books for sensitive children can be found in Judith Wynn Halsted's book *Some of My Best Friends Are Books: Guiding Gifted Readers from Preschool to High School*, 2nd edition (2002).

Key Points

☑ Precocity, intensity, creativity, and sensitivity are key indicators of giftedness.

☑ Gifted learners function ahead of their age peers in one or more areas; areas of precocity can be traditional subjects, such as math or reading, or non-traditional, such as understanding mechanical systems or expertise in nature or animals.

☑ Young gifted learners often speak with advanced syntax and vocabulary.

☑ Gifted children's own levels of cognitive, physical, emotional, and social development are often out of sync; this *asynchronous development*, common to gifted, creative learners, results in unique and specific education and social needs.

☑ Intensity shows itself in superabundance of the intellect, imagination, emotions, psychomotor system, and senses.

☑ Superabundance in children is sometimes misunderstood, even punished by adults; parents should make a conscious effort to accept and support their child's intensity.

☑ Intense gifted children often prefer to follow their own course and do things their own self-determined way, but this inner drive is often not taken seriously by adults.

☑ Intensity continues throughout the gifted person's lifespan.

☑ Creativity is part of human nature, and for many gifted children, divergent or creative thinking is an inherent part of the way they experience and contribute to the world.

☑ Highly creative children do not necessarily receive high test scores.

☑ Creativity can be nurtured as well as inhibited; parents and teachers should be careful to accept and support children's divergent, creative thinking.

☑ Highly creative people often have complex personalities that resist categorization; highly gifted children often have the ability to learn with two or more learning styles.

☑ Parents can support complexity by refusing to limit or define children with words or actions; instead, adults can accommodate seemingly opposite traits, such as masculinity and femininity or imagination and logic in their children.

☑ High levels of sensitivity can cause discomfort for children.

☑ Sensitivity is necessary for appreciation of beauty.

☑ Adults can refrain from thinking of sensitive children as difficult or thin-skinned.

☑ Children can learn to manage aspects of their environment so as better to handle high levels of sensitivity; bibliotherapy can be a good way to address the issue of sensitivity.

Questions for Reflection

Think again about each of the traits of giftedness mentioned in this chapter: precociousness and asynchronous development, intensity and self-determination, a creative nature and complexity, and high sensitivity.

1. How often do you notice these traits in your child? Daily, occasionally, rarely?

2. Has the frequency changed with age?

3. Can you think of specific examples of when your child has shown a particular trait?

4. Is it important to you that your child "have" any trait on the list? Why or why not?

5. Do you feel that you can see your child for who he or she is apart from who you want your child to be?

Resources for Families of Gifted Children

Books

Clark, Barbara (1997). *Growing Up Gifted: Developing the Potential of Children at Home and at School*, 5th ed. Prentice Hall.

Delisle, Deb, & Delisle, James (1996). *Growing Good Kids: 28 Activities to Enhance Self-Awareness, Compassion, and Leadership.* Free Spirit Publishing.

Delisle, James R. (1992). *Guiding the Social and Emotional Development of Gifted Youth: A Practical Guide for Educators and Counselors.* Longman.

Kerr, Barbara (1997). *Smart Girls: A New Psychology of Girls, Women and Giftedness, revised edition.* Great Potential Press (formerly Gifted Psychology Press).

Kerr, Barbara, & Cohn, Sanford (2001). *Smart Boys: Talent, Manhood, and the Search for Meaning.* Great Potential Press (formerly Gifted Psychology Press).

Kurcinka, Mary Sheedy. (1991). *Raising Your Spirited Child: A Guide for Parents Whose Child Is More Intense, Sensitive, Perceptive, Persistent, Energetic.* HarperCollins.

Rogers, Karen (2002). *Re-forming Gifted Education: Matching the Program to the Child.* Great Potential Press (formerly Gifted Psychology Press).

Saunders, Jacquelyn (1991). *Bringing Out the Best: A Resource Guide for Parents of Young Gifted Children.* Free Spirit Publishing.

Smutny, Joan Franklin; Walker, Sally Yahnke; & Meckstroth, Elizabeth (1997). *Teaching Young Gifted Children in the Regular Classroom: Identifying, Nurturing and Challenging Ages 4-9.* Free Spirit Publishing.

Strip, Carol A. (2000). *Helping Gifted Children Soar: A Practical Guide for Parents and Teachers.* Great Potential Press (formerly Gifted Psychology Press).

Takacs, Carol A. (1986). *Enjoy Your Gifted Child.* Syracuse University Press.

Vail, Priscilla (1979). *The World of the Gifted Child.* Walker.

Webb, James T. (2000). *Is My Child Gifted?* VHS Video. Great Potential Press (formerly Gifted Psychology Press).

Webb, James T. (2000). *Parenting Successful Children.* VHS Video. Great Potential Press (formerly Gifted Psychology Press).

Webb, James T.; Meckstroth, Elizabeth; & Tolan, Stephanie (1982). *Guiding the Gifted Child.* Great Potential Press (formerly Gifted Psychology Press).

Winner, Ellen (1996). *Gifted Children: Myths and Realities.* Basic Books.

Magazines and Journals

Gifted Child Today
Prufrock Press
P.O. Box 8813
Waco, TX 76714-8813
www.prufrock.com

Gifted Education Communicator, A Journal for Educators and Parents
15141 East Whittier Blvd., Suite 510
Whittier, CA 90603
Phone: (562) 789-9933
www.CAGifted.org

Parenting for High Potential
National Association for Gifted Children
1707 L Street, NW Suite 550
Washington, DC 20036
Phone: (202) 785-4268
www.nagc.org

Understanding Our Gifted
Open Space Communications
P.O. Box 18268
Boulder, CO 80308
Phone: (303) 444-7020 or (800) 494-6178
www.openspacecomm.com

Organizations and Websites

Davidson Institute for Talent Development
www.ditd.org/ditd.ph
ERIC Clearinghouse on Disabilities and Gifted Education. This government agency provides numerous articles on gifted education, most available on the Internet free of charge

ERIC EC, The Council for Exceptional Children (CEC)
1110 North Glebe Road
Arlington, VA 22201-5704
Phone: (800) 328-0272
http://ericec.org
Gifted-Children.com Website. A web-based newsletter. Monthly fee
www.gifted-children.com
Hoagies Gifted Website. The web resource and support for families of gifted children.
www.hoagiesgifted.org
National Association for Gifted Children
1707 L Street, NW Suite 550
Washington, DC 20036
Phone: (202) 785-4268
www.nagc.org

The National Foundation for Gifted and Creative Children
395 Diamond Hill Road
Warwick, Rhode Island 02886
Phone: (401) 738-0937
  www.nfgcc.org
Serving Emotional Needs of the Gifted (SENG)
P.O. Box 6550
Scottsdale, AZ 85261
Phone: (206) 498-6744
  www.sengifted.org

At Home with Home Schoolers

Claire, Age 14

I am 14 years old and would be finishing up eighth grade. I have been home schooled for about eight or nine years, ever since my dad took me out of school halfway through kindergarten. At that point, my dad was interested in the idea of home schooling, and I was having a bad time in kindergarten. I already knew how to read simple texts, and the teacher was still teaching us the alphabet, which made sense for some kids but not for me.

My dad brought up the subject of home schooling at the dinner table: "How would you like to stay home and learn with Mommy and Daddy?" I was all for it and said, "When do we start?" That was where it began.

My Home Schooling Day

Our schedule varies from day to day. On a day when we don't have any out-of-home activities, I generally begin my day with cello practicing. I usually practice about four hours every day in the morning, from about 8:00 a.m. until noon. Then my dad, my brother, and I often read books together about physics, chemistry, or historical fiction. After lunch, my brother and I usually work on learning German, and my brother practices piano. He also practices violin in the morning. I work on biology and algebra, or occasionally we will go to the YMCA. Late in the afternoon, my brother will often watch an educational video while I work on editing my recently finished first novel, write more on the history for my fantasy story, or work on a new song I am writing.

That is pretty much our day, although recently my dad and I have been working on recording my first CD album while my brother and my mom read a biology book together.

I take cello lessons for an hour every Tuesday morning, and I also participate in a theory class, a cello group, and a string quartet on Saturday mornings at The String Academy of Wisconsin at the University. I also occasionally volunteer at the Humane Society where I feed, play with, exercise, and socialize the animals. I used to shadow a small animal vet a year ago, too.

Over the years, we've looked at curricula and experimented with trying to follow very set schedules. I think that by now we've got a technique that works well. We don't use any comprehensive curriculum right now, although I do use biology and algebra textbooks. You could say we take every day as it comes, but we know what we have to accomplish and we make sure we accomplish it.

What I Like about Home Schooling

Home schooling allows me to concentrate more on what I'm interested in. My parents can help me individually instead of dealing with a big class of people at different levels, so everything goes more quickly and more efficiently. Or if something isn't going well and I'm getting frustrated, we can take a break, maybe work on something else, and come back to it later. That is very helpful for me.

I learn some things best by myself. Algebra is one example. I need help sometimes, but I feel good figuring something out for myself. Some things I get really interested in and I go after them. Examples are dinosaurs and America's Space Program. Learning science is a bit more difficult, and I need someone there to help me get started. After that, I'm generally okay. It really varies by subject.

What I Don't Like about Home Schooling

If there's one thing I don't like about home schooling, it is that almost everyone I meet assumes that I am in school. It sometimes gets frustrating when people ask, "Are you off school today?" or "What grade are you in?" To us, grade levels don't matter. I also feel left out when school kids I know start talking about someone at school or a teacher or a test, because I'm not experiencing those things. Occasionally I feel like I'm some sort of "oddball" and that I ought to be experiencing all that school stuff.

A Good Education

If you don't learn anything, it's not a good education. I consider a good education to be enjoyable, exciting, and to make a difference in how you think. In algebra, for example, I realized what amazing things you can do when you don't even know what number you're dealing with! I want to go to college and become someone who makes a difference in others' lives. To me, a good education allows you to *live* life and not just get by. There are certain things you need in life to stay on top and make it. You *need* math. You *need* to know how to read. But there's a lot more you can explore with additional knowledge. There are new frontiers, and somebody has to explore them. There is space and nature and all sorts of things out there.

My Future

At the moment, I want to grow up to be a professional cellist. I've been practicing four hours a day. I also hope to have my novel published. Right now I'm in the editing phase. I want to write my own songs, something that I've already been doing for awhile. I also hope to know just about everything I can find out about space and our environment. I guess you could say I'm ambitious. I don't know. I just really want to know things and make a difference.

My advice for other home schoolers would be this: "Don't get frustrated." When you start, it can be hard. You have to find exactly what works for you and your family. But I think it's worth it. I've learned a lot. The comfortable environment has allowed me to grow. I still play with my younger brother. I'm proud of that. I think I'm a lot closer to my family than some kids in school. And I think that in school, it's cool not to like your parents, especially in high school or junior high. I love my family.

3 Social and Emotional Needs

These children have no greater obligation than any other children to be future leaders or world class geniuses. They should just be given a chance to be themselves, children who might like to classify their collections of baseball cards by the middle initials of the players, or who might like to spend endless afternoon hours in dreamy reading of novels, and to have an education that appreciates and serves these behaviors.

—Jane Piirto (1999)

Certainly a child's social and emotional needs are important, but just what do we mean by healthy social and emotional development? Does it mean getting along with everyone or having a lot of friends? Handling your emotions well? Being happy? Is emotional development the same for everyone? Are social and emotional needs of unusually bright children unique or different?

Often we think of the well-rounded, emotionally healthy child as the child who fits in, the child who doesn't stand out in any embarrassing way, the child who cooperates and participates willingly. The advanced and sensitive learner, however, often does *not* fit in with other children and *does* stand out whether he wants to or not, has a different understanding of cooperation, and may prefer to participate on his own terms. What does emotional and social development mean for this kind of child?

Defining Social-Emotional Needs

To begin, we must consider three important truths about social and emotional needs and development of gifted children:

- Many of the social and emotional needs of the gifted child are no different from those of any other child.

- What may be normal for gifted children will at times be different from what is normal for their same age peers.

- A child's social and emotional life is never separate from the rest of the child's life.

First, many of the social and emotional needs of the gifted child are no different from those of any other child (Webb, 1993). The goals of acceptance and understanding of self and others, a sense of community and feeling accepted by others, and fulfillment of personal potential are common to us all. In other words, knowing oneself, tolerating differences, having friends, being able to acknowledge and express feelings, working toward personal goals, and generally being happy are simple yet important social and emotional needs for gifted and for all children. The needs and goals themselves are not complicated, but gifted children can be at greater risk for not having their needs met.

Gifted children can be socially and emotionally vulnerable, however, usually because of one or more of the gifted child's characteristics—e.g., precociousness and asynchronous development, intensity, perfectionism, sensitivity, or complexity—or to the child's inappropriate environment (Webb, 1994). A child who enters kindergarten being able to multiply may not be easily accepted by other children who feel threatened by the child's high ability and "differentness." A child who becomes paralyzed by perfectionism during tests will have difficulty fulfilling or living up to the potential expected by teacher and parents. The social and emotional needs of acceptance and self-fulfillment are not being met. Children like these need an extra dose of understanding, as well as academic accommodations, if they are to succeed and see themselves positively.

As the examples show, the interaction of gifted traits with the environment often makes it difficult for children to accept and value their own differences. Sometimes an environment, whether at home or school, is unhealthy or toxic for a gifted child because it does not match the child's needs or even punishes the child for characteristics that are simply a part of giftedness. When a precocious reader is made to feel that being able to read better than other children is something to hide or be ashamed of, her learning environment is toxic. When a curious child is belittled or punished for asking difficult questions, the environment is toxic. In cases like these, the environment, not the child, needs to change.

Second, what may be normal for gifted children will at times be different from what is normal for their same age peers (Meckstroth, 1992). The gifted child's excitability may be mistaken for ADHD, his questioning of life's mysteries seen as a mood disorder, his love of organization as obsessive-compulsive behavior, or his discrepancy between the speed of this thoughts and his ability to write them down, while normal for many gifted children, may be diagnosed as a learning disability

(Webb, 2000b). Understanding and acceptance of self is thus more complex because the gifted child feels or knows from an early age that she is different—sometimes extremely different—from the norm.

Knowledge and understanding of the common traits and behaviors of giftedness help parents to know when—and when not—to worry and will prevent inappropriate comparisons with other children. Parents should also know that gifted children can be as different from each other—in fact, perhaps more so—than from average learners. Parents of *highly gifted*, *exceptionally gifted*, or *profoundly gifted* children will notice that their children's gifted characteristics are present in the extreme; these parents, then, must resist the temptation to try to fit their children into the mold of the *moderately* gifted child. While a moderately gifted child usually exhibits sensitivity and high energy, a profoundly gifted child will show a high degree of emotional sensitivity that seems always present and will have an extraordinarily high energy level. Parents of gifted children often become experts in giftedness, both the academic and the social-emotional aspects, out of pure necessity.

Third, a child's social and emotional life is never separate from the rest of the child's life. It is not a subject area like math or spelling or physical education. A child's social and emotional self is fully integrated in every activity, every thought, every experience, whether or not we plan for it or recognize its presence. It is how the child feels about who he is and what he is doing, and how he interacts with his work, his environment, his peers, his teacher, his family, his world. A walk to the grocery store to buy some bread, a phone conversation with a grandparent, some play time at a local park, and an afternoon alone in his room reading a favorite book are all part of the child's social life. He is experiencing and learning about how he fits in with the world, whether he is by himself or with others. Tears of frustration, words of anger, peals of laughter, sly smiles, and quick wit are all part of the child's emotional life. He is learning what it is like to be human with a full and varied range of feelings.

Usually, parents can easily see how social and emotional health is intricately bound up with academic needs. For example, when a child is challenged and able to learn at an appropriate pace and level, the child is closer to knowledge of self and acceptance of others than if the child is tied to a lockstep or inappropriate curriculum. Children who are not adequately challenged may not understand the full extent of their abilities, and because they do not need to *work* to master academic material, they may have difficulty accepting and understanding the different needs of more average learners.

Sometimes we fool ourselves into thinking that certain educational experiences contain within them a social and emotional component, while others do not. The truth is that *all* learning environments shape the child emotionally in some way. An educational environment in which adults are always in control of what, when, where, and how subjects are learned carries with it a social and emotional agenda as well as an academic one. A student in an inflexible environment, whether in a school classroom or at home, is being taught that social obedience and emotional compliance are as important as multiplication or American history. An education that defines success in terms of public performance and competition also teaches specific social and emotional lessons. A student whose academic learning is valued *only* when it results in good grades, spelling bee championships, high SAT scores, and eventual entrance to select colleges may be internalizing that learning for its own sake has no place in education. Although achievements and honors can be a highly valuable and enjoyable part of a child's educational journey, they are neither necessary nor should they be the end goal Home school can help students to de-emphasize grades and value learning for its own sake.

Likewise, an educational setting that offers the child some real educational choice and encourages risk-taking within safe boundaries promotes yet a different kind of social and emotional growth. When a student in this setting is given a choice of what branch of science to focus on for the next few months and how to approach the topic—whether through hands-on experiments, Internet sources, traditional textbooks, or a combination of these approaches—the student learns that taking responsibility for one's own education is as valuable as the specific science information one ultimately acquires. This kind of responsibility is important in college and is critical in later life, when we must rely on ourselves, rather than teachers or parents, to help us realize our dreams.

In summary, gifted children have many of the same social and emotional needs of other children. Gifted children's differences, however, such as intensity and sensitivity, will mean that normal social and emotional development may look different for them than for other children their age. And certainly, social and emotional needs are intricately connected to all parts of the child's life, including academics.

Home Schooling for Positive Social and Emotional Growth

The isolated, lonely, even awkward home schooled child is a common stereotype. But in fact, home schooling probably offers families a greater opportunity than traditional schooling for children to widen their social horizons and to experience positive social and emotional growth. Meeting social and emotional needs such as finding friends and peers is often easier for home schooling families because of the flexibility of mixed-age socializing, as this parent relates.

In addition to finding friends and understanding differentness, home schooling for gifted students can help with social and emotional growth in still other ways.

> *Social and emotional development is much easier to deal with in home schooling than it would be in a traditional school. We have been able to find real peers for our children and to arrange for them to spend time together. Also, through our local support group, we interact with a wide range of children of many ages, degrees of giftedness, and so on. This facilitates social interaction with people who are different and de-emphasizes the "differentness" that many schooled gifted children struggle with.*
>
> —Josh, home school parent

Take perfectionism, for example. When an adult acknowledges and values work a student does on his own and which the student evaluates himself based on real-life needs (such as teaching himself HTML to create a web page), the adult helps to temper perfectionism by encouraging realistic standards that stem from the child's own values. This reinforces for the student a sense of lifelong, independent learning and self-evaluation. Parents of children in traditional schools can also promote such activities and real life evaluation, but home school parents can make them a central part of the child's curriculum, rather than an add-on or enrichment activity. In doing so, parents are fully integrating academic and social-emotional development and are offering their children a holistic, individualized education plan.

Karen Rogers recommends that parents—who know the child best—put together an educational plan for their child based on the child's unique needs and then work with the school to have the plan implemented (Rogers, 2002). How much of the plan will be accepted by the school, of course, depends heavily on the school's budget, understanding of giftedness, staffing, and other factors outside of the parents' and the child's control. As Dr. Rogers (2002) writes in *Re-forming Gifted Education: Matching the Program to the Child*, schools don't always take parents' concerns and knowledge into full account.

> *Regrettably, schools often simply don't believe that parents could accurately recognize a gifted child or that such children have special academic or other learning needs. Even more regrettably, schools seem to know very little about gifted children, and worse, they seldom know what to do with a gifted child if they do acknowledge that a child could be one (Rogers, 2002, p. 7).*

Parents, who have watched *how* their children learn from birth, often have valuable insight into the kinds of learning experiences their gifted children need.

Often, implementing an individualized educational plan in a home school setting may be easier and more effective than negotiating with a school for an appropriate education, particularly for families who have done the necessary work and research to understand their child's needs. Academic educational options such as subject acceleration (working at a faster pace in one or more subjects), dual enrollment, or even grade skipping are not only possible in home schooling, but can be implemented without red tape or adherence to academic schedules, such as having to wait until the beginning of a semester or year. These academic accommodations go far toward helping the child to know herself, and to find and realize her potential.

Practical Strategies for Home School Parents

Deirdre Lovecky (1992a, p. 20) suggests the following strategies to guide the child toward positive growth and self-actualization:[3]

- Adopt an attitude of play and joy in creativity.
- Focus on the creative process more than the creative product.
- Encourage children to find work they can love.
- Study social conventions so that children can freely choose appropriate conformity if desired.
- Help children to accept and identify their intense feelings and to learn to separate those feelings from the feelings of other people.
- Explore issues of ethics, empathy, justice, and moral efficacy.
- Seek to understand the strengths and weaknesses of the child's will and the reactions of other people to the child's self-determination.

In a home schooling environment, the above strategies can be deftly interwoven into both the curriculum and daily life. Some practical ways to do so are these:

- Accommodate uneven development.
- Understand and manage perfectionism.
- Keep achievement in perspective.
- De-emphasize grades.
- Socialize with a wide variety of ages.
- Treat feelings as friends.
- Use bibliotherapy in a natural way.
- Refuse to limit children with unnecessary labels.
- Expose your child to a banquet of careers.

Let's look at each strategy in more detail.

Accommodate Uneven Development

Children who learn quickly sometimes have areas of uneven (asynchronous) development. For example, many gifted children can converse about high level ideas and complex arguments yet are unable to put those ideas or arguments in writing due to undeveloped small-motor or spelling skills. As noted previously, the gifted child is more likely than other children to experience a mismatch between intellectual and psychomotor development, language ability and reasoning development, or intellectual skills and emotional development (Terrassier, 1985). Such a child usually thinks faster than he can write, speaks with more sophistication than he can judge the appropriateness of what he is saying, or learns about events and ideas that are too intense for his still developing emotional maturity. These

---

3   Reprinted by permission of *Roeper Review*, Volume 15 (1), ©1992, P.O. Box 329, Bloomfield Hills, MI, 48303.

mismatched traits and behaviors can cause problems for the child with others when he asks inappropriate questions of strangers such as, "Are you married? Do you have a lot of money?" or when he tells sophisticated jokes and puns to other children and is met with blank stares.

Home school parents can help children through these mismatches in development in three important ways: (1) by not forcing the child's development to meet a generic timetable, (2) by being flexible and creative with curriculum materials, and (3) by encouraging self-directed, child-initiated study. Consider, for example, the uneven development of a gifted seven-year-old whose spelling and verbal skills are at a middle school level, but who has an emotional meltdown when she tries to copy spelling words or write a story because of her still developing handwriting skills. Rather than expect the student to use middle school level handwriting skills to do middle school level work, a home school parent can suggest that she dictate to an older, willing sibling, or that she use a whiteboard and dry erase markers, or that she record her stories and do oral spelling using a tape recorder. Meanwhile, the child can continue to develop handwriting skills on her own timetable without sacrificing higher level learning in content areas. In the home school setting, the child's developmental course sets the pace, rather than a generic timetable, as this parent explains.

> *My first-grade son tends to be intensely interested in one or two subjects at a time and works far ahead of grade level in those areas. By the time he's ready for college, I think he'll have covered the basics of a solid education, but not in the order prescribed in the grade-level guides.*
>
> —Myra, home school parent

A first grader in school does not have the option of focusing on math and science for a year, followed by a year of intense work in history and literature, but for the home schooled child, there are few limits on the order or depth of study.

> *My son's reading skills are such that he can read anything. However, his emotional level leads me to have to be extremely selective in the literature he reads or I read to him. So whereas other home school parents with gifted (and other) kids may tackle history in depth, I cannot because history is full of violence, death, sadness, etc. He's simply not emotionally ready for these tragic themes and topics even though his academic reading level would tell you otherwise. It is a big challenge finding material.*
>
> —Barbara, home school parent

For the home school parent, a child's uneven development means that much of the generic curriculum material and educational advice in books and teacher supply stores may not meet the child's needs, not just because of ability level, but also because of complex emotional factors.

Home schooling allows this parent to tailor her son's reading and curriculum materials to his unique developmental needs. She might use humor-based history resources, such as *The History News* series by Candlewick Press, or she might search for historical fiction aimed at a younger audience. Or her son can study geography in depth, using maps that he makes himself as well as globes and pre-made maps, and wait a year or two before studying wars and other sensitive topics. Flexible and creative use of curriculum materials means that the child is not tied to someone else's idea of *what* needs to be learned *when*.

Another way that parents can accommodate gifted children's uneven development is by giving the child greater choice in topics, allowing her to self-regulate levels of challenge and progression of study. In the classroom, the amount of student control may be relatively small, given the necessities of classroom management and various local, state, or national standards to be met. A truly self-directed education (with plenty of adult support and facilitation) is an idea that holds promise but is ultimately impractical in most school settings. At home, however, parents and children can experiment with how much control children can effectively handle.

For children who have been labeled underachievers, self-directed learning may be a critical component of rekindling a love of learning. Joanne Rand Whitmore (1980), expert on underachievement in gifted children, suggests that adults *gradually* incorporate self-direction into a child's education by beginning with one or two subject areas, such as math or reading. Home school parents might ask a child to help set learning goals for an area of strength (e.g., math) and even work with the parent to choose curriculum resources. As the child becomes more comfortable with taking responsibility for his learning, he can slowly add more subjects.

LeoNora Cohen and Judith Gelbrich (1999) have found that children's interests, especially those expressed through play, help children gain equilibrium by leading the child to seek answers to questions that arise within the child. For example, if a young child suddenly becomes fascinated by insects, learning all he can about their species, habitats, and behaviors from field guides, and playing for hours with plastic ants and spiders, he may be seeking answers to questions of feeling small in a big world, or he may be wondering about life's infinite diversity and complexity. In either case, his interest guides him to seek information in a way that integrates his development levels. The child, on his own, reconciles his age-appropriate fears and high-level need for philosophical thought. Or if a sensitive child takes an intense interest in fantasy novels, the child may be seeking answers to philosophical questions such as, "What is reality?" or "Is this all that life can be?" The interest allows the child to address such issues on her own terms, in her own way, and at her own pace. Self-directed study is more than a pedagogical strategy; it is important to the child's sense of self, development of independence, and fulfillment of potential, all of which are important social-emotional goals.

Carefully developed self-directed study allows the child to learn according to unique internal growth patterns without external pressure to perform according to a generic model of development.

Understand and Manage Perfectionism

©Copyright PEANUTS. Reprinted by permission of United Feature Syndicate.

Many parents are familiar with their children's painful struggle with perfectionism when letters are not formed correctly, projects are inevitably flawed, or games are lost. Many gifted learners are almost by nature perfectionistic, in part because they can so easily discern the discrepancies between what is and what could be. They are able to envision perfect achievement, whether or not such achievements are realistic.

Consider, for example, a young perfectionistic child who is learning to print. She sees the flawless examples in her handwriting workbook and does her best to copy the letters on the lines provided for practice. But as hard as she tries, her letters never look as good as the examples. If she receives grades on her work, a less than perfect grade may cause her to panic. Whereas her classmates accept a "B" or "C" as adequate work, she may drive herself to develop perfect penmanship at the expense of deeper learning. A perfect set of letters is her proof that she is indeed smart, that she is a good writer. Or she may give up, refuse to write anything that is not strictly required, and thus avoid facing her inevitable imperfection. The child then thinks of herself as a non-writer, a belief that becomes self-fulfilling. In either case, perfectionism leads to the confusion of effective verbal communication—writing—with the mechanics and aesthetics of handwriting.

This "drive to perfect," whether it be in handwriting or any other endeavor, is, according to Mary-Elaine Jacobsen (1999b), a "hard-wired" trait of the gifted. It is not always a bad thing. Who would want to be in the hands of a surgeon or a pilot who was not a perfectionist? Linda Silverman (1989) reminds us that perfectionism is "the root of excellence." The urge to perfect is what allows for the joy of learning to play a Chopin etude or to be able to build a bridge that doesn't collapse.

Uneven development often leads parents and other adults to confuse a healthy urge to perfect with unrealistic expectations for the child, which can in turn exacerbate a child's tendency toward unhealthy perfectionism. That is, if a child excels in one area, often there is an expectation for the child to be superior in all areas. Donna, who has been a home school parent for three years, writes:

> *I am still grappling with the issue of writing. My eight-year-old son, like many gifted boys, hates to put his thoughts to paper. Part of it is a sense of perfectionism—he doesn't want to write the wrong or "boring" thing. Additionally, he refuses to use invented spelling, and as he is not a natural speller, he is limited to the words he knows, can sound out, or get someone else to spell for him.*
>
> —Debra, home school parent

This student's perfectionism with spelling is obvious, but parents and teachers often do not recognize the tendency of the gifted child to expect too much from himself. For example, a child who is actually paralyzed by perfectionism is labeled "lazy" or "uncooperative," and the high-achieving perfectionistic child is perceived as "a bit uptight but okay." Adults might assume that they have the responsibility to set high goals and standards for children, unaware of the potential dangers to the child's self-concept. Or adults might treat perfectionism as something that can be cured or, if it is ignored long enough, something that will just go away.

Jacobsen (1999b) writes that neither pathological perfectionism nor chronic procrastination—one outgrowth of perfectionism—is a necessary characteristic of giftedness. The urge to perfect can actually be healthy as long as we don't adopt an all-or-nothing attitude. A *pragmatic perfectionism* allows us to keep in mind overall goals, realistic timeframes, and expectations of quality. It means being able to say "enough" when necessary and move on to the next activity or day, as well as knowing when it is right to persist toward high goals and standards.

Silverman (1989) suggests that we can help children develop healthy perfectionism by *helping them to set realistic rather than unreachable goals* and by *building their self-confidence*. Parents can support children's confidence in their abilities by allowing them to be involved in complex activities without fear of excessive evaluation, by supporting their desires to set reasonably high goals for themselves, and by encouraging them to appreciate and develop their own unique abilities.

We can also help children understand that whatever high standards we set for ourselves should not be imposed on others, and that perfectionism is a tool to use when we need it and to put aside when we don't. Finally, children should not be ashamed of being able to see how things should be or of having an urge to perfect (Silverman, 1989). When a child becomes anxious about handwriting that isn't neat, we can both accept his feelings and provide some perspective by saying, "I see that you want to be able to write more neatly. It is difficult right now. In time, it will get easier." Parents can also share with their children times in their own lives when they thought they would never get something right but eventually did, times when they made mistakes, big and little, or times when their expectations were unrealistic.

Children love to hear stories about when their parents were younger. Parents can think of examples of when they had to practice a long time to learn a sport or a musical instrument. They can relate to their children how it felt at the beginning of learning a new skill. What were the factors in their continuing? How did the experience of success in one area lead to the ability to take risks in a new area? Were there times when giving up was the right thing to do? If so, why?

As useful as these stories of past experience are, they will not replace parental modeling through real-time action and examples. Does your child ever see you practice skills or try new activities? One home school parent sets a dual goal for herself of: (1) developing skill in an area in which she already has some level of accomplishment, such as piano playing or cooking, and (2) learning a new skill that doesn't come easily, such as ice skating or drawing. The important thing is that children see their parents practice skills, try new things, struggle, fail, and succeed, even when doing so results in something that is less than perfection, and that parents are able to laugh at mistakes and failures rather than model an attitude of anxiety and being "uptight." Everyone needs areas in which standards of perfection can be relaxed.

One of the most challenging aspects of perfectionism in the home school setting may in fact be the *parents'* tendency toward perfectionism rather than the child's. With seemingly no limits of how fast and how high a home schooled child can soar, it is often hard to know when appropriate encouragement and support crosses the line into a debilitating pressure to succeed. Ellen Winner (1996) writes that while a child-centered home school that is individualized, progressive, and challenging has "the potential to be the best of what school can be," she also warns that some parents have a personal investment that causes them to never be satisfied with how their children are educated. Such parents choose home schooling because they see their children as "brilliant victims" of the school system. Parents who bring this dangerous attitude to home schooling do so through attitudes and behaviors such as never feeling that the child is learning enough, by going from one curriculum to another in an effort to cover all bases, by home schooling year round—not to promote a continual love of learning but to cram in as much education as possible—and by feeling that being average even in one or two areas can never be an option for their children. Chapter 6 offers some suggestions for ways that parents can make home schooling both meaningful and relaxed, and it discusses how to know what expectations are appropriate for home schooled gifted children.

Keep Achievement in Perspective

Understanding and dealing with perfectionism is inextricably tied to how we understand achievement. In our society, we celebrate high achievers and worry about low achievers. The student who performs schoolwork above expectations is publicly recognized, awarded, and encouraged to continue, while the student who performs below potential is evaluated, diagnosed, and counseled. But is the low-achiever the only student at risk?

Alfie Kohn, who has crusaded for years against the abuse of rewards and punishments in homes, schools, and the workplace, warns us of the hidden costs of our nation's preoccupation with achievement. In *The Schools Our Children Deserve*, he writes that not only do students' interest in learning and quality of learning suffer, but we also set the stage for increased unhealthy perfectionism and avoidance of challenge *regardless of the level of student achievement* (Kohn, 1999).

In *Learning Together: How to Foster Creativity, Self-Fulfillment, and Social Awareness in Today's Students and Teachers*, Elizabeth Drews (1972) questions the value of achievement for the purpose of meeting outside expectations.

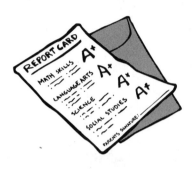

Achievement judged solely by the individual's compliance with some-one else's expectancies and standards may be the very opposite of finding the self. Good students know that generally they will not receive high grades if they spend their time learning how to think, discovering what they think, or voicing their own opinions. Instead, they will do "best" if they read what is assigned—and little more—and shape their opinions (and answers on tests) to conform to the teachers' pre-stated judgments or the textbook's pontifications (Drews, 1972, p. 42).

When I taught writing to college students, often the students most concerned with getting an "A" or "B" were the ones who took the fewest risks with their writing. They used only vocabulary, syntax, and punctuation with which they were comfortable, and their essay topics never strayed far from the handbook's generic suggestions. Their writing showed little improvement from the beginning of the quarter to the end, but this lack of improvement still fit their notion of high achievement, predicated almost entirely on grades.

Students in the class who seemed less concerned with good grades and more involved with improving their writing, however, attempted to use new vocabulary words, more complicated syntax, and unfamiliar punctuation such as dashes, colons, and semicolons. They risked writing about topics that interested them and were important to them rather than following the handbook's list of suggested themes. They didn't always get it right, but they usually showed much improvement over the course of the quarter. Sometimes their grades were very good, sometimes average.

Students who didn't have a perfect G.P.A. to begin with seemed to have less to lose and therefore more room to take risks with new learning. Unlike the students who were concerned only with grades, they experienced social and emotional development through increased self-knowledge because of their choice of writing topics and greater use of their abilities. By taking greater risks, they gained more skill and confidence in their writing.

It seems to me that young children prone to obsessive perfectionism need a wide range of freedom in which to experience being *im*perfect without fear of ridicule or rebuke or of not "making the grade." The path of creative thinking requires acceptance of missteps along the way. Kohn (1999) points out that even when we think we're comforting a perfectionist (e.g., "a 92% is still very good, dear"), we often only reinforce the message that achievement is what counts. The result is often a preoccupation with doing even better, getting excellent grades, rather than learning deeply and meaningfully. And with every "A," every spot on the honor roll, every standard mastered early, or every grade skipped, the child can prove once again to the world and to herself that she really is very good.

What happens when the gifted learner becomes an adult with fewer opportunities to prove herself? When there are no more SATs, no more possible Summa Cum Laudes, the individual as an adult is now faced with the often debilitating task of seeing herself separate from her achievements. If she has experienced positive social and emotional growth along the way, she can realize that her self-worth is not measured only by awards and accomplishments; she can then continue on life's journey, regardless of whether that journey includes public recognition or visible benchmarks of success. She develops an "interest in the world" that leads to a state of flow (Csikszentmihalyi, 1990). If, however, she did not learn to see herself separate from external evaluations, she will feel lost and will have difficulty experiencing the pleasure of life experiences for their own sake. Perhaps she will turn to getting as thin as possible as a substitute for achievement, or perhaps she believes that she is a fraud—not really bright after all—just as she had always secretly suspected. Or she may become a paralyzed perfectionist, incapable of exerting any effort that includes even the tiniest element of risk without tremendous stress (Adderholdt-Elliott & Goldberg, 1999).

If your child is not achieving or seems stymied, before you assume that your child is lazy or unmotivated, ask yourself whether he could simply be so scared of inevitable imperfection that doing nothing is easier than trying anything new. Some children need gentle yet specific guidance in learning to deal with risk and failure in order to participate fully in all that life offers.

Learning to fail and to deal with *necessary* risk may be one of the most difficult but one of the most important tasks for young gifted home schoolers (Adderholdt-Elliott & Goldberg, 1999). This does not mean that parents should push their children to fail any more than they should push them to succeed, but parents of gifted children need to work harder than other parents to find opportunities for their children to experience failure and, more important, to see that life goes on, that failure is sometimes necessary for growth, and that it is okay to pursue an activity "just for the fun of it." Encourage a gifted math student to write poetry in a personal journal without worrying about whether it is "any good." Support a budding interest in tap dance or soccer, even if your child was born with two left feet. Sometimes being a good parent means saying, "You don't always have to try your best," or "Let's sing using our worst voices!" or even "An 80% on that test is fine for now."

Home school parents can take *unnecessary* risk out of learning by looking for ways to de-emphasize competition while at the same time encouraging excellence of thought. James Webb (2000c) recommends that parents find just a few minutes on a regular basis to spend one-on-one time with each child, with a rule that the shared activity be non-competitive in nature. Conversation, nature walks, singing, playing catch, or doing a puzzle together are some ideas for parents to try. Favorite board and card games can also be played in a non-competitive spirit. Try playing Scrabble® by sharing each other's letters and without keeping track of points. Play card games such as SET (a matching game) by putting the discovered "sets" in one pile rather than awarding them to individual players. In this way, parents can encourage their children to strive for excellence, even when no individual stakes are involved.

One home school parent of five children found that participation in sports allows her son to practice risk-taking and to enjoy an activity for its own sake, not in order to be "the best."

> *Playing on winning or losing teams enables one to experience success and failure in a less intense way since a win or loss is a team effort, not the sole result of one person's performance. Participating on a sports team may not work for all gifted children, but for some it is worthwhile. I suspect my 14-year-old son may be the only gifted classical pianist, trigonometry whiz on his baseball team, but he can enjoy the feeling of camaraderie sitting on the bench waiting for a turn at bat, encouraging teammates, etc. He can learn persistence and self-control when he is the pitcher and his team's fielding errors are costing him valuable outs. And he can learn that it's okay to be average at something and still enjoy it.*
>
> *Additionally, sports are a bridge activity—a way to relate to other boys his age in a fun way, even though they may not share his more intense interests.*
>
> —Nina, home school parent

Not all gifted children will enjoy organized competitive sports, but they might enjoy the camaraderie of being part of a team through youth symphonies, youth choirs, chess teams, drama clubs, debate groups, or other less physical, less competitive "teams." Some gifted children will need group activities that still allow them to learn new skills in private, where they can practice until they reach what they consider an acceptable level of performance. For example, a child learning to ski may want to take a private lesson to practice on his own until he can navigate his skis without falling, before letting anyone in the group see him. A child learning a foreign language may prefer to practice with an audio tape before having to converse with others.

Achievement is not a bad thing, but it must be kept in perspective. The child must choose it freely; it cannot be forced. Home school parents can be careful not to confuse a child's achievements with her lovability or worth as a human being.

De-Emphasize Grades

If your child has been a chronic underachiever in school, as evidenced by grades, for example, don't look at home schooling as a way to "shape him up" and suddenly change him into a high achiever. You may consider doing away with grades and other objective measures of learning. Annemarie Roeper writes:

> *[O]bjective measurements imply that we do not try to see who a child is, but think of children in terms of what they can do, academically, physically, or socially. This leads to a partitioning of the individual—the math part, the reading part, the social part, the organizing part. As a result, we confront children with a variety of expectations, and then draw conclusions about each child without truly understanding them as complete individuals. We never put Humpty Dumpty together again (Roeper, 1995, p. 136).[4]*

---

4   Reprinted by permission of *Roeper Review*, Volume 18 (2), ©1995, P.O. Box 329, Bloomfield Hills, MI 48303.

Objective measurements such as report cards that break the child's learning into parts can make it harder to see the big picture in terms of a child's educational needs and achievement. Barbara Clark (1997, p. 440) writes that "under the threat of grades, bright students balk at venturing into the unknown or trying any area in which they are not sure they will succeed." There is little, if any, correlation between high school or even college grades and eventual success (Clark, 1997). In addition, an emphasis on grades and other extrinsic motivators may put students at risk for the Performance Syndrome, where looking smart and not making mistakes are more important than learning and doing one's best (Amabile, 1989).

The most dramatic result so far of our family's decision to de-emphasize grades can be seen in our son's handwriting and writing. Having been taught two different printing styles at two different schools and also being left-handed, he began home schooling with barely legible handwriting. Most concerning to me was that he thought of himself as having "bad" handwriting, which I feared could easily become a self-fulfilling prophecy.

Home schooling allowed us the freedom to focus on the long-term goal of a child who writes easily and comfortably and who is able to choose the appropriate writing style and quality for the specific writing task he faces, rather than the short-term goal of producing several pages of perfect practice letters by the end of the term. For one full year, we said nothing, not a word, about his handwriting, whether he was writing a letter to his grandfather or scribbling notes for himself. We made a conscious effort to encourage him to use writing in many ways throughout the day, and I allowed him to see me writing messy rough drafts and using better writing when there was a reason for doing so. He had the freedom to choose from several writing tools—traditional pens and pencils, word processing programs, and an old manual typewriter from his father's college days. He began to understand that writing and handwriting are not the same and that rewriting is an integral part of the writing process.

The result is that writing became a regular part of his day, and after several months, he found his own style of printing that is both highly legible and attractive—most of the time. We know our approach is working because he is excited about writing, he willingly shows his unfinished and imperfect writing to us, he understands the value and necessity of revision, and he pays attention to the writing of his favorite authors so as to learn from them. He will probably learn cursive later than his classroom peers, because for now he writes quickly and easily with his newfound manuscript style—a response to his individual needs rather than a curriculum standard that requires cursive to be learned in third or fourth grade. In home schooling, there is no reason that cursive writing can't be saved for middle school or later, just as there is no reason not to introduce it in first or second grade if a child is ready and eager.

Parents may be amazed at just how little formal assessment and evaluation of learning is actually necessary in home school for learning to move forward. Often, learner feedback is an integral part of a learning activity, such as when a very young child learns how tall he can build a tower before the blocks all fall down, or when an older child sees highlighted misspelled words in the draft of a computer e-mail message. Children who are learning long division can be encouraged to multiply to check their answers and then revise them, if necessary, *before* showing the work to adults. We routinely give our son the answer key or teacher's edition to any textbooks or workbooks he is using and encourage him to check his own work upon completion and to read the teacher's notes for deeper understanding. When learning—not grades—is the goal, cheating becomes meaningless.

Simple family conversation provides natural and enjoyable opportunities for children to see gaps in their learning as well as areas in which they've grown. Card and board games can provide scaffolding for math and logical thinking skills in a way that is more effective in teaching math to young children than computer programs (Healy, 1998). If your child needs practice in mental addition and subtraction, making time for "unplugged" interactive board and card games may be better than buying the latest CD-ROM or curriculum book.

When evaluation or assessment is necessary, either for legal or personal reasons, parents can think carefully about exactly what needs to be measured and what form is least intrusive in the learning process. Portfolios of student work, self-evaluation (not in comparison to other children in the home), and allowing students to set and track their own learning goals are alternatives to number or letter grades. For example, if a child uses batteries, wires, switches, and lights to make his own personal nightlight and door alarm, the parent can simply take a photo of the creation and note what skills and understanding were necessary for the work that was done. This can then be placed in the child's learning portfolio. One home school parent uses comprehensive grade-based computer games (Jump Start Adventures® and Clue Finders® are popular choices), which her son enjoys and which give her a rough idea of whether he's learning what is normally expected at his grade level. She can record the level of the computer program, the date of completion, and the percentage of correct responses, which is usually available when the child finishes the program, to add to the child's home school records.

Parents can also help their children see the positive aspects of pursuing excellence. Careful and consistent practice of a violin solo, honing the physical skills necessary to do a back flip, and taking the time to learn to bake a flawless loaf of bread can give children a feeling of joy and success. These pursuits of excellence, however, should not be the basis for the child's sense of self-worth. If the violin solo misses a beat, if the back flip results in a fall, or if the bread collapses, the child needs to be able to put the events in perspective and not see himself as a failure.

By de-emphasizing grades, parents encourage children to love learning for its own sake, to get to know themselves better as learners, and to understand when evaluation is useful and when it is not. These children are in a better position to seek the flow of appropriate challenge and thus fulfill their potential, rather than work only for good grades.

Socialize with a Wide Range of Ages

Gifted children often seek friends from various ages, especially older children. As one parent explains, multi-age socializing can be both challenging and successful.

> *Finding friends is a constant issue. My seven-year-old son is an extravert and enjoys the company of others very much, regardless of their age. He is most comfortable socializing with children about twice his age. He is working on learning how to interact with same-age peers. He now has a group of neighborhood boys with whom he rides bicycles, but he wants deeper friendships. He does have one "best friend" his age who is a true friend, but he longs for others, regardless of age.*
>
> —Casey, home school parent

In school, a seven-year-old would have little opportunity to interact with other children twice his age, but home schooling allows parents to seek a variety of friends for the children.

Parents can help children who differ markedly from age peers seek understanding and acceptance both of themselves and others. The chance to interact with a wide range of ages and abilities gives asynchronous children a broader scope of reference within which to develop self-understanding. Because asynchronous children are often several ages simultaneously, they can learn to recognize in themselves the part that identifies with age peers, the part that identifies with younger children, and the part that enjoys the company of older children and adults. Mixed age socializing is also more in keeping with how life *outside* of school normally exists. When you stop to think about it, the K-12 classroom setting is one of the few times in our lives when we spend the majority of our time with people who are exclusively our own age.

If possible, gifted children should also socialize with age mates who share their interests and abilities. Parents can search for possibilities for friendship with one or two age mates who share some of the child's sensitivity, intensity, or creativity: "[T]he gifted child often needs several different kinds of peers…some for sports, different ones for intellectual pursuits, and still others for emotional friendships" (Webb, Meckstroth, & Tolan, 1982, p. 15). Chess clubs, science fiction book groups, Saturday and summer enrichment classes, and talent search programs are all places where you might find like-minded children. If your child strikes up a conversation with or seems interested in pursuing a friendship with another child, do whatever you can to facilitate the relationship according to your child's wishes, even if it means extra driving or rearranging your schedule. Phone conversations and correspondence, either through the postal system or e-mail, also help maintain and develop long-distance friendships.

Annemarie Roeper (1992, p. 52) writes that adults need to create for children an environment that "keeps young children from developing feelings of being on the outside and separated from the world, from feeling excluded rather than being included." Whether face to face or by e-mail, friendship allows children to feel included and is as important for the gifted child as for any other child. Gifted children, however, may have some friends that are older or that fulfill a specific need—a chess buddy, a swimming buddy, or a computer buddy. Parents of gifted children often must work harder than other parents to facilitate meaningful friendships for their children.

Treat Feelings as Friends

Feelings should be friends to children. Parents often deny or in other ways negate gifted children's feelings, sometimes without meaning to, by saying things such as, "How could you say such a thing!" or "You don't really mean that." When children have very strong emotions or existential fears, parents may not understand or can even be frightened by the intensity of the child's feeling, but parents should work hard to offer a safe and non-judgmental place for children to grow into their big and powerful feelings without shame. They can do this by accepting and talking about feelings. Children need to be able to recognize, accept, and give names to their feelings (Webb, Meckstroth, & Tolan, 1982). As Annemarie Roeper (1995) has pointed out, children's trust in parental reactions is crucial to a healthy parent-child relationship and allows children to develop internal control free from anxiety.

How can parents accept children's feelings and build trust? One way is to allow your child a regular time when you are all ears, when nothing else is competing for your attention, when the child can talk about anything without fear of repercussion. James Webb, in the SENG-Model (Supporting Emotional Needs of Gifted) parent support groups (Webb & DeVries, 1998), recommends this as "special time" to be set aside for each child in the family, even if it's only five or 10 minutes per child per day. Listen to what your child says without showing undue anxiety. If at bedtime your five-year-old says, "I'm afraid that I might die before you," resist the natural temptation to placate her with an answer such as "Oh, of course that won't happen!" or "That's not something you should be thinking about." Instead, ask gentle questions to elicit more information, but don't push for details. Say, "Did something that happened today get you thinking about that?" Talk about the unlikelihood that such as situation would occur without promising that it won't. Share some fears you had as a child. Similarly, if a child is angry at a sibling and says, "I wish Jake were dead," don't answer by saying, "No you don't." Say instead, "You sound like you're pretty angry at Jake right now." This kind of response acknowledges the child's angry feelings. What you don't want to do is negate, belittle, or ignore the child's very real feelings or fears.

Eda LeShan's *What Makes Me Feel This Way: Growing Up with Human Emotions* (1974) is a sensitively written book (unfortunately out of print) that helps children to recognize, understand, and give names to feelings. Look for it in your library or used-book store. Older children can study philosophy as a way to come to terms with existential questioning. David White has written an excellent series of articles for *Gifted Child Today* magazine about helping gifted children to learn about philosophy. James Delisle (1992) advises that adults can help children develop a satisfying philosophy of life by helping them to appreciate the fact that they think deeply, allowing them to imagine possible futures for themselves, empowering them to be agents in their own world, and encouraging them to have the courage of their convictions.

Children who can acknowledge and discuss their feelings and who are comfortable with their feelings can better discover what they want to be and do, and they can interact more freely with others. Home schooling allows parents to take advantage of the teachable moment—whether it comes at midmorning, noon, or in the evening—to help children to express and accept what they feel.

Use Bibliotherapy in a Natural Way

Bibliotherapy—that is, using books to enhance both intellectual and emotional development—is an effective strategy for home schoolers. Discussion of themes in selected books can be used to address strong feelings and concerns that a child is currently experiencing, such as adjusting to a new sibling or having difficulty with friends. Reading books is also a wonderful way for children to feel more connected to the bigger world of people of ideas. Perhaps because many children's book authors were gifted children themselves, they often write about themes or issues of giftedness in a way that touches the heart and soul as well as the mind. *Some of My Best Friends Are Books: Guiding Gifted Readers from Preschool to High School, 2nd edition*, by Judith Wynn Halsted (2002), offers short summaries and detailed suggestions for using over 300 books that contain situations and characters of interest to intense and creative children. An index of themes directs readers to books with themes of perfectionism, aloneness, differentness, idealism, and other concerns familiar to gifted children.

For bibliotherapy to be most effective, of course, children should come to the books because they are good or interesting books, not because they address social and emotional issues. Parents can use the technique of sprinkling these good and interesting books in the child's path—leaving them on the coffee table or in the child's room—rather than giving them as assignments. You may wish to borrow the books or buy them for yourself and allow your child to see you reading them, which may naturally pique the child's interest. Buy the books as gifts for your child. But whatever you do, don't give the book to a child saying it will help the child to deal with a problem.

For example, a 10-year-old child, new to home schooling, feeling unsure about home schooling, and simply feeling out of step with the world, might enjoy the novel *Skellig*, by David Almond, where a 10-year-old boy befriends a home schooled girl, Mina. Mina is a free spirit, and both children have emotional and imaginational superabundance. This is a good book to read aloud as a family in the evening or, as one home school parent suggests, to read aloud in installments during lunchtime. Some children will be eager to discuss the book right away; others may need time for the book's meaning to sink in. When the child seems ready, parents can initiate a conversation by saying something like, "What did you think of Mina in *Skellig*?" or "Did the book say why Mina learns at home instead of learning at school?" You might review the book together to look for answers.

Children can also be encouraged to keep a reading journal to record their thoughts and feelings about books they read. Keep in mind, however, that many children will be reluctant to share their thoughts in writing if they suspect they will be graded or otherwise evaluated. For some children, simply reading the book together is a good start. Discussion may come with time. Other children may enjoy participating in a book discussion group, perhaps facilitated by home school parents. The Junior Great Books Discussion Program can be helpful in participating in or facilitating a book discussion group. For more information about Junior

Great Books, visit the website, www.greatbooks.org/programs/junior, or phone (800) 222-5870.

Movies are also valuable for exploring social and emotional issues. The website at www.teachwithmovies.org offers a searchable database of movies by title, key word, minimum age, cultural heritage, and character development. The movie *October Sky*, for instance, can be found by looking under cultural heritage topics of Aviation & Space Exploration, U.S./1945-1991, West Virginia, Science & Technology, and under character development topics of Father/Son, Perseverance, Breaking Out, and Friendship. An on-line learning guide for the movie includes a description, background information, and discussion questions. The site also includes a list of movies not recommended as teaching tools and an insightful essay on the effect of violent films on children.

Two excellent examples of book and movie combinations that address important issues for young, visual-spatial, and sensitive learners are Albert Lamorisse's award-winning 1965 movie *The Red Balloon* and its companion book, published by Doubleday (1997), and the classic wordless picture book *The Snowman*, by Raymond Briggs (1978), and corresponding video produced in 1982. Both stories deal with the journey and feelings of a young child who becomes attached to a seemingly inanimate friend and then must deal with loss. Both offer uplifting endings and use visual storytelling in a way that appeals to readers of all ages.

Bibliotherapy helps children find peers in characters similar to themselves and thus gain deeper self-understanding and self-acceptance. Books also allow children to understand others better and explore the world's diversity and complexity. Home school parents can easily make bibliotherapy an integral and large part of their child's education, including both fiction and non-fiction. When a child has books as friends, the child is never lonely (Halsted, 2002).

Refuse to Limit Children with Unnecessary Labels

Labels allow us to simplify complex ideas and can be useful shorthand for referring to a constellation of traits and behaviors. By referring to the "visual-spatial learner" or the "gifted learner," we immediately confer a complex meaning to the reader or listener without having to go into a more time-consuming explanation. However, the very complexity of an idea and a child can easily be reduced and misunderstood by the unnecessary use or overuse of labels. Learning styles and personality traits are as varied as are individual children, and no two gifted children are alike.

An educational environment that respects the complexity of children does not force a particular learning style or characteristic but will encourage children to explore all facets of their personalities and will resist the temptation to limit children's views of themselves. While understanding a child's preferred modes of learning or dominant personality traits—such as a visual-spatial learning style—can be valuable for both parents and children, a creative learning environment presumes that such "diagnoses" are never ends in themselves, but rather jumping-off places for broader understanding and inclusivity, paving the way for the possibility of fuller integration of dimensions as the child grows to adulthood.

For example, if a child has demonstrated a preference for rational thinking and staying within the lines, the parent can accept and value this preference, while at the same time being sure to offer the child opportunities to explore safely the passionate side of learning, to extend herself beyond the lines without fear of "not being herself." The adult will be very careful not to call the child "left-brained" in the child's presence or to show the child overtly or covertly that divergent or more creative behavior is unexpected (Liedloff, 1977). This approach is very different from the notion of strengthening a child's weaknesses, because the non-preferred dimensions are not seen as weaknesses, only as options previously seldom chosen. The child remains in control of the choices; the adult provides options, guidance, support, and acceptance.

Complexity is one of the more difficult traits of giftedness to understand, but supporting complexity can be as simple as not acting overly surprised when your usually introverted daughter asks to take a theatre class, or offering an outgoing child time for solitude and daydreaming, or making available a wide range of materials and approaches to learning. Parents should also refrain from making defining or "referential" statements in children's presence, such as "Joe is my logical child, but Jane is my creative one," or "Hannah just isn't a math person," or "Sam is so messy!" or "Jordan has ADD, you know" (Rimm, 1997). Such statements set up and reinforce the child's expectations for and sense of self and often prevent the child from necessary risk and personal development. Likewise, parents should be careful not to compare a child to other children in the child's hearing (Webb, 2000c). When a child feels no artificial boundaries to his personality or thought processes, when expectations are neither too low nor too narrow, when there are no labels, that child is free to experiment with many new ways of being and learning.

Expose Your Child to a Banquet of Careers

> [L]et me tell you a secret. For successful people, work is like play. That's right—play. That's because they've found the work that is best suited to who they are.
>
> —Barbara Sher in her introduction to *Working in Music*

For intense and creative learners, finding a satisfying career can be both easier and harder than for other children. It can be easier because these children often have passionate interests that lead them to merge work and play. However, it can be harder because gifted children can be so good at so many things. Having the ability to do many things well is called *multipotentiality.*

Multipotentiality can result in problems for gifted individuals. It can result in spreading oneself too thin in high school because a student has difficulty choosing between honors math, jazz band, and being editor of the school newspaper. Multipotentiality can result in several changes of majors in college or a variety of graduate degrees in several fields. For adults, it can lead to a series of jobs in several different fields, none of which is pursued to the point of personal fulfillment or to one's capability. Some adults never learn to prioritize or to make necessary choices from several available options. They change careers every five years or jump from job to job, always vaguely dissatisfied with what they've chosen.

To avoid these problems, home school parents can begin early to encourage the child to discuss interests, values, and areas of strength and to talk about which kinds of careers might be appealing. Exposure to careers can be done very informally for young children without pressure to choose just one. Family members and friends can be good, informal sources of information for a variety of careers. A grandparent or an aunt can talk about her career. A family friend who is an artist can allow your child to spend an hour or so watching him work. Uncle Bill might be willing to let your child shadow him for a day at the car dealership. If you know an engineer or a doctor or a lawyer, ask for a short tour of the workplace. Let your children into the world of your own work by talking about the interesting things you do and why you chose the field or how it chose you.

Young children can also begin to make choices about how to spend their time and energy. When a play date, museum trip, and day at home are all possible activities for a Sunday afternoon, allow the child to make the choice and to experience the inevitability of *not* being able to do everything, rather than reschedule the play date and museum trip so as to make all choices possible. If a child has numerous hobbies and interests, all in stages of semi-completion, help the child to prioritize and to focus on fewer interests in greater depth, with the understanding that some hobbies and activities can be "shelved" for later.

Older children can think more seriously about what kind of future they envision for themselves. Home school families can include a course in "Career Awareness" or "Career Education" as part of their curriculum. Encourage children to learn more about training required and advantages and disadvantages for various jobs and how jobs relate to personal interests. While exploring careers and jobs, discuss with children how all jobs are important and contribute to society. Which jobs involve work outdoors? Work with computers? Are there jobs that combine two or more interests? Which jobs require college? Which require apprenticeships and hands-on training? How do values affect choice of jobs? A child who shows a lasting interest in and aptitude for science can learn about the various branches of science, the variety of careers available, and differences between laboratory and field science. The book *Autonomous Learner Model: Optimizing Ability*, revised edition (Betts & Kercher, 1999) includes information about college and career planning activities. Libraries offer career publications for all ages. Lerner Publications' Exploring Careers series is good for elementary age students and includes several books about jobs and vocations. Titles in the series include *Working in Music, Working in Health Care and Wellness, Working in Law and Justice, Working in Sports and Recreation, Working in the Environment*, and *Working with Animals*.

High school age children can also begin to focus on one or two intense areas of interest to specialize in a topic or skill area. The complexity of some gifted children's abilities and interests may mean that they may need to creatively find ways to combine and integrate fields of otherwise exclusive study, such as technical writing for someone who is both a writer and a technical whiz, or biomedical ethics for a scientist who also has a passion for philosophy. Or someone gifted in math and also in music might combine the two by working as an engineer but playing oboe in the community orchestra as a hobby. For students with multipotentiality, sometimes the second interest can be valuable as an avocation or leisure time activity.

Some older children will be ready for more extensive mentorships and apprenticeships. Kathleen describes how she found a mentor in the field of dog breeding for her teenage daughter, Alison.

> *On my own, I probably wouldn't have considered seeking a mentorship for Alison, since she is just 13, but she brought it up to me several times, and her interest spurred me on. When she expresses that kind of interest and desire, she is usually ready to take on whatever task she has in mind.*
>
> *I decided to contact a woman who had helped us with some dog training when our dog was young. Her business is relatively small, and my daughter remembered her. I have to admit that I was somewhat nervous about approaching someone to take on a 13-year-old to help in the dog breeding business; I had to force myself to pick up the phone and call her. Fortunately, it went well. The breeder remembered her own passion and interest in dog breeding when she was Alison's age and said that she wished she had had the opportunity to learn more about the business as a teen. We decided to meet to discuss the possibility.*
>
> *We have begun with a very loosely arranged schedule—approximately a half day or so per week. Alison's experience there is still in the very early stages, but so far it has been positive. I see this particular mentorship as a relaxed, low key way for a younger person to get some practical experience. When I see the excitement in my daughter's eyes on her "kennel days," I know that it was worth a few minutes of discomfort to take a risk and call a business person to propose the mentorship.*
>
> —Kathleen, home school parent

As this parent's experience shows, some mentorships can be informal. Others are more formal and rigorous, depending on the age of the child, the child's personality and particular interest, and the adult or business acting as mentor. *Mentorship: The Essential Guide for Schools and Business*, by Jill Reilly (1992), offers ideas and further examples of mentorships for young people.

Career guidance should not stop as soon as a student enters or even graduates from college. Gifted people often have several careers during their lifetime, and a variety of careers does not necessarily indicate indecision or failure. It often indicates an ever-developing sense of purpose or a need for new or greater challenge. The most recent edition of the popular book, *What Color Is My Parachute? A Practical Manual for Job-Hunters and Career-Changers*, by Richard Nelson Bolles, can be a valuable resource for young and old adults who are trying to answer the question, *What do I want to do with my life?*

The more gifted children with multipotentiality can learn about careers—including the training, the salaries, the working environments, and the number of career possibilities—and the more they learn about themselves, their own abilities and interests, the better chance they will have to find a way to merge work and play and the better career and life choices they will make. Career education can be a part of every home schooled child's curriculum from early grades on.

Conclusion: Rethink the Child's Place in Society

Some behaviors and patterns of development that can cause social-emotional problems for gifted children are uneven development, perfectionism, non-conformity, poor peer relations, excessive self-criticism, avoidance of risk taking, and multipotentiality (Webb, 2000a; 2000b). All of these areas can be addressed particularly effectively in a home schooling environment through flexible and self-directed study, emphasis of learning over grades, mixed-age socialization, acceptance of feelings, bibliotherapy, refusing to label children unnecessarily, and exposing children to a variety of careers. To realize home schooling's great potential, however, parents must be willing to examine ideas of a child's appropriate place in both the child's own communities and the larger world, and they must be willing to do things in ways that differ from classroom education. This often means venturing out into the world during the day rather than working at home at a desk.

Home school parents must be prepared for the fact that other adults may expect that a child's place is out of sight and out of mind during what are considered normal school hours. Children who frequent libraries, bookstores, parks, and zoos at 10:00 a.m. on a Monday morning are sometimes assumed by adults to be nuisances or even truants. Many adults in our culture feel that as long as children are safely tucked away in a classroom, they are "in their place," but children who venture into the real world of multi-aged living and learning upset the balance and challenge the usual notion of what is or what should be.

Home schooled children should thus be prepared to answer such questions as "Why aren't you in school?" or "Do you have a day off today?" Often, a simple "I learn at home" will suffice and is better than trying to defend or explain, unless you are reasonably sure that the person is truly interested in learning about home schooling. These adults may not understand that your child has already spent several hours reading in the early morning hours or that she stayed up late working on building a radio. Both you and your children should think and talk about how you will respond to such questions.

Home school families can take comfort in the fact that home schooling offers possibilities for social and emotional growth that are not available to classroom schooled children.

- Whereas the classroom child spends most of the day in the company of age peers, the home schooled child has the opportunity to interact with people of all ages, not just on weekends, but every day. The child thus gains a better sense of herself and how she is similar to and different from the people around her.

- Whereas the classroom child is cut off from the day-to-day work and business of adult life, the home schooled child can observe and participate in weekday life of the real world, such as running a household or home business, shopping for groceries, standing in line at the post office, or spending a lunch hour at the local library. The child thus has a better understanding of real life work and what kinds of jobs might one day allow for the merging of work and play.

○ Whereas the classroom child views issues of importance to his community from the perspective of classroom windows, the home schooled child may choose to understand and explore those issues, and so may volunteer time at a library or animal shelter or get involved in civic issues important to his community, such as learning about the effects of local zoning laws or the opinions of local elected officials. The child thus is actively involved in his community and feels a greater connection to the world around him.

In these and many other ways, home schooled gifted children can experience positive social and emotional growth.

Key Points

☑ Many social and emotional needs, such as self-understanding, self-acceptance, having friends, and feeling connected to the world, are the same for all children, gifted or not.

☑ Social and emotional development are integrated with all other aspects of the child's life.

☑ All educational environments have within them inherent social and emotional lessons; environments that don't acknowledge giftedness or that punish children for their giftedness are unhealthy or toxic.

☑ Uneven development can occur in several combinations, such as intellectual-psychomotor, language-reasoning, or intellectual-emotional discrepancies.

☑ Home schooling reduces many artificial struggles related to uneven development because it can be flexible with grade levels.

☑ Self-directed study and modified curriculum allow children who are gifted to better work within their unique development patterns.

☑ Perfectionism is often misunderstood and misinterpreted as laziness, manipulation, or refusal to cooperate.

☑ The drive to perfect is an inborn trait; it comes from the heightened ability to see what could be.

☑ Chronic high achievers as well as low achievers may be at risk for unhealthy perfectionism.

☑ Parents should be honest with themselves about how their own perfectionism may affect their children.

☑ Parents can address negative perfectionism by helping children to set realistic goals and to build their self-confidence; in addition, de-emphasizing grades is an effective and healthy way for home school parents to encourage excellence.

☑ Home school parents can promote social and emotional health through mixed-age socialization, acceptance of feelings, bibliotherapy, refusing to label children unnecessarily, exposing children to a variety of careers, and rethinking the child's place in society.

Questions for Reflection

1. What are my child's areas of uneven development? How can I accommodate these mismatches so that my child can use them as strengths?

2. Is my child prone to perfectionism? Do I have realistic expectations for my child? Am I prone to perfectionism? Do I model healthy risk-taking and acceptance of imperfection?

3. Do I have a special time each day with each of my children? Do I accept all their feelings without judgment? Do I label my child unnecessarily?

4. Will I use grades in home schooling? What are some alternative evaluations I can use?

5. How will I plan for social development in home schoolings? How will I help my child to find friends who are peers intellectually and emotionally?

6. How will I respond to family members and friends who disagree with our choice to home school?

People with great passions,
people who accomplish great deeds,
people who possess strong feelings,
even people with great minds and a strong personality,
rarely come out of good boys and girls.

—Lev Vygotsky

Resources for Social and Emotional Development

Books

Davis, Gary (1996). *Teaching Values: An Idea Book for Teachers (and Parents)*. Westwood Publishing.

Delisle, James R. (1992). *Guiding the Social and Emotional Development of Gifted Youth: A Practical Guide for Educators and Counselors*. Longman.

Elyé, Beatrice J. (2000). *JUMPSTART: Ideas to Move Your Mind. A Teen Guide to Developing Important Life Skills that Will Help Dreams to Come True*. Great Potential Press (formerly Gifted Psychology Press). Encourages writing as a path toward self-discovery.

Galbraith, Judy (1998). *The Gifted Kids' Survival Guide (for ages 10 and under)*. Free Spirit Publishing.

Galbraith, Judy, & Delisle, James (1996). *The Gifted Kids' Survival Guide: A Teen Handbook*. Free Spirit Publishing.

Halsted, Judith Wynn (2002). *Some of My Best Friends Are Books: Guiding Gifted Readers from Preschool to High School, 2nd edition*. Great Potential Press (formerly Gifted Psychology Press). An important resource for home schooling families that explains how to use books for intellectual and social growth. Summaries of books are organized by grade level and include discussion questions. Indexes for author, title, grade, and theme make it easy to find a book on "aloneness" or "friendship" for a particular reading level.

Lewis, Barbara (1997). *What Do You Stand For?* Free Spirit Publishing. Real life stories about children who are true to themselves and make a difference. Several useful checklists for self-discovery. Ages 11 to adult.

Maglione, Robin S. (1986). *Alyndoria—Tales of Inner Magic*. Gifted Education Press. Three fairy tales for ages preschool through grade five explore themes of sensitivity, intelligence, and friendship.

Mosatche, Harriet S., & Unger, Karen (2000). *Too Old for This, Too Young for That! Your Survival Guide for the Middle School Years*. Free Spirit Publishing. This sensitively written manual for the awkward "tween" years covers everything from sweat to sadness, friendships to goal setting.

Packer, Alex J. (1997). *How Rude! The Teenagers' Guide to Good Manners, Proper Behavior, and Not Grossing People Out*. Ages 13 to adult. Free Spirit Publishing. An amusing and useful guide for understanding, living in and contributing to a civil society.

Reilly, Jill (1992). *Mentorship: The Essential Guide for Schools and Business*. Great Potential Press (formerly Ohio Psychology Press).

Rimm, Sylvia (1997). *Dr. Sylvia Rimm's Smart Parenting: How to Parent so Children Will Learn*. Crown Publishing.

Webb, James T. (1993). Nurturing Social-Emotional Development of Gifted Children. In K. A. Heller, F. J. Monks, & A. H. Passow (Eds.), *International Handbook of Research and Development of Giftedness and Talent* (pp. 525-538). Pergamon Press.

Webb, James T.; Meckstroth, Elizabeth; & Tolan, Stephanie (1982). *Guiding the Gifted Child*. Great Potential Press (formerly Gifted Psychology Press).

Favorite Fiction for Sensitive Children (in order of suggested age)

Wells, Rosemary (1988). *Shy Charles*. Dial Books for Young Readers. Written in enchanting verse, this is the unforgettable story of Charles, whose shyness often proves an embarrassment to his parents, but whose resourcefulness, in the end, saves the day. Picture book.

Lobel, Arnold (1979). *Frog and Toad Are Friends*. HarperCollins. The stories of the quintessential odd couple Frog and Toad are rich with gentle wisdom and dry wit about friendship and life. Ages 4-8. Other books in the series: *Days with Frog and Toad, Frog and Toad Together, Frog and Toad All Year*.

Howe, James (1998). *Pinky and Rex*. Simon & Schuster. Easy reader. Pinky, a boy whose favorite color is—you guessed it—pink, is smart and loves books and stuffed animals. Rex, his best friend, is a dinosaur-loving girl who likes nothing better than a good game of soccer. Together, they appreciate each other's differences while finding common human experiences to share. Written with warmth and elegance. Other titles in the series: *Pinky and Rex Get Married, Pinky and Rex and the Spelling Bee, Pinky and Rex and the Mean Old Witch, Pinky and Rex Go to Camp, Pinky and Rex and the New Baby, Pinky and Rex and the Double-Day Weekend, Pinky and Rex and the Bully, Pinky and Rex and the New Neighbors, Pinky and Rex and the School Play*.

Rylant, Cynthia (1985). *Every Living Thing*. Aladdin Paperbacks. Twelve stories explore the complex and moving relationships between human beings and animals. A wonderful introduction to the short story and a must-read for animal lovers and any child who has felt a special connection with a pet. Reading level grade four and up.

L'Engle, Madeleine (1962). *A Wrinkle in Time*. Bantam Doubleday Dell. This classic first book of L'Engle's Time Quartet (*A Wrinkle in Time, A Wind in the Door, A Swiftly Tilting Planet, Many Waters*) tells the story of the Murry family, starring Meg and Charles, children who have a hard time fitting into usual society because of their giftedness. In this first adventure, they travel through space and time to save their father and to face themselves. Reading level grade six and up.

Almond, David (1999). *Skellig*. Yearling. Delacorte. Ten-year-old Michael is facing a move to a new house, his baby sister's illness, a new home school friend named Mina who quotes William Blake, and an extraordinary being living in their dilapidated garage. This story for reading level five and up is magical tale of love and intuition.

Tolan, Stephanie (1999). *Ordinary Miracles*. Morrow Junior Books. Matthew and Mark are the identical twin sons of a minister and are expected to become preachers just like the four generations of Filkinses before them, so when Mark befriends a scientist with a secret whose research goes against their father's beliefs, Mark must reassess his own beliefs and his identity. Young adult.

Philosophy Resources

Bender, David L. (1993). *Constructing a Life Philosophy: An Examination of the Alternatives*. Greenhaven Press's Opposing Viewpoints Series. Greenhaven Press. Not for the faint of heart, this series for young adults looks frankly and without bias at several points of view, from Christianity to Situation Ethics and Yoga. Discussion activities included.

Gaarder, Jostein (1996). *Sophie's World, A Novel about the History of Philosophy*. Translated by Paulette Moller. Berkley Books. Young adult and up.

Hester, Joseph, & Vincent, Philip (1987). *Philosophy for Young Thinkers*. Trillium Press. A program of critical thinking and analysis of philosophical and moral concepts for grades K-12.

White, David (2000). *Philosophy for Kids*. Prufrock Press.

At Home with Home Schoolers

James, Age 6

"I learn best if it's tough stuff and it gets my brain working."

Q: How long have you been home schooling?

A: *All my life. I've never gone to regular school.*

Q: Why are you home schooling?

A: *Well, because I like it. I get more time with my family. I have friends who are home schooled, and I have more fun so I think every child should be home schooled. But if they want to go to school, that's their choice; it's fine with me.*

Q: Describe a typical day of home schooling.

A: *Well, a typical day of home school is like this: I get up, do my chores, water the grass, do stuff, do my grammar, finish my grammar, have my mother read to me, have lunch, then we go out somewhere. We come home, have dinner and then play a game and get ready for bed. I might play with a friend at 3:00.*

Q: What outside-the-home activities do you participate in (examples: lessons, play groups, volunteer work, and so on)?

A: *I go to a Spanish lesson and I might be taking ice skating lessons (again). I go to a park day once a week that is like a playgroup. I go to a Natural History Museum class on Sundays. I go to a book club every month. The book club is on Mondays. We read books like Mouse and the Motorcycle, etc. You get the picture. [James' mom adds here that he also takes a sports class, a geometry class, gymnastics class, and science club once a month.]*

Q: What do you like about home schooling?

A: *It's really fun and I get to play games a lot and have more time with my family.*

Q: What don't you like about home schooling?

A: *That's a tough one. Nothing really. Well, sometimes I feel that I could make more friends at school. It's kind of tough to decide, but I'm sticking to home schooling for now.*

Q: How would you describe yourself as a learner? What are your learning styles and strengths? How do you learn best?

A: I learn best if it's tough stuff and gets my brain working and it takes 15 minutes to an hour (to complete). Once, I was working on a puzzle for an hour. I like to do books like Puzzlemania and Mensa books of challenges. They have easy, medium, and tough levels. It's really fun.

Q: What advice do you have for other children who are considering home schooling?

A: Well, that it's a lot more fun than public school or private school and you learn more.

Intellectual Needs

Gifted children who are satisfied as adults are those whose ideas were encouraged as children, as compared to others who had the wind taken out of their sails by adults telling them how it could be better.

—Elizabeth Meckstroth (1992)

Gifted students need to know. They learn quickly, with few repetitions needed for mastery. They probe subjects deeply, questioning big ideas and seeking connections. But they are not easy to "teach" in the conventional sense. Jessie offers the following description for understanding how gifted children learn.

> *Teaching Roberto, age nine, is like wrestling a fire hose into a barrel with the water turned on full blast. If I were handed a random child to home school, my job would still be to tap into interests and to manage the flow of curiosity. Another child might "turn on" well, have a steady stream of questions, and be great fun to teach. But Roberto is like that fire hose. No way does the parent lead such a child! I guess it is like a rush of water—you manage it according to how strong the flow.*
>
> —Jessie, home school parent

Their need to know can happen in any area of interest or in several. Some children are insatiably curious about nearly everything around them; while other children focus on one subject area, such as animals or history. When the interest is in an area highly prized by adults and society, such as mathematics or creative writing or playing the violin, we're more likely to support the child's interest and provide the necessary education and resources than if the subject has little apparent value to society, such as inventing games or building kites.

Let's look at three children with a need to know—Jorge, Brianna, and Carla. Jorge's world revolves around dinosaurs. He wakes up thinking about T-Rex, discusses theories of the dinosaurs' demise over lunch, and spends his evening reading dinosaur books. His first-grade teacher is concerned that Jorge is too focused on one topic, but for him, the classroom easy reader books on other topics do not compare to what he considers his *real* dinosaur books and encyclopedia articles. The teacher doesn't see Jorge at home, where his parents can barely keep up with his questions and need for resources, where he'd rather assemble his latest stegosaurus model than watch cartoons on TV.

Brianna's artwork is all over her room—pencil drawings scattered on the floor, clay sculptures on her dresser, paintings framed in cardboard on the wall. In school, she doodles on the edges of her worksheets and invents cartoons instead of taking notes, yet she struggles in art class where she is expected to follow specific instructions for drawing the head of a horse using pre-determined shapes. Brianna's parents worry that she is too easily distracted by her own thoughts and is not living up to her potential. Rather than do an assignment correctly by writing five sentences for five spelling words, she writes a Haiku (poem). Her insistence on doing things her way often causes discomfort for adults. Her teacher considers her inattentive, but Brianna concentrates for hours at a time on projects of her own choice.

Carla spends much of her time outdoors, listening to music through headphones while watching clouds, or writing in her journal. She enjoys the company of animals, especially her horse, and knows just how to soothe an injured stray. In her school work, she usually knows the right answer but often can't explain exactly how she knows it; her grades are only average. Her sensitivity allows her to anticipate and absorb other people's emotional responses so that when there is tension or an unspoken problem, she is the first to "tune in" and say something to help the situation. Other people enjoy being around her, though sometimes she prefers to be alone.

These three students are composites, based on several parents' descriptions of their gifted children. Their real-life counterparts inhabit homes and schools throughout the country. Jorge engages in immersion learning—that is, learning in a particular interest that seems to consume the child's every waking moment. Brianna exemplifies creative learning; she is a child whose divergent thinking cannot be molded to fit others' expectations. And Carla embodies intuitive learning; she is a child guided by impressions and internal antennae rather than by external or sensory cues. Many gifted learners will show their "need to know" in a combination of two or even three of these ways of knowing.

Home school parents can learn to recognize and nurture these specific, frequent learning strengths of gifted and creative children by offering an educational environment that celebrates and accommodates all three types of learning—immersion, creative, and intuitive.

Immersion Learning

When gifted children learn by immersion, in the words of psychologist Deirdre Lovecky, they are involved with "investigation that has no more point than the sheer joy of learning about the world and one's place in it" (Lovecky, 1992b). Once immersed in a topic, they will study it "to the point of vanishing interest," which may be hours, weeks, or longer. Sometimes gifted learners move from one topic to another, and only in hindsight can parents discern a pattern of study, such as the science fiction thread that eventually links a preoccupation with robots, physics, philosophy, Star Wars, and comic book heroes.

Immersing oneself in a single topic of interest requires concentration, dedication, and above all, time. When a child is allowed to fulfill a personal need for immersion learning, whether in literature or the latest trading card game, she learns the joy of delving deeply into a subject and making connections with previous knowledge. She learns to love learning.

Whereas immersion learning may be difficult in a school within a structure of pre-determined classes and topics, schooling at home offers children a chance to explore an interest in depth, even if the study lasts longer than a classroom unit might last. Children can freely follow their natural train of thought as they make connections and become interested in new topics. As Colleen discovered, allowing her daughter to use her natural learning process often results in deeper and more meaningful learning.

> *I think it is hard to get gifted children to follow the path of learning you set for them. They want to follow their own path.... Gifted kids are going to have more of their own opinions on things and not just take what the book says as truth (or parents or teachers for that matter).*
>
> *Jenny (age eight) has the ability to make connections that other kids don't seem to make. She can think about two or three things at one time. So if I'm reading something about weather, her mind may be on something else at the same time, and she may pop in with a question for me about the Ancient Egyptians and weather or their weather gods, and she will want to explore that for awhile and leave the weather book until later, and it is almost impossible to guide her back to finish the weather book because her mind has gone off to Ancient Egypt and is working out the answer to her questions. She challenges things that she doesn't think are true more often than most kids and can challenge them intelligently, and she takes the time to research why she's right and someone else is not, even at age eight.*
>
> —Colleen, home school parent

By allowing Jenny the freedom to follow her own train of thought and to immerse herself in the topic according to her own needs and questions, her teacher (Mom) opens the doors to higher level thinking skills—analyzing, evaluating, and synthesizing. In this kind of learning, Jenny is free to notice patterns, ask questions, and divert from the well-trodden path. However, if Colleen assumes that her most important role as a home school parent is to keep her daughter "on task," then Jenny may reluctantly go along with finishing the weather book or unit, and although they both may have the satisfaction of checking off pre-selected goals or objectives, what is lost in the meantime?

Another parent, Kathleen, explains how she now adjusts her home school approach to accommodate her 13-year-old daughter's need for immersion learning.

The approach we began using initially with home schooling (more of a formal curriculum) did not work with my gifted children. Their drive to learn about what interests them is so strong that to force a curriculum changes who they are as learners. We have had to adjust our thinking to a place where their sense of self is being served by how they are learning. For example, we allowed our 13-year-old daughter, Allison, to be consumed with reading all four volumes of Harry Potter over and over until she had found every correlation and related detail between the books to her satisfaction, a task that took her weeks and weeks.

There are many times when Allison will totally immerse herself in a new venture and not come up for air unless we force her to. She became interested in a website called "Neopets," which combines fantasy animals with the opportunity to create a self-contained world, complete with newsletters, shops, banks, and websites. She learned the principles of advertising, pricing, inventory, banking, the stock market, interest, and bankruptcy all from this site in a way that enraptured her with its use of animals. She would spend as much time on it as we would allow, finding new and different ways to go farther in the project. She focuses completely on one area of interest until she feels she has exhausted it (temporarily) and then moves on to something else, maybe to return to it a few weeks or months later again in a different way.

After such episodes (which are unpredictable in length), she will jump right back into an old interest or start something new (such as a several week adventure in making homemade kites and putting them to the test). But she will generally return to an old favorite, like Neopets, for a period of time before finding something completely new to dive into.

Not having had any experience home schooling other children, I can only guess that there may be children who desire a more structured learning situation at home, but in our case, the "differentness" that is so huge in gifted children required that we offer a very different learning environment. Otherwise, it seems to me that regular school would have worked!

—Kathleen, home school parent

Parents can support immersion learning by allowing plenty of time for children to follow their own interests, by supporting interests that are untraditional or odd, as well as those that are more academic in nature, and by assisting the child in finding resources. Parents can also keep in mind that not every project a child starts must be finished before moving on to something else. Sometimes children return to unfinished work later with a fresh perspective and new ideas. And sometimes the child has learned all that he or she needs to know from the work that was done. If parents feel uncomfortable or out of control when their children do not finish activities, they can help children learn the habit of persistence and the ability to follow through on projects and ideas in small steps. For example, if a child routinely writes stories and poems that are never finished, the parent can help the child choose one or two pieces of writing that will be expected to be completed and then guide the child through the process of breaking the task into steps and setting goals, rather than expect that all writing projects of the child's own choice reach completion.

Creative Learning

Creative learning may seem an oxymoron. Doesn't creativity come *after* learning? When we learn, aren't we consciously following a linear thought process and making an effort *not* to be creative?

Creative learning is very different from the kind of learning required to memorize a list of facts or repeat the thoughts of someone else. Creative learning is instead based on *divergent thinking*, which is open-ended and has more than one correct answer or no absolute answer. Divergent thinking moves away from what is obvious or standard. Think of a small stream that breaks from a river to chart its own path. *Convergent thinking*—i.e., learning that offers a single correct answer—is what we generally find in classrooms. Convergent thinking moves *toward* what is standard or expected. Think of an on-ramp to a highway that allows a smaller road to join with a larger one. A student listening to a lecture about the causes of the Civil War and taking notes on what the speaker says is thinking convergently, staying within expected guidelines. When a student (or teacher) asks open-ended discussion questions such as, "What would have happened if President Lincoln had been assassinated at the *beginning* of the war?" or "How might life today be different if the South had won the war?" he or she is using divergent thinking in which there is no single correct answer. There are many possible answers. Some people might say the problem is "messy." Others refer to this kind of thinking as "thinking outside the box." Whatever the descriptor, divergent thinkers use creative thinking.

Divergent thinkers prefer "the unusual, original, and creative aspects of any topic" (Lovecky 1992a). Because such thinking gets "off track," it is not always welcome in the classroom and is, at times, annoying to adults or peers. Because of this, gifted children who think creatively may learn to hide their true nature behind a false "conforming, ungifted" self (Lovecky, 1993), especially if they possess convergent thinking skills as well. It is often easier to conform and give the expected answer than to behave in ways that draw attention or disapproval. Perhaps precisely because some gifted children can switch so easily between convergent and divergent thinking, they sometimes conform all too easily to the classroom convergent model, especially when such conformity is routinely encouraged and rewarded. Some creatively gifted children are at risk of "losing" their creativity (at least temporarily).

But some divergent thinkers have a hard time "switching off" their creative side in the classroom, either because they *choose not* to learn according to the convergent model (Kohl, 1994) or because they are *unable to* conform. Unfortunately, these students, who include the class clowns, are likely to be viewed by their teachers as being "less ambitious, hard working and studious" than convergent thinkers (LeShan, 1967), and are less likely to be recommended for screening or placement in gifted and talented programs.

Because gifted children are precocious and learn faster than other students, home school parents may be tempted to use curriculum packages and home schooling approaches that focus on preparation for high scores on college entrance exams. However, creative thinkers prefer to question, manipulate, and transform what they know, rather than learn one bite after the other in logical sequence. Because this can cause the old order of things to break down along the way (Eby & Smutny, 1990), creative learning is "messier" than learning by authority. Temporary chaos is a normal stage of the creative learning process, and children may have long periods with nothing tangible to show for their efforts. A helpful resource for home school parents is the Future Problem Solving Program (www.fpsp.org), a non-profit program of creative thinking for children ages 9-19.

Creative learning is important for every discipline, from science and math to the arts and humanities. Creativity enhances our quality of life. That is not to say, however, that creative learning is all fluff and no substance. Mihaly Csikszent-mihalyi (1996) reminds us that "divergent thinking is not much use without the ability to tell a good idea from a bad one," or good judgment and evaluation. After the divergent phase, then, comes a convergent thinking phase, where the ideas generated are evaluated and judged by criteria. Both types of thinking are needed. Likewise, children may need guidance for knowing how to make their dreams come true, or in the words of Mary-Elaine Jacobsen, how to become creative producers.

> *The difference between the creative person and the creative producer is hard work. Those who actually produce the play, build the rocket, find the cure, and write the novel don't let their ideas collect dust on the "tomorrow" shelf. They dig in, often before they feel completely ready, and keep digging until they unearth what they are searching for* (Jacobsen, 1999b, p. 158).

Home school parents can help their children learn convergent skills, such as study skills and organization, by including these as an integral part of learning without sacrificing divergent thinking. Study skills can be learned in any subject matter and through any interest. A child who does the work necessary to design and publish a personal web page or write a science fiction story is learning both study skills (convergent thinking) and higher level skills (divergent, creative thinking) that will be useful throughout the child's life. These self-initiated projects are just as valuable as a completed math workbook or an essay. When parents give children the time and space to work on and complete their own projects as well as assigned work, they offer valuable practice in creative production and organization. (See Chapter 15 for resources that show children how to organize their time and space.) E. Paul Torrance and Kathy Goff (1990) offer these guidelines for fostering and nurturing creative learning (ERIC Digest #E484):

Guidelines for Creative Learning

- Be respectful of the unusual questions children ask.

- Teach children to appreciate and be pleased with their own creative efforts.

- Be respectful of children's unusual ideas and solutions; children will see many relationships that parents and teachers miss.

- Show children that their ideas have value by listening to their ideas and considering them. Encourage children to test their ideas by using them and communicating them to others. Give them credit for their ideas.

- Provide opportunities and give credit for self-initiated learning. Too much supervision, too much reliance on prescribed curricula, failure to appraise learning resulting from a child's own initiative, and attempts to cover material with no opportunity for reflection interfere seriously with self-directed learning.

- Provide chances for children to learn, think, and discover without immediate evaluation. Too much evaluation, especially during practice and initial learning, makes children afraid to use creative ways to learn. Accept honest errors as part of the creative process.

- Establish creative relationships with children—encourage creativity while providing adequate guidance and being a model of a creative learner.

- Avoid insisting that children do things the "right" way.

- Do not pressure children to be realistic, to stop imagining.

- Avoid comparing children with others.

- Refrain from discouraging or ignoring children's natural curiosity.

Intuitive Learning

When gifted children are engaged in their need to know, either through immersion learning or creative learning, they do learn differently from other children. Sometimes they skip steps or use intuition first before more logical reasoning (Strip, 2000).

What exactly is intuition? The dictionary might define it as "knowledge outside of reason or experience." Some describe it as an inner voice or a sixth sense or a gut feeling. Whatever the definition, highly intuitive people rely on introspection more than observation to make sense of the world (Keirsey, 1998).

Barbara Clark (1997) writes that intuition is an integrative function, bringing together various other modes of thought such as convergent and divergent thinking. In this respect, intuition is a high level of thought. The development and use of intuition results in accelerated learning, greater retention and recall of what is learned, and a higher level of interest in the subject matter. Techniques that help to develop intuitive ability, such as fantasy and imagery, are important for problem solving and emotional development (Clark, 1997).

Parents can nurture their children's intuition by helping them quiet their minds, focus attention, and have a receptive attitude (Clark, 1997). Ellen J. Langer (1997) describes this approach as "mindful learning," characteristics of which are "the continuous creation of new categories, openness to new information, and an implicit awareness of more than one perspective." When we struggle with a problem, such as thinking of just the right metaphor for a poem, only to have the answer come to us while we're doing something mindless like exercising or taking a walk, we've experienced intuitive learning.

For children to take advantage of this kind of intuitive leap, they need time—unhurried time to take in information, focused time to mull over the problem, then quiet time for intuition to work. It is hard to tap into intuition when the TV is on, the dog is barking, and our minds are trying to force order on chaos. When we can reduce sensory distractions, we can breathe deeply and more readily accept whatever thoughts or ideas come to us. For many families, home schooling automatically offers a reduction of stress and a more relaxed way of life.

We find home schooling to be so much easier than traditional school. School had many meetings, fund raisers, homework requirements, and these seemed to take up the entire afternoon in addition to any lessons or activities, so that the only down time was on the weekends. That meant we were stressed from Monday through Friday and tried to recover and have fun each weekend. Now, we have a relaxed pace from Monday through Sunday, and the days seem to be so much calmer.

Our mornings were the first area to improve. No more stress about backpacks, clothes, lunches, homework, and the like every morning of the week. Next to improve was the afternoon. The girls still participate in several lessons and activities after school, but homework does not interfere with our family evenings. We tend to finish school before the activities, so that the evenings are so much calmer. Any schoolwork done in the evening is in the form of a family activity like reading or games and does not have the pressure of having to be finished for the next day. Much of the school homework seemed trivial and pointless. Even now, when I see homework from our neighbor friends, I am so thankful that my kids do not have to do it. Neighborhood kids spend hours in the afternoon/evening doing work that seems like it should have been done during the school day. Meanwhile, my kids are playing outside, reading for pleasure, or doing some other activity.

We also have the benefit of having the kids find each other for a best friend. They rarely fight, and I think that is a direct benefit of a more relaxed atmosphere.

—Monica, home school parent

Creativity and Intuition

Creativity and intuition seem to come more readily in relaxed, "unthinking" moments—during a leisurely walk, in the hazy aftermath of sleep, or while staring out a car window—than in high stress settings. The ability to relax is crucial to the development of both creativity and the use of intuition (Clark, 1997). Creating a home environment that is conducive to these kinds of learning requires only small changes in attitude and perspective in areas such as these:

○ Focus on long-term growth and development rather than short-term behavior as a way to reduce family tension and to promote relaxation. If a child is having difficulty falling asleep, tap into your stores of patience before saying or doing something that will cause a stressful response in the child. The long-term goal is to help the child to manage time, and himself, effectively and independently. Brainstorm with the child for ways to get to bed at a reasonable hour. Lying quietly in a dark room with soft music might make the transition from activity to rest easier for the child and would provide a chance to visualize and daydream. Help the child to view this quiet time as a wonderful opportunity to ponder ideas for the next day's activities.

○ Provide time and opportunity for children to fantasize, not just when there is nothing else to do or at the end of a long, busy day, but also during peak learning times. Children who awaken early (too early for their parents!) can be encouraged to use this as their imagination time, perhaps with some quiet dress-up clothes, a sketchbook, or a writing pad.

○ Be a good role model for intuitive learning. Barbara Clark (1992, p. 354) challenges parents to ask themselves, "How many times have you known, really known, how you wanted to do something, but for whatever reason allowed yourself to do it another possibly more 'sensible' way, only to discover later that your original idea would have worked much better?" Trust your inner voice more often. Share with your children times in your life when you "went with your instincts."

○ Help children to view mistakes as opportunities rather than ends or failures. Each false step is a step in a new and different direction.

○ Older children can be encouraged to imagine their futures and the many possibilities ahead of them, to predict how they might react to a certain way or life or career (Clark, 1997; Delisle, 1992).

○ Whether with family or with friends, provide opportunities for children to engage in open-ended philosophical discussion of ideas. One friend of mine who is a home school father leads a philosophy discussion group for children and adults. He begins by asking simple questions such as, "What is gossip?" or "What are human rights?" and then allows participants to explore their own and others' thoughts and responses. Science fiction and fantasy books offer another, slightly different outlet for intuitive and philosophical thought, as well as a topic of discussion for like-minded thinkers. Ask about starting a fantasy book club group for children at your local library or bookstore, perhaps starting with Madeline L'Engle's *Wrinkle in Time* trilogy, J. K. Rowling's *Harry Potter* series, C. S. Lewis' *Narnia* books, or J. R. R. Tolkien's *Lord of the Rings* and *Hobbit* books).

Mary, Mary, Quite Contrary: How Does Your Argument Grow? Putting Argument to Good Use

When parents of gifted and creative children get together, before long, they begin to commiserate about their children's love of argument. Gifted children often disagree, protest, refute, nitpick, and just plain love to argue. Linda Silverman writes that the urge to argue is rooted both in the gifted child's intelligence and personality,[5] and she quotes Leta Hollingworth, a psychologist who in 1927 noted the gifted child's love of precision:

> *Exactness in all mental performances is characteristic, and keen love of precise facts. Allied to this is the perception of things in their multitudinous relationships, with frequent use of the phrase, "Well that depends." A young child who spontaneously utters the phrase, "That depends," is sure to catch the attention of one who thoroughly knows gifted children* (Hollingworth, 1927, p. 4).

While it is easy to see the positive side of many traits of giftedness—e.g., sensitivity and perfection—we don't always enjoy the child who loves to argue. We melt at the understanding of a sensitive child who notices we are having a bad day, and we appreciate the flawless piano recital of the young, hard-working perfectionist. But understanding the value of the performance of the child skilled in argument and refutation takes quite a bit of patience and insight.

The Positive Argument

How can we better understand and appreciate the value of analysis, argument, and refutation? We can start by thinking about how the development and use of argument and refutation may be important to both critical insights and creative production (Lynch & Harris, 2001). The ability to detect errors and to trust one's judgment in finding and correcting mistakes allows us to produce new ideas and improve upon old ones. A well developed sense of refutation is necessary in several careers apart from the obvious one of lawyer. Proofreaders, reporters, researchers, historians, mechanics, engineers, mathematicians, scientists, and doctors all must have excellent skills in error detection. Nearly any job done well requires the ability first to recognize and second to resolve problems. Because some children readily notice errors, they are also overly quick to have strong opinions about what (and

---

5   Silverman, L. "The Walking Argument," www.gifteddevelopment.com/Articles/The%20Walking%20Argument.html.

who) is right. They often, however, need help using evidence and logical reasoning to support their many opinions, as this home school parent explains:

> *I was raised without necessarily learning how or when it is appropriate to state opposing views so that they can be well received. Consequently, as a college student, I had trouble with my faculty advisor and had to learn at that point what could have been taught to me as I was growing up.*
>
> *One important aspect of learning to use argument appropriately is learning when it's acceptable to detect errors and express opinions, and when one needs to use self-control and refrain from refuting. The child may be creative and gifted, but refutation can be seen as disrespect and can get a child in trouble if done with authority figures such as a policeman, school principal, employer, some teachers, a coach, etc. Gifted children need to learn to keep emotions in check and perhaps even ask permission to share another perspective, as part of learning to use argument appropriately.*
>
> *Sometimes we need to be able to accept what they are told. Arguing with a coach on a sports team, for example, may get a player benched or off the team.*
>
> —Nina, home school parent

Gifted children may need to be asked respectfully, "What are your reasons for believing so?" and "How did you come to that conclusion?" and "What would someone who disagrees with you say?" The grade school years provide the training ground for this process. Unfortunately, many young gifted and creative children are not shown how to make the best use of refutation skills and are instead discouraged from or even punished for detecting errors or expressing strong opinions, especially when doing so makes the adults around them uncomfortable. Rather than being helped to use tact or to moderate their refutation when appropriate and necessary, they are told to "stop arguing" or "just do as I say." This does not help the child learn how to use argument appropriately. For the creatively gifted child in particular, knowing how to cope not only with one's own refutation but also that of others is an important part of social and emotional development (Lynch & Harris, 2001).

One way for parents to help their children to use and develop refutation skills is to allow mistakes to be an integral part of the curriculum. Children can be asked to find errors rather than to produce error-free work (Lynch & Harris, 2001). Parents can use their own mistakes as ways to help children learn how to offer corrections or advice with good humor and tact. When your child catches you in the wrong about a fact or theory, show your delight in learning something new. This may require a bit of shoring up of one's ego, but the example you set by modeling acceptable human imperfection is well worth the effort.

Gifted children who learn at home can start earlier than other students to develop skills in critical thinking. Several home school resources exist for learning logic, including the highly recommended materials from Critical Thinking Books & Software listed at the end of this section. Parents can also use real life to develop logical thinking skills. If a child wants a puppy, for example, the parent can ask for a T chart of reasons both pro and con for why the family should get a puppy. If the reasons are valid, then the child can research which kind of dog would be a good fit for the family rather than choosing randomly.

Another good strategy for home school parents is to include materials with multiple perspectives in the curriculum. Does everyone agree with the Human Genome Project? Why or why not? What is the stereotype of Americans in other countries? Parents can encourage children to see other points of view and perhaps even learn how to agree to disagree. For example, if a child believes very strongly that animals should not be used in lab experimentation, he can research the reasons for the *other side*, as well as doing research to back up his own opinion. A good writing exercise is to write opposing viewpoints, even for the position with which he disagrees. The child need not change his mind, but he will have a better understanding of why some people may disagree with his position; he will also learn to have more tolerance for other people's ideas and perspectives.

These strategies are important, of course, for all children but are of particular importance for gifted children who are quick to notice mistakes and equally quick to comment. Without guidance in thinking through one's arguments carefully and expressing one's opinions with tact, gifted children may grow into adults who equate fault-finding with helpfulness and hurtful sarcasm for friendly teasing. Gifted children have the intelligence, creativity, and courage to note mistakes, but they lack the caring to tolerate other people's differing opinions or weaknesses. James Webb (2002) calls gifted persons who lack caring but who are otherwise courageous and creative *unguided missiles*: "These are the gifted 'hackers' who break into computer systems, or who in other ways courageously or outrageously pinch the noses of authorities around them." Webb reminds adults that we have a responsibility to influence children "to become more caring and compassionate" and to cultivate and model such traits and behaviors in ourselves.

Resources that Use Refutation

Mystery and detective stories are obvious resources that require children to detect clues and errors. Parents can look for popular detective series books for children:

- *Einstein Anderson, Science Detective*, by Seymour Simon
- *Encyclopedia Brown*, by Donald J. Sobol
- *Match Wits with Sherlock Holmes*, by Murray Shaw, adapted from the original Sir Arthur Conan Doyle stories
- *The Stevie Diamond Mysteries*, by Linda Bailey

Children who are strong visual learners may enjoy "what's wrong with this picture" books, such as *Art Fraud Detective*, by Anna Nilsen. This book provides hours of engaging investigation as the child uses a magnifying glass—included with the book—to distinguish real paintings from fakes. Usborne Books publishes several excellent interactive puzzle books and adventure quest books for all ages that integrate text and graphics. Look for books in these series: *Young Puzzles* (ages 5+), *Puzzle Journey* (ages 8+), *Fantasy Adventure* (ages 8+), *Puzzle Adventures* (ages 8-13), *Whodunnits* (ages 9+), *Science Puzzle Adventures* (ages 10+), *Solve It Yourself* (ages 12+), and *Advanced Puzzle Adventures* (ages 12+). Usborne books are available in many libraries and some bookstores, or via the website www.ubah.com.

Critical Thinking Books & Software offers several books, programs, and CD-ROMs that capitalize on a child's need for precision and love of refutation (on-line descriptions, samples, and ordering are available at www.criticalthinking.com). Some of these are:

- *A Case of Red Herrings: Solving Mysteries through Critical Questioning*, by Thomas Camilli, grades 4-6, 7-12.

- *Red Herrings Science Mysteries: Solving Problems through Critical Questioning*, grades 4-9.

- *Critical Thinking, by Anita Harnadek*, grades 7-12, 10-12. Children use real-world examples from news, advertisements, and politics to develop logical thinking skills. Teacher's manuals available.

- *Editor in Chief: Grammar Disasters & Punctuation Faux Pas*, grades 4-6, 7-8, 9-12. Available in both book form and on CD-ROM, this innovative program uses copyediting rather than drill and practice to develop grammar and language skills as children are asked to analyze and find errors in pictures, captions, and stories.

- *Reading Detective: Developing Skills for Reading Comprehension*, grades 4-6, 7-8. Excerpts from award-winning authors and original fiction are used to practice and develop reading comprehension skills. The program builds confidence and is an enjoyable way for children who shy from analytic reading to focus on details and to question what they read.

- *You Decide! Applying the Bill of Rights to Real Cases*, grades 7-12. By putting themselves in the role of judge, children analyze arguments logically in order to make the best decision.

Learning with Humor

A sense of humor is nearly always mentioned on lists of traits of gifted, creative children and visual-spatial learners. Some gifted children display a quick sense of humor at a very early age; they enjoy the incongruous and the absurd and never seem to tire of puns. After taking a snapshot of an open door with a lid from a peanut butter jar perched on the top, one young girl delighted in asking her friends and family what the photograph meant. Then she would shout gleefully, "The door is a-jar!" Parents and teachers of gifted children are familiar with such punnish "groaners."

©Copyright PEANUTS. Reprinted by permission of United Feature Syndicate.

Humor and Health

Contrary to some stereotypes about gifted children, many gifted children delight in the silly bathroom humor of early and middle childhood and greatly enjoy—often to their parents' dismay—books like Dav Pilkey's popular early reader series or *The Stinky Cheese Man and Other Fairly Stupid Tales*, by Jon Scieszka. Parents should be cautious not to expect their gifted child to be "too smart" for such silliness or to see this as an indication that their child is not gifted. Pilkey himself was a gifted child humorist, whose first book, *World War Won*, was published when he won a writing contest (The National "Written and Illustrated by…" Contest) at age 19. Hearty laughs, even at silliness, are physically and mentally healthy, help temper perfectionism, strengthen the immune system, increase oxygen intake, and lower blood pressure (Monson, 1994; Holt, 1996).

Humor can also promote healthy social and emotional development. The authors of *Guiding the Gifted Child* recommend that adults teach children to use humor to diffuse tense situations by looking at situations from a different perspective (Webb, Tolan, & Meckstroth, 1982). For example, if a child is worried about an upcoming test or performance, an adult can encourage the child to imagine the most unlikely, fantastical thing that could go wrong, the more outrageous the better. Perhaps all of the pencils in the room will turn into carrots, or Martians might land on stage in the middle of a piano recital. Then the adult can help the child to use imagination or visualization in a more positive way, to imagine everything going very smoothly, that she knows all the answers to the test, or that she remembers all of the keys and cadences of the musical piece and performs perfectly. Or perhaps the adult can say, "Here are a few tricks I have used when I have had to perform." Humor used in this way must be done with a gentle touch so that the child does not feel she is being made fun of.

Gifted children should be taught to use humor to cope with stress, which increases in the adolescent years. Watching a funny movie or favorite sit-com or just being silly with friends is a much healthier antidote to a rough day than drugs or alcohol. Humor employed skillfully is also a valuable social skill. Being able to make other people laugh goes a long way toward making friends, and a shared laugh is a unifying social force (Webb, Meckstroth, & Tolan, 1982; Holt, 1996; Monson, 1994). Learning to laugh is also a powerful ally against unhealthy perfectionism (Adderholdt-Elliott & Goldberg, 1999). Games like Pictionary ® in which we have fun laughing at ourselves, can help children to see that other people can enjoy being with us even when we're not perfect.

The Gifted Young Comic

Some children create or perform the comical with unusual skill and wit. Barbara, a home school parent, writes of her son:

> *James, age six, loves comedy, loves to laugh. It is a challenge finding humor that's not too adult and yet that's sophisticated enough and funny enough. Because of his sensitivities and intellect, he makes up his own jokes, riddles, and brain teasers to satisfy himself (and to share with others).*
>
> —Barbara, home school parent

Gifted child humorists often prefer humor normally appreciated by children or adults several years their senior (Fern, 1991). Like other characteristics associated with giftedness, a sense of humor can be complicated by issues of asynchronous development. A child's sense of humor may become a liability if he will do anything for a laugh, such as making fun of others in demeaning ways.

Bibliotherapy—using themes in books to address issues and developmental stumbling blocks—can help youngsters learn to self-regulate humor, understand why some humor is not always appreciated by others, and understand and accept their particular humor gifts. In Louis Sachar's *Dogs Don't Tell Jokes*, seventh-grader Gary Boone's parents offer him $100 if he won't tell a joke for three weeks. And in *The Great Gilly Hopkins*, by Katherine Paterson, the self-proclaimed "Gifted Gilly—a funny female of the first rank" learns a valuable lesson about the difference between benevolent humor and cruel sarcasm.

Home schooling offers a specific challenge for these funny youngsters because many adult comedians and clowns say that school gave them the audience they needed to practice and perfect their craft (Fern, 1991). Families who home school potential humorists may need to make a special effort to provide the social component needed by these young comedians. This could mean being a patient and loyal audience themselves and seeking opportunities for the child to use his wit and humor with others. Perhaps your home school group would like to form a comedy club where children can do stand-up comedy or stage plays (Gleason, 1991). The book *Improvisation, 2nd Edition: Use What You Know—Make Up What You Don't!*, by Brad Newton, is full of impromptu games, skits, pantomime, and other improvisations that can be used in group settings.

Of course, adults sometimes need comic relief as well. A teacher of gifted, Jean Watts, has written *In Search of Perspective* and *Off Hours*, two books of cartoons that can help parents laugh at situations in everyday life. One home school parent of a highly gifted child finds it helpful to use imaginative role play when life gets hectic. She simply asks herself what is funny in the current stressful situation that could be used in a TV sit-com. This keeps her from overreacting to mild annoyances. The authors of *Bringing Out the Best: A Resource Guide for Parents of Young Gifted Children* (Saunders, 1991) suggest that, when tensions run high, parents ask themselves, "What would Bill Cosby do with this?"

Learning to Laugh, Laughing to Learn

Used wisely, a sense of humor—whether deceptively subtle or wild and wacky—can be a powerful learning tool, engaging and sustaining the child's interest while at the same time encouraging critical and creative thinking. Political cartoons, for example, are an excellent pathway to history and government, and verbal word play helps to develop vocabulary and linguistic skill. Humor can engage all of the senses and styles of learning, from auditory puns to visual cartoons and kinesthetic charades.

Children who are reluctant readers may come eventually to a love of books through comic strips such as *Garfield* or *Peanuts*. One home schooled boy learned to read through the humor of *Calvin and Hobbes*, a comic strip that contains rather sophisticated vocabulary and much commentary on education and family life. (Note that Calvin's antics and the fact that the strip was written for adults may make it inappropriate for some young children.) James Howe, author of several children's books including the funny and popular Bunnicula series, remembers that he was a very slow reader, but in the sixth grade moved straight from comics to adult books (Marcus, 2000).

Reluctant writers may enjoy writing and drawing comics as a way to demonstrate understanding of topics or to express ideas. The fine lines and lettering required in comic art offer enjoyable practice in fine-motor control. If your child resists journal writing, suggest that she draw a picture or cartoon instead. Or suggest that children use new vocabulary words in funny sentences, the sillier the better, or they can make up their own funny words based on Greek and Latin roots and common prefixes and suffixes. In creating their own comics, children will learn small-motor control, writing and drawing skills, and the value of revision. Two resources for budding comic strip artists grade four to adult are *The World of Cartooning with Mike Peters*, by Mike Peters, and *Drawing on the Funny Side of the Brain*, by Christopher Hart.

If you're interested in using humor to motivate learning, consider the following ways in which comic strips can be paired with topics of study for older children:

- *Superman* & American Heroes: Why did the character of Superman appeal to the public when he was created in 1938? What other comic strip heroes arose at the same time? Why?

- *Peanuts* & the Changing Times of 1950-2000: How did the Peanuts gang change to reflect the social changes in the United States in the second half of the Twentieth Century? What other popular comics were created in the years following World War II?

- *Garfield* & the "Me" Decade of the 1980s: How does the Garfield strip reflect the "me" culture of the 1980s?

- *Asterix* & Ancient Rome: Make your own collectible trading cards based on the Asterix adventures, including main characters and their characteristics and place in the society of Ancient Rome.

- *Tintin* & Geography: Draw a map of Tintin's various adventures, including routes of travel.

- Political Cartoons & Twentieth Century American Politics: For older learners, explore the books *Drawn & Quartered: The History of American Political Cartoons*, by Stephen Hess and Sandy Northrop, and *Herblock: A Cartoonist's Life* by Herbert Block. Collect and analyze current political cartoons from newspapers. Draw your own political cartoons to comment upon current events.

- Comics, Humor &World Culture: Photocopy, collect, and compare comic strips from different countries or from a specific country such as Japan or England, and analyze the culture from a "comic" point of view. Many libraries carry newspapers from around the globe (hint: college and university libraries offer the widest selections and usually allow independent scholars—you!—to use their materials with a special pass).

Richard Shade (1999) has taught summer classes on humor to gifted tenth graders; he offers these suggestions for helping gifted children to learn about humor:

- Create an atmosphere that accepts all forms of age-appropriate (taking asynchronous behavior into account) and socially appropriate humor. Promote risk-taking.

- Collect examples of a wide variety of humor, especially those that relate to subjects about which the child is learning.

- Distinguish between productive and benign humor on the one hand and sarcasm and ridicule on the other.

- Use the book *License to Laugh: Humor in the Classroom*, by Richard Shade (1996) as a way to understand and analyze different forms of humor.

- Encourage humor production. Shade suggests such forms as skits based on television shows, radio plays, parodies of songs, original humorous songs, stand-up comedy routines, captions to cartoons, comic books, and caricatures.

Key Points

- ☑ Gifted children have a strong intellectual drive, a "need to know."

- ☑ Immersion learning, creative learning, and intuitive learning are three common ways (other than the usual ways taught in school) that gifted children need to know or prefer to learn.

- ☑ Immersion learning may seem obsessive or pointless to casual observers, but there is usually a need that drives a child's particular interest or a common thread that links together a string of interests.

- ☑ Creative learning involves divergent thinking, thoughts, and behaviors that veer from the usual and expected.

- ☑ Divergent thinking is not always valued in traditional learning environments; most classroom learning is convergent.

- ☑ Intuitive learning is a synthesis of creativity, intuition, and convergent thinking.

- ☑ A relaxed state of mind is necessary for intuitive learning to occur.

- ☑ Gifted children often love to argue and find errors.

- ☑ The ability to find mistakes and argue well is a skill used in many careers.

- ☑ Children can be taught how to argue effectively, how to give reasons to support their arguments, and how to be tolerant of differing opinions and viewpoints.

- ☑ Curriculum resources that use critical thinking skills and error detection can take advantage of a child's argumentative nature.

- ☑ Adults have the responsibility to be models of caring, compassionate, and creative learners.

- ☑ An early and strong sense of humor is a common trait of gifted children.

- ☑ A gifted child may enjoy corny jokes and bathroom jokes as much as sophisticated humor.

- ☑ A sense of humor helps promote both mental and physical health.

- ☑ Home school parents of young gifted humorists may need to make a conscious effort to provide their children with social outlets or an audience.

- ☑ Humor can help adults to gain perspective on challenges of parenting and teaching.

- ☑ Many curriculum resources use humor as an introduction to specific subjects.

Questions for Reflection

1. Think about your child's intense interests. What areas of immersion learning would your child enjoy? How might you more fully support your child's favorite interest?

2. Choose one or more of the Guidelines for Creative Learning listed in Chapter 4 to implement in your home. In what specific ways can you put the guideline(s) into practice?

3. Do you think of yourself as being highly intuitive or not very intuitive? Why or why not? When was the last time you trusted your intuition to help you to make a decision?

Non-Fiction Bibliotherapy for the Creative and Intuitive

Older children and adults can gain valuable perspective on creativity and how to adapt to change through the best-selling book *Who Moved My Cheese? An Amazing Way to Deal with Change in Your Work and in Your Life*, by Spencer Johnson.

The following books by Nathan Aaseng, published by Lerner Publications, offer many examples of creativity, intuition, courage, and perseverance:

Better Mousetraps: Product Improvements that Led to Success
Close Calls: From the Brink of Ruin to Business Success
From Rags to Riches: People Who Started Businesses from Scratch
Midstream Changes: People Who Started Over and Made It Work
The Fortunate Fortunes: Business Successes that Began with a Lucky Break
The Problem Solvers: People Who Turned Problems into Products
The Rejects: People and Products that Outsmarted the Experts
The Unsung Heroes: Unheralded People Who Invented Famous Products

Lerner Publications also publishes Kids' Ventures books, written by Arlene Erlbach, which profile children ages six to 16 who have learned to trust their creative and intuitive impulses:

The Kids' Business Book
The Kids' Invention Book
The Kids' Volunteering Book

Special Section: Comic Resources

It is extremely important for a cartoonist to be a person of observation. He not only has to observe the strange things that people do and listen to the strange things that they say, but he also has to be reasonably observant as to the appearance of objects in the world around him.

—Charles M. Schulz

Peanuts Comic Strips

The beloved cartoon creations of Charles M. Schulz reflect astounding insight into human nature and the world and are appropriate for all ages. Several books that offer collections of strips are available in your local library. Three anniversary books—*You Don't Look 35, Charlie Brown; Around the World in 45 Years*; and *Peanuts: A Golden Celebration*—combine the strips themselves with commentary about the author and the history of the strip. If your child is a real Peanuts fan, look for these additional resources:

Charlie Brown's Super Book of Questions and Answers, Random House. Packed with information, these books skillfully integrate education and entertainment. Published in the 1970s, they are, unfortunately, out of print, but look for them at the local library and used-book stores. Each of five volumes covers a different subject area and is appropriate for all ages (reading level approximately fourth grade).

Charlie Brown's Super Book of Questions and Answers: About All Kinds of Animals

Charlie Brown's Second Super Book of Questions and Answers: About the Earth and Space...from Plants to Planets!

Charlie Brown's Third Super Book of Questions and Answers: About All Kinds of Boats and Planes, Cars and Trains, and Other Things that Move!

Charlie Brown's Fourth Super Book of Questions and Answers: About All Kinds of People and How They Live!

Charlie Brown's Fifth Super Book of Questions and Answers: About All Kinds of Machines and How They Work!

This is America, Charlie Brown Video Series. Paramount Videos. Widely available in libraries and video stores, this entertaining series provides a wonderfully humorous introduction to history for visual-spatial learners (and a good refresher course for adults!). All ages.
The Mayflower Voyagers
The Birth of the Constitution
The Great Inventors
The Building of the Transcontinental Railroad
The Wright Brothers at Kitty Hawk
The Smithsonian and the Presidency
The Music and Heroes of America
The NASA Space Station

What Have We Learned, Charlie Brown? Paramount Video. A memorial day salute: Peanuts and the World Wars. All ages.

Home of Peanuts on the Web: www.snoopy.com. Strip archives, games, and information.

Picture Books for Reading Aloud (Ages 4 and Up)

Barrett, Judith (1982). *Cloudy with a Chance of Meatballs*. Aladdin. What if food fell from the sky? Excellent illustrations.

Henkes, Kevin (1996). *Lilly's Purple Plastic Purse*. Greenwillow. A wonderful combination of humor and sensitivity.

Marshall, James (1972). *George and Martha*. Houghton Mifflin. Perfect for the sensitive child who enjoys subtle and wry humor. The books also provide valuable lessons of true friendship between two very lovable hippos. Other books in the series include:
George and Martha: One Fine Day
George and Martha: Back in Town
George and Martha: Encore
George and Martha: Rise and Shine
George and Martha: Round and Round
George and Martha: Tons of Fun

Pilkey, Dav (2000). *The Silly Gooses*. Scholastic. Humor at its corniest.

Prelutksy, Jack (2000). *It's Raining Pigs and Noodles*: Poems. Greenwillow. Be prepared for big hearty laughs from the whole family. All ages.

Scieszka, Jon (1996). *The True Story of the Three Little Pigs by A. Wolf* as told to Jon Scieszka. Puffin. From the book: "Everybody knows the story of the Three Little Pigs. Or at least they think they do. But I'll let you in on a little secret. Nobody knows the real story, because nobody has ever heard *my* side of the story." All ages.

Shaw, Nancy (1988). *Sheep in a Jeep*. Houghton Mifflin. "Beep! Beep! Sheep in a jeep on a hill that's steep." A favorite read-aloud book.

Early Readers (Approximately Grades 1-3)

Marshall, James (1997). *Rats on the Roof and Other Stories*. Puffin. Seven silly stories about animals with unusual problems. A good introduction to short stories and an inspiration for children to write their own.

Parish, Peggy (1992). *Amelia Bedelia*. HarperCollins. Each Amelia Bedelia book in this extensive series is punnier than the last, as Peggy Parish describes the life of a housekeeper who takes all of her instructions literally.

Yolen, Jane (1996). *Commander Toad in Space*. Paper Star. As Jane Yolen says in her website (www.janeyolen.com): "I began the *Commander Toad* books because I saw an article in the local newspaper about a boy and his frog who had just won a jumping-frog contest. The frog's name was 'Star Warts.' I thought it would be funnier if the frog had been a toad, since the old superstition is that toads give you warts. (It isn't true, of course.) So I invented frogs and toads in space on a ship called 'Star Warts.' Every book is riddled with puns. (I love puns!)" Other books in the series are:
Commander Toad and the Voyage Home
Commander Toad and the Space Pirates
Commander Toad and the Planet of the Grapes
Commander Toad and the Intergalactic Spy
Commander Toad and the Dis-Asteroid
Commander Toad and the Big Black Hole

Fiction: Intermediate Readers (Approximately Grades 3-6)

Blume, Judy (1981). *Superfudge*. Dell. No, it's not a cookbook. It's a hilarious story about sibling rivalry. Also look for Blume's *Tales of a Fourth Grade Nothing* and *Otherwise Known as Sheila the Great*.

Dahl, Roald (1998). *Charlie and the Chocolate Factory*. Puffin. Some sensitive children find Dahl's books scary, but others are enchanted by his odd-ball and deft sense of humor. If your child enjoys this book, follow it with the classic movie, *Willy Wonka and the Chocolate Factory*, then discuss the differences and similarities between the book and the film adaptation.

Howe, Deborah, & Howe, James (1996). *Bunnicula: A Rabbit-Tale of Mystery*. Aladdin. This first book in a popular series is told from the point of view of a dog named Harold. Is the family's new pet bunny really a vampire, as Chester the cat suspects? Bunnicula fans may also enjoy these books:

Bunniculas Wickedly Wacky Word Games

Bunnicula's Frightfully Fabulous Factoids: A Book to Entertain Your Brain!

Bunnicula's Pleasantly Perplexing Puzzlers: A Book of Puzzles, Mazes, & Whatzits!

Bunnicula's Long-Lasting Laugh-Alouds: A Book of Jokes & Riddles to Tickle Your Bunny-Bone

Milne, A. A. (1957). *The World of Pooh: Winnie the Pooh* and *House at Pooh Corner*. Dutton. These perennial favorites hold a special appeal for children who enjoy word play. Be sure to get the original rather than the more recent Disney versions. Read aloud for the best effect.

Sachar, Louis (1998). *Sideways Stories from Wayside School*. Avon. The silly adventures that take place in this 30-storey high school are therapeutically funny for children who have had less than ideal classroom experiences. Other books in the series:
Wayside School Is Falling Down
Wayside School Gets a Little Stranger
Sideways Arithmetic from Wayside School: More than 50 mindboggling math puzzles
More Sideways Arithmetic from Wayside School

Television, Videos, Games

Bill Nye, The Science Guy Television Program and Videos. This science show is informative and fun for all ages. The fast pace will appeal to some children but may be too frenetic for others. Check your television guide for times and channels. Videos available in most libraries. Titles include:
Dinosaurs—Those Big Boneheads
The Human Body—The Inside Scoop
Outer Space—Way Out There
Powerful Forces—All Pumped Up!
Reptiles and Insects—Leapin' Lizards!

Kidsongs: Very Silly Songs (1991). Sony. This video is no longer being produced, but you should be able to find it in libraries or video stores. Lots of fun songs performed by children. Ages 2-6.

Meet the Mentor Video: Robb Armstrong, Cartoonist (1996). Scholastic. Look for this short video (8 minutes) about the creator of *Jump Start* comic strip in your library or video store.

Non-Fiction: Humorous Academic Materials

Can't get your elementary-age child to touch math or grammar or writing? These humorous resources will tempt the most reluctant students. They are also good for review of basic concepts and skills.

Burchers, Sam. Vocabulary Cartoon Books. New Monics Books. These delightful and effective vocabulary books are designed to capitalize on brain research and learning and memory theory. Each vocabulary word is presented in mnemonic cartoon form with phonetic pronunciation, common definition, and three sentences in which the word is used. Available in most major bookstores. Go to www.vocabularycartoons.com for on-line samples.
Vocabulary Cartoons, Elementary Edition, 3rd-6th Grade
Vocabulary Cartoons, SAT Word Power, 7th-12th Grade
Vocabulary Cartoons, SAT Word Power II, 7th-12th Grade

Costello, Bill (1998) *Cartooning with Math* (Ages 9-12) and (1995) *Cartooning with Letters, Shapes and Numbers* (Ages 4-8). Thinkorporated. Learn to draw cartoon characters while practicing math or writing skills.

Doolittle, John (1994). *Dr. DooRiddles Associative Reasoning Activities*. Critical Thinking Books & Software. Rhyming riddles develop reasoning and language skills. Grades K-3, 4-8, 7-adult. Go to www.criticalthinking.com for on-line sample activities.

Fritz, Jean. Historical Books. Paper Star. Children who resist history may be lured by Jean Fritz's light writing touch and the delightfully comic illustrations. Solid elementary-level historical information. Appropriate for both young precocious readers and older reluctant readers.
And Then What Happened, Paul Revere?
Around the World in a Hundred Years: From Henry the Navigator to Magellan
Bully for You, Teddy Roosevelt
Can't You Make Them Behave, King George?
George Washington's Breakfast
George Washington's Mother
Make Way for Sam Houston
Shh! We're Writing the Constitution
The Great Little Madison
What's the Big Idea, Ben Franklin?
Where Do You Think You're Going, Christopher Columbus?
Where Was Patrick Henry on the 29th of May?
Who's that Stepping on Plymouth Rock?
Why Don't You Get a Horse, Sam Adams?
Why Not, Lafayette?
Will You Sign Here, John Hancock
You Want Women to Vote, Lizzie Stanton?

Gonick, Larry. *The Cartoon Guides*. HarperPerennial.
The Cartoon Guide to Physics (also available on CD-ROM from HarperCollins Interactive)
The Cartoon Guide to Genetics
The Cartoon Guide to the United States
The Cartoon Guide to the Universe (I and II)
The Cartoon Guide to Statistics
The Cartoon Guide to (Non) Communication

Note: While these popular books are packed with valuable information and high school level concepts, the humor is sometimes bawdy and adult-oriented. Most appropriate for older teens.

Greenberg, Dan. *Comic-Strip Grammar*. Scholastic Professional Books. Forty cartoons with practice exercises, parts of speech, punctuation, possessives. Grades 4-8.

Greenberg, Dan. *Comic-Strip Math: Mini-Story Problems*. Scholastic Professional Books. Forty cartoons with story problems, multiplication, division, fractions, decimals, money, mental math. Grades 3-6.

The History News. Candlewick Press. These creative books offer historical information in the form of a comic newspaper. Suitable for elementary and middle school ages. Titles include:

The History News: Explorers
The History News: In Space
The History News: Medicine
The History News: Revolution
The History News: The Egyptian News
The History News: The Greek News
The History News: The Roman News
The History News: The Stone Age News
The History News: The Viking News

Usborne Books publishes a similar series for ages 10 and up titled Newspaper Histories.

Kellaher, Karen (2001) *Comic-Strip Writing Prompts*. Scholastic Professional Books. Fifty favorite comic strips (*Garfield, Peanuts, Dennis the Menace, Claire and Weber, Citizen Dog,* and *Nancy*) with writing prompts. Designed for grades 3-5, but appropriate for older ages as well, since the level of writing is controlled by the student.

Kirkland, E. (1988) *Cartesian Cartoons* and (1990) *Cartesian Cartoons: Holiday Book*. Mystery Media. Cartoon graphing activities for middle school and high school students. Ages 9-12. See also *Lil' Gridders* (1993), Mystery Media. Cartoon graphing puzzles. Ages 4-8.

Mad Libs®. This classic party game in which participants supply words for a story is a great way to learn and practice parts of speech. Look in your local bookstore or teacher supply store for volumes suitable for children.

Rosenthal, Paul (1992). *Where on Earth: A Geografunny Guide to the Globe*. Knopf. Out of print but worth looking for. Check libraries and used-book stores for this comic look at geography.

Ross, Stewart (1996). *And then…A History of the World (Squashed-up Into 1991/2 Pages, Without the Boring Bits)*. Copper Beech Books. A witty and wonderful overview of world history.

Standard Deviants Videos. Cerebellum Corporation. These fast-paced, humorous videos are available for nearly every high school and college level subject, from basic math and Spanish I to calculus and physics. You can find Standard Deviants videos in most libraries and many retail stores. The website, www.standarddeviants.com, offers practice tests, information for teachers, sample video clips and activities.

Tang, Greg (2001). *The Grapes of Math: Mind-Stretching Math Riddles*. Scholastic. Children will learn new ways of perceiving math through computer-generated art and delightful rhyming riddles.

Weyland, Jack (1992). *MegaPowers: Can Science Fact Defeat Science Fiction?* Kids Can Press. A cartoon book on physical science (comics interspersed with reading material). Ages 8-12.

Websites

ComicsPage.com. Tribune Media Services syndicated comics on the web, including editorial cartoons. Parental supervision suggested.
www.comicspage.com

Emmett Scott's Cartoon Corner Website. Visit the art studio, puzzles, stories, or funny pages for hours of fun. All ages.
www.Cartooncorner.com

Mark Kistler's Imagination Station. Information about Mark Kistler's television program and videos, books, teacher resource guide, and free on-line drawing lessons. All ages.
www.draw3d.com

The Periodic Table of Comic Books. This entertaining and well-designed website from the Department of Chemistry, University of Kentucky, allows you to click on an element to see a list of comic book pages and stories involving that element. Click on Oxygen, for example, and you'll find at least 10 comic book references, including a 1958 *Batman* cover: Robin: "Batman! You mean you can breathe the oxygen in the water but can't survive on the surface!" Batman: "Yes, Robin, I've become a human fish." Parental supervision suggested.
www.uky.edu/Projects/Chemcomics

United Media Comics.com. United Media syndicated comics on the web. Here you'll find Ziggy, B.C., Peanuts, New Yorker Cartoons, and much, much more. Parental supervision suggested.
www.unitedmedia.com

Advanced Study of Comic Strips

Glubok, Shirley (1979). *The Art of the Comic Strip*. Macmillan. Explores newspaper comic strip art, with lots of examples from the 1890s to the present (1979). Grade 4 and up.

Harvey, Robert C. (1998). *Children of the Yellow Kid: The Evolution of the American Comic Strip*. Frye Art Museum. This beautifully illustrated book traces the 100 year history of American comic strips, including several original drawings from our country's best known comics. Plenty of intellectual and historical fodder. Young adult reading level and above who are passionate about the history of comic strips.

McCloud, Scott. (1993) *Understanding Comics: The Invisible Art* and (2000) *Reinventing Comics: How Imagination and Technology Are Revolutionizing an Art Form*. HarperPerennial. These two books investigate the definition of comics and describe in great detail the art of comics, including such concepts as abstract art, perspective, and closure. Best for young adult reading level and above.

Comic Resources for Parents

Fakih, Kimberly Olson (1993). *The Literature of Delight: A Critical Guide to Humorous Books for Children*. Bowker-Greenwood Imprint.

Loomans, Diane, & Kolberg, Karen (1993). *The Laughing Classroom: Everyone's Guide to Teaching with Humor and Play*. H. J. Kramer. Foreword by Steve Allen. Lots of practical suggestions.

Shade, Richard (1996). *License to Laugh: Humor in the Classroom*. Teacher Ideas Press.

At Home with Home Schoolers

Aaron, Age 8

"I like using my imagination."

Q: Why do you home school?

A: *Because it is fun and flexible.... We started it when we traveled round Australia for three months. I had gone to school before that, but the teachers didn't teach the way I learn.*

Q: Describe a typical day of home schooling.

A: *Math, English, which includes handwriting, grammar, and puzzles (these are the starters), then* Writing Strands, *history, or science. In the afternoons I do more science or art until 4:00 p.m. Then I have dance classes two afternoons. I do some of my work on the computer. Every few weeks we do some Latin or French.*

Q: What outside-the-home activities do you participate in?

A: *I go to Cubs (scouting activities). I learn jazz and tap dancing, and I go to weekly piano lesson. I join in a kids club on Friday at our church, and I also go to Sunday School. Once a month, I go to the park with other home schoolers in our area.*

Q: Has your home schooling routine changed as you've grow older?

A: *Yes, it has changed. I can work on my own more now. I really like my new* Writing Strands *book. Mum can now trust me to do a task she tells me to do, though I sometimes get distracted. We do some different subjects; for instance, we started Latin when Mum figured out that in one of my favorite books,* Harry Potter, *the spells are in Latin.*

Q: What are the best things about home schooling?

A: *The very best thing is not having to go to school—school comes to me! I like being able to jump on the trampoline during my breaks. I like having a teacher that really loves me (I know my Mum does).*

Q: What are the worst things about home schooling?

A: *Not having friends to play with during breaks.*

Q: How would you describe yourself as a learner?

A: *I learn well by watching and doing. I'm good at science and math and the trampoline. I like using my imagination. I like making up who I am and where I am and who's with me. I have heaps of imaginary friends, pets, and family members. Sometimes my family or friends play with me too.*

Q: What are your short-term and long-term goals, if any? How are you working to meet them?

A: I want to be a bareback rider, Olympic trampoline artist, paleontologist, and zoologist. I practice on my trampoline every day. I'm trying to persuade my parents to give me riding lessons. I study hard so that I can get into university one day.

Q: What advice do you have for other children and young adults who are considering or starting home schooling?

A: Work hard at your subjects and think positively. Always keep going, but just don't stay up too late.

Q: Would you consider home schooling your own children some day? Why or why not?

A: Yes! I think it's good because you know your children's learning styles and limits, so you can teach them that way.

Learning Styles: Learning With A Difference

As described in the last chapter, gifted children have a strong "need to know," and often they fill this need through immersion learning, creative learning, and intuitive learning. These are "ways of knowing" that many gifted children have in common.

However, children also have individual preferences for *how* they learn, regardless of whether they are using immersion learning, creative learning, or intuition. We call these preferences *learning styles*. A child who immerses himself in the world of dinosaurs, for example, might do so by listening to books on tape about dinosaurs (auditory learning style), studying anatomical diagrams of dinosaurs (visual learning style), pretending to be dinosaurs (kinesthetic learning style), or building clay models of dinosaurs (tactile learning style). Or a child who loves to draw creatively may do so with quick, deft sketches (impulsive learning style) or slow, careful illustrations (reflective learning style).

Many parents never encountered the idea of learning styles when they were in school. Generally, all students were expected to learn the material in the manner in which it was presented, often in textbook form with a lot of repetition, drill, and pencil-and-paper tests. If a child had difficulty learning, the child was assumed to have been at fault. Some of those children may have been underachievers, or later became dropouts, or felt as if they were failures because they didn't learn concepts the way the teacher presented them. We now know, for example, that some children grasp math concepts better using math manipulatives, small objects they can move around, to "see" the addition or subtraction concepts that in earlier teaching methods were being presented only in abstract, numeric form. Other children need more than the usual time to contemplate ideas and problems, resulting in relatively poor performances on timed tests, even though the children know the material well.

Today we know that *how* we learn has a big impact on whether we learn at all, and that the same material can be presented and evaluated effectively in a number of different ways—learning with a valuable difference—depending on the needs of the child. Mismatches between a child's learning style and the learning environment are a frequent cause of learning difficulties. A child who learns best visually or by using her hands may breeze through preschool and kindergarten, where the hands-on activities and visual stimulation support the child's natural way of learning, but beginning in the grade school years, the student will probably be expected to sit still and *listen* more in order to learn. Some students do learn well this way, especially strong auditory learners. Other students, however, struggle to pay attention in an environment that neither understands nor accommodates their learning needs. Their style of learning may be viewed as a disorder rather than a normal difference. Many children labeled with ADD and ADHD learn best visually; they are creative and their thought patterns are random (think of a web of ideas) rather than sequential (as in a list) (Freed & Parsons, 1997).

Conversely, a child who naturally prefers to learn by sound and sequence, who is already reading fluently at age five, and who enjoys following directions and participating in grown-up conversations may be frustrated by the freedom, "babyishness," and seemingly random nature of a preschool classroom. His attempts to engage the teacher in meaningful dialogue may be viewed as attention-seeking and manipulative, and his struggle to bring order to the free-form play of his classmates may make him seem "bossy." The teacher may not recognize or understand the asynchronous traits of his development. His need for dialogue as a way to understand his world, rather than viewed in terms of learning styles, may instead be interpreted as a lack of verbal self-control.

More important than any other tool in your home schooling toolbox is an understanding of learning style theory and your child's and your own preferred learning styles. This knowledge and understanding will pave the way for both successful home schooling and a future lifelong love of learning. Home school parents should take time at the beginning of home schooling to read about and understand learning style theory, beginning with some of the Learning Styles and Personality Types Resources listed at the end of the chapter. You will find several ways of categorizing and understanding how we learn, and some of them will overlap. This chapter offers an introduction to three very useful approaches to learning styles. For home school parents, a combination of these is usually helpful.

- Learning through the Senses: Visual, Auditory, Kinesthetic, Tactile
- Learning in Space and Time: Visual-Spatial and Auditory-Sequential
- Learning in Tempo: Reflective and Impulsive

Learning through the Senses:
Visual, Auditory, Kinesthetic, and Tactile

One of the easiest and most productive ways to understand and apply learning style theory is by asking ourselves through which senses we learn best. Think about how your child spends leisure time, what kinds of learning experiences are frustrating and what kinds are enjoyable, how and what she sees, hears, moves, and touches. The following questions are designed to offer some clues.

1. Imagine your child in a museum room where several exhibits are available. Which exhibit would your child go to first?
   A. An art display with colorful abstract paintings
   B. A listening corner with a variety sounds and musical selections available on headphones
   C. A physics demonstration with ropes for pulling and climbing
   D. An exhibit that allows children to guess the identity of unseen items using the sense of touch

2. Which of the following ways to learn about art would your child enjoy the most?
   A. Looking at art from several vantage points for several minutes
   B. Listening to and participating in an interesting art discussion
   C. Using dramatic role play to re-enact how artists create paintings
   D. Sculpting figures from clay

3. Which of the following leisure activities would your child choose during free time?
   A. Watching a video
   B. Listening to a book on tape
   C. Playing active, physical games such as tag
   D. Putting together a puzzle

4. By what means does your child prefer *initially* to learn a new game such as chess?
   A. Studying diagrams of chess moves and games
   B. Reading books about chess players and strategy or asking questions
   C. Playing the game, even if it is unfamiliar
   D. Handling and arranging the pieces and board

Do your answers follow a pattern? If most of your answers were A, your child probably learns best by seeing (visual learning). If most of your answers were B, your child probably learns best by listening, including reading (auditory learning). If most of your answers were C, your child probably learns best by doing and experiencing (kinesthetic learning). If most of your answers were D, your child probably learns best by touching and manipulating (tactile learning).

Was it difficult to choose answers, or did you find yourself wanting to answer "all of the above"? While some children will have a definite preference for learning in a specific way, many children will learn best with a combination of two or more of the senses, such as listening to music while drawing or being allowed to use his or her body while reading or writing. Some of the answers use more than one sense, such as playing a game of chess (visual, kinesthetic, and tactile) or watching a video (visual and auditory). Kinesthetic learners, in particular, may exhibit either visual or auditory learning characteristics as well (or both) (Vitale, 1982). The point is not to place a limiting label on children, but to begin to get a sense of how the child prefers to learn in various situations.

A home school parent can offer children activities that allow the child to find what learning approaches work best for different tasks. Imagine an ever-changing buffet from which your child samples and chooses and savors. You might experiment with helping your child to learn something new using his or her dominant mode of learning, then use other modes of learning to reinforce or practice (Vitale, 1982). For example, your predominantly visual learner might learn phonics (auditory learning) with words he has already learned by sight (visual learning). Music theory for your auditory learner can serve as an introduction to math. A kinesthetic learner might benefit from some experiments with kitchen science before she reads about chemistry. Children who like to use their hands can build models of historical scenes *while* they are learning history, rather than as an end-of-the-unit project.

Try to provide as wide a variety of learning experiences as possible while keeping an eye on how your child responds to different approaches. You will also want to think about your own learning preferences and how they affect the learning environments you provide for your children. If you are most comfortable with books and discussion, you may unconsciously provide relatively few opportunities for your child to use the tactile or kinesthetic approach, hands and body, to learn. Conversely, if you naturally learn by doing and favor a "hands-on" approach, you may want to remind yourself to offer your child books and tapes and time for reflection.

Following are some ideas for learning based on visual, auditory, kinesthetic, and tactile learning styles adapted from *Teaching Young Children through Their Individual Learning Styles*, by Rita Dunn, Kenneth Dunn, and Janet Perrin (1994), and *Growing Up Learning: The Key to Your Child's Potential*, by Walter Barbe (1985).

To Facilitate Visual Learning:

- *Videos* – check both the children's and the non-fiction adult sections of your library

- *Books* – with plenty of pictures, even for older students

- *Chalkboard* – a combination chalkboard and dry erase easel with plenty of colored pens and chalk works well

- *Paints and Other Art Supplies* – for creative experimentation and play

- *Charts, Photographs, Pictures* – encourage the child to hang maps and posters around the house; cut colorful photos and graphics from magazines to put in a scrapbook

- *Art Museum Field Trips* – also smaller local art galleries and art shows

To Facilitate Auditory Learning:

- *Tapes and CDs* – start early in allowing the child his or her own music collection based on personal taste

- *Books on Tape* – books on tape or CD are excellent for car rides or bed-time relaxation

- *Tape Recorders for oral book reports* – mini tape recorders are convenient; encourage children to make their own books on tape for themselves or as gifts, complete with sound effects

- *Musical Toys and Instruments* – encourage children to make their own

- *Plenty of Opportunities for Informal Discussion* – mealtime, car time, anytime—as much and as often as parents can handle!

- *Permission to Talk to Themselves* – while studying or drawing

To Facilitate Kinesthetic Learning:

- *Floor Puzzles* – use cardboard or stiff foam sheets to make your own

- *Large Blocks* – and plenty of small blocks and building materials for older children

- *Blackboard and Chalk* – try a sidewalk and thick chalk, too

- *Step-On Number Lines* – use these for learning multiplication facts; you can make your own with butcher paper; step-on letter lines work well for letter recognition and spelling

- *Cooking and Building* – real life skills of cooking, building bird houses, and planning a garden are great home school activities

- *Field Trips* – in addition to zoos and museums, ask your local baker or librarian or firefighter if you can get a behind-the-scenes tour

- *Nature Walks* – plan to spend plenty of time and pack snacks, notebook and pencil, colored pencils for sketching, field guides, and a magnifying glass

○ *Dramatization and Role Play* – daydreaming and fantasy play are powerful learning tools for some children

○ *Puppet Shows* – encourage children to write and produce their own puppet shows based on either favorite books or original ideas

To Facilitate Tactile Learning:

○ *Manipulatives* – if your child doesn't enjoy a particular brand or type, try something else or make your own

○ *Puzzles* – thick wood puzzles are worth the extra money; also look for three-dimensional puzzles

○ *Sandpaper Letters and Numerals* – cut letters, numbers, and shapes from ordinary sandpaper, foam, heavy construction paper, felt, or assorted fabrics such as denim and corduroy

○ *Lotto and Bingo Games* – purchase, or make your own

○ *Art Projects* – the more the better; as the child gets older, invest in high-quality "real" art materials such as pastels and charcoal pencils

○ *Chalkboard, Magnetic Board, Flannel Board* – look in teacher supply stores for ideas

○ *Typewriter, Computer Keyboard* – an older, inexpensive model works fine

○ *Sand and Water Tables* – if possible, keep a small permanent sand and water area outside or, if you live in a cold climate, in the kitchen or playroom

Learning in Space and Time:
Visual-Spatial and Auditory-Sequential Learning

Another way to approach the idea of learning styles is to ask whether we learn best by seeing (visual) or by hearing (auditory) and whether we arrange things and ideas best in space (spatial) or in time (sequential). A visual-spatial learner will be able to "see" patterns and connections in space. People with this learning style often excel in art, architecture, physics, aeronautics, pure mathematical research, engineering, computer programming, or photography (Silverman & Freed, 1991). An auditory-sequential learner will be able to "hear" patterns and connections in the realm of time. Writers, musical composers, and lecturers must have strong auditory-sequential skills.

Neither auditory-sequential nor visual-spatial learning is a better learning style than the other. Likewise, the point isn't to strive for a diluted balance that forces the child to conform to an average status quo. Rather, we can understand each child's unique style of learning, support and nurture that style, and gently provide opportunities for the child to explore and strengthen other modes of learning.

So if each style is necessary and valuable, why all the recent fuss about visual-spatial learning?

The traditional school model favors an auditory-sequential style. Children are expected to learn in a step-by-step sequential manner—each lesson must be followed in turn, without skipping ahead or jumping around. In school, children are usually surrounded by words rather than pictures as the primary information source. Thus, to learn about a subject area, children are assigned chapters to read and essays to write. In school, the emphasis is on rote memorization and reiteration of details; being about to recite the multiplication table quickly is the sign of a "good" math student.

The visual-spatial learner, however, often learns best by *not* following the usual sequence of steps, by thinking and doing in three dimensions—with design and construction and experimentation—rather than with pencil and paper, and by exploring "big picture" concepts before delving into details and facts. Visual-spatial learners often learn best by with a sight approach to reading, a visualization approach to spelling, inductive reasoning, and mastery of higher-level concepts (Silverman, 1998). Whenever we blindly or unthinkingly follow a traditional classroom model, such as using a phonics-only approach to reading, we are putting the visual-spatial learner at a disadvantage.

Home school parents of visual-spatial learners are often surprised to realize that real life is often visually and spatially oriented—that without the restraints of school walls, their children are free to use their strengths more fully and to develop at their own pace. These children navigate complex hiking trails of a nature park with ease, remember with precision how to rebuild a block tower that was toppled by the family dog, or focus for hours on weekend design projects of their own choosing. They may learn to write later than other children, but in the meantime can dictate enchanting stories or draw complex comics. They may learn long division a year or two later than other children the same age but often master high level algebraic concepts before that. Visual-spatial learners in particular need to experience success in order to find motivation, and they should be encouraged to use any skill at which they excel (Silverman & Freed, 1991).

Home schooling allows parents of visual-spatial learners to structure the learning environment to remove the obstacles that prevent their children from realizing their full potential. Parents can use the Visual Spatial Toolbox, created by David G. Lazear,[6] to support and develop visual-spatial learning. While tools such as these may be crucial for the highly visual-spatial learner, they are also effective for other children as well. Since many highly gifted children have both visual-spatial and auditory-sequential abilities, visual-spatial learning techniques may help to provide balance and a whole-brain approach to learning for children who otherwise would rely too heavily on traditional, linear pathways.

Visual Spatial Toolbox

- *Guided Imagery/Visualizing* – create pictures/images of different items in the mind (e.g., characters in a story, a period of history, a scientific process)

- *Active Imagination* – associate/find connections between visual designs/patterns and prior experiences/knowledge

- *Color/Texture Schemes* – associate colors and texture with various thoughts, ideas, concepts, and processes

- *Patterns/Designs* – create abstract patterns and designs to represent the relationships of different pieces of knowledge

- *Painting* – express understanding of concepts using the medium of paints or colored markers (e.g. mural creation)

- *Drawing* – create graphic representations of items being studied (e.g. diagrams, illustrations, flow charts, etc.)

- *Sculpting* – demonstrate understanding of concepts by creating models in clay

- *Mind-Mapping* – create "visual webs" of written information

- *Pretending/Fantasy* – creation of new, fun scenarios in the mind based on factual information

- *Montage/Collage* – design a collection of pictures to show various aspects or dimensions of a concept, idea, or process

---

6   David G.Lazear, 1998. Reprinted with permission. For more information, see Lazear's website, New Dimensions of Learning, at www.multi-intell.com, or call (800) 726-8605.

Lazear also offers these visual/spatial lesson plan ideas for individual subject areas:[7]

History:

- Have imaginary talks/interviews with people from the past.
- Make visual diagrams and flowcharts of historical facts.
- Imagine going back in time—see what it was like "back then."
- Paint a mural about a period of history.
- Imagine and draw what you think the future will be like.

Mathematics:

- Do a survey of likes/dislikes, then graph the results.
- Estimate measurements by sight and by touch.
- Add, subtract, multiply, and divide using various manipulatives.
- Imagine using a math process successfully, then really do it.
- Learn metric measurement through visual equivalents.

Language Arts:

- Play vocabulary words "Pictionary®."
- Teach "mind-mapping as a note taking process."
- Draw pictures of the different stages of a story you're reading.
- Learn to read, write, and decipher code language.
- Use highlight markers to "colorize" part of a story or poem.

Science and Health:

- Draw pictures of things seen under a microscope.
- Create posters/flyers showing healthy eating practices.
- Create montages/collages on science topics (e.g., mammals).
- Draw visual patterns that appear in the natural world.
- Pretend you are microscopic and can travel in the bloodstream.

Global Studies and Geography:

- Draw maps of the world from your visual memory.
- Study a culture through its visual art—painting and sculpture.
- Make maps out of clay and show geographical features.
- Make décor for the classroom on a culture you are studying.
- Use a map to get around an unfamiliar place or location.

---

7   David G. Lazear, 1998. Reprinted with permission.

Practical Arts and Physical Education:

- Draw pictures of how to perform certain physical feats.
- Create visual diagrams of how to use shop machines.
- Practice drawing objects from different angles (drafting).
- Learn a series of "spatial games" (e.g., horseshoes, ring toss).
- Imagine your computer is human—draw how it works.

Fine Arts:

- Watch dancers on video and imagine yourself in their shoes.
- Pretend you can enter a painting—imagine what it's like.
- Listen to music with eyes closed and create a sculpture from clay.
- Draw the sets for the various scenes of a play you are reading.
- Draw the visual and color pattern of a dance.

Parents can remember that no child is made according to a mold and that not all children who are considered visual-spatial learners will benefit from the advice meant for them. Some visual-spatial learners resist the use of math manipulatives, for example. This resistance may mean that the child needs a different kind of manipulative, perhaps one that she creates herself, or it may mean that for some reason, this particular visual-spatial learner will learn math better through verbal math resources or math discussions. Or perhaps the child is simply not ready to appreciate and use the manipulatives. The parent may simply need to wait a year or two and try again.

When parents understand the way in which their particular visual-spatial learner thinks about and experiences the world, they can design an education plan to fit the child. They can use the child's visual spatial interests to connect to the subject being studied. For example, a middle school age student who loves art may enjoy activities from the book *Art in Chemistry; Chemistry in Art*, by Barbara R. Greenberg and Dianne Patterson (grades 7-12). The book was conceived when the authors were teaching, as separate subjects, introductory art and chemistry and found that many art students were not engaged by the traditional approach to chemistry. The result is a fascinating book that offers such activities as analyzing both the chemical and artistic composition of photography and applying principles of cubism and surrealism as they create molecular models—connecting visual-spatial learning with the study of science.

Some subjects that would seem a natural fit for the visual-spatial learner can contain hidden obstacles either in terms of the subject matter itself or the specific materials that are used. Plane geometry, for example, offers the visual-spatial learner a chance to use spatial understanding in a meaningful and enjoyable way, but its verbal, formal proofs may prove both frustrating and discouraging (Dixon, 1983). The answer may be to allow younger children to explore the spatial nature of geometry and to save geometrical proofs for a later age. Or parents can use an inductive approach to high school geometry such as Key Curriculum Press's *Discovering Geometry*, which uses graphic flowcharts to introduce students to geometrical proofs, or *A Visual Approach to Algebra* (Dale Seymour Publications), which begins with the visual big picture of algebra before moving onto abstract equations.

A Word about Brain Hemisphere Theory

The two sides or hemispheres of our brains are not the same. Our left side controls the right side of our body, and vice versa. Also, the hemispheres have different areas of specialty. The left hemisphere specializes in language (and much more), while the right hemisphere specializes in images (and much more).

Children who have a visual-spatial learning style are often referred to as having right hemisphere brain dominance. They are sometimes simplistically called "right brained" and are thought to be highly creative. Auditory-sequential learners, on the other hand, are assumed to be left hemisphere dominant. They are called "left brained" and are thought to be primarily convergent thinkers.

Many very insightful and useful books and articles have been written based on this theory, but the artificial dichotomy of "right-brained" and "left-brained" learners is a good example of how learning styles can be misused in a reductive way that may ignore the complexity of real children. Used as a starting point in understanding broad patterns of learning, such theory certainly has its uses and merits. But as Jane Piirto (1998, p. 56) reminds us, "[W]e now know we use our whole brain unless we have had a brain injury, and the right-left brain fad has passed, with phrases *right brain* and *left brain* becoming codes for 'more creative' or 'flakey,' and 'less creative' or 'dull and logical'" [author's emphasis]. Thus, once a child is labeled "left brained" or "right brained" in an educational setting, certain expectations and limitations, both spoken and unspoken, are immediately conferred upon the child. A child thought of as "left brained" may not be offered fantasy novels to read, or a child thought of as "right brained" may not be encouraged to use sequential reasoning skills. Home schooling allows parents to introduce the child to other modes of learning while recognizing learning strengths.

Knowing my son's strengths, weaknesses, learning styles, intelligences, and the like have helped me be more precise about materials we use and how we use them. It's been a vital part of our home schooling journey to understand how my son (and I) learn. It helps to know because I can see what challenges lie ahead for him. For example, knowing that neither my son nor I are linguistically oriented will probably prompt me to afford him opportunities to be exposed to better literature and grammar skills than I had....

—Barbara, home school parent

We have not applied learning style theory formally in our home schooling, but for a very long time, we used a lot of videos and computer games because that's what seemed to work best. I tend not to think in terms of specific learning styles because my sense with my 13-year-old daughter is that she needs to use different styles at different times.

—Jan, home school parent

Very few people fit one dominant learning style model completely, and highly creative people may switch from one learning style to another more often than less creative people, depending on the task involved (Csikszentmihalyi, 1996). This switching includes the use of supposedly left brain skills and traits. Creatively gifted children are more likely to be both introverted and extraverted (which is different from being somewhere in the middle); that is, they may be highly introverted at some times and highly extraverted at others. This all makes sense when we think of the skills necessary for creative people to be successful. They prefer and perhaps even crave solitude while creating, but they must also seek feedback and an audience for their work at various stages of completion (Csikszentmihalyi, 1996).

Learning in Tempo: Impulsive and Reflective Thinkers

In addition to preferring certain means of learning, we all have our own preferred pace or tempo of learning and thinking. Some people are more impulsive; given a multiple choice test, for example, they choose the first answer that seems right, then move quickly on to the next question. Other people are more reflective; given the same multiple-choice test, they study all of the responses carefully before making a decision.

Both kinds of thinking—impulsive and reflective—are useful, but if the preference for one over the other is extreme, it can pose challenges for the child and parent. A child whose natural tempo is impulsive may need to learn to pause and reflect before saying the first thing that comes to his mind or reaching for the first object that catches his attention. Of course, impulsivity does not necessarily imply hyperactivity. It is possible to think and choose both quickly *and* carefully.

A child whose tempo is reflective may need practice making timely decisions. She may need to learn how to systematically choose between alternatives so as not to become paralyzed into indecision. She will also benefit from knowing that "reflective" does not mean "slow" or "unintelligent." She can learn to appreciate her ability to think thoroughly and deeply.

Card games and board games that reward specific thinking tempos can help children to appreciate their own individual strengths. Chess, for example, rewards and encourages reflective thought, while a fast card game like Apples to Apples® (Out of the Box Publishing) allows an impulsive thinker to appreciate quick thinking. Books are also a good way for children to understand thinking styles and tempos. Compare the thoughtfulness of Meg in *A Wrinkle in Time* with the quick thinking of Gilly in *The Great Gilly Hopkins*, for example. With which character does your child most easily identify? How can each one's learning style be misunderstood by others?

Putting It All Together:
Using Learning Styles in Home Schooling

Learning style theory is as much an art as a science. You can't get it wrong; you can only keep experimenting and responding to your children's reactions. And it's not as much work as it may at first seem. Understanding how children learn best and prefer to learn saves time and energy in the long term; learning is more efficient and frustration reduced.

Once you know your child's styles and preferences, you can think of creative ways to introduce new subjects and reinforce previous learning. A child who loves language and literature may enjoy learning history through historical fiction, or science through reading biographies of scientists. A visual-spatial learner might use architecture as an avenue to history, while an auditory-sequential learner might like to read historical fiction. A child who prefers art and music may approach math through tessellations, or science through the physics of musical instruments. Fulcrum Publishing, Teacher Ideas Press, and Scholastic Professional Books offer resources that combine learning styles and subject areas.

It is important to know the kinds of learning your child prefers, but equally important is knowing which types of learning he avoids. For example, if you are working with a child who strongly prefers convergent, sequential learning, think of ways to introduce the child to divergent, random thinking as well. For instance, this child might first learn about great painters of history through books, *then*, after she feels comfortable with the topic, enjoy experimenting with hands-on or visual activities. A visual-spatial learner can learn math computation with an abacus, *then*, after he has a comfortable knowledge base, move on to pencil and paper math problems.

Why bother exposing a child to less preferred ways of learning if one or a few learning styles work best? There are several advantages to *starting with* and *focusing on* preferred learning styles and then *gradually introducing* less preferred learning styles. First, using several approaches to learning provides the child with a more complete understanding of the topic being studied. Supplementing non-fiction history resources with historical fiction, or a visit to a living history museum, or making crafts of the period is a more comprehensive study than one approach by itself. Second, many people whom the child will encounter in life, including future teachers and fellow learners, will *not* share the child's preferred learning style. Being able to adapt to other styles when necessary is an important skill, as well as a way to understand others' differences. Finally, gifted children often benefit from activities and ways of thinking that do not come easily for them. These challenges encourage children to persist in the face of difficulty and to take risks with the unfamiliar. The important difference is that children who learn at home can do *most* of their learning in a way that is natural for them, rather than adapt to someone else's learning style. Children's learning differences are often the key to successful home schooling.

Learning styles have definitely played a role in our home schooling. For instance, for my nine-year-old kinesthetic learner who must be moving and touching, I am able to make many subtle accommodations to our learning that help her get through the day. Her assignments include drawing and illustrating sometimes instead of writing. She needs to touch Mom lots throughout the day, so many times she does her EPGY math [a distance learning program through Stanford University] while sitting on my lap. When I read aloud, I either make it short or have a quiet activity for her to work on while listening. For something that is new, I show her how to do it rather than just tell her. Without some validation through the learning style books, I would not have felt that this was a proper way to learn. The learning style books had some good tips that helped.

My older child, age 10, likes to get information by reading. This has freed us up to let her read some information without doing additional studying for a test. When she reads for pleasure, she retains an enormous amount of information.

—Monica, home school parent

My son has to be personally (and physically) involved in whatever he is studying. He has to draw, write, touch, arrange, flip through pages himself. He loves interrupting and offering his ideas and thoughts. He hates it when he has to sit down calmly and listen to a lecture. So I adjust our lessons to fit his learning style. Through trial and error, I have tested various presentation methods and lesson approaches. With only one student, I can build the environment to best suit him. You can say that his learning style dictates the curriculum and our whole home schooling experience.

—Jon, home school parent

Key Points

☑ Children and adults have preferred ways of learning called *learning styles*. Being able to use our preferred learning styles results in easier, deeper, and more meaningful learning. Being prohibited from using preferred learning styles often results in great frustration, decreased learning, underachievement, and lowered self-concept.

☑ Children differ in their preference for learning through the senses. *Visual learners* prefer to use their eyes to learn, *auditory learners* prefer to use their ears to learn, *kinesthetic learners* prefer to use their bodies to learn, and *tactile learners* prefer to use their sense of touch to learn.

☑ Children differ in their preference for learning in space and time. *Visual-spatial learners* prefer to learn by seeing in the realm of space. *Auditory-sequential learners* prefer to learn by hearing in the realm of time.

☑ Children differ in their preferred learning tempos. *Reflective learners* prefer to take their time before reaching a conclusion or sharing their thoughts. *Impulsive learners* prefer to come to quick conclusions and share first impressions.

☑ Creatively gifted children may exhibit several learning styles and resist easy categorization. Parents and other adults can keep an open mind about how children learn best.

☑ Home school parents can take these steps toward using learning style theory:

  1. Read about learning style theories using some of the resources listed at the end of this chapter.

  2. Observe their children to see how they usually prefer to learn and how they learn best.

  3. Allow their children to use preferred learning styles as the main avenue to learning.

☑ Reinforce learning by introducing other, non-preferred learning styles in gentle and fun ways.

Questions for Reflection

1. Answer the questions on page 133 for each of your children. Which of the five senses does your child enjoy learning with?

2. Which of the ideas on pages 135-136 might help facilitate and enrich your child's learning? Which ideas would your child choose as the most enjoyable?

3. Whether or not your child is a strong visual-spatial learner, review David Lazear's visual/spatial lesson plan ideas on pages 139-140. Which ideas will your child enjoy?

4. If your child normally does not choose or prefer visual-spatial activities, think of ways to introduce such activities for variety and to stretch mental muscles.

5. Think about your own learning tempo. Is it usually reflective or impulsive? Has it changed since your childhood? If your learning tempo is different from that of your child, how can you best support your child's learning needs?

Learning Styles and Personality Types Resources

Barron-Tieger, Barbara, & Tieger, Paul D. (1997). *Nurture by Nature: Understanding Your Child's Personality Type—And Become a Better Parent.* Little Brown & Co.

Dixon, John Philo (1983). *The Spatial Child.* Charles C. Thomas.

Keirsey, David (1998). *Please Understand Me II: Temperament, Character, Intelligence.* Del Prometheus Nemesis.

Kincher, Jonni (1995). *Psychology for Kids: 40 Fun Tests that Help You Learn about Yourself.* Free Spirit Publishing.

Vitale, Barbara (1982). *Unicorns Are Real: A Right-Brained Approach to Learning.* Rolling Jalmar Press.

West, Thomas (1997). *In the Mind's Eye: Visual Thinkers, Gifted People with Dyslexia and Other Learning Difficulties, Computer Images and the Ironies of Creativity.* Prometheus Books.

Williams, Linda Verlee (1983). *Teaching for the Two-Sided Mind: A Guide to Right Brain/Left Brain Education.* Simon & Schuster.

Special Section: Verbal Math Resources

Picture Books for Young Readers (Ages 5-10)

Anno, Mitsumasa (1995). *Anno's Magic Seeds.* Philomel Books. From the author: "I called this book *The Magic Seeds* because, in fact, there is a mysterious power in even one tiny seed that seems beyond our understanding." See also *Anno's Math Games* (1989) and *Anno's Mysterious Multiplying Jar* (1999).

Birch, David (1993). *The King's Chessboard.* Penguin. How much rice would result from a grain for each square of a chessboard, the amount to be doubled each day? A good companion book for *One Grain of Rice.*

Demi (1997). *One Grain of Rice: A Mathematical Folktale.* Scholastic. This beautifully illustrated story weaves together art, math, literature, and culture.

Lasky, Kathryn (1994). *The Librarian Who Measured the Earth.* Little Brown and Company. Part math, part biography, part historical fiction, this beautiful book about a largely unknown historical figure is for all ages.

Marilyn Burns Brainy Day Books. These books for young readers include an appended section for parents that discusses the mathematical concepts and suggested activities.

Amanda Bean's Amazing Dream: A Mathematical Story, by Cindy Neuschwander (1998). Scholastic.

A Cloak for the Dreamer, by Aileen Friedman (1995). Scholastic.

The Greedy Triangle, by Marilyn Burns (1995). Scholastic.

The King's Commissioners, by Aileen Friedman (1995). Scholastic.

Spaghetti and Meatballs for All: A Mathematical Story, by Marilyn Burns (1997). Scholastic.

Neuschwander, Cindy (1997). *Sir Cumference and the First Round Table: A Math Adventure*. Charlesbridge Publishing. See also *Sir Cumference and the Dragon of Pi: A Math Adventure* (1999) and *Sir Cumference and the Great Knight of Angleand: A Math Adventure* (2001). A trio of delightful witty stories set in the Middle Ages. A good introduction to geometric ideas.

Schwartz, David M. (1993). *How Much Is a Million?* Mulberry Books, and (1999) *On Beyond a Million: An Amazing Math Journey*. Bantam. "No matter what number you have, there is always one bigger." By the author of *G Is for Googol*, these books are packed with mathematical tidbits about big numbers.

Scieszka, Jon (1995). *Math Curse*. Viking. Children and adults will enjoy this humorous story of a girl cursed to see everything in her day as a math problem.

Elementary-Age Reading Level (Approximately Grades 3-6)

Adler, Irving (1990). *Mathematics*. Doubleday. This oversize picture book introduces the rich world of math, from square numbers and Fibonacci numbers to computer programming and the golden ratio.

Bauer, Joan (1997). *Sticks*. Bantam. A young adult novel about the game of pool in which the protagonist is helped by a math whiz to understand how to use geometry and physics to be a better player.

Burns, Marilyn. Brown Paper School Math Books. Little Brown & Co. No one does verbal math better than Ms. Burns. The Brown Paper School Book series is an inexpensive resource that invites creative responses and is adaptable for a wide variety of ages.
The Book of Think, or How to Solve a Problem Twice Your Size (1976).
Math for Smarty Pants (1982).
The I Hate Mathematics! Book (1976).
This Book is about Time (1978).

Enzensberger, Hans Magnus (2000). *The Number Devil: A Mathematical Adventure*. Henry Holt. This colorful story uses wordplay and humor to introduce advanced mathematical principles.

Math Word Problems for Children Website. There are lots of word problems here, many based on contemporary and classic children's books.
www.mathstories.com

Mathnet (aka Math Patrol). Television show from Square One Television, Children's Television Workshop. With the motto "To Cogitate and To Solve," this Dragnet spoof uses both humor and story telling to present solid mathematical concepts and problem solving. Thirty episodes aired between 1987 and 1992. Look for videos of "The Case of the Unnatural" (1994) and "Treasure in Monterey Bay" (1994) in your library or video store. Book versions of several episodes are available as *Mathnet Casebooks*, published by Scientific American Books for Young Readers/W.H. Freeman.

Pappas, Theoni (1997). *The Adventures of Penrose the Mathematical Cat: The Mathematical Ca*t, and (1993) *Fractals, Googols and Other Mathematical Tales*. Wide World Publishing/Tetra. Delightful stories and simple drawings engage both children and adults. Use as a way to interest children who think they "don't like hard math."

Pappas, Theoni (1997). *Math for Kids: & Other People, Too*. Wide World Publishing/Tetra. Stories, puzzles, and challenges for a relaxed approach to math.

Pappas, Theoni (1991). *Math Talk: Mathematical Ideas in Poems for Two Voices*. Wide World Publishing/Tetra. Light-hearted poetic dialogues about such topics as integers, imaginary numbers, and tessellations are best enjoyed when read aloud by two people.

Ross, Catherine Sheldrick (1993). *Circles: Fun Ideas for Getting A-Round in Math*. Addison-Wesley. See also *Squares* (Kids Can Press, 1997) and *Triangles: Shapes in Math, Science and Nature* (Kids Can Press, 1997). An amazing amount of information is packed in these deceptively small books. Nicely illustrated with suggested activities.

Sachar, Louis (1997) *Sideways Arithmetic from Wayside School: More than 50 mindboggling math puzzles*, and (1995) *More Sideways Arithmetic from Wayside School*. Scholastic. These very funny books are companions to Sachar's Wayside School books, but can be enjoyed on their own as well.

Schwartz, David M. (1998). *G Is for Googol: A Math Alphabet Book*. Tricycle Press. Children and their parents will enjoy the many math words and ideas in this inventive book, from A is for Abacus to Z is for Zillion.

St. John, Glory (1975). *How to Count Like a Martian*. Henry Z. Walck (out of print). Check your library for this problem-solving book that explores counting and codes from many countries and cultures. This book, written for older elementary, provides an excellent explanation of the importance of zero and place value by presenting ancient numbering systems.

Young Math Books Series. Books in the Youth Math Books series, published by Thomas Y. Crowell in the 1970s, are appropriate for a wide range of ages, from precocious preschoolers all the way through early middle school, but are especially good for children ages 6-9. Advanced mathematical concepts are introduced in a precise yet relaxed and interesting manner. Most titles are out of print, although a few have been reprinted with other publishers. Look for these selected titles in libraries or used bookstores.

3D, 2D, 1D, by David A. Adler
666 Jellybeans! All That? An Introduction to Algebra, by Malcolm E. Weiss
Angles Are Easy as Pie, by Robert Froman
Area, by Jane Jonas Srivastava
Averages, by Jane Jonas Srivastava
Base Five, by David Adler
Binary Numbers, by Clyde Watson
Building Tables on Tables: A Book about Multiplication, by John V. Trivett
Circles, by Mindel and Harry Sitomer
Exploring Triangles: Paper-Folding Geometry, by Jo Phillips
Graph Games, by Frédérique Papy
The Greatest Guessing Game: A Book about Dividing, by Robert Froman
How Did Numbers Begin?, by Mindel Sitomer
How Little and How Much: A Book about Scales, by Franklyn M. Branley
Lines, Segments, Polygons, by Mindel and Harry Sitomer
Maps, Tracks, and the Bridges of Königsberg: A Book about Networks, by Michael Holt
Mathematical Games for One or Two, by Mannis Charosh
Measure with Metric, by Franklyn M. Branley
Number Ideas through Pictures, by Mannis Charosh
Odds and Evens, by Thomas C. O'Brien
Probability, by Charles F. Linn
Right Angles: Paper-Folding Geometry, by Jo Phillips
Roman Numerals, by David Adler
Rubber Bands, Baseballs, and Donuts: A Book about Topology, by Robert Froman
Shadow Geometry, by Daphne Trivett
Solomon Grundy, Born on One Day: A Finite Arithmetic Puzzle, by Malcolm E. Weiss
Spirals, by Mindel and Harry Sitomer
Straight Lines, Parallel Lines, Perpendicular Lines, by Mannis Charosh
Venn Diagrams, by Robert Froman
Yes No, Stop Go: Some Patterns in Mathematical Logic, by Judith L. Gersting and Joseph E. Kuczkowski
Zero is Not Nothing, by Mindel and Harry Sitomer

Zaccaro, Edward (2000). *Challenge Math: For the Elementary and Middle School Student.* Free Spirit Publishing. From the publisher: "Difficult concepts in statistics, probability, algebra, physics, trigonometry, and calculus are explained in easy-to-understand language and illustrated with cartoons. Kids enjoy discovering the connections between math and science. Includes 1000 problems at three levels of difficulty—Challenging, Very Challenging, and Einstein." Grades 4-8.

Late Elementary to Young Adult Reading Level (Approximately Grades 6 and Up)

Agnesi to Zeno: Over 100 Vignettes from the History of Math. Key Curriculum Press. Designed for grades 9-12, these one-page introductions to people and concepts from math history include suggestions for discussion questions and projects. www.keycurriculumpress.com.

Amdahl, Kenn (1996). *Algebra Unplugged*. Clearwater Publishing. No pencil-and-paper problems, just an easy discussion of first-year algebra with some review of previous math. Some teen-oriented references may go unappreciated by younger readers. Science fans may also enjoy There Are No Electrons: Electronics for Earthlings (1991).

Downing, Douglas A. (1996). *Algebra the Easy Way; Trigonometry the Easy Way; Calculus the Easy Way.* Barrons Educational Series. Math is tied to a fantasy storyline in this series designed for high school and college students. Widely available in bookstores.

Hanadek, Anita (1976). *Critical Thinking: Problem Solving, Reasoning, Logic and Arguments.* Critical Thinking Books & Software. Grades 7 and up. Rigorous verbal logic. Visit www.criticalthinking.com for on-line sample pages.

Harnadek, Anita (1996). *Math Word Problems* (Grades 3 and up) and (1998) *Algebra Word Problems* (Grades 6 and up). Critical Thinking Books & Software. Short and to-the-point word problems. Highly divergent and visual thinkers may do better with *Mind Benders* and *Math Mind Benders*. Visit www.criticalthinking.com for on-line sample pages.

Harnadek, Anita (2000). *Mind Benders* (Grades K-12) and *Math Mind Benders* (Grades 5 and up). Critical Thinking Books & Software. Effective combinations of verbal and graphic reasoning. Also available on CD-ROM. Visit www.criticalthinking.com for on-line sample pages.

Isdell, Wendy (1993). *A Gebra Named Al: A Novel.* Free Spirit Publishing. "Julie, Al, and the Periodic horses journey through the Land of Mathematics, where the Orders of Operations are real places and fruits that look like Bohr models grow on chemistrees." Teacher's guide available.

Jacobs, Harold (1994). *Mathematics: A Human Endeavor.* W. H. Freeman and Company. A liberal arts approach to math, with entertaining and enlightening prose, relevant comic strips, a leisurely pace, and a friendly tone. Also available by Harold Jacobs, (1995) *Elementary Algebra* and (1987) *Geometry*. Visit www.whfreeman.com for on-line tables of contents and summaries.

Pappas, Theoni (1989). *The Joy of Mathematics*, and (1991) *More Joy of Mathematics: Exploring Mathematics All Around You.* Wide World Publishing/Tetra. Fun books for reference browsing or an intro to more serious study.

Verbal Math Resources for Parents

Historical Connections in Mathematics and *Mathematicians Are People, Too*. The AIMS Education Foundation. Math history programs for elementary through high school. www.aimsedu.org.

Isdell, Wendy (1996). *Using a Gebra Named Al in the Classroom* (Teacher's Guide). Free Spirit Publishing. See *A Gebra Named Al*, above.

Kaczmarski, Kathryn (1998). *Exploring Math with Books Kids Love*. Fulcrum Publishing. This excellent resource book shows how to explore middle school math concepts with over 20 popular trade fiction and non-fiction books, such as *Math Curse, The Westing Game, In the Year of the Boar and Jackie Robinson, Dogsong, A Wrinkle in Time, Flat Stanley*, and *Julie of the Wolves*.

Thiessen, Diane, et al. (1998). *The Wonderful World of Mathematics: A Critically Annotated List of Children's Books in Mathematics, 2nd ed*. National Council of Teachers of Mathematics. Over 500 trade books are reviewed and analyzed for content and accuracy, illustrations, the author's writing style, and the included activities.

At Home with Home Schoolers

Brandon, Age 12: "Home schooling offers a much greater challenge."

Sean, Age 10: "Sometimes I go a little 'outside the lines'...because I see a better way."

Ali, Age 8: "I learn things faster in home schooling."

Juliann describes what it's like to home school three children, each of whom has a different learning style:

> *Each of my children learns differently. Thus, each is individually tutored, and I am the tutor. Just as my three children will, unfailingly, never eat the same things, they will not learn in the same manner either. Brandon took the PLUS test last week as part of the Johns Hopkins University talent search, and he qualified for the summer workshops, so he is now officially gifted. My middle child, Sean, is quite gifted, both verbally and in math, and if he were the oldest, I think he would more fully appreciate his own talents. He is the most introspective of my three children with the highest E.Q. (Emotional Quotient). He dictated his answers to me, as the computers were in use at the time. I have tried to be faithful to his responses. Ali is left-handed, very creative, very kinetic, and visual. She either gets it right away, in which case you had better get out of the way 'cause she's on fire, or she refuses to undertake the exercise at all! She overflows with stubborn creativity. Of my three children, she most loves to chat with other children and perform for an audience. She is my extrovert.*
>
> —Juliann, home school parent

Here is what Juliann's three children, Brandon, Sean, and Ali, have to say about home schooling.

Q: How long have you been home schooling?

Brandon: 12 years; all my life.
Sean: 10 years; all my life.
Ali: 8 years; all my life.

Q: Why are you home schooling?

Brandon: Because I felt my brain was wasted in public school.

Sean: Because I think I will get a higher level of schooling and teaching.

Ali: Because in a public school, there are 30 other students that the teacher is teaching.

Q: How would you describe a typical day of home schooling?

Brandon: I start school after breakfast at about 9 or 10 o'clock. I like to warm up with Latin and my journal, both on the computer. Then my mother sits down with me and we start math, my best subject. Math takes about an hour to an hour and a half. Then I will do my guitar and anything else I am assigned to.

Sean: First I do my math, then I do my Latin, then I do my guitar. I don't usually read specific, assigned books. I usually read Roman Empire books, science fiction, Calvin & Hobbes, my sister's stories (I don't think that counts), books about World War II and World War I. I read after my other schoolwork is done. I like to play Legos® chess, video games, and Axis & Allies® I like to scooter, swim, and bike.

Ali: I get out of bed, get dressed and eat, then start on my homework.

Q: What outside-the-home activities do you participate in?

Brandon: A few months ago, I was taking saxophone and guitar, but I had to quit because we moved. We also go ice skating every week, and about two or three times a month we find a museum or a field trip.

Sean: We visit museums and historical and nature sites. We ice skate once a week with other home schoolers. My brother and I take guitar lessons. My sister and I used to take karate. My sister and I want to take horse riding. My mom says I can start an animal **project this spring, like guinea pigs or mice.**

Ali: Hiking is what I like to do, because you are not in a room and you see all kinds of plants and animals.

Q: What do you like about home schooling?

Brandon: I like not having to get up so early and still get a lot accomplished. I tried regular school once when I was six, and I couldn't stand it. It was so boring; I had known everything they were teaching for years. Home schooling offers me a much greater challenge.

Sean: The learning is easier because the teacher has more time to spend with you.

Ali: I like home schooling because I know my teacher, and I will always have her in every grade I am in.

Q: What don't you like about home schooling?

Brandon: There aren't a lot of kids around, so I don't have a lot of friends.

Sean: You don't have as many friends. You don't interact with kids.

Ali: You know everybody there, because they are your brothers and sisters, so you don't have many friends.

Q: What does a "good education" mean to you?

Brandon: Having the knowledge to do anything on earth. There is nothing that I will not be smart enough to do.

Sean: I'll get my college degree easier and move on to my job.

Ali: It means a lot to me because I know I can be what I want when I am an adult.

Q: How would you describe yourself as a learner?

Brandon: I am a very good learner. I like to understand what I am doing, so if anything goes wrong, I know what I did and I know how to avoid it next time.

Sean: I like reading and following directions. Sometimes I go a little "outside the lines" and don't do it the way they say because I see a better way. I like to do old things, but new things I like to do more. (Juliann's note: Sean is a very linear learner, and I suspect that he views departure from the prescribed routine as "cheating," or as he puts it, "easier." But he learns so rapidly that a great deal of review would be boring and even counterproductive.)

Ali: My learning style is to look at the subject and see what it says, and then I know what it means. My strengths are my thoughts.

Q: What are your long-term goals, if any? How are you working to meet them?

Brandon: I am not sure exactly what I want to be when I grow up, but I will not be limited by any lack of information.

Sean: I want to be a marine biologist.

Ali: I would like to be a horse veterinarian.

Q: What advice do you have for other children and young adults who are considering or starting home schooling?

Brandon: Home schooling is a lot of hard work, especially for the teacher, because he or she has to organize everything. If you stick with it and really try to learn, there is potential for greatness.

Sean: Work hard and don't get upset easily.

Ali: For starting home schooling, my advice is to make sure you want to do it and study and think more because your teacher will go faster because she does not have 30 other students to teach. Home schooling is really nice and I think that other people should do it too and that everybody in the world should be allowed to do it.

6 The Full-time Parent/Teacher

The greatest joy of home schooling has been having a relaxed and happy family. The stress level in our home went down so much. I love being around my children and watching them love learning.

—Monica, home school parent

I have these spirited kids. What happened to all my ideas about these cozy family "learning times" with compliant learners? Why did I buy into the idea that home schooling would create this wonderfully harmonious and calm lifestyle? We are not calm and easygoing people. And giftedness creates its own challenges. Our children were considered different (i.e., not socially acceptable) because of their differences, which include being home schooled, being environmentally sensitive, being educationally and mentally more advanced. The more asynchronous and individualistic the child, the more isolation becomes an issue. It is very hard to convince a child he is a worthwhile person when he feels rejected or not accepted by most people outside his family, or even just by his peers.

—Sarah, home school parent

I have found it somewhat difficult to get used to this job as home school parent. I stay at home during the day while most fathers are working away from home, which has felt awkward. Taking care of the house is hard. Trying to find peers for our kids has been very hard.

—Martin, home school parent

> *I have learned a lot about myself since starting home schooling. First and foremost I have learned that I am capable of facilitating my children's education. I have also learned that I am not patient and how to be more patient. I have learned to ask questions before jumping in to solve problems. I have learned to listen with my heart, as well as my ears. I have learned to make sure I understand the girls before jumping in with suggestions. And I've learned to have more fun with learning and life.*
>
> —Joan, home school parent

"I could never be both parent and teacher to my child!"

"I don't know what expectations I should have for my child."

"I'd like to home school, but I'm afraid home schooling will swallow up my life."

If these are some of your concerns about home schooling, you're not alone. Education at home is not the best choice for every family. Linda Dobson (1998), in *The Homeschooling Book of Answers*, suggests that parents thinking about home schooling ask themselves honestly whether they enjoy being with their children most or all of the time, if they themselves have a curiosity about the world and love of learning that they can share and pass onto their children, and if they are willing to work to have a strong and satisfying relationship with their children. If you answer "no" to two or more of these questions, home schooling is probably not for you. Perhaps educational options other than home schooling are more appropriate for your children, your family, and you (and congratulate yourself for your honesty).

On the other hand, perhaps you don't feel you can answer "yes" because you're confused by the questions or unsure of your answers. Perhaps you believe you can *learn* to enjoy being with your children more, you can rediscover a sense of curiosity about the world, and you can start now to have a positive relationship with your children that can last a lifetime. If so, then home schooling may be a realistic option.

Let's take a closer look at some of the common concerns of new home school parents.

I Could Never Be Both Parent and Teacher to My Child!

When we read stories to preschoolers or show them how to tie their shoes, when we answer a seven-year-old's questions about where babies come from or help a teenager learn how to change oil in the car, we are being both parent and teacher. But if we feel we must drill a seven-year-old on addition facts or instruct a 13-year-old in algebra, suddenly the scene changes. The children are no longer relaxed. We expect them to be eager to learn (and if they are not, we are disappointed). We feel we must hold them (and ourselves) accountable for the results. No longer are we involved in the "informal apprenticeship" that was present in changing oil or tying shoes, and that informal apprenticeship is what we want; it is one hallmark of creative parenting (John-Steiner, 1997).

What changed? The attitude toward the task changed. If a home school parent tells a child to sit at the kitchen table to do a worksheet about circumference and area with an expectation that the parent will review the work after 30 minutes, the adult is very aware of his role as teacher, and the child may resist being taught. If the setting is less formal, and if the parent explores the ideas of circumference and area with the child by initiating a discussion during an afternoon walk, or suggests a hands-on activity from the book *Circles*, by Catherine Sheldrick Ross, or reads the picture book, *Sir Cumference and the First Round Table*, by Cindy Neuschwander, then parent and teacher roles are once again joined in a way that facilitates learning.

Relationships Come First

"My child would never listen to me talk about circumference," you may be thinking. That may be true—for now. Right now your child may need and want more independence and control. Give him a protractor, ruler, compass, and some paper, and allow some free exploration. Find an interesting geometry software program your child can use without adult oversight. The eventual goal is to help your child feel that he can *afford to cooperate* with you, but this is not a process that can be forced. Annemarie Roeper (1995) reminds us that an uncluttered parent-child relationship must come first, even before meeting other learning needs and standards, before test scores or filling out home school forms.

Forcing a child to do academic work at the expense of your relationship with the child or the child's relationship with learning is simply not worth it. That's not to say that you should give up, but rather than authoritarian control, think in terms of "wooing the child" (Maté, 1999).

Suppose your nine-year-old is having difficulty learning multiplication tables. Your first instinct, based on your own education and your concern that your child learn math, may be to drill the child more with flash cards, at which point she begins to resent both math and you. What do you do? If you can see that continuing with more drill will cause more resentment, you have other options. Take a break for a few days or weeks; time off from a difficult task often results in renewed willingness to work. If after a few weeks she still resists the curriculum, you can be creative in the ways you approach math tasks. Woo the child to math by playing games such as Yahtzee® cribbage, or Monopoly® look in your library for the video *Schoolhouse Rock! – Multiplication Rock*, which uses rhyme and song as memory aids or the book *The Number Devil*, by Hans Magnus Enzensberger, a colorful foray into the world of mathematics. Such resources take away the bias against math by making it fun. Explore other facets of math that do not require arithmetic in order to nurture and sustain your child's confidence in her ability to "do math." Design patterns and tessellations; watch the Nova video The *Shape of Things*; create your own probability games or experiments with dice.

Your child will continue to learn, you will strengthen your relationship through enjoyable activities, and you'll experience less stress and have more fun

Cooperation Rather than Conformity

Sometimes children resist complying with adults. They usually have their reasons. Gabor Maté (1999) describes the knee-jerk defiance of many children as *counterwill*, and he argues that it is the natural response of a highly sensitive child to an inappropriate environment. Although we think of counterwill as an *excess* of will and power, it actually points to a *weak* self-concept and a need to defend the self against perceived threats, whether real or imagined.

> [T]he various epithets such as stubborn, willful and so on indicate not a strong will but the lack of one. An emotionally self-confident person does not have to adopt an oppositional stance automatically. She may resist others' attempts to control her, but she will not do so rigidly and defensively. If she opposes something, it is from a strong sense of what her true preferences are, not a knee-jerk reflex. A child not driven by counterwill does not automatically experience any advice, any expression of the parent's opinion, as an attempt to control. Registering deep in her psyche is a sense of solidity about her inner core, this nucleus of the self, so there is no necessity to defend the will against being overwhelmed. I will be able to hang on to myself, an inner voice reassures her, even if I listen to what somebody else thinks, or do what someone else wants me to do. I won't lose my identity, so I don't have to protect myself through resistance. I can afford to cooperate. I can afford to heed *(Maté, 1999, pp. 188-189).

The question then becomes not "How can I get my child to cooperate?" but rather "How can I get my child to a level of emotional safety and comfort so that he can afford to cooperate with me?" For a child who has either routinely denied her "self" in order to fit in, comply, or conform, *or* who automatically adopts an attitude of defiance, a period of re-discovering her unique self may be necessary before she has the self-understanding and strength to cooperate effectively with others.

Cooperation is not the same as habitual conformity. Habitual conformity is a default position of continually trying to fit in and do what others want us to do. Cooperation is voluntarily chosen. There is a difference between a child's doing what he thinks everyone wants for fear of being disliked or reprimanded and the same child's choosing at specific times and places to accommodate or compromise because doing so is good for himself and those around him. The latter self-directed way of behaving is, of course, preferred because it helps the child be self-sufficient and learn for the sake of learning.

Maté suggests that parents of sensitive children can make a big difference in diffusing and preventing counterwill by re-thinking the nature of their relationship with their child. By keeping a strong parent-child attachment foremost in their minds, parents reassure the child that he or she is valued and accepted regardless of behavior, regardless of whether the child chooses cooperation. He cautions parents not to mistake "acquiescence for voluntary 'good behavior.'" Routine compliance with a parent's wishes is healthy only if the child is not doing so out of fear or for lack of other options. When a child does display defiance, the parent can choose not to take it personally and to see the opposition as not entirely within the child's control, but part of a larger growth process. By expanding the idea of the parent-child relationship to include occasional resistance and opposition, parents can give the child the gift of freedom of expression without fear of emotional punishment or emotional blackmail such as withholding affection on the part of the parent. Unacceptable behavior does not have to be encouraged, but neither does it have to result in parental "looks" and subtle sulking in the form of the silent treatment or skipping routine signs of caring.

Integrating Compliance and Control

Elizabeth Meckstroth (1992) offers strategies that parents can use to foster resiliency in their children, help them integrate self-control, and freely choose compliance. By changing our own behaviors and attitudes and modeling new behaviors, we can encourage positive behaviors in our children. Gifted children are quick to see the hypocrisy in, "Do what I say, not what I do."

- Use stressful situations as signals to solve problems rather than to react to injustices.

- Be a goal finder rather than a fault finder. Explore how you can make a situation work for you instead of against you.

- Consider choices to experience control of your life. Replace thinking that you have to do something with thinking that you choose to do something.

- For inspiration, study the lives of exceptional people and how they overcame the stresses they encountered.

- Be aware of your body's messages. Listen as if nothing else matters at that moment as much as what your child is telling you.

- Take your children seriously! Feel the situation their way and listen to understand rather than to respond. Accepting and understanding do not necessarily mean agreeing.

- Arrange private time together. Plan an appointment when you want to share your time.

- Make time for your personal self-expression (art, music, dance) that helps you understand who you are.

- Accept that people may not always understand your feelings and perceptions.

- Recognize and evaluate the "shoulds" in your life. How much is based on other people's needs and on outgrown habits?

- Reward yourself and others for trying; expect progress, not perfection.[8]

What Expectations Should I Have for My Child?

Knowing what and how much to expect from children is never easy. For parents of precocious and creative children whose possibilities seem limitless, the task is more complex. When children's intellectual development is significantly higher than the child's chronological age, parents may be confused as to what kind of behavior to expect from the child (Webb, Meckstroth, & Tolan, 1982). Home school parents may face an even greater challenge because our children look primarily to us for guidance as to who they should be.

Avoid Perfectionism

Perfectionism wreaks havoc on expectations if we feel that it is our job to create the perfect home school and give our child the perfect education. The urge to perfect *can* result in an excellent educational environment for one's children, but perfectionism can also lead to feelings that you're not doing enough. Look closely at whether you have a tendency to overemphasize your children's achievement and performance. There is no shame in admitting that your own adult perfectionism affects your children. Recognizing the temptation to expect too much is far better than turning a blind eye to potential problems from a child who feels excessive parental pressure.

Home schooling is always a work in progress, so know from the beginning that you will never feel a total sense of completion. Many days you will go to bed knowing you could have done more or your child could have learned more. That's okay. There is always another day, and perhaps your child *did* learn enough for this day. Learning can't always be orchestrated and directed from the outside. Sometimes it needs to unfold according to its own timetable.

If you feel that your child should always be engaged in useful activities or "educational" play, be cautious about making home schooling an arena in which the child has no room or time for leisure and no space in which she is not under an adult's watchful eye. You may need to make a conscious effort to allow a certain block of time every day for your child's safe (but relatively unsupervised) play or daydreaming. The child must know that he is valued whether or not he is producing or performing; he must also have time for free thinking and play in order to develop his creative self.

Gifted children, who already feel so different from others, need encouragement and support. If you yourself are intimidated by high achievement either in yourself or in others, if you feel threatened by the enormous potential in your children, or if you are fearful of being branded a pushy parent in the eyes of the world, you may unconsciously offer your advanced and creative child too little support and encouragement. You may allow your child to find her own way without letting her know that she is free to soar as high as she wishes, or you may in subtle ways encourage her to settle for mediocrity only because it is more comfortable and safe than taking the risks that might lead her to self-actualization.

For example, take the parent who allows a child to quit swimming lessons because the child thinks she may not pass the test at the end. Although the parent's intention is to support the child's feelings, the child may learn from the situation that fear of failure is a valid reason to quit. However, the solution is not to say to the child, "Oh, come on. You can do it. It doesn't matter if you fail," because it *does* matter to the child if she fails.

A better course of action is to help the child acknowledge, understand, and verbalize her feelings. Being able to say, "I'm scared of failing" in the safe presence of an understanding adult is wonderfully therapeutic. The parent can then share stories of his or her own fears of failure and whether the result was success or not. More importantly, parent and child can talk about why the child is taking swimming lessons—to enjoy swimming, to be safe in the water, to be able to attend swim parties. If the child's anxiety is extreme, a vacation from lessons may be the answer, perhaps with more leisurely practice and pool time. The important thing is that the parent's attitude is one of problem solving, rather than reacting with anger or without sensitivity to a child's painful emotions.

Parents who are unsure of what constitutes normal behavior for specific ages may wish to read from a series of books on child development written by Louise Bates Ames and Francis L. Ilg, with titles such as *Your Seven Year Old: Life in a Minor Key*, or *Your Eight Year Old: Lively and Outgoing*. Some parents of gifted children find it useful to read not only the titles aimed at their children's current age, but also volumes for ages a few years older and younger, not just to know what to expect, but to get a better idea of how a gifted child can be several ages at once. Parents will be less likely to punish children for simply "acting their age," or in the case of asynchronous children, "acting their ages" (Webb, Meckstroth, & Tolan, 1982) if they are aware of what is normal for certain ages.

Find a Balance

In *Right-Brained-Children in a Left-Brained World*, Jeffrey Freed stresses the importance of the parent's being "totally nonjudgmental" with regard to home learning tasks: "[The child] will sense your expectations and frustrations, and will either 'check out' or refuse to work with you. Don't let home schooling become a test of wills; if something isn't working, try another approach." (Freed & Parsons 1997, p. 201),

Give your child as much control as possible over what, how, and when to learn. The amount of control will be different for each child, depending on family dynamics and the child's personality and needs, but parents can start by relinquishing a little more control than they feel comfortable with. Children who have control over their assignments complete more work (Clark, 1997). They also learn valuable study and time management skills that will be useful in their later lives.

By sitting down with your child to brainstorm and plan the home schooling schedule by day, week, or month, you are giving your child a message that her opinion counts, that education isn't directed from above. Your state may require certain subjects, or you may feel strongly that one or more academic areas should get special attention. Decide which items are non-negotiable before your planning session. Keep your list of non-negotiables as small as possible—include only those items for which you are not willing to compromise—two or three at most. Then ask your child what, how, when, and where he or she would like to learn. Work together to design a learning path that is agreeable to both of you.

Will Home Schooling Swallow up My Life?

There is no question that home schooling will take up a lot of your time, and it is a lot of work. It *will* be harder to find private space for yourself. Home school parents are frequently "on call"—answering questions, asking questions, searching for the right resources, going on outings, allowing themselves to become involved in a healthy way in their children's interests, helping the children widen their interests to include some they may not have come across on their own. In short, you are an active parent not just before and after school and on weekends, but every hour of every day.

The positive side of home schooling is you'll have more opportunities to develop your relationships with your children in more relaxed and thoughtful ways. It is hard for parents to guide their children effectively during rushed mornings and tired evenings. It is much easier to be a good listener, patient, flexible, and responsive when a parent has an entire day.

On the other hand, you can easily feel you are drowning in a sea of responsibilities, especially if you have more than one child. You may feel you need to be always on, always available, always "at the ready" to be a good home school parent. But it is important to block in time for your own personal needs, too. Here are some tips.

Arrange Planning Time

You can save time and anxiety by making an appointment with yourself to plan. Just as classroom teachers have planning time, you need regular time to plan a schedule. Choose a regular library day when you and your children will find books and other resources for the coming week. On the weekend—maybe Sunday evening—check television listings for the week and note the programs you want to view or tape. If you keep daily records (for yourself or for the state), plan a time each day when you will jot down necessary details. This is easier than trying to remember what everyone learned in the last week, and you'll feel less stress.

Keep a notebook of ideas for resources or study; set aside one evening a week to review curriculum on the Internet; then when you something interesting, store it in a folder on your computer. Later, when you need math ideas, go to the math folder and review items there.

Find Time Alone

It is crucial that you find a way to have some time alone—and not just when you are planning your home school curriculum! If you are an introvert, this may mean time truly by yourself, because you need more time alone than other people. You might enjoy an afternoon at a local art museum, bookstore, or just walking around the zoo. If you are an extravert, your "time alone" may consist of a weekly book discussion group (for adults) or a weekend lunch with friends. Regular exercise is another good way to recharge mental and physical batteries. Insisting on time for you is not selfish. It is necessary and sets a good example for your children. You may need to be inventive and assertive to get this time for yourself. A spouse may need to give up some time to spend an evening or afternoon with the children. Perhaps you and a home school friend can take turns keeping all of the children for one morning each week. When your children are old enough to stay by themselves at community classes, take advantage of the time they are in class to enjoy a leisurely cup of coffee rather than waiting in the car.

One home school parent of five tells how she finds time alone:

It has helped to designate certain times of day as times I am "off duty." Before 8 a.m., if children are awake, they know they need to occupy themselves quietly in their rooms. This gives me time for classical piano, my personal creative outlet. Then, during the little ones' afternoon nap, the older children do silent sustained reading, assuring all of us a quiet break.

—Nina, home school parent

Like this parent, plan half an hour each day when your children read quietly while you read or do something else that is primarily for you. There is an Internet mailing list for parents of gifted children called TAGMAX.[9] You may find support, ideas, and virtual energy from others who are struggling with similar issues. One home school parent writes, "I couldn't do it without the on-line support I get from various e-mail lists specifically for families with gifted children. They have kept me from feeling strange and isolated."

Work as a Team

In most home school families, one parent is the primary "teaching" parent while the other parent works to bring in the income. It is important that parents share basic parenting and educational philosophies, even when one is with the children the majority of the time. Parents should work together and discuss their views on home schooling so that they use the same basic approach in both home schooling and parenting. If one parent is the primary home school parent, the other parent can take an active role whenever he or she is available.

As the primary income parent, my role is limited because I spend less time with the children. But on evenings and weekends I play a very similar role to my wife—acting as a facilitator, helping the kids find resources, working with them on specific problems or projects, bouncing ideas off them and letting them bounce ideas off me.

—James, home school parent

9   For a complete list of Families of the Talented and Gifted (TAGFAM) e-mail lists, go to www.tagfam.org.

You can ask other home school parents for suggestions of how to foster a joyful and successful home school experience. At the same time, keep in mind that what works for one family may be different from what works for your family. Jon offers this advice based on his experience:

> *Personality traits that I consider very important for a teacher are patience, creativity, ability to improvise, sense of humor. Be supportive of your child. Don't criticize. Let your kid make mistakes and correct them. Offer advice or assistance and resist the temptation to do it yourself because you know how and you can do it better. Patience is paramount. You cannot allow yourself to lose your temper, even when your child is making the same mistake repeatedly day after day and doesn't seem to learn. Just try to find new ways to solve the problem, memorize the rule, or organize the information. Something is bound to work, sooner or later.*
>
> *If there are two parents, then they must be in agreement on home schooling. The person who is not the primary teacher should be very supportive, or the burden will be too heavy for the other one.*
>
> —Jon, home school parent

If possible, both parents should be familiar with the family's basic home school approach (see Part II: Creating Your Home School Approach). Often, one parent is the reader or Internet junkie in the family, doing most of the research necessary to begin home schooling. The primary home school parent should keep the other parent informed of decisions and activities, successes and concerns; parents who work outside the home can make an effort to ask about the home school day without taking on the role of home school principal! Both parents may want to view together James Webb's videos, *Is My Child Gifted?*, *Parenting Successful Children*, and *Do Gifted Children Need Special Help?* from Great Potential Press (formerly Gifted Psychology Press), then discuss your reactions to the videos and the implications for home schooling. Other parenting resources are recommended at the end of this chapter.

Cultivate Intellectual and Creative Outlets

Some home school parents give up a job to stay home with their children. Often more stressful than the loss of income is the loss of intellectual and creative outlets. Most of us are aware of the dangers of over-stimulation and over-scheduling in the workplace, but we might not be as cognizant of the dangers of *under*-stimulation for the gifted parent. Mary-Elaine Jacobsen (1999a) advises gifted adults to cultivate several areas of interest—intellectual, educational, musical, artistic, social recreational, and spiritual pursuits—"usually far more than the average person." Although it can be a challenge to keep intellectual and creative pursuits alive while home schooling, it is not impossible, and the example you will set for your children is invaluable. If you like to read, schedule an hour for a silent reading after lunch when everyone—including you—enjoys a book of his or her own choosing (the dishes can wait). If you are a writer, reserve an hour before everyone gets up or after they are asleep to put words on paper. Whatever your professional interests, keep up by reading professional journals and perhaps joining Internet lists as a way to "talk shop." Home schooling can offer the space you need to explore your passions from different angles and on your own timetable.

If your job is flexible, you may be able to integrate your interests with those of your children. An artist can teach a bi-weekly home school art class which his own children can attend. A lab technician can delve into elementary science from the perspective of broader knowledge and experience.

Home schooling may also provide you time to experiment with new interests. Maybe you've always wanted to learn to draw but your career always came first. This is the perfect time to get pencils and drawing paper and see what you can do. Return to one or more of your interests and enjoy exploring it once again. Whether you see home schooling as a burden or opportunity is mostly up to you.

> *As I gradually gave up the role of being "teacher" and became a learner, I found joy in a different sense from before. I began learning right along with my children in whatever we were doing. It became exciting for me, and now I look forward to new ideas and challenges along with my children. I feel like I am learning so much for the first time and loving it. Interestingly, I have found that the more we work together as learners, the more the children are willing to follow a lead I might suggest, which was not the case at first when I was trying to force a direction or an activity.*
>
> *To my amazement, home schooling afforded me the opportunity to learn more about myself than what I have learned about anything else put together. When I was faced with being with my children 24 hours a day every day, my sense of self was really challenged. Until I tried as hard to understand myself as I did my children, we didn't get very far. I learned how to manage those days of frustration as I learned more about my own past and present expectations; I had to learn first how my own school experiences had affected me and my decisions in home schooling.*
>
> —Kathleen, home school parent

Self Discovery

As parents learn more about gifted traits in their children, they will slowly understand and accept the giftedness in themselves. They begin to re-evaluate their own potential and perceptions of self. Face-to-face with giftedness in all its glory and frustrations, home school parents have no choice but to come to terms with what giftedness means and how it affects their lives.

Many of the personality and learning traits we've discussed thus far—sensitivity, complexity, intensity, creativity, immersion learning—are familiar to home school parents. If our own giftedness and creativity have been nurtured and developed, we can identify with the positive aspects of those qualities—the sensitivity that provides for deep and meaningful relationships, the complexity and intensity that keep life from getting boring, the creativity that drives us to forge new and exciting paths, and the immersion learning that results in hours of joyful focus.

Some parents, however, may have painful memories of being "too" sensitive, being misunderstood because of their complexity, being too intense for others to handle, and experiencing creativity as a liability.

> *Home schooling has reminded me that the things I remember most in life were not things learned in school; rather, they were life experiences. I've learned about my own learning styles, about my own tendency toward excitable behavior, about my own random way of learning. I've learn that to think out of the box is okay. I was always labeled a free spirit, and now I know why! I've learned that I, too, can be self-educated.*
>
> —Barbara, home school parent

Painful memories can lead to frustration or sadness, but gifted parents should follow a "call to wholeness" (Aron, 1997) rather than be weighted down with unrealistic expectations. This does not mean trying to be perfect or to make our lives perfect. It is instead a call to be who we were meant to be, to discover our potential and not be afraid to fulfill it. Stephanie Tolan (1998, p. 214) challenges us to examine "our own wish to fit in and be comfortable, to avoid standing up and standing out. We need to challenge our own temptation to build our lives to benefit only ourselves, only our immediate families and 'tribal' groups…." A call to wholeness offers the opportunity to take more risks, to love more freely, to grow bigger in our capacity to live a meaningful life without fear of making mistakes or looking foolish.

Key Points

☑ Education at home is not the best choice for every family; home schooling is often time-consuming and difficult.

☑ Successful home school parents enjoy being with their children most or all of the time, have a curiosity about the world and love of learning that they can share and pass onto their children, and are willing to work to have a strong and satisfying relationship with their children.

☑ A healthy parent-child relationship must have priority over before meeting other learning needs and standards; parents can see themselves as "informal mentors" rather than taskmasters.

☑ Parents should value voluntary cooperation over habitual conformity.

☑ Parental perfectionism wreaks havoc on expectations; parents can work to find a balance by giving children as much control as possible over what, how, and when to learn.

☑ Home school parents can save time and anxiety by setting aside regular time to plan for curriculum and scheduling.

☑ It is important that home school parents share basic parenting and educational philosophies, work together, and discuss their views on home schooling so that they use the same basic approach in both home schooling and parenting.

☑ Home school parents should place a high priority on time to recharge and time for their own intellectual and creative needs.

☑ Home school parents often come to terms—perhaps for the first time—with their own giftedness, how it affects their lives, and how to use it as a strength instead of experiencing it as a struggle.

Questions for Reflection

1. To what extent is your educational dream for your children that they sustain their love of learning?

2. Are there times that you resist displaying your children's gifts and talents to others?

3. When are you willing to allow your children freedom to decide when, how, and even whether to seek public recognition and awards for their accomplishments?

4. Were you a gifted or creative child? Do you consider yourself a gifted adult? Do you consider yourself creative? Why or why not?

5. How can you separate your own needs and goals as a parent from those of your child?

Resources for Sensitive, Intense, Creative, and Otherwise Gifted Adults

Advanced Development. Institute for the Study of Advanced Development. A Journal on Adult Giftedness.

Aron, Elaine N. (1997). *The Highly Sensitive Person: How to Thrive when the World Overwhelms You*. Broadway Books.

Csikszentmihalyi, Mihalyi (1996). *Creativity: Flow and the Psychology of Discovery and Invention*. HarperCollins Publishers.

Csikszentmihalyi, Mihaly (1990). *Flow: The Psychology of Optimal Experience*. Harper & Row.

Jacobsen, Mary-Elaine (1999). *Liberating Everyday Genius: A Revolutionary Guide for Identifying and Mastering Your Exceptional Gifts*. Ballantine Books. (Published in 2000 under the title *The Gifted Adult: A Revolutionary Guide for Liberating Everyday Genius*.)

Kerr, Barbara (1994). *Smart Girls: A New Psychology of Girls, Women and Giftedness, revised edition*. Great Potential Press (formerly Gifted Psychology Press).

Kerr, Barbara, & Cohn, Sanford (2001). *Smart Boys: Talent, Masculinity, and the Search for Meaning*. Great Potential Press (formerly Gifted Psychology Press).

Piirto, Jane (1998). *Talented Children and Adults: Their Development and Education*. Prentice Hall.

Piirto, Jane (1998). *Understanding Those Who Create, 2nd ed.* Great Potential Press (formerly Gifted Psychology Press).

Streznewski, Marylou Kelly (1999). *Gifted Grownups: The Mixed Blessings of Extraordinary Potential*. John Wiley and Sons.

Parenting Resources

Covey, Stephen, & Covey, Sandra Merrill (1998). *The 7 Habits of Highly Effective Families: Building a Beautiful Family Culture in a Turbulent World*. Golden Books.

Dreikurs, Rudolf & Soltz, Vicki (1964). *Children: The Challenge*. Plume.

Faber, Adele, & Mazlish, Elaine (1999). *How to Talk So Kids Will Listen & Listen So Kids Will Talk*. Avon.

Rimm, Sylvia (1997). *Dr. Sylvia Rimm's Smart Parenting: How to Parent So Children Will Learn*. Crown Publishing.

Walker, Sally Yahnke (2002). *The Survival Guide for Parents of Gifted Kids: How to Understand, Live with, and Stick Up for Your Gifted Child*. Free Spirit Publishing.

Webb, James (2000). *Do Gifted Children Need Special Help?* Video. Great Potential Press (formerly Gifted Psychology Press).

Webb, James (2000). *Is My Child Gifted?* Video. Great Potential Press (formerly Gifted Psychology Press).

Webb, James (2000). *Parenting Successful Children*. Video. Great Potential Press (formerly Gifted Psychology Press).

Webb, James, & DeVries, Arlene (1998). *Gifted Parent Groups: The SENG Model*. Great Potential Press (formerly Gifted Psychology Press).

Webb, James; Meckstroth, Elizabeth; & Tolan, Stephanie (1982). *Guiding the Gifted Child*. Great Potential Press (formerly Gifted Psychology Press).

At Home with Home School Parents

"Thoughts on Being Gifted for a Year" by Sarah, Home School Parent

It has been about a year and a half since I happened across the website for the Gifted and Talented in my search for answers to questions about my oldest son. I have two sons (whom I home school), both of whom are, of course, unique and special. But it is my older son who has challenged me the most. Quick to learn but unwilling or unable to go through the usual educational hoops, he has been at times an old man in a child's body and different from other kids his age. He has also had, and continues to have, difficulties with his health and has many of the symptoms of ADD.

My entry into the world of the gifted through an e-mail list resulted in culture shock, to put it mildly. I stumbled through the first few months, finding that my old assumptions about what it meant to be "smart" were challenged. I'd never heard the expression "gifted" used in the context of intelligence when I was a teenager. At first, I have to confess that I was a bit put off by some parents' descriptions of their kids—you know, the types that read quantum mechanics as leisure reading. While I felt sure that my son was highly intelligent, he showed no signs of the single-minded focus that drives some of these gifted kids to university at age 13 (except for computer games, which he loves!).

I read as much as I could find on the Internet on giftedness. I hadn't realized that giftedness came with particular character traits affecting the emotional and even spiritual life of the gifted—traits like heightened emotional sensitivity, intensity, empathy, imagination, and even sensitivity to seams in socks! Some of the Linda Silverman articles hit too close to home. I also found, to my surprise, many pieces of the puzzle that described me as a child; often characteristics that other people had tried to encourage me to change. It was as if I had been an alien, and then I found that there were other life forms that were similar enough to be related to me and who could provide me with a mythical history and identity.

I've spent a lot of time in this last year (the year that I have been gifted) going through the process of grieving, not for opportunities missed or great things I "could" have done, but for having lost my vision, for not trusting and speaking my own truths. For having lost myself....

This time continues to be a process of growth and personal challenge to integrate my "lost" self with my present understanding. My relationship with my older son has undergone many changes, mostly for the better. His new understanding of himself is helping to heal some of the pain of his "differentness."

At this rate, what great changes will be wrought by the time I have been gifted for two years—or three or four!

Part 2

Creating Your Home School Approach

7 Getting Started

One learns quickly in home schooling a gifted child that the shortest distance between two points may be not a straight line.

—David Albert, author of *And the Skylark Sings with Me: Adventures in Homeschooling and Community-Based Education*

Home school parents are often asked, "How do you home school?" The person asking usually wants a recipe, as if there were a list of ingredients that, when mixed in the right proportions and prepared using exact instructions, will produce well-educated home schooled children. The recipe might start with a schedule such as: "We get up at 7:00 a.m., do math from 8:30 until 9:30 using this specific workbook, take an exercise break, then read from a history book until lunch," and so on, with the hourly schedule mapped out until bedtime. In other words, if you follow this routine, you, too, will be able to home school successfully. But one family's outline describes only one family's experience; it does not reflect the many important questions that must be answered according to each family's unique needs and circumstances—questions like these:

- Should we take a break from school before starting home school, or should we plunge right in the first day with assignments and formal curriculum?

- What kind of home school approach will work best for our family— self-directed learning, traditional subject study, classical education, unit studies, or a combination of approaches?

- What are my child's strengths and areas of struggle? How should these influence our approach and the curriculum materials we use?

- As a parent/teacher, what are my own areas of expertise that I can use to help my child learn? What subjects will require me to study or seek resources, mentors, or other help?

- What are my child's preferred learning styles? How will these influence my choice of materials and methods?

- Will we use grade levels and grade-based curriculum to determine what our child will learn?

- How will we assess our child's needs and evaluate his or her learning? How much time will we spend home schooling each day? Each year?

- How much money should we plan to spend on home schooling?

Each of the chapters in Part II will help guide you through these questions and decisions. You will read examples from real home school families who have created their own self-directed home school approach. You will learn how they structure their day, combine approaches based upon the needs of their child, individualize learning for different subjects, and evaluate what their children are learning. You'll learn how parents assess their children's academic needs and how they budget their money and time. Because each family's needs are different, each family's home school experience is unique.

How do you home school? We can only offer a few general guidelines—a few favorite ingredients and recipes—but each person wanting advice will need to use just what works for them and discard the rest. *There is no one right way to home school.* Having said that, let's look at some creative ways to approach home schooling.

Creative Home Schoolers

The home school families I interviewed are all creative home schoolers—an approach different from many other kinds of home schooling. These families exemplify what Teresa Amabile (1989) writes in *Growing Up Creative*—that creativity is both *novel* and *appropriate*. Creative home schooling is *novel* in that it is *unique to each child*, created anew every day as the best match between learner and subject. It is *appropriate* in that it *addresses real, individual needs*. Further, the effectiveness of creative home schooling is continually assessed in an ongoing, informal basis, with the parent making small but important changes when necessary to maintain appropriateness. In creative home schooling, you don't follow anyone else's idea of what's best for your child unless it works for your child. You can choose from several home schooling approaches and from many resources, depending on your child's academic needs and emotional development.

Creative home schooling requires that you, as a home school parent, inform yourself about options that are available and make careful choices based on what will best serve your child, and not what may look good to others. A particular textbook or approach cannot be blamed for a child's learning difficulties, because you will now have the power to try something else. You will have the flexibility to change course if your child's needs change or if things just aren't working as expected.

Creative home school teachers are a varied lot. Their self-described approaches range from "very relaxed" and "interest-led" to "relatively academic" and "very structured for certain subjects." "Eclectic" was the descriptive word used most often by the families I interviewed. Many home school parents seem reluctant to limit their approach by restricting themselves to a single model or theory. As one parent writes: "I don't like to categorize us too much because then you risk putting the category before the needs of the child."

Kim, whose nine-year-old daughter attended a Montessori school for first and second grade before home schooling in third grade, describes her approach as a blend of philosophies: "I'd say our approach…is a combination of child-directed learning, unit study, and Montessori, with some collaborative learning thrown in, too."

Amira, home school parent of three children, explains it this way:

> *Our approach is forever changing as I learn more, and as we adapt to the needs of each child and to the busy schedule of our family. We could call it an evolving approach, or a "let's try it and see if it works" approach.*
>
> —Amira, home school parent

Melinda Roth writes in an article for *Home Education Magazine* (2001), that a strict adherence to specific home school labels leads to divisiveness within the home schooling community and to criticism of other home schoolers whose approach might be at a different end of the spectrum from our own. Such divisiveness can then prevent us from combining seemingly incompatible approaches in new and exciting ways.

Juliann has home schooled her three children since her oldest, now 12, was in first grade doing fourth-grade work. She notes three important aspects of her creative home schooling approach:

> ■ *Eclectic. We move around in both method and objective. Things stay busy and interesting.*
>
> ■ *Academic and Traditional and Well-Rounded. We love books and read constantly; we write and solve and keep portfolios and records; we follow a calendar. We cover everything a college-preparatory classroom would cover. For assessment, we use the ITBS (Iowa Test of Basic Skills), the CogAT (Cognitive Abilities Test), and the Johns Hopkins Talent Search qualifying exams.*
>
> ■ *Relaxed. You won't always have a great day! We recently moved across the country. Seventy-five percent of our teaching materials and 90% of our books are still in storage, so home schooling has been a new kind of challenge this semester. I decided to just go with the flow and pull out a few boxes. "Well, let's learn this!" I said. We've indulged in a lot of field trips in our new location. We should be in our house soon, and re-shelving our library will be like finding old friends. We can't wait!*
>
> —Juliann, home school parent

Juliann has given herself the freedom to choose what works for her family. She has combined what many people might think of as opposite educational styles—traditional and interest-based. She uses academic testing and other traditional resources such as textbooks when they serve her family's needs, but she also gives her children a voice in what they study, encouraging development of her children's self-directed learning that will last a lifetime. She says:

> *When we began to home school, Trevor, then age six, and his dad and I sat down and wrote up a list of things that we would like Trevor to learn for the remainder of the first-grade year. Karate, typing, and guitar were on the list, in addition to the academic subjects.*
>
> Juliann, home school parent

Juliann recommends that new home school parents "*search constantly for resources and ideas, and never stop trying new topics, new approaches, and new techniques.*" Like snowflakes, no two home school learners are alike, even within the same family.

> *We are pretty relaxed, and our approach varies according to the child. Our highly motivated 13-year-old needs almost no help from us beyond transportation and an occasional suggestion, such as, "Here's a brochure with some interesting art courses—see if they appeal to you." But our 10-year-old needs some guidance, as in, "It's time to do some math."*
>
> —Carol, home school parent

Principles of Creative, Self-Directed Home Schooling

Creative and self-directed home schooling is both easier and harder than one might expect—easier because home school approaches can be tailored to fit each family, and harder because there is no *User's Manual*. It will be a continual work in progress as you adapt methods and materials to fit the changing needs of your child and family. There are no specific rules to follow except to maintain curiosity and excitement of discovery; however, successful experiences of other families and ideas from gifted education curriculum and research can provide the basic foundation for your own unique approach.

Creativity

Creative home schooling rests on the idea that creativity is an important part of being human. Each of us has the ability to invent and to think in entirely new directions. In *Understanding Those Who Create* (1998), Jane Piirto asserts that creativity is not so much a skill that can be taught as it is instead a basic human instinct that is too often stifled rather than enhanced. She reminds us that creativity is the foundation of talent development and invention. Without creativity, for example, a talented young athlete will not be able to visualize future goals or success. Without creativity, a young computer whiz will not have the vision to develop new software and other technology. An education that promotes rather than hinders our natural creativity is not just valuable, but essential for all children, regardless of a child's individual talents.

Piirto (1999) writes that highly creative people know how to take risks, value complexity, and see the world with fresh eyes. Children naturally see the world with fresh eyes and show high levels of creativity in small, everyday ways. In talking recently with a six-year-old friend on the phone—to plan for our next home school group lunch—I gave her several traditional suggestions for how to shape the home-made bread we were going to make together, e.g., a braid, a peasant-style loaf, or individual rolls. She interjected, "How about a star? We can all break off the points and taste-test them." This six-year-old made a new suggestion, different from my options; her "fresh eyes perspective" allowed her to wonder before she asked "Is it possible?" By the way, it was possible, though not easy, and the taste test worked beautifully!

Just as any human trait manifests itself in degrees and variations, creativity is often more intense in some children than in others and is not limited to the fine arts—music, dance, drama, writing, or painting. The world also benefits from creative leaders, problem solvers, inventors, scientists, mathematicians, and creative individuals in every area

Parents and others who work with children may find it more helpful to think of creativity as *divergent thinking*, or "out of the box" thinking, rather than a final, tangible product. Divergent thinking means moving away from what is usual and expected, taking a new path instead of the well-worn road. Unfortunately, when children display creative and divergent thinking as a part of their learning, whether at school or home, adults often react to their ideas in a negative fashion with subtle, evaluative statements such as, "Well, that isn't quite what I had in mind." To support and encourage divergent thinking, we must first consciously change the way in which we respond to children's ideas and actions. Let's suppose an eight-year-old girl is asked to write a book report based on a biography. She asks if the book can be an autobiography instead of a biography. Next, she asks if it has to be about a real person or if it can be about a fictional character, such as a fictional journal of favorite *Star Wars* characters. And finally, she asks if the book report can be in the form of a play that she performs herself. The parent's response to these questions will make an enormous difference in how the child views her own divergent thinking. The teacher/parent who assumes the child is "just being difficult" may shut down all future suggestions with, "No, you have to follow the assignment," or "Why do you always make things so complicated!" or even a sarcastic, "Don't try to be so smart."

With responses like these, the child may learn to bury her divergent thinking or channel her creativity into other, less desirable arenas where she knows she won't "get caught."

On the other hand, if the significant adult listens carefully to the child's creative ideas, the child learns that she can take the risk of offering her own ideas, that complexity is sometimes a good thing, and that there is room for fresh perspectives and challenges. If the adult feels that part of the assignment is non-negotiable—that the subject of the biography be a real person, or that the report be written—he can honestly talk with the child about his concerns, and together they can negotiate a compromise. The adult may realize that learning is a long-term enterprise and that the positive lessons of divergent thinking may be more important for *this moment* than having the child do a traditional biography book report. The child will still learn important skills from reading a fictional autobiography and performing a play, and a written book report can always be scheduled for another time. In situations like these, the home school parent has much more flexibility than a classroom teacher.

Of course, when children propose the impossible simply as a way to get an adult's attention, something else is going on. When we say green, they say red. When we say yes, they say no. Then when we say no, they say yes. What is going on is not divergent thinking; it is a power struggle. The authors of *Children: The Challenge* (Dreikurs & Soltz, 1992) recommend that in such cases, the most important and often the most difficult thing parents have to do is to realize their own role in such power struggles. For example, when parents act with the mistaken belief that they can *make* their children behave or cooperate, the result is often a knee-jerk rebellion from the child. If, in the example above, the parent thinks that the child is testing limits and is looking for a power struggle, go ahead and call her bluff. Say something like this: "Sure, that sounds like a good plan. When do you think you'll have the play ready to perform? We can even videotape it if you'd like." If the child truly wants to do the play, she will be thrilled. If she was waiting for a different reaction, she will be perplexed. Perhaps she will give the play a try anyway, just for fun, or maybe she will withdraw her suggestion and agree to try the book report. In any case, there is no winner or loser, so there is no need for her to feel threatened.

To encourage and support their children's divergent thinking, home school parents can keep in mind the following principles important to understanding creativity.

○ *Creativity involves the whole person, all of the time.* Creativity is not a separate activity reserved for art projects or story writing but is infused in everything a child does, says, and thinks (Piirto, 1998).

○ *Creativity is inner-directed.* It arises and emanates from within the child (Starko, 1995). Creativity does not consist of prepackaged "creative activities" in which the child colors complex designs or follows someone else's idea of being creative (although these activities may be enjoyable). The focus needs to be on the child's use and development of creativity for the child's needs and goals, and how adults can best facilitate the process.

- *Creativity is complex.* Creative persons often have "dimensions of complexity" that break the boundaries between introversion and extraversion, intelligence and naiveté, playfulness and discipline, fantasy and reality, and passion and objectivity (Csikszentmihalyi, 1996). Parents can keep an open mind about who their child is and offer opportunities to stretch beyond confining labels and expectations.

- *Creativity is a significant and integral part of learning.* Creativity does not preclude rigorous learning or critical thinking or problem solving. Creativity is an integration of thinking, feeling, and sensing and, along with intuition, may be an expression "of the highest level of human intelligence" (Clark, 1997).

Gifted Education

Along with creativity theory, gifted education theory also provides valuable direction and ideas for creative and self-directed home schooling. For parents whose children are divergent and intense thinkers with high levels of sensitivity and self-determination, a home school approach that incorporates gifted education theory is essential. The gifted learner, like any other learner, has specific needs that require understanding and planning. Many home school parents do this intuitively, as they allow their children to do accelerated work in subject areas of strength, or as they provide a wide range of choices for independent study. Home school parents need to consider how best to meet the academic, social, and emotional needs of their gifted child, such as making an extra effort to allow the child more of a say in what they study, or spending more time looking for curriculum alternatives and appropriate peer interaction (Whitmore, 1980). But with practice and time, such home school strategies become almost second nature.

Even if your child has not been formally identified as gifted or if you choose not to label your children as such, gifted education theory can still be an important part of your overall approach to home schooling. Ellen Winner, in *Gifted Children: Myths and Realities*, writes, "when teachers take materials designed for gifted programs and use them in ordinary classrooms, all children thrive" (Winner, 1996, p. 274).

Gifted education experts recommend, as a minimum amount of accommodation to the gifted learner, a differentiated curriculum for all grade levels, thematic instruction, flexible pacing of instruction, and the possibility of skipping levels already mastered (NAGC, 1998; Ronvik, 1993). These principles can easily be part of every home schooled child's education. Some students will move at a faster pace than others, need greater breadth of material to satisfy their thirst for knowledge, or work several grade levels ahead of age peers in some or all subjects. The more highly gifted the child, the more extreme these differences will be.

In home schooling, some children will teach themselves to read at a very young age, or fly through math concepts, or will be ready for independent learning tasks far earlier than other children. It is not unusual for highly gifted children like these to be able to read articles in newspapers at ages six or seven. Or, if they learn to read later than age peers, they may be able to do algebra problems in third grade.

Home schooling based on the following gifted education principles gives all children a chance to thrive according to their unique needs.

○ *Gifted education is differentiated for every child.* Educators trained in needs of gifted children recommend an education that is naturally accelerated when necessary and both enriched and individualized (Eby & Smutny, 1990). This means that a child who learns quickly will not be held back by a lockstep curriculum; a child who has deep and wide interests will be exposed to a banquet of learning experiences; a child who has specific interests and passions will be provided time and resources to pursue them.

○ *Gifted education encourages development of multiple perspectives* within and across areas of knowledge (Van Tassel-Baska, Johnson, & Boyce, 1984). Rarely is knowledge isolated as a subject separate from the rest of human experience. By organizing learning around themes, parents and teachers can help children to make connections with previous knowledge. By asking, "How else might someone view this?" we can encourage tolerance for and understanding of different viewpoints. Learning about the automobile can include a study of the effect the automobile has had on the environment and landscape, as well as some of the issues of automobile safety and fuel economy.

○ *Gifted education is not limited by generic classroom subjects and standards.* Gifted education should allow students to "venture away from the basic curriculum in areas in which they excel" (Strip, 2000, p. 70). Because gifted children can master some academic subjects very quickly, this frees up time for them to pursue individual interests, even if those interests do not seem to fit into the general framework of school curriculum. Parents will find that most interests do include the study of one or more core subjects. For example, when he was nine, our son spent several months on a self-selected study of "classic science fiction" with an emphasis on the short stories of Isaac Asimov. His independent work included reading, writing, and science. During this time, he worked on math, history, and geography for about half an hour each at least every other day. This was enough for him to keep up in those subjects while still allowing him to follow his own strong interests. Other children might be more interested in nature studies or taking apart car engines or learning about dog breeding.

○ *Gifted education does not separate social and emotional needs of the child from academic needs*, but considers them holistically. The needs of the whole child are tied intricately together in a way that meets the child's inner agenda, which is to develop oneself (Roeper, 1996). For example, if a child studies spelling words only with great frustration, one can't say that academic needs have been met and that emotional needs can be addressed later, separately, because then the child is not moving toward wholeness. Instead, the adult should look for the reasons behind the child's frustration and search for possible creative solutions. Perhaps the child's learning style does not match rote learning of a list of words, or the child needs to learn words that are more directly tied to topics of his interest, or the level of challenge of the spelling program is too high or too low, or the child is engaged in a power struggle with the adult. By looking at the needs of the whole child instead of just the need to learn to spell, the adult helps the child move forward in both academic and social-emotional growth.

In addition to principles of creativity and gifted education, experiences of families who have "been there, done that" can offer helpful advice and suggestions to make creative home schooling easier and more effective. The first step that many veteran home schoolers advise for families is, in fact, to take a break.

Take a Break

The most important advice I can give for the first year of home schooling is to take things slowly and not try to cover everything. There is so much adjustment in the first year, especially if you are removing children from public schools. You need to adjust to everyone being home all the time, and you need to learn how to get along, how to cope with each other. It's not a good time to try to "do it all" academically or socially. Take it slowly, and learn to enjoy your family again.

—Gerry, home school parent

When children change from formal schools to home schooling, families go through a period—days, weeks, even months—when they consciously have to remove themselves from school both physically and mentally. Cafi Cohen, author of *And What about College? How Homeschooling Leads to Admissions to the Best Colleges and Universities*, calls it a time of "decompression," a time for children to nullify the negative effects of classroom environments.[10] The negatives include acceptance of a "one-size fits all" curriculum, emphasis on conformity, reliance on extrinsic motivation, obedience to authority, lack of privacy, and dependence on the judgment of others to determine worth (Gatto, 1992).

Before a child can reap the full rewards of a home-based education, these negative lessons and beliefs must be unlearned and replaced with lessons of self-determination, personal responsibility, and joyful learning. During the initial home schooling period, parents can help their children to internalize the following new beliefs.

10   See Cafi Cohen's website at www.homeschoolteenscollege.net.

○ *Learning happens all the time.* Whether in the classroom or in the world, I can choose to learn from the people and the environment around me.

○ *Learning sometimes requires immersion in a single topic or area of interest instead of moving on to the next class or lesson or subject.* Immersion learning is one of the best ways to learn, because it means I am interested in and focused on what I am learning.

○ *Learning requires inquiry and reflection.* I can choose to respect the advice and intentions of adults who are helping me learn, and at the same time, express my own opinions and needs.

○ *Learning is active rather than passive.* I can help choose my own curriculum by expressing my interests and needs. I can also learn *how to learn* by seeking resources, asking questions, looking for connections, and creating things and ideas.

○ *Learning belongs to the learner; it is not for others to determine my worth.* Self-respect depends on knowledge of self and my innate worth as an irreplaceable human being.

○ *Learning requires some quiet space and "off" time,* sometimes just by myself and sometimes with one or two close friends—time when I can daydream, doodle, read, play, be silly, or just do nothing.

A book that promotes such self-directed learning is *The Teenage Liberation Handbook,* by Grace Llewyllen (1998), written for teens and preteens about how home schooling and self-directed learning can offer a high quality education. Llewyllen states, "Before you start your new life, you have to let go of the old one" (p. 125). She calls the initial home schooling period "the vacation" and recommends students do nothing academic for a minimum of one week—longer if necessary. This vacation is necessary; it helps students get to know themselves all over again—their interests, their dislikes, their energy levels throughout the day—without the influence of school schedules or peers. Although *The Teenage Liberation Handbook* is written for the student, parents can also read it for a refreshing new perspective on learning.

Some children will be coming to home school from a negative or painful school experience. Because a formal classroom is simply not a good fit for many intense and creative learners, these children may feel lost, rebellious, depressed, or angry about their learning. For them, taking a break from "school" is absolutely necessary. It usually does not work to go immediately to a full-speed home school schedule. Not only will the parent not have enough time to plan for home school curriculum, but the child will have no time to adjust to a new pace of life. The only exception should be when a child is eager to start learning at home right away, because the child felt held back from learning in the classroom. This was our experience. Our son wanted to start learning at home on the first day, so we began with self-directed learning, careful to follow his lead.

Parents, too, need to decompress during this period. Adults about to be their child's teacher need plenty of time to sort through their beliefs on achievement, education, assessment, and learning. What does a good education mean, now that schools and classroom teachers are no longer setting the standards? What is important for your child to learn? What must be learned in order to keep educational and career options open? How will you measure success in home schooling?

The Sabbatical

You might find it useful to think of the first weeks or months of home schooling as a "sabbatical" from formal, structured school—a time to reflect, to rest, and to rejuvenate. When a teacher takes a sabbatical, he or she does not stop learning. Rather, the learning is of a different nature—self-directed study on chosen topics, leisurely reflection and writing, opportunities for self-knowledge, assessment of the past, and planning for the future. When the sabbatical is over, the teacher returns to former tasks, but with renewed energy, new knowledge, and a new perspective.

The goal during the child's sabbatical will be to re-kindle his passion for learning and to help him begin to see himself as an independent, self-directed learner. He can choose to read a book that is not on a reading list and no one will ask him to discuss, analyze, or write a report about it. He can choose to write a story or poem—just for himself. He can choose to play the piano for two hours, or draw for an entire morning, or take a walk in order to study the colors of leaves. By giving him this freedom, you will be rekindling his curiosity, observation, and discovery. Many parents find that limiting television and computer time helps speed up the process of discovery. You may want to experiment with entire "black out" days, in which everyone in the family, including parents, goes without electronic media.

At first, during their sabbatical, your children may not know how to direct their own time and may appear to do "nothing" or "goof off." However, they may be living in a rich imaginary world, particularly young children. Avid readers may devour books from morning until night. Teens may sleep for hours. But at some point, parents will see their children's old interests come back to life, or new interests emerge. When this occurs, parents will notice their child becoming a bit restless, looking for things to do, or even asking when he or she is going to start learning something.

During the sabbatical time, parents should be busy researching home school options (see recommended reading at the end of the chapter). They should also consider carefully what changes they want to make in their approaches to parenting (review Chapter 6). Depending on state home school laws, parents may wish to plan for several weeks, a semester, or even a year of time off from formal education. Keep in mind that this is not a sabbatical from learning. The parent may wish to think of it as a time of unschooling (see Chapter 9), when the child is using the world as her classroom and is learning according to intrinsic need and interest. When a sabbatical lasts several weeks or longer, you may want to keep a learning log (see Chapter 13), so activities are noted for state and personal records.

Parents can also use the sabbatical as a time to get to know their children all over again, to watch them, to re-learn their preferences and habits. John Holt writes in *How Children Learn*:

> My aim…is to persuade [educators and psychologists] to look at children, patiently, repeatedly, respectfully, and to hold off making theories and judgments about them until they have in their minds what most of them do not now have—a reasonably accurate model of what children are like (1967, p. 173).

In other words, how do your children choose to spend their time when no one is directing their attention? How do they learn? Play? Relax? Challenge themselves? Laugh? Have a good cry? Let off steam?

> *I believe the steps necessary in making home schooling successful start with a variety of different trials with different approaches. An open mind and knowing that tomorrow is another day is a must in the beginning.*
>
> *I know that I struggled with this concept myself in the beginning. I read many recommendations to do this very thing, and I found it hard to do…that is, to take time to get to know your child and let your child find out more about himself.*
>
> *Gifted children with a strong interest in one specific area will most likely gravitate to that interest, which is a great way to start home school learning. Eventually, you get a feel for how quickly things can be learned or "covered" and how much time there really is to let go. Enjoy the absence of struggles that existed in the former regular school day before trying to add new ones.*
>
> —Kathleen, home school parent

The length of your sabbatical will be affected in part by how long you plan to home school. If you plan to home school long-term—several years or more—you have the freedom to allow for a relatively longer sabbatical period. If you plan to home school for only a year, you may need to keep a closer eye on what your children will need to have covered academically before entering or re-entering school.

You may also choose to take a sabbatical for a year as a way to take a break from school, during which time you focus on self-directed learning. Some families use a year off from school to travel, so as to get a different kind of education and a fresh perspective on life and learning. See *A Family Year Abroad: How to Live Outside the Borders*, by Chris Westphal (2001), and *No More School: An American's Experiment with Education*, by Howard Rowland (1975), for examples of families who have traveled abroad with young, intense learners.

The Sabbatical and Giftedness

Whether you think of it as decompression time or a break from formal academic lessons, the need for a sabbatical may be greater—and the period may be longer—for families with a gifted child, because they must rethink not only their beliefs about education, but also their understanding of what giftedness means for their family and how giftedness will affect and guide their children's education. The children, who may be emotionally and intellectually bruised from inappropriate school practices, may need time to heal.

Parents whose children have been in school can be confused about what gifted education should be. Carol Strip, in *Helping Gifted Children Soar* (2000), writes that an expanded curriculum for gifted students does *not* mean MOTS (More Of The Same)—more worksheets, more busywork, or more analytical reasoning at the expense of practical life skills. She advises further that gifted children should not be expected to excel in every subject. Parents new to home schooling may need to de-brief themselves from the MOTS attitude or the idea that their gifted child should always "close the gap" between areas of strength and areas of struggle. Gifted children need plenty of room to find and explore individual passions and interests and, like all children, may be "just average" in one or several areas.

Jessie, home school mother of two, offers sabbatical advice based on her experience with her gifted children:

> *My son attended kindergarten and half of first grade. It took me two years after only kindergarten and half of first grade to "bounce" my son back. My daughter is as good as new, because she has always been at home.*
>
> *Take a break; don't even think about skimping there. Expect the first year to be hard, and know that each year after that gets easier. Remember that social contact is as important as learning the three R's, so plan on a lot of your time being used that way. Know that kids need to be taught social skills, that this is part of the whole. Find as many home schoolers in your area as possible before you begin. If possible, meet with them socially a few times so you and your child can have friends from the start.*
>
> —Jessie, home school parent

Key Points

☑ There is no one right way to home school.

☑ Taking a break is an important first step for new home school families.

☑ Creative home schooling encourages parents to design a home schooling approach that is unique to their family's needs.

☑ Creative home schooling presupposes that inner-directed creativity is an integral and significant part of a child's education.

☑ Creative home schooling is based on principles of gifted education, such as differentiation for every child, multiple perspectives, interdisciplinary study, expansion of standard curriculum, and integration of social and emotional development.

Questions and Activities for Reflection

1. Spend a full day with your child in which you have no expectations for learning or planned activities. Offer your child the chance to play games, take a nature walk, go to the library, listen to music, or whatever else sounds like fun.

2. Think back to your own childhood.

    ○ How much unstructured time did you have to play or do as you pleased?
    ○ As a child, did you wish you had more or less time alone?
    ○ Did you enjoy those times when no one controlled your activities?
    ○ How did you spend that time?
    ○ Do you wish an adult had taken a greater interest in what you were doing?

3. Think about your day-to-day life as a parent now. Do you have any time that is reserved just for you—time when you can think without interruption or choose activities you enjoy?

4. Imagine you have time alone in your home for an afternoon.

    ○ How do you feel? Relaxed? Anxious?
    ○ What will you do?
    ○ How can you create private time for yourself?

> *Learning to use time alone, instead of escaping from it,*
> *is especially important in our early years.*
> *Teenagers who can't bear solitude disqualify themselves*
> *from later carrying out adult tasks that require serious mental preparation.*
>
> —Mihaly Csikszentmihalyi
> *Flow: The Psychology of Optimal Experience*

Home Schooling Reading Lists

Sabbatical Reading List

Csikszentmihalyi, Mihaly (1990). *Flow: The Psychology of Optimal Experience.* Harper & Row.

Csikszentmihalyi, Mihaly (1996). *Creativity: Flow and the Psychology of Discovery and Invention.* HarperCollins.

Elkind, David (1988). *The Hurried Child: Growing Up Too Fast Too Soon.* Addison-Wesley.

Gardner, Howard (1991). *The Unschooled Mind: How Children Think and How Schools Should Teach.* Basic Books.

Gatto, John Taylor (1992). *Dumbing Us Down: The Hidden Curriculum of Compulsory Schooling.* New Society Publishers.

Guterson, David (1992). *Family Matters: Why Homeschooling Makes Sense.* Harcourt Brace Jovanovich.

Holt, John (1967). *How Children Learn.* Pitman Publishing.

Holt, John (1995). *How Children Fail.* Delacorte Press/Seymour Lawrence.

Holt, John (1995). *Freedom and Beyond.* Boynton/Cook Heinemann.

Illich, Ivan (1983). *Deschooling Society.* Harper Colophon.

Kohn, Alfie (1999). *The Schools Our Children Deserve: Moving beyond Traditional Classrooms and "Tougher Standards."* Houghton Mifflin.

Llewellyn, Grace (1998). *The Teenage Liberation Handbook: How to Quit School and Get a Real Life and Education.* Lowry House.

Moore, Dorothy, & Moore, Raymond, et al (1979). *School Can Wait.* Brigham Young University Press.

Smith, Frank (1998). *The Book of Learning and Forgetting.* Teachers College Press.

Books about Mentors and Community-Based Education

Albert, David (1999). *And the Skylark Sings with Me: Adventures in Homeschooling and Community-Based Education.* New Society Publishers.

Sheffer, Susannah (1992). *Writing Because We Love To: Homeschoolers at Work.* Boynton/Cook Heinemann.

Books about Specific Families' Experiences

Colfax, David, & Colfax, Micki (1992). *Hard Times in Paradise*. Warner.

Colfax, David, & Colfax, Micki (1998). *Homeschooling for Excellence*. Warner.

Dobson, Linda (2000). *Homeschoolers' Success Stories: 15 Adults and 12 Young People Share the Impact that Homeschooling Has Made on Their Lives.* Prima Publishing.

Lande, Nancy (1996). *Homeschooling: A Patchwork of Day: Share a Day with 30 Home Schooling Families.* WindyCreek Press.

Leistico, Agnes (1997). *I Learn Better by Teaching Myself; and, Still Teaching Ourselves.* Holt Associates.

Llewellyn, Grace (1993). *Real Lives: Eleven Teenagers Who Don't Go to School.* Lowry House.

Llewellyn, Grace (1996). *Freedom Challenge: African American Home-schoolers.* Lowry House.

Riley, Dan (1994). *The Dan Riley School for a Girl.* Houghton Mifflin.

Internet and Web Resources

Ann Zeise's A to Z Home's Cool Homeschooling Website
www.gomilpitas.com/homeschooling

Eclectic Homeschool On-line
http://eho.org

The Homeschool Zone
www.homeschoolzone.com

Jon's Home School Resource Page
www.midnightbeach.com/hs

At Home with Home Schoolers

Olivia, Age 21, Graduate Student

"I asked my mother to home school me."

Learning at Home and at School

I was home schooled for a total of eight years, including second, fourth, fifth, and seventh grade through eleventh grade. Age three to five, I attended two kindergarten programs, one in the morning and one in the evening. When I transferred to a French Immersion School at age five, I was required to complete another year of kindergarten before proceeding to the first grade (all in French). While the language training at the French Immersion School was excellent, I took a bus at 7:30 in the morning with an unpleasant hour-long commute and did not return home until 4:30 in the afternoon. I asked my mother to home school me for second grade for two reasons: (1) the stress of the school day, and (2), the positive example of some neighbors who were home schooling.

During second grade at home, I read from the *McGuffey Readers*, studied Spencerian penmanship, and used *Ray's Arithmetic*, all of which were used in one-room schoolhouses in the 1800s. While I enjoyed the year, my mother and I were both unsure about my progress; was I at the same level as other students my age? For this reason, my mother sent me to an elementary school for third grade. Our question was answered. I received all A's in my schoolwork and participated in various programs for gifted learners. While the year was a positive one, I again asked to be home schooled for fourth grade because my mother was expecting a baby and I missed the time spent with my family.

Over the next two years, we followed a similar home school program, while increasing the level of difficulty. My mother convinced me to attend school for sixth grade; she wanted me to see what I was missing so that I could make an informed decision about being home schooled for middle school or high school. Once again, I excelled academically. However, two students in the class who were experiencing personal problems made the year especially difficult for me by constantly teasing me. One of them came to visit me four years later to apologize for her actions during sixth grade. Their actions during my sixth grade year made it easier for me to choose home schooling for seventh and eighth grades. While I visited various high schools at the end of eighth grade, I again chose home schooling.

As I grew older, my home schooling routine became more independent. My mother trusted me to accomplish the tasks that I set for myself. At the same time, I began to need some outside help as I attempted more advanced mathematics. My mother found students from a local university to come on a weekly basis to help me with problems I found particularly difficult to solve.

During my high-school years, I set goals for the progress I hoped to make each day—one lesson of math, one chapter in each of the books I was reading, etc. While I often attempted to make a schedule, I found it was more effective to determine a number of pages to be read or exercises to be done. In that way, I could do some work and then help my sisters with their lessons, or practice the piano, or help around the house. This flexibility helped me enjoy learning; it also helped prepare me for the independent learning style required in college. When I was 16, I spent two months at a high school in the Republic of San Marino, located on the east coast of Italy; there, I audited classes in philosophy, art history, theology, history, Greek, Latin, French, and Italian literature. At age 17, I took the SATs and was accepted at Marquette University.

While home schooling, I participated in many outside-the-home activities. During my elementary years, the Gifted and Talented coordinator at the elementary school continued to invite me to participate in Young Authors' Conferences. Later, my family helped form a club for several home schooling families in our area. We called it the C.A.T.S. Club, or Children And Teachers Socializing. As the oldest member, I adapted, directed, and acted in a play we presented to over 150 people; I created a role for all the other club members, ages three to nine, highlighting their talents. We also took "field trips" as a group. In addition, I became very active at my church, where I served as lector, youth representative on the Parish Council, and co-coordinator of the Prayer Network. My sisters and I also visited a local nursing home regularly and made friends with some of the residents.

On Being Gifted

I consider myself to be a gifted learner because I strive to do my best in all areas of study. I enjoy learning and have been blessed with the ability to do so. In addition, my parents have provided me with exceptional opportunities to develop my talents, and I am grateful for the privilege of receiving an education.

Giftedness, in my opinion, is often linked to one's desire to learn. I have always been enthusiastic about learning. While I was home schooling, this enthusiasm led me to pursue certain interests, including various languages. I read Alessandro Manzoni's *I Promessi Sposi*, an 800-page Italian classic, aloud to my mother in Italian. I enjoyed the book so much that I proceeded to read an English translation aloud to my little sisters. I learned French by reading the stories of Guy de Maupassant aloud to my mother and discussing their meaning with her. In addition, I audited Greek 001 and 002 at Marquette University during my high school years. My interest in creative writing led me to attend various continuing education courses for adults offered by a local technical college and Marquette University when I was 13 and 16 years old. Academically, these activities have enhanced my college experience greatly. Such experiences also helped me develop emotionally.

The challenging aspect of giftedness for me has been its social impact; sometimes other students are not truly interested in learning as much as possible, but in just getting through their required courses. I find that some students resent someone who invests serious effort in learning. At the college level, I experienced this negative response much less, as many more students there begin to enjoy learning for its own sake.

The Best and Worst Things about Home Schooling

In my opinion, some of the best things about home schooling were its relaxed pace and its flexibility. I was able to pursue special interest areas, like foreign languages and writing. The opportunity to spend more time with my family and to forge friendships with my parents and sisters was priceless. In addition, I believe that home schooling helped me develop socially, since it allowed me to interact with younger children and with adults instead of relating primarily to other students my own age.

Interestingly enough, one of the most difficult things about home schooling was also its flexibility, because it was challenging to stay on task and achieve the goals I set for myself. Sometimes it was difficult to measure my progress. Finally, without the formal structure of a school setting, I had to learn to create my own opportunities for socialization.

How I Prepared for College

To prepare for the rigors of a formal classroom education, I completed all of the tests that were included in the materials that I used to study. I often timed myself in order to develop speed and focus. One skill which especially helped me at the college level was stream-of-consciousness writing; I learned about it in several writing courses, and I continued to practice on my own as a home schooler. It greatly increased my speed and coherence on essay examinations.

While I worried about my preparation for college, I actually found that being home schooled made many things easier for me as a college student. I was able to manage my time well since I was already used to studying independently. I was eager to learn and to do my best in each class. My foreign language background provided insights into the subjects I studied. I continued to pursue the same interests that had motivated me as a home schooler, obtaining a double major in classical languages and English literature, as well as a minor in theology.

I believe that a "good education" not only provides a student with a well-rounded base, but also allows that student to pursue his or her own interests. Every student has certain talents, which should be focused on and developed so that each student can train his or her unique voice. Home schooling encourages independent research; if a certain topic interests you, you have the time to pursue it in depth. In this way, genuine learning occurs. A good education teaches you to learn; it is your job to continue learning as long as you live.

Advice for Other Home School Students

I would suggest that students who are considering home schooling make sure they can work well with their parents. Even if they complete most of their work independently, it is important to have a good relationship with their primary instructors. While I think it is essential to make consistent progress in basic subjects, I would encourage new home schoolers to explore their interests and to discover what they really enjoy. Finally, I think that home schoolers should incorporate service to others as part of their curriculum; so much can be learned by visiting the elderly, for example. By socializing with people of all ages, home schoolers can gain insights into what is important in life.

I would consider home schooling my own children some day, even if only for a year or two. Home schooling gives children a chance to learn at their own pace. Instead of being forced to move at the speed of the class, the home schooled child has an opportunity to find his or her own rhythm and to discover his or her own talents. In addition, home schooling creates a deeper bond between parents and children as they learn and grow together. Home schooling can turn learning into an adventure instead of an exhausting routine. Yet the success of home schooling depends largely on the personality of the child; some children probably do need the structure of school in order to learn effectively.

I would like to thank my parents for being courageous enough to allow me to home school. I would like to thank them for their patience and their encouragement, for all the learning opportunities that they created for me, and for their faith in my ability to learn and to succeed.

8 Curriculum Matters

In life's curriculum students are faced each day with only glimpses of the pieces of things which they have to assemble and reassemble into a comprehensive, personally meaningful order, one that accomplishes something not just for its own sake, but also for the greater good. Schools, and especially schools for gifted students, need to organize curriculum creatively, and not just in the arts, so that students have not only the opportunity, but also feel an urgent responsibility to construct meanings that are elegant solutions to worthy problems. This is the best possible curriculum for them, for us, and for our future.[11]

—Ken Seward (1998)

Every home school parent is asked more than once, "Whose curriculum are you using?" The questioner means: "What math texts? What social studies program? What book(s) for reading?" The person usually assumes that there is one best company that supplies curriculum materials to home school parents. The answers to questions about curriculum for home schoolers may come as a surprise to many readers.

First, what is curriculum? Is curriculum different for each learner? The word *curriculum* comes from the Latin root *currere*, which means *course of action*. Your child's curriculum is simply a course of study or outline of topics to be learned. An afternoon in the park talking about the first signs of spring or a book read in bed is as much a part of the curriculum as a science chapter read at a desk in school.

---

11   Reprinted by permission of *Roeper Review*, Volume 21 (2), ©1998, P.O. Box 329, Bloomfield Hills, MI 48303.

Unschoolers—those home school families who follow their child's own leads and interests—have a curriculum, though it may be hard to explain and can change from day to day. Other home school families have a curriculum that consists of different materials and activities for each subject. Distance learning and special programs are part of the curriculum. Music, karate, and other regular activities are, too.

Some home school families do use packaged or "canned" curriculum, in which a company provides nearly all of the material and guidance needed for a particular year of study; however, parents of gifted and highly creative children don't find such materials very useful unless substantially revised.

A child who learns differently from most children—including the gifted child—will probably *not* have academic needs met by a generic curriculum designed for average learners, any more than that gifted child will have social and emotional needs met by traditional beliefs about fitting into a same-age group. He needs curriculum with sufficient rigor and challenge, as well as opportunities to interact with a mixture of age groups. While packaged materials, traditional textbooks, and classroom-designed standards *can and do* have a role in home schooling, they are by no means the only or the most effective pathway to successful home-based education.

Carol Strip (2000), in *Helping Gifted Children Soar*, suggests that the standard school curriculum may actually be harmful to gifted children, stunting social and emotional growth and acting as a barrier to further learning. Because schools must find an orderly way to move children from grade to grade, standards and learner outcomes are written for the hypothetical average child, both in terms of learning style and ability. Classroom practices and materials are designed for groups of 20 or more children and are by no means the best way to learn outside classroom walls. Most home schooling advocates agree that standard school curriculum is the optimal curriculum for few if any students, because it forces children—each of whom has unique and individual needs—into a one-size-fits-all mold. One parent, considering home schooling her three children, believes, "Someday we will see that it is the classroom that is holding children back."

As a home school parent, you are about to teach one or more children whom you know intimately and whose educational needs and preferences will lead to a truly individualized curriculum. Individualized curriculum for each child will, of course, depend upon several factors:

- Your own knowledge base, curiosity and comfort levels.
- Your children's goals and needs.
- Your budget.
- The extent to which you will use grade levels.

Prior to making any major purchases or mapping out an extensive plan of study for your child, take some time to review each of the following factors as they relate to your family, and realize that no packaged curriculum will be able to meet all of your child's needs.

Parent Knowledge, Curiosity, and Comfort Levels

Your own education background, travel and life experiences, interests, and comfort levels with particular subjects will greatly influence both the subject content and the kinds of materials and approaches you use. For example, interest-based and child-led learning, sometimes called unschooling, will be most effective if you take an active interest in learning along with your child. When your child asks questions you cannot answer (which will happen sooner, rather than later), you simply find an outside mentor in the subject or in other ways help your child to study the content in greater depth. Whatever home school approach you use, it is a good idea to start with a subject area in which you are comfortable.

Where to Begin?

If you have an area of expertise such as science, math, history, literature, or foreign language, you may want to begin with that. For example, if you have a science background and are comfortable with science, you may want to customize your child's course of study in science. When your child asks questions about a more advanced science concept, you will be able to facilitate more in-depth learning through your own knowledge and without much help from other resources. On the other hand, if you remember little from your science classes and are uncomfortable with the subject, you may wish to use a science tutor, an on-line science course, or a current text that offers a good teacher's edition.

In our family, both parents have literature backgrounds, and our home is filled with books. Library visits are a favorite family activity, and we spend many hours each week in leisure reading. We have been able to provide a strong and effective language arts curriculum for our child by reading to him, guiding his reading choices, starting a book discussion group for home schooled children, and both encouraging and facilitating his writing. However, if you are uncomfortable with language arts curricula and the idea of helping your child learn to read, speak, and write with fluency, you may want a comprehensive language arts program or text as a guide.

In our case, we put extra effort and thought into subject areas with which we were not so familiar. Workshops at nature centers and visits to science museums help to address the fact that neither parent has a strong background in science. As our son grows older, I will need to put even greater effort into finding appropriate science materials and programs, while other areas, especially language arts and social sciences, will be easier to plan for. I have discovered that community classes for children through a local university, as well as group physical activities such as open gym and plenty of free time to play with other children, help our son, an only child, to experience socializing and playing in a group.

Your Children's Goals and Needs

Just as your own interests and skill areas will affect your home school approach and curriculum, your child's interests, goals, learning strengths, and unique learning needs will have a great influence on the materials and course of study that will work best for your family. Consider two dissimilar home schooled children with different learning styles, both age 11, both studying math. The first student, a math whiz, sees the world in numbers and wants to be a scientist when she grows ups. This student will enjoy a math program that allows her to move quickly through basic concepts and delve into complex college-preparatory mathematics sooner rather than later. She may get involved in distance learning programs such as Stanford University's Education Program for Gifted Youth (EPGY), or she may use a workbook program such as *Singapore Math* she can complete at her own pace. The text that will work best for her will depend on her level of comfortable independent learning as well as the amount of in-depth explanation she requires. Gifted students with strong math skills often need rapid acceleration in math—that is, higher level work and a faster pace than their age peers.

Our other 11-year-old student is not interested in math; he prefers to read fiction, study history, and write stories. While achievement scores show that he is capable of doing advanced math, he prefers a more leisurely approach. A language-based math program such as Harold Jacobs's *Mathematics: A Human Endeavor* may satisfy his learning needs while preserving an interest in math. CD-ROM math programs such as *Math Workshop Deluxe* or *Geometry Blaster*, while not rigorous enough for a math whiz, may be perfect for our humanities-interest student. Fulcrum Press's *Exploring Math with Books Kids Love* has ideas for how to integrate middle school math with a child's love of literature.

A child's own interests and goals are as important as his or her aptitude. Although a child with obvious talent in math should be encouraged to develop that area, he or she should not be forced into an early career track just because of potential. David Albert (1999) suggests that it is a mistake for parents or teachers to push the gifted child hard in areas of seeming potential: "There's nothing wrong with this if it is what the child really chooses. But I know too many 40-year-old gifted children who were pushed into math and science because they were good at it, who wake up discovering they would have preferred to be dancers, or mental health counselors, or horse trainers."[12]

12   Albert, David, personal interview, March 2000.

Your Family Budget

Is home schooling expensive? Yes, it can be. But it doesn't have to be. It depends on your definition of expensive, your family budget, and your children's particular needs. Whether home schooling is considered expensive is largely a matter of how individual families define the term, as the following examples show.

> *Well, so far, I wouldn't say it's expensive if I consider that our only other alternative was private school. I would say costs are significant, but they don't have to be. We spend $2,000-$3,000 a year for one school-age child. This includes books and the costs of lessons and special classes.*
>
> —Barbara, home school parent

> *Both of our girls really need to be doing more challenging work than what a standard curriculum offers, especially Sarah. Her challenge comes from classes offered on the Internet and correspondence courses. They cost money. So do the textbooks she needs to challenge her. Both girls are stimulated by outside activities that encourage skill development, such as computer classes or music lessons. These cost money. Even unschooling cost us a lot of money when they were younger. They were interested in so many things, and we were always buying supplies for various activities. I know some people say they can home school a child for under $200 a year, but we have never been able to do it for less than $700.*
>
> —Joan, home school parent

Here are some additional responses to the question of whether or not parents find home schooling to be expensive.

> *We spend about $600 per year for curriculum and supplemental materials, averaging about $200 per child. We are fortunate to live in a large metropolitan area with an excellent library system, so many needs can be met through the library. In a large family like ours, there is also an economy of scale, since many materials can be reused with other children. For instance, this year we spent $200 for a high quality microscope, but as each child uses it, the cost per child decreases. When we look at the cost of private school and the advantages of home schooling over private school, home schooling seems a bargain by comparison.*
>
> —Nina, home school parent

Actually, for us, home schooling is less expensive than participating in public school. When I think of the money we donated to the school (it seemed like there was a fundraiser every month), we're actually ahead of the game. And don't forget the back-to-school supply list. The other thing, especially with girls, is the wardrobe. Our clothing needs are now very basic, as we don't need to compete with peer pressure or buy uniforms.

—Anne, home school parent

We find home schooling to be rather expensive for our family for several reasons. Our local library doesn't carry many of the books we'd like to read or study. We live in Canada, so as a result, anything we order from the United States is expensive due to the exchange rate, which currently favors the U.S. We find that many of the less expensive programs and curricula and books do not meet the demands of our voracious and asynchronous learners. The rate at which we go through materials leaves us always looking for more. It's not very often that we find the right book at the right level with appropriate content, so I feel a slight thrill when we do…but then the book is completed in one or two days and we have to begin the hunt all over again.

—Joyce, home school parent

Materials are not that expensive. The library is free and resources there are abundant. The main expense for our family is the reduction in income that we have taken in order to home school. I still work part-time, but I have lost a lot of income, since I was working as a well-paid consultant. Looking at it that way, home schooling is costing more than any private school would cost us. But I believe that it is still worth it. We still have enough income to live comfortably, and my child is happy. I am sure that it is better in the long view to home school your child than to leave him a bigger estate. No amount of money in the world can buy happy childhood memories.

—Jon, home school parent

Home School with One Income or Two?

If your family income is diminished as a result of home schooling, as when one parent gives up an outside job, consider that a high quality education at home can be achieved without costing a lot of money. Where one family might spend thousands of dollars on distance education, summer programs, and expensive books and materials, another family may achieve the same results with less expensive options such as adult mentors from the community, free Internet independent study programs, local classes organized by home school parents, and supplies purchased second-hand or made at home. If you are not able to afford tuition for your child to take advanced calculus at age 16, there are other ways for him to continue learning and to stay challenged. Perhaps he can audit the class in a community college or work as an unpaid intern at an engineering firm for a couple of years. Educating a highly gifted child does not have to be expensive, and you do not need to go into debt to meet your child's academic needs. Parent or child or both can usually find creative ways to continue academic and social-emotional growth.

Although most home school families are two-parent, single-income families, it is not always necessary for a second parent to give up a paying job. Many of the families interviewed for this book have two incomes. One parent might work part-time and schedule work hours so that a parent is always home. Many careers lend themselves to working from home—teaching music lessons, consulting, computer data entry, writing, tutoring, or running a web-based business.

Keisha's family looks for creative ways to accommodate two jobs:

I am an adjunct professor at a local university. I teach one class per term, and it is always a one-day-a-week, three-hour evening class. I rotate between two courses and have been doing so for the last two and one-half years, so I've got my routine down pretty well. I also have my own one-person consulting company, and I work out of my basement. The work is sporadic but pays well. For example, I have two contracts about to start in the next month that will require a half-time commitment on my part and possibly three-quarter time through the summer. In summer, my children will be in a daycare/camp at the same place where both attended kindergarten.

We try to get our academic work done before noon. After that, my son can do as he pleases for the most part, while I do my contract work or teaching prep. At 3:30, I take him to after-school daycare, where he sees friends and plays.

My husband provides additional support. He owns a retail establishment, but his schedule is such that he is home all day three days during the week, Tuesday through Thursday. If I have a meeting or work commitments, he can help out with the children. Additionally, my in-laws live 40 minutes away and can watch the children at times.

—Keisha, home school parent

Single-parent, single-income home school families are less common, but they do exist. If you feel that home schooling is important for your child or children and you are a single parent who must work, consider possible creative and flexible ways to home school before assuming that home schooling is not an option for your family. Is there a room or space at your workplace where your child can do independent study while you work? Can you arrange work from home part- or full-time? Can you use childcare during work hours and home school either early in the morning or in the evening? Many home school families find that two or three hours of uninterrupted, focused academic work is all that is needed to accomplish as much as is usually learned in a full school day. Do you have relatives or friends who are willing to provide both childcare and tutoring or oversight while your children do independent studies or computer-based learning?

Single home school parents can find support and advice at the VegSource Single-Parent Message Board: www.vegsource.com/homeschool/singleparent/index.html.

Try Before You Buy

One budget-saving strategy is to look and wait before you buy. A common mistake of new home school parents is to buy too much material too soon, thinking the right curriculum or educational game or other product will be the answer and therefore must be purchased right away. Another common pitfall is to purchase material before you have a clear idea of what kind of learner your child is or what kind of home schooling approach will work best for your family. Many home school families have enough unused and unwanted curriculum materials in their garage to open a resale store!

It is best to spend a lot of time exploring options. The sabbatical period is perfect for this (see Chapter 7). View samples on-line whenever possible. Request print catalogs to browse at your leisure. Ask about return policies before you buy, and always ask for recommendations from other home school parents whose opinions you value. Ask your home school friends if you can borrow and try their materials for a week. Browse bookstores, teacher supply stores, and home school curriculum fairs to get a preview of materials before you buy. Used book stores often carry textbooks, games, and videos in addition to paper and hardbound books in many categories, including encyclopedias, books on tape, magazines, and music. Many on-line sites offer used curriculum materials for sale as well. If you know other home school families who have children with similar interests and abilities, consider purchasing materials as a group.

Not every resource needs to be purchased. Many home school families use the library almost exclusively as their source of home school materials. Talk to your librarian about starting a home school bookshelf or resource area. One home school parent found that her library was willing to order almost any book she needed that the library didn't already have as long as she put in the request (called a patron request). College and university libraries often have a wide range of curriculum materials available for their teacher education majors. If you have no affiliation with a university, you may be able to acquire borrowing privileges by paying a small yearly fee.

Getting a Handle on Home School Costs

Brainstorm as a family about how much money per month, semester, or year you plan to budget for home schooling. Keep a record of school-related expenses for a few months, then review your earlier estimate to see if it is reasonable. As your children grow older or develop strong interests or talents in an area requiring special tutoring or instruction, you may need to adjust your budget. If you were paying private school tuition prior to home school, consider the total yearly cost of tuition, uniforms, lab fees, field trips, etc. that you were paying. If your family could comfortably pay this amount, it may be reasonable to allocate the same amount to home school. If your children previously attended public school, consider costs of school clothes and supplies, lunches, school fund drives, teacher gifts, and miscellaneous fees. The total of these items can provide a baseline figure for home school costs.

Check your state home school laws and local school system guidelines to see if the guidelines allow home schoolers to attend school part-time. Many states allow home schooled children to take one or more classes at their local public school. This may be a good way to address academic needs that you would otherwise meet through private lessons or tutors.[13]

When figuring the cost of home schooling, be sure to make a distinction between expenses you would bear regardless of whether your child was home schooling versus those specific to home schooling. For example, if your child will take gymnastics lessons whether home schooled or not, that cost is not included. If those gymnastics lessons are to take the place of a school P.E. class, then they can be considered a home school cost.

Ask bookstores and teacher supply stores if they offer a discount for home school parents. Many do.

If you can't afford the manipulatives and other hands-on learning materials you'd like to have, make your own, or better yet, challenge your children to make them. One home school family made a three-dimensional model of the human body from papier-mâché using one of the children as a mold, sponges for the lungs, thick "finger jello" for the liver, colored yarn and string for the vascular, nervous, and lymphatic systems, and so on. A commercial model from a teacher supply store costs from $50 to $100 dollars.

Before you buy, ask yourself if the same learning outcomes can be obtained from materials you already have. For example, instead of play money, use the real thing. Use checkers, coins, beans, or empty coin rolls as math manipulatives for computation. Make tangrams from cardboard or construction paper, and math manipulatives from small paper boxes, marbles, dried beans, buttons, pieces from

---

13   Some home school advocates advise against participation in such tax-funded classes or programs because of an implicit threat to home school freedoms, while other home school advocates encourage a fuller cooperation between schools and home school families. To learn more about each side of the issue, read articles by Helen Hegener and Susan and Larry Kaseman in past issues of *Home Education Magazine* (www.home-ed-magazine.com) about unnecessary regulation, and see David Guterson's book *Family Matters: Why Homeschooling Makes Sense* (1992), for reasons to seek a new kind of education system that encourages innovative school-home cooperation.

old board games, and other odds and ends. Measuring cups, scales, timers, funnels, whisks, food coloring, baking soda and vinegar, chopsticks, and small glass jars to use as beakers, all from your kitchen, make a treasure trove of science equipment. Gifted children do not necessarily require expensive materials; they are often able to do more and go farther with whatever is available.

The book *Homeschooling on a Shoestring: A Jam Packed Guide*, by Melissa L. Morgan and Judith Waite Allee, contains a wealth of suggestions for ways to make use of community resources, preview curriculum materials, and get a top-notch education at home without spending a lot of money.

For home schooling inexpensively using the Internet, look for the book *Homeschool Your Child for Free: More than 1,200 Smart, Effective, and Practical Resources for Home Education on the Internet and Beyond*, by Laura Maery Gold and Joan M. Zielinki.

Home school consultant Kathi Kearney offers numerous ways to use the Internet to educate home schooled children. See her Free Firewood site at www.ignitethefire.com/freefirewood.html.

Finally, it is probably wise to keep in mind that sometimes we *do* get what we pay for, and in the long-term, some educational investments will pay for themselves in time saved, better quality, and effectiveness. Because gifted children often learn better with a variety of approaches and materials that can be easily adjusted for pace and level, basic grade-level curriculum materials may not be as useful as curricula for gifted students that is carefully designed, tested, and updated. Extra money spent on a high-quality, multi-media foreign language program may be a wiser long-term choice than trying to piece a program together from less expensive sources. On the other hand, if a parent already knows the foreign language, or if the child is highly motivated to learn the language, the more expensive program may not be necessary. Use your own knowledge and abilities, family budget, and children's needs as a guide.

Special Section: Working with Your Librarian

A home school family's best friend is a good librarian. Work to build a good working relationship with your local librarian or children's librarian. Introduce yourself and your children to your librarian early on so you know each other by name. Help your children to feel comfortable approaching the librarian with questions. If you belong to a local home school group, invite the librarian to attend a meeting, or set up a meeting when your group members and the librarian can talk about needs of local home school families.

Home school parents and children can make the librarian's job easier by volunteering. Duties vary by library but might include shelving books, leading book discussions, helping with fund drives, assisting new computer users, and reading to young children. Another idea for your library is to design and print inexpensive bookmarks for the children's room that include lists of good books to read or "Top Ten Reading Lists" for different reading levels, genres, or interests.

By showing that they are committed to high quality library services for all patrons, home school families can build a level of trust and mutual support with their librarian. Home school families should also provide a positive example by avoiding behaviors that make the librarian's job unnecessarily difficult (Masters, 1996), such as:

○ Objecting to age ratings and materials on evolution and the occult.

○ Checking out all of the materials on a certain subject.

○ Making too many requests for service, software, hardware, curricula, and textbooks at once.

○ Demanding a lot of personalized service.

○ Using out-of-print booklists.

○ Neglecting supervision of children in the library.

Remember that the library offers materials with a wide range of perspectives, that other children both at home and in school may need to do research on any given topic and may need access to resources, that limited library budgets usually prevent extensive ordering of new books or hiring of new staff, that out of print books are sometimes difficult and expensive to order, and that all young children in libraries need adult supervision and should respect the needs and rights of fellow patrons.

Another way to assist your local librarian is to offer to put together a Home School Resource File of information to be used by the librarian and patrons. Individual home school families or home school groups can gather the following resources in a sturdy, large folder or expandable "accordion" file (Brostrom, 1995). Here are some ideas for the folder[14]:

○ General information on home schooling—different styles, methods, positive and negative aspects, personal experience anecdotes (these can be in the form of original articles or magazine articles and newspaper clippings)

○ Current bibliographies of home school books and other resources (highlight titles owned by your library)

○ Copies of state laws regarding compulsory education and home schooling

○ Samples of compliance forms required in some states for home school registration

○ Phone numbers and addresses for the state department of education

○ Local public school rules and regulations, and legal cases involving home education

○ Curriculum guides from the local public school district

○ Phone numbers and addresses of home school liaison and curriculum administrators employed by the local school districts

○ Lists of local, regional, statewide, and national home education groups

14   Resource list reprinted by permission of the author, David C. Brostrom, from his book, *A Guide to Homeschooling for Librarians*, 1995.

- Local home schooling support group leaders

- Home school publisher and supply house catalogs

- Samples of home schooling newsletters, magazines, and articles

- Handouts with "electronic connections"—home schooling discussion and news groups on the Internet, local and regional electronic bulletin boards, and companies that sell educational software

- Articles on teaching theory and differing educational viewpoints

- Phone numbers and addresses of people authorized to give accredited tests in your state (some states require standardized testing)

- Library card application procedures and brochures spelling out special services for educators

- Library volunteer forms

- Questionnaire from the librarian to library patrons asking for recommendations regarding library programs, services, policies, and procedures

- Information on high school equivalency tests and college entrance examinations

You can present your librarian with one or more copies of the completed Home School Resource File along with a donated copy of this book or other home schooling books. A good book to donate is *A Guide to Homeschooling for Librarians*, by David C. Brostrom (1995), published by Highsmith Press. Brostrom offers a positive description of home schooling and provides numerous ideas and examples of how libraries can better serve the needs of the growing home school population. Home school parents or groups can also present their librarians with a "wish list" of curriculum reference materials, available for check-out, that can be used by home school parents and other families, as well as classroom teachers. If the library budget is tight, your home school group can offer to raise money to get the collection started. Below are some good books and magazines to include on an Educators' Reference Shelf in your local library.

About Teaching Mathematics: A K-8 Resource, second edition, by Marilyn Burns, Solutions Publications, 2000.

American History through Earth Science, by Craig A. Munsart, Teacher Ideas Press, 1997.

Art in Chemistry; Chemistry in Art, by Barbara R. Greenberg and Dianne Patterson, Teacher Ideas Press, 1998.

Book Links: Connecting Books, Libraries, and Classrooms, a magazine published by the American Library Association.

Cooking Up U.S. History: Recipes and Research to Share with Children, second edition, by Suzanne I. Barchers and Patricia C. Marden, Teacher Ideas Press, 1999.

Discovering Geography of North America with Books Kids Love, by Carol J. Fulher, Fulcrum Publishing, 1998.

Discovering World Geography with Books Kids Love, by Nancy A. Chicola and Eleanor B. English, Fulcrum Publishing, 1999.

Family Math Books, by Jean Kerr Stanmark, et al. Titles include: *Family Math*, 1986, (grades K-9), *Family Math for Young Children: Comparing* (Equals Series), 1997, (grades PreK – 3), and *Family Math—The Middle School Years: Algebraic Reasoning and Number Sense*, 1998, (grades 5-8). Lawrence Hall of Science, University of California.

From Butterflies to Thunderbolts: Discovering Science with Books Kids Love, by Anthony D. Fredericks, Fulcrum Publishers, 1997.

The Horn Book Magazine. Horn Book, Inc. Articles and book reviews about children's and young adult literature.

Literature Connections to American History K-6 and 7-12: Resources to Enhance and Entice (two volumes), by Lynda B. Adamson, Teacher Ideas Press, 1997.

Literature Connections to World History K-6 and 7-12: Resources to Enhance and Entice (two volumes), by Lynda B Adamson, Teacher Ideas Press, 1998.

The Mailbox Bookbag: The Teacher's Idea Magazine for Children's Literature. Education Center, Inc. A magazine for teachers of primary and intermediate readers.

Marilyn Burns Talks about Math Teaching Today. Three audiocassettes for K-8 teachers: "What's Reform All About?" (60 minutes), "Teaching the Basics" (65 minutes), "Linking Assessment and Instruction" (70 minutes). Math Solutions Publications.

Math: Facing an American Phobia, by Marilyn Burns, Math Solutions Publications, 1998.

Mudpies to Magnets: A Preschool Science Curriculum, by Robert A Williams, Robert E. Rockwell, and Elizabeth A. Sherwood, Gryphon House, 1987. Also, *More Mudpies to Magnets: Science for Young Children*, 1990.

Notes from a Scientist: Activities and Resources for Gifted Children: Some Suggestions for Parents, by Beverly T. Sher, The College of William and Mary, Center for Gifted Education, 1993.

Of Bugs and Beasts: Fact, Folklore, and Activities, by Lauren J. Livo, Glenn McGlathery, and Norma J. Livo, Teacher Ideas Press, 1995.

Science through Children's Literature: An Integrated Approach, by Carol M. Butzow, John W. Butzow and Rhett Kennedy, Teacher Ideas Press, 2000. Also, *More Science through Children's Literature: An Integrated Approach*, 1998, and *Intermediate Science through Children's Literature: Over Land and Sea*, 1994.

Some of My Best Friends Are Books: Guiding Gifted Readers from Preschool to High School, 2nd edition, by Judith Wynn Halsted, Great Potential Press (formerly Gifted Psychology Press), 2002.

Teaching Art with Books Kids Love: Teaching Art Appreciation, Elements of Art, and Principles of Design with Award-Winning Children's Books, by Darcie Clark Frohardt, Fulcrum Publishing, 1999.

Teaching Physical Science through Children's Literature: 20 Complete Lessons for Elementary Grades, by Susan E. Gertz, Learning Triangle Press, 1996.

Teaching Science with the Internet: Internet Lesson Plans and Classroom Activities, by Marc Rosner, Classroom Connect, 1998.

Teaching U.S. History through Children's Literature: Post-World War II, by Wanda J. Miller, Teacher Ideas Press, 1997.

Through Indian Eyes: The Native Experience in Books for Children, by Beverly Slapin and Doris Seale, American Indian Studies Center, 1998.

U.S. History through Children's Literature: From the Colonial Period to World War II, by Wanda J. Miller, Teacher Ideas Press, 1997.

What Else Should I Read? (Volumes 1 & 2), by Matt Berman, Libraries Unlimited, 1996.

When home school families have educational resources that they no longer need, such as fiction and non-fiction books, educational videos, textbooks, educational games, math manipulatives, magazine collections, and other curriculum materials, rather than allow them to collect dust in the basement or garage, families can donate to their library. Donations like this enhance the library collection for all users and free up library funds for other books and supplies.

Grade Levels and Standards

Covering less in more depth, however, is only the first step toward better education. Ultimately, we want to call into question the whole idea of a curriculum to be "covered" and to think instead about ideas to be discovered.

—Alfie Kohn (1999)

Most classroom educational resources and materials are designed to be used for a certain grade or grade range, for example, K-3, or fifth grade, or middle school. Recently, because of the move toward state standards for every grade level, classroom materials are increasingly being written to comply with specific standards and benchmarks for specific grades. For example, if one of the standards for fifth-grade math states that students will "recognize and generate equivalent forms of commonly used fractions, decimals, and percents," then math teaching materials for this grade level will emphasize this skill. Standards can be very useful for parents new to home schooling; they demystify the education process and help parents feel confident that their child is learning the right skills for his age and grade level. Standards can also help parents find topics they might not think of on their own.

Using minimum standards in a rigid way, however, has definite drawbacks. For one thing, standards are written for the average fifth grader and sometimes the slightly below average fifth grader—that is, standards set the minimum level of competency that all fifth graders are expected to achieve before moving on to the next grade. Because some children learn slowly and others more rapidly, and because some children may have difficulty mastering a particular math computation skill, all standards should be used with caution. They should be used only as a guide. For example, while we expect most third graders to know their times tables and to do multiplication problems of two digits, we know that some students will achieve these skills later and other students will achieve them earlier. Most gifted students can handle curriculum two or three grade levels above other children in their age group. Children who are highly gifted can work at even higher levels (Rogers, 2002). What is worrisome about standards is that when used to define curriculum, either for gifted or for any other exceptional students, such use will lead to unnecessary (and inappropriate) dumbing down of the curriculum for all.

Because standards are often designed for a single grade level, school resources designed for grade levels are often limited in their content and expectations for the child. For example, in a history book that is designed to meet a state second-grade standard of being able to list the tribes of American Indians by their geographic region, there is no mention of how climates affected the ways different tribes lived, because that is a fifth grade standard. But what if your child is curious about these things? Do you then use the fifth-grade material as well? Or do you wait until you've finished "covering" second grade before moving on?

Standards have other drawbacks, too. Barbara Clark cites research that shows that when teachers were reminded even in small ways about meeting standards and being accountable for what their students learn, they controlled and criticized students more and allowed less freedom and experimentation in the classroom. Students who feel freer in their learning environment solve more problems than students who are more controlled. When students are given more control over the content and completion of assignments, they complete significantly more work (Clark, 1997).

While academic materials designed to cover standards for particular grades offer peace of mind and structure for an anxious parent, non-graded resources allow the flexibility of not being bound by particular grade levels and give children the opportunity to learn without an imposed "ceiling" on the information presented. Non-graded resources include trade books written for a general audience rather than for classroom use, education trade books not geared to a particular grade level (such as the Brown Paper School books), and curriculum materials that do not restrict themselves to one grade (such as Key Curriculum Press's *Key to...* math workbooks). There are some advantages to combining graded material with non-graded material.

> *Sometimes we use textbooks and sometimes not. Right now, Sarah, who is 13, is using grade seven writing mechanics workbooks, a grade eight science book, a grade six English book, and non-graded material for everything else. Lynn, age 15, is using non-graded material only, though she has used graded material in the past.*
>
> *Lynn usually works at several different levels at the same time. Last year, she was alternating between college-level texts, adult fiction and science fiction, and comic books and picture books for art ("fascinating illustrations," she said). I think the girls have their own reasons for working at a variety of levels, and I think it helps them assimilate new information, too. It allows them to accommodate their natural rhythm of interest as well as development. I don't think Lynn would have gained as much from the college-level material if I had wanted her to work at that level all the time. This year, she's alternating between pulp teen fiction, university texts, adult science fiction, and adult non-fiction material. I strongly believe my job is to stay uncritical and discuss their reading with them. I find that the pulp fiction roughly correlates to the audience Lynn writes to when she writes her own science fiction. I think the adult material stimulates her intellectually.*
>
> —Joan, home school parent

If you choose to follow grade-based education standards, at least to start, look for materials that are flexible in terms of challenge and pacing or that are specifically designed for gifted and creative children.

What Grade Are You In?

Unless a state home school law requires you to follow a grade-based curriculum, there is no need to think of home schooled children as being in a particular grade unless they are more comfortable doing so. This is one of the great benefits of home schooling. A 10-year-old child can be in eighth grade for math and science but in fourth grade for language arts. Another 10-year-old can do high school level writing assignments and fifth-grade math. Home schooling solves many of the problems associated with whole grade skipping because the child can learn at several grade levels at the same time. Schools find this much flexibility difficult.

Here are some home school parents' thoughts regarding the use of grade levels:

> *We do not follow a grade-based curriculum, since the "levels" of learning are different for the various subjects and vary greatly. For example, my 12-year-old easily enjoys and understands high school or college level science, but needs a writing program geared to middle school level and work that is only a year or two ahead in math. One of the major problems she had with traditional school was that it was all one grade level, and an enrichment program could only provide a small adjustment in concept level. We do not keep track of her grade levels in any particular subject, but we do make notes of the ideas and concepts that are being learned, especially for those we consider to be possible high school level.*
>
> —Kathleen, home school parent

I don't use a grade-based curriculum though I do refer to several curriculum guides for book ideas and the like. That's the challenge of having a gifted child. I cannot use just one curriculum for one grade because my six-year-old son is all over the board with every subject. For example, I have math books and other textbooks, which range from third to eighth grade. I do not keep track of his grade level because grade level is entirely arbitrary. When people ask what grade my son is in, I tell them he's the age equivalent of first grade if he were in a public school.

—Barbara, home school parent

We do keep track of grade levels (in our family) because the school board form we fill out each year asks for them and because it makes our home schooling a bit more understandable to people who've only experienced public school. By that measure, our two girls are in grades eight and 11; however, our girls are not just in grade eight or grade 11. For example, our eldest is working grade 10 geometry, grade 12 language arts, grade 12 and university level physics, etc. Our younger daughter is doing a grade 10 language arts program, as well as a grade eight science program. We base what we do on what they need or want to know, not on what grade they are in.

—Joan, home school parent

Being flexible with grade levels removes many barriers to a child's learning at a natural and individuated pace. Home schooling offers many children their first experience of learning at a pace and at a level that is appropriate for them.

We have an extremely bright, eager, eight-year-old child who loves to learn and is interested in everything. In school, she was held back by curriculum that was two or three years more advanced. She didn't do it. She needed more. She needed to be able to explore and find out things for herself, not just read about them in a book and answer some questions. She didn't want to read two paragraphs about cats and stop. She wanted to really dig into information about cats…and apply what she's learned to real life. Discovery is an important part of learning. Too many school materials are written with the constraints of the classroom in mind. For the rapid learner who absorbs knowledge like a sponge and is ready to take it to the next level, school curriculum will never be enough. These children are always going to need more, more challenge than memorization of facts can give them, more stimulation than the average classroom can allow, more freedom to explore, to ask questions, to find out for themselves, to make a hypothesis and follow it through.

—Rose, home school parent

The Luxury of Being Able to Wait

©Copyright PEANUTS. Reprinted by permission of United Feature Syndicate.

Although parents of children who have remained unchallenged in the classroom may immediately recognize the benefits of being able to work at a faster space, there is another benefit of home schooling for gifted learners—that of being able to slow down when necessary. A child may want to delve deeply into subjects of interest without having to move on to the next benchmark, or a child may need to wait until his or her body and mind are more in sync before exploring the rigors of formal study.

The luxury of being able to wait is a powerful educational advantage, especially for children who may naturally learn to read later than other children, arrive at social maturity later than their friends, or achieve sensory integration later than average. Some children are late bloomers, but such delays are not necessarily negative. In fact, later maturity can be beneficial in at least three ways: (1) by allowing for the possibility of increased neurological development and capacity as the result of prolonged non-specialization of brain hemispheres, (2) by preserving a child-like sense of wonder crucial to adult creative thinking, and (3) by giving the adolescent a deeper and more meaningful store of direct experience with life rather than second-hand experience through books (West, 1997). This is not to say that maturity should be artificially delayed any more than it should be rushed. However, for a child whose internal timetable naturally ticks at a relatively slower pace, parents can know that there are definite advantages to allowing the child to follow that rhythm.

In an article for *Harvard Educational Review*, William J. Rohwer, Jr. (1971) has argued that prior to adolescence, the education of children should be one of "satisfactory work and play," in which "mastery would not be required at a particular early age, but rather at the time the child can acquire the skills (and the prerequisite sub-skills) readily and successfully." In this view, there is no magic year for mastering reading or multiplication tables or cursive writing. Rohwer is careful to point out that he is not advocating "training in techniques of self-indulgence and mediocrity." Rather, he is advocating a radically different approach to old notions of age- and grade-based standards and definitions of achievement and excellence.

Rohwer's vision has exciting and profound implications for both home schooling and gifted education. By delaying formal education—i.e., what we think of as traditional classroom instruction—until age eight or later, children are more likely to have matured both emotionally and intellectually enough to handle the demands of the classroom. Also, the freedom to work at one's own pace removes the artificial ceiling inherent in materials designed for grade level classroom use. While some gifted children move quickly through grade levels in a linear fashion, other gifted children, especially visual-spatial learners, learn to read at a later than average age, or they have difficulty learning to write, even though they are absorbing information at an astounding rate. For these children, home school parents can delay formal education—that is, classroom study that requires them to work as a group, following the instructor's pace, or individual study that requires adherence to a strict linear train of thought—until the child's own levels of development are more in sync. In the meantime, exploratory, early childhood education could be prolonged past first grade into the middle school years. David Elkind argues, "What intellectually gifted children need most, then, is not early formal instruction, but rather a prolongation of opportunities to explore and investigate on their own" (Elkind, 1987, p. 154).

This slow-down-and-wait approach to home schooling does not mean that a child would not engage in deep learning or rigorous or even accelerated study, or that she would not be expected to learn how to read, write, and do math. It does mean, however, that the child can wait until her individual sensory and motor systems are more fully integrated before formal learning constitutes the bulk of her education. Parents who have witnessed this developmental process note that the child gradually becomes better able to follow the direction of others, concentrate on assigned work, and write and calculate in a way that supports rather than interferes with higher level thinking. Until that time, often at about age eight to 10, learning can happen according to the child's internal timetable and unique learning style. A highly reflective 10-year-old may not be able to recite multiplication facts in the time allowed on most standardized tests, but will still be allowed to explore the beauty and complexity of high school level geometry, or to learn a visual approach to algebra. An impulsive eight-year-old may not be able to do science worksheets, but can explore concepts of simple machines and force with hands-on experimentation and videos.

Even for a child who is reading fluently, a prolonged period of exploratory learning offers a chance to use and develop all of the senses, possibility preventing vision problems and allowing for fuller integration of sensory systems (Rowher, 1971; Moore & Moore, 1979). Much of the therapy recommended for promotion of sensory integration involves the kinds of physical and multi-sensory learning activities prohibited by desk learning and long bus rides to and from school—for example, using hopscotch to review multiplication tables, or skipping rope while reciting the alphabet, or spending an afternoon at a petting zoo.

We used the delay approach when we allowed our son to take a break from formal math study for one and one-half years beginning when he was seven. Although a placement test showed that he was "ready" for advanced math, he had been resisting his math textbook, which focused on computation and word problems, and we could see that he was not ready to attend to number work for its own sake. Instead, we read informal math books (see Verbal Math Resources, Chapter 5) and played card and board games. He continued to work at advanced levels in his favorite subjects—language arts and history. When we saw that he was becoming better able to handle formal learning (at age eight and one-half), we reintroduced regular math work with materials from Key Curriculum Press and the textbook *Mathematics: A Human Endeavor*, by Harold Jacobs. He was able to learn and study in a way that had been impossible just one year before, and a new placement test showed that he had somehow gained two years in math skills during the break! Now he loves math and computation, is working several grade levels ahead of his age that are appropriate for his ability, and regularly does more math work than assigned just because he wants to. I suspect that if we had not taken a break while his sensory systems were maturing and becoming more integrated, his attitude toward math would be much more negative.

Parents who adopt the delay approach need to be aware that friends and relatives may strongly disagree. Rowher acknowledges that such opposition is inevitable and that its root cause is an understandable fear of "generations of students who, intellectually and socially, are self-indulgent know-nothings" (1971, p. 338). This delay approach will not be a good choice for parents who think that their children may return to school before the developmental process is complete. For long-term home schoolers, however, a prolonged period of exploratory learning may give children the time they need to develop to their unique and fullest potential.

Your child's home school curriculum or course of study will be much more than a company name or workbook series. It will include all materials and experiences from and through which your child learns and will be shaped by your child's needs and interests, your own strengths and knowledge, and your family's unique circumstances and way of life—a truly individualized curriculum.

Key Points

☑ Grade-based curriculum seldom meets the needs of gifted students.

☑ Grade-based standards are useful as guides but pose serious problems when used as a definitive list of what to learn and when to learn it.

☑ Home schooling offers the opportunity to work in several grade levels at the same time.

☑ Parents use different approaches and materials for different subjects, depending on their own levels of knowledge, curiosity, and comfort.

☑ Children's interests, goals, and aptitudes help direct the choice of curriculum materials for each subject.

☑ Single-parent families and two-income families can home school successfully with careful planning and flexibility.

☑ Parents often combine home schooling with work from home.

☑ Parents can avoid unnecessary or mistaken purchases by researching curriculum and previewing materials before buying.

☑ Parents can keep costs down by borrowing, creating, and taking advantage of free or inexpensive materials.

☑ The public library can be a valuable resource for both parents and children.

☑ Home schooling families can make patron requests at their libraries.

Activity for Reflection

Make a list of the subjects you plan to include in home schooling, and think about your own personal knowledge and comfort level for each, your child's aptitude and interest in each, family budget and resources, and whether you plan to use grade-based materials.

Table 8.1: Curriculum Planning Grid

	Knowledge	Comfort	Child's Interest	Budget	Materials
Math					
Language Arts					
Science					
Social Studies					
Fine Arts and Foreign Languages					
Other					

Self-Directed Learning and Common Home School Approaches

Most of the home school families I interviewed for this book used one of the following approaches as their primary framework: (1) unschooling (interest-based, child-led learning), (2) studying subjects individually, (3) classical home schooling, or (4) unit studies. Self-directed learning, explained in Chapter 9, combined with other learning approaches such as the four above, seems uniquely suited to the learning styles and needs of gifted children.

To help you tailor and create a home schooling approach to meet your family's needs, the next four chapters explore the concept of self-directed home schooling and how it can be used within a variety of home school approaches. The chapters are as follows:

O Unschooling and Self-Directed Learning	Chapter 9
O Studying Individual Subjects	Chapter 10
O Classical Home Schooling	Chapter 11
O Unit Studies: What's the Big Idea?	Chapter 12

You'll notice that several of the various popular home school approaches overlap. Home schoolers often take the best elements of each approach and use them to meet their children's unique needs. Some families use unschooling as their primary home schooling approach. Other families study subject areas individually or follow the classical education model, with an underlying emphasis on self-directed learning. Some families do self-directed unit studies in language arts or science, but study math as a separate subject with traditional textbooks and assignments.

There are, of course, several other home school approaches that are not covered in this book. If you are interested in learning more, Linda Dobson, in *The First Year of Homeschooling Your Child*, describes several methods of home-based education (Dobson, 2001):

O Traditional School at Home
O Classical Education
O Charlotte Mason
O Unit Studies
O Eclectic (or Relaxed)
O School-Sponsored Home Schooling Programs
O Independent Cooperative Learning Situations
O On-Line Learning

If you are interested in a particular home school method or approach that is not covered in the next four chapters, such as Charlotte Mason or School-Sponsored Home Schooling Programs, you may look for these on your own in Dobson, in other books, or on the Internet.

The next chapters *will* give you enough understanding of self-directed learning to integrate aspects of it into your daily home school routine, regardless of other approaches used.

Following is a list of the major advantages and disadvantages of the four approaches to home schooling covered in the next four chapters.

Advantages and Disadvantages of Home School Approaches for Gifted Children

Unschooling

Advantages:

+ Reduces pressure to perform
+ Encourages independent learning
+ Allows for immersion learning
+ Removes barriers to natural acceleration

Disadvantages:

− Sabbatical period may be long for chronic underachievers
− Requires trust, patience, and ongoing involvement from parents
− Some students may resist taking responsibility for their learning

Studying Subjects Individually

Advantages:

+ Facilitates record keeping and state compliance
+ Allows students to vary resources according to areas of strength
+ Is familiar to parents

Disadvantages:

− May not hold student's interest
− Does not encourage interdisciplinary learning
− May neglect non-traditional topics of learning

Classical Home Schooling

Advantages:

+ Emphasis on logic, literature, and languages may be enjoyable for some students
+ Can offer high level of challenge and rigor
+ Is comfortable for parents and children who want more structure

Disadvantages:

− May inhibit creativity
− May have too much outside-imposed structure for some students
− May not leave adequate time for student's own interests

Unit Studies (Thematic Studies)

Advantages:

+ Facilitates global, interdisciplinary learning
+ Recognizes important role of child's interests
+ Easily adjusts for learning styles, rates of learning, and varied resources

Disadvantages:

− Pre-packaged unit studies may not offer adequate challenge or depth
− May overlook a child's area of strength or weakness (such as math or writing)
− Can easily be overly orchestrated by the parent

At Home with Home Schoolers

"Stealth Home Schooling" by Janice, Home School Parent

The following comments from a home school parent show how self-directed learning can fit in and around other methods with a very positive result. She calls it "Stealth Home Schooling."

In our family, we tend to be a combination of both scheduled and relaxed home schoolers. The scheduled part comes in by providing a structure for my boys. "School" begins no later than 9:00 a.m. in our house, unless we have visitors, or we're down at the beach, or hiking, or, well, you get the picture. Assuming nothing else is planned, the children are prepared to sit down and do school work. Understand that my children equate "school work" with something that is evaluated on paper—math problems, writing, spelling, etc. Everything else is NOT school.

So I generally sit down with them for an hour or two, and we work on math (*Singapore* curriculum is our current favorite), handwriting (Getty Dubay), grammar, and writing (we use a mishmash of various books/curricula and Inspiration software).

This year I'm farming out science. We lucked out and discovered a wonderful science program for home schoolers. The teacher is wonderful, and my children have acquired an instant social group in our new town.

In the past, I've done formal science using the AIMS materials. We of course do significant "stealth science" by watching a lot of science television shows. Thanks to the wonders of a satellite dish, we can access Bill Nye several times a day. We are smitten with the Animal Planet channel, and most Tuesday nights find us viewing NOVA on PBS. Then there is the garden. My dear boys are fascinated by the success of their various seeds, especially the sunflowers. And we do plenty of food science around here; we have two Ph.D. biochemist/food science specialists in the family, so they are always coming up with strange and unusual stuff for the boys.

With the exception of *Simon Spells* (a spelling program for Macintosh systems only), in our family, educational software is not thought of as "school" (more stealth home schooling). My children are big fans of the various *Sim* games (*SimAnt*, *SimTheme Park*, *SimSafari*, etc.), which qualify as science/business simulation (more stealth home schooling). We've been through almost all the Davidson software and Learning Company software. The children tend to race through all of these programs in short order. I'm not certain that heaps of learning is occurring with these software programs, but the boys have fun.

My eldest no longer views reading as "school." In fact, he will typically read several books per week; it is a battle to get him to turn off the reading light at 10:00 p.m. He is such a voracious reader now that he will generally read most anything I plop in his lap without complaint, unless the book is truly boring.

My youngest, age 10, reads at a seventh/eighth-grade level but thinks of reading in terms of time or number of pages read. I blame the public schools for this.

There, children were required to read one hour per day in class and another 10 pages per night at home. Prizes were given for number of pages read, regardless of content. I don't know how long it will take to unschool this concept out of him! It is driving me nuts. This child has yet to discover the pleasure of reading!

We have yet to really jump into history. Last year, because we were following our state's fifth-grade standards, where U.S. history was the subject matter, we worked our way through the first three books of Joy Hakim's *A History of US* (1999). I highly recommend the series, but found a concentration on U.S. history to be too narrow, even though the author views U.S. history in a global context. So next year, or perhaps this summer, I hope to use many of the resources recommended by the classical education community and begin with studies of ancient history.

In many ways, I like the concept of the classical education approach, although for me it seems somewhat dated. We really like *Singapore Math*, my boys adore the home schooler's science classes, and they are chomping at the bit to learn Java or some other programming language.

So as always, we continue to zigzag from one point to the next and stay adaptable. I quickly learned that curriculum guides based on state standards simply didn't work, no matter how varied in level. My sons love to go off on tangents, which is probably the way most folks learn! And I eagerly supported their various ancillary interests as they popped up. 'Tis a grand method for joyous learning, but beastly for staying on prescribed plan.

Resources Mentioned by Janice

AIMS Educational Foundation: Activities Integrating Math, Science, and Technology.
   www.aimsedu.org

Animal Planet Channel
   http://animal.discovery.com

Bill Nye the Science Guy television program and videos.
   www.billnye.com

Davidson software programs – now produced by Knowledge Adventure.
   www.knowledgeadventure.com/home

Discovery Channel
   www.discovery.com

Getty-Dubay Handwriting

   Italic Letters: Calligraphy & Handwriting (1994) by Inga Dubay & Barbara Getty. Continuing Education Press.

   Italic Handwriting Series: A Comprehensive Handwriting Program for Children and Adults, Third Edition (1994) by Inga Dubay & Barbara Getty. Continuing Education Press.

Hakim, Joy (1999). *A History of US*. Oxford University Press. A 10-volume U.S. history series.

Inspiration Software
    www.engagingminds.com/inspiration

Learning Company Software
    www.learningco.com

NOVA television program and videos by PBS
    www.pbs.org/wgbh/nova

Simon Spells. Don Johnston, Incorporated
    www.donjohnston.com

Sims Software – produced by Maxis
    http://simcity.ea.com/us/guide

Singapore Math
    www.singaporemath.com

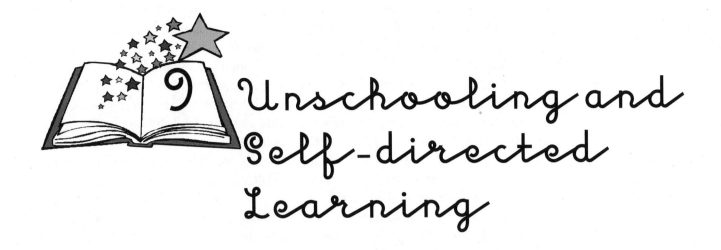

9 Unschooling and Self-directed Learning

[A] child whose self-directed learning is interfered with, who is forced to follow adult learning priorities, may acquire a strong sense of guilt about any self-initiated activities. One risk of early formal instruction, then, is that it may encourage a sense of guilt at the expense of a sense of initiative.

—David Elkind (1989)

Although similar, self-directed learning and unschooling are not necessarily the same thing. The first half of this chapter describes self-directed learning—what it is, why it is particularly effective for gifted learners, and how it is often misunderstood. The second half describes unschooling, shows some examples of unschoolers, and highlights some areas of similarity and difference. *Both approaches place the responsibility for learning in the hands of the child.*

Self-directed learning is an educational philosophy that emphasizes the child's role as an active learner. Recent years have seen a great interest in self-directed learning, both as an approach to adult education for lifelong learning and as a form of gifted education. Self-directed learning is very different from the traditional model of learning in which teachers and other adults decide *what* will be learned, *when* it will be learned, *how* it will be learned, and *whether* it was learned or not.

Students can be self-directed in several ways and in varying degrees. Children are self-directed whenever they:

- O decide *what* they need or want to learn,
- O set *goals*—their own goals,
- O identify and find *resources* for learning,
- O choose and use *strategies* for learning, or
- O *evaluate* their own learning (Lowry, 1989).

Home school parents can decide to make self-directedness an integral and key part of their child's education. Of course, no one is self-directed 100% of the time. Self-direction includes assistance and guidance from others. All children will benefit from training in self-directed learning, but it is particularly useful for gifted learners, because as a group, these students prefer tasks that are self-instructional. Gifted students learn more when they control their pace of learning, have a strong internal drive to do things their own way, and have intense, broad areas of interests they want to explore (Maxwell, 1997; Rogers, 2002, Winner, 1996).

Not only is self-directed learning well-suited for the way gifted children learn, but it also helps prepare them to use their skills and talents more effectively. About 70% of adult learning is self-directed (Lowry, 1989), for example, when we decide to teach ourselves how to fix a sink or how to operate a computer program. In the workplace, employees who can identify what they need to know and then find the resources to solve problems have an advantage over workers who are dependent on others for direction.

Self-Directed Learning Myths and Realities

Many home school parents might like to incorporate more self-directed learning into their home schooling approach, but are unsure of how to start or are concerned about the long-term effectiveness of such an approach. Indeed, many myths surround the idea of self-directed learning.

- **Myth:** Self-directed learning can't be taught.
- **Reality:** *While some children are naturally more self-directed than others, all children can learn techniques of self-directedness and self-instruction.*
- **Myth:** Self-directed learning is the same as unstructured learning.
- **Reality:** *In self-directed learning, the student has a role in the selection of content and materials and in the pace of learning. Learning may or may not be highly structured.*
- **Myth:** Self-directed learning lacks depth and rigor.
- **Reality:** *Self-directed learning may or may not be more rigorous, or it may result in deeper learning than teacher-directed learning.*
- **Myth:** Self-directed learning is all or nothing.
- **Reality:** *Self-directed learning is usually only one part—though an important and integral part—of a child's overall education.*

Let's look at each reality more closely.

Self-Direction Can Be Learned

Self-directed learning requires skills and self-confidence. While some home schooled children will jump at the chance to have more of a say in their education, others will balk at the idea. Children who have been viewed as underachievers will need a gradual incorporation of self-directed learning, beginning with only one subject area or interest (Whitmore, 1980). Some children will be eager to direct their own learning, but will need guidance to do so.

George Betts (1985) developed the Autonomous Learner Model as a way to meet the cognitive, social and emotional needs of gifted elementary and high school students. The model is designed to help gifted students become self-directed learners.

An autonomous learner is one who solves problems or develops new ideas through a combination of divergent and convergent thinking, and functions with minimal external guidance in selected areas of endeavor. (Betts, 1985, p. 4)

Betts cautions that students usually do not become autonomous learners overnight or even in a few months. The process requires patience and dedication on the part of adults, as children learn more about themselves, explore new subject areas, practice both individual and group learning, and develop skills of independent study (Betts, 1985).

One aspect of the Autonomous Learner Model that adapts particularly well to home schooling is the fifth dimension of the program, called In-Depth Study, where learners choose an area of passion or high interest, design a project or unit, share it with others, and finally evaluate their own learning (Betts & Kercher, 1999). Areas of passion or interest can be traditional topics in math or history, or they can be non-traditional, such as car engines or comparative religions. The Big Ideas for Big Thinkers approach described in Chapter 12 loosely follows this model.

Betts recommends that young students, ages five to nine, begin with an awareness of the skills needed for in-depth study, and that the teacher (or parent) "capitalize on opportunities for incidental learning" (Betts, 1985, p. 58). For example, a parent might notice and then comment to a child on the child's interest in maps, then help the child learn how to find more information about reading maps and the history of map-making—by reading library books, looking at maps used for many purposes, and making one's own maps.

Older children, grades four through six, are introduced more formally to skills and concepts of self-directed learning and begin to develop such skills as asking effective questions, finding information, finding mentors, working in groups, and determining mastery (Betts, 1985). Parents of a 10-year-old who want to encourage their child to spend more time learning about an area of interest—geography, for example—can offer the child some choice in what curriculum materials to use, what aspects of geography to focus on, and how to share knowledge with others. At this age, the child can also check his or her own work using an answer key or teacher edition. Later, when the child is ready—at about high school age—he or she can apply the skills learned in many or most areas of study (Betts, 1985).

These learners can, with minimal assistance, determine what they need or want to learn, seek and select resources for learning, and evaluate whether their learning is successful. Some home schooled children will be ready to apply aspects of self-directedness at an earlier age in specific topic areas or interests, but parents are wise not to pressure children to take on more responsibility for their learning than they are prepared to handle. Parents who want more information about this model can read *Autonomous Learner Model: Optimizing Ability*, by George Betts and Jolene Kercher (1999).

Some home school families find that their approach naturally changes over time from *awareness* of self-directed learning and an informal, interest-based approach to more *formal applications* of independent learning as children mature. A parent who home schools three children, ages seven to 14, explains how she encourages the development of self-directed learning according to each child's development and age, and how she combines self-directed learning with a more traditional, subject-based approach for the older children.

For each subject, at each level, each year, we choose the approach that best meets the needs of that child. At the younger ages, our approach is primarily interest driven. My seven-year-old daughter does some math each day (at about a fourth/fifth grade level), much of which consists of word problems derived from our family experiences and interests. She also writes a paragraph or two a day, about things she is interested in. Beyond that, her current intense interest is reading several biographies a day and adding each person about whom she reads to her laminated timeline, which fills one wall of her room. We also include other subjects as she expresses an interest.

During the early elementary years, I plan only about half of what I know will be learned in an average day. That leaves time for spontaneous learning as circumstances arise, as well as time for following intense interests.

My approach is more traditional with my 12- and 14-year-old sons who are now earning high school credits. For high school subjects, such as Spanish, Algebra 2, Biology, or Medieval History, I feel more secure using a well-regarded textbook or curriculum, knowing that the subject has been covered thoroughly and at a depth appropriate for high school credit. At this age, I see myself more as a learning facilitator than as a teacher. I oversee their work and discuss concepts with them, but they learn fairly independently.

—Nina, home school parent

Note that the progression used by Nina ranges from informal learning based on the child's interests to a gradual development of the skills necessary for self-directed, independent study. The amount of self-direction and specific ages when autonomous learning can be fully applied is unique to each child.

Selection of Content, Materials, and Pace

An easy way for parents to introduce self-directed learning to their children is to give their children input into the *content*, *materials*, and *pace* of study. One parent uses an interest inventory to help determine areas of study.

> *Once a month I'll ask my daughters to write down or tell me a list of interests, and once a year I get them to fill out an interest inventory which is much more complete and detailed. Then I research materials and get their input on what resources we should use to study their areas of interests. The time of year I have them fill out the inventory is variable and depends on how long each plan of study lasts.*
>
> —Joan, home school parent

Joan's approach is interest-based and introduces skills and concepts of self-directed learning, but it is not without structure. Children and parents vary in their preference and tolerance for structure. Some work best with a highly structured environment in which activities follow a schedule and the day's events unfold according to plan. Others need less structure and more freedom to act on spontaneous ideas. All children benefit from some scheduled activities.

Mihaly Csikszentmihalyi, author of the books *Creativity* and *Flow*, writes that creative people need some structure in order to free their minds from the clutter of having to re-invent the wheel every day. Mary Sheedy Kurcinka, in *Raising Your Spirited Child* (1992), writes that routines are very important for children who are slow to adapt to change and who struggle with transitions (a characteristic of many gifted children, as well as children diagnosed with ADD (or Asperger's Disorder). By being able to predict what is coming—wake-up time, meal and snack times, and so on—these children can save energy that would have otherwise be spent worrying about uncertainty. Some sort of schedule seems beneficial. Likewise, at least some unstructured learning seems to be beneficial for gifted learners. Parents can experiment with time periods of less structured learning throughout the week and see how their children react.

Begin by asking your children want they want to do or learn. Make it an open-ended question, and give them time to think of and write down some topics. Then, allow the child's interest area to become a key part of learning. To provide focus, ask the child to come up with a project idea that will help organize the learning experience and show what was learned. The project is limited only by the imagination—a series of educational posters, a model, a board game (a popular choice), a card game (use index cards to make a matching game or trivia game), a book, a photography exhibit (great for nature enthusiasts).

A child's interest provides a key to joyful and successful education, especially with children who are full of self-determination and creative ideas. L. S. Vygotsky (1997) wrote that a teacher's job is to find a child's interest, then organize the environment and provide scaffolding in such a way that the child can use that internal interest as a way to learn. The interest can be almost anything. I know a seven-year-old who turned an obsession with a trading card game into a monthly newsletter. This project required learning computer skills, writing, proofreading, art and graphics, copyright law, layout and design, communication, and business sense, and the child in no way felt that he was doing "schoolwork."

An interest in the Titanic could lead to building a model of the ship to scale, learning about the history of the time (*Hakim's History of US* series), writing an imaginary diary of a child on the ship, listening to music popular at the time, studying what went wrong structurally, gathering facts about the numbers of passengers, lifeboats, and so on. The child's learning style will influence how the interest takes shape. A detail-conscious child may enjoy using graph paper to sketch the ship and its compartments, whereas another creative child may use watercolors to portray the ship in the dark night waters.

An important caution for parents who use the self-directed and interest approach is to keep the focus on the *child's* interest, the *child's* initiative, and the *child's* work, not the *parent's* interest and planning. For example, if a child expresses an interest in learning about Egypt, parents should avoid the temptation to orchestrate, rather than facilitate, the child's study by buying every available book and kit about Egypt, filling the house with posters of hieroglyphs, "taking over" the interest with a detailed plan of activities, and doing every project along with the child. Instead, parents should help the child locate resources, plan visits to museums, etc., all the while remembering that the interest belongs to the child.

Gifted children will skip from one interest to another, driven by a curiosity to understand all parts of their world and a desire to make connections. By letting the child determine the intensity and scope of the interest, parents can save themselves a lot of time and money and still keep alive the child's love of learning.

An older child may be ready to have even more control over what he or she learns, including what materials to use. If you are contemplating which algebra program to use, for example, talk with your child about different options—CD-ROM, traditional or non-traditional text, workbook, on-line course, manipulative-based program, and so on. Spend some time sampling and researching options, and then ask your child for her preference, which may be a combination of two or three options. Discuss the reasons for her choices, and together set up a schedule for using the materials.

With self-directed learning, children learn how to pace themselves. If a child is doing math pages that contain several practice problems for a concept already mastered, encourage the child to do every other or every third problem. If those problems are correct, the child can then go on; if some of the problems are incorrect, explain that this is an indication that doing the full set of problems is probably necessary. By including the child in these kinds of learning strategies and choices, the child will be better able to direct the pace of his or her own learning in future years.

Depth and Rigor

Self-directed learning does not mean that the child's education will lack depth or rigor. Because no constraints are put on how much or how fast the child learns, self-directed learning can allow a highly motivated learner to master difficult subjects with more depth, in far less time, and with more challenge than is possible in a more outer-directed environment. No artificial standards limit the amount of learning per grade level. Children may cover what might be considered two or even more years of a subject's curriculum in a single year. Likewise, a child may pursue a topic in greater depth, making more meaningful connections than are possible in a typical classroom setting that tells him how far he may go and when he must stop.

The parent below allows her children to pursue their own interests as deeply as they wish without relying on textbooks. She believes that this approach allows her children to learn at a deeper level than if they used a traditional curriculum plan.

> *Recently, we had a sixth-grade home schooled girl over to help plan an Egyptian festival for our upcoming conference. This girl is gifted but uses a very academic curriculum. As the children discussed the type of tables to set up (it's going to be like a market with a table for food, cosmetics, religion, and so on) my two children suggested a math table. Their friend asked why, and they explained the Egyptian's role in geometry.*
>
> *When they were discussing the other tables and what would be available, it became obvious to my children that their friend's knowledge of Egypt was very limited and that it was mostly topics usually found in textbooks—pyramids, mummies, and cat gods. My children asked her if she had studied Egypt. Her reply was, "Yes, but all this wasn't in my textbook!" My children were shocked! Without ever have "studied" Egypt formally, my children knew so much more and at a deeper level.*
>
> —Mary, home school parent

In this case, self-directed learning resulted in study that was both deeper (covered in greater detail, e.g., daily habits of everyday Egyptian life) and more rigorous (at a more challenging level, e.g., the history of mathematics and geometry).

Self-directed learning, practiced conscientiously, implies extensive parent-child interaction. A parent who encourages self-directed learning knows that home schooling duties sometimes know no limits. You never know what questions or topics might come up. You must take seriously a child's questions about why World War I started—even if the question comes at 7:30 in the evening—then assist the child in finding answers which will no doubt lead to more questions.

For self-directed learning to "take hold," it also requires parents to serve as models of lifelong learning. How can we expect children to become interested in geography, history, science, or literature if they never see adults continuing to pursue these subjects for the joy of learning?

How to Encourage Self-Directed Learning

Parents need to have curiosity and flexibility if self-directed learning is to work. Many times you'll find yourself learning right alongside your child, as you provide a model of someone who loves to learn and who seeks answers to questions. But some advance planning and parental homework doesn't hurt and can make you a more effective facilitator.

Real life provides all sorts of opportunities for learning. For some ideas, see the PUMAS (Practical Uses of Math and Science) website at http://pumas.jpl.nasa.gov, which offers a collection of examples written mostly by engineers and scientists of how K-12 math and science topics are found in everyday life.

The following activities, habits, and strategies are reported by home school families to be especially effective in supporting self-directed learning.

- Read aloud to your children or to the whole family on a regular basis. You can read picture books, classic stories, non-fiction books, newspaper articles—anything that is interesting.

- Keep a wide variety of reading material in the house and easily accessible to children.

- Provide leisure reading time for children when they can immerse themselves in books of their own choosing.

- Make library visits a regular part of errands. Allow enough time for children to browse the shelves in addition to looking for specific books.

- Be a model of someone who writes for different purposes throughout the day. Let your children see you writing grocery lists, to-do lists, instructions for caretakers, journal entries, letters, poetry, short stories—anything that requires putting pen to paper or fingers to keyboard.

- Keep a variety of writing instruments and paper in different rooms of the house. Remember, not every piece of children's writing needs to be evaluated or even commented upon.

- Start a collection of interesting maps, such as those from *National Geographic*, and have an up-to-date globe in a common area of the house.

- Play board games and card games regularly—daily if possible.

- Keep puzzles available for pleasant self-challenge and relaxation.

- Expose your children to a wide variety of music through CDs, live performances, and making music at home.

- Encourage children to create their own art, and expose them to art forms from different cultures and eras of history.

- Watch high quality television programs that explore biographies, history, current events, and science. Don't call it "educational."

- Enjoy age-appropriate movies as a family.

○ To show that math is a part of everyday life, encourage your child to help you look for bargains in the grocery store, adjust amounts in recipes, make a floor plan of his or her room so as to arrange furniture most effectively—any activity that involves mathematical thought in real life.

○ Encourage children to participate in everyday household activities such as cooking, cleaning, and yard work. Make it fun! Prepare a favorite recipe together; make a game of dusting the furniture or choosing new flowers for the garden. These activities may be cherished childhood memories.

○ Encourage your children to "try out" sample curriculum resources before you make a decision to buy. Ask for their input in educational materials purchase.

○ Show your children how to adjust their pace of learning; explain ideas of compacting and telescoping (see Chapter 10) and the theory of self-directed learning.

○ Allow your children to check their own work when possible; ask them what percentage of correct answers they consider adequate for mastery. Talk about their answers, and experiment with the best way to make corrections (Re-do the problem? Re-read the passage? Find a different approach to the material?).

○ Enjoy your children every day. Learn with your children every day. Learn from your children every day.

Unschooling

Home schooling based on the child's interests and needs is often referred to as unschooling. Although unschooling can be understood as a specific form of home schooling, for many parents, it is more of an attitude toward learning than a specific method. Grace Llewellyn (1996) writes in *Freedom Challenge: African American Homeschoolers*, "I often use the term 'unschooling.' 'Homeschooling' can sound like doing *school* at *home*, while the kind of home schooling that excites me does not resemble school and often takes place as much out in the world—museums, workplaces, riverbanks—as in the home."

There are nearly as many definitions of unschooling as there are people who consider themselves unschoolers. Mary Griffith (1998), in *The Unschooling Handbook: How to Use the Whole World as Your Child's Classroom*, defines it this way: "Unschooling, to me, means learning what one wants, when one wants, where one wants, for one's own reasons." Unschooling is sometimes referred to as child-led learning, and most dedicated unschoolers advocate a non-coercive education in which the child has a significant role in choosing both the content and the pace of learning. Perhaps most importantly, unschoolers believe that children will learn what they need to learn if allowed to seek answers to their own questions. For example, an unschooling family would trust that a child would learn geography because geography is a part of life, not because it is included in a "what needs to be learned when" list or other learning schedule. Rather than use a geography curriculum, the unschooling family encourages the child to learn about his neighborhood, country, and world as questions arise from travel (How far is it to Grandma's house?), news (What countries are affected by the hurricane?), reading (Where is the real Paddington Station?), and other aspects of everyday life.

Many people are suspicious of unschooling. They think unschooling parents let their children run wild, or provide no educational guidance, or are ignoring their children's learning needs. However, few people who call themselves unschoolers fit the stereotype. Some use the child's interests as a base for cooperative learning activities and projects. Some do use textbooks. Some require music lessons. Sandy, for example, says she "sort of" follows a grade-based curriculum, "but only in terms of a convenient suggestion or topic areas to cover and nice books to read. We do take note of grade-appropriate skills."

Some parents prefer to use the phrase *self-directed learning* to *unschooling* as a way to describe their home schooling because it is a more positive description of what actually occurs. Self-directed learning and unschooling are not necessarily synonymous, however. A child who does independent study using a distance learning course or some other formal curriculum chosen by adults may not be unschooled, but *would be* using skills of self-directed learning. Likewise, an unschooled child may have much freedom in terms of time, but if adults neither listen to the child's questions nor guide the child to find answers, she may develop few skills of self-directed learning.

Unschooling does not imply a lack of education, nor is it an abrogation of parental responsibility, nor is it an excuse to ignore children's educational needs. Parents who use the unschooling umbrella as a cover for educational neglect are doing a grave disservice both to their children and to the many conscientious proponents of unschooling and self-directed learning. The "un" in unschooling refers only to traditional classroom school methods of teaching, not to education itself.

Even though unschooling, like any educational choice, can be misused or abused, it is important to state that unschooling *can* be a highly effective approach to home schooling for some children and is often a particularly effective option for highly motivated learners with a wide range of interests. Many children can soar well above the expectations and boundaries of any outside-directed curriculum. Unschooling allows children to get to know themselves as learners—their likes and dislikes, strengths and weaknesses, rhythms and plateaus. Some families use unschooling for subjects in which their children are strongly motivated and then use more traditional approaches for other subjects. Some families practice unschooling during the summer, effectively making for a year-round education. Other families find that unschooling is the perfect match for young children, but that older children prefer more formal educational approaches. Summer offers a good time to experiment with self-directed learning. So is your sabbatical period. If you are tempted to skip the sabbatical stage, re-read Chapter 7.

Advantages and Disadvantages of Unschooling for Gifted and Creative Students

Advantages:
+ Reduces pressure to perform or compete
+ Encourages self-initiated learning
+ Allows for immersion and intuitive learning
+ Removes barriers to natural acceleration

Disadvantages:
− Sabbatical "resting" period may be long for underachievers
− Requires trust, patience, and intensive involvement from parents
− Some students may resist taking responsibility for their own learning

 # Key Points

☑ Self-directed learning fits the way many gifted children prefer to learn and prepares children for the role of lifelong learners.

☑ While some children are naturally more self-directed than others, all children can learn techniques of self-directedness and self-instruction.

☑ In self-directed learning, the student has a role in the selection of content and materials and in the pace of learning. Learning may or may not be highly structured.

☑ Self-directed learning may or may not be more rigorous or result in deeper learning than teacher-directed learning.

☑ Self-directed learning is usually only one part—though an important and integral part—of a child's overall education.

☑ Unschooling is a home school approach that presumes children will learn what they need to know by following their interests and asking their own questions.

☑ Unschooling may or may not include a large degree of self-directed learning.

☑ Unschooling is particularly effective for highly motivated children with a wide variety of interests; many families begin with unschooling and gradually incorporate more traditional learning approaches.

Questions and Activities for Reflection

1. Give your child the choice of spending a day alone in his room or outside. Resist the temptation to direct his activities or to convey hidden expectations or preferences.

   - What do you notice about your child's choices of activities?

   - Is it easy or difficult for your child to have unstructured time?

   - Is it easy or difficult for you to allow your child to have control over what to do and when to do it?

2. Think about what subjects and interests your child would want to pursue on her own.

   - What level of self-directed learning might be appropriate for these subjects?
   - What subjects is your child unlikely to pursue on her own?
   - How might you encourage more self-directed learning in these areas?

Unschooling Resources

Books about Self-Directed Learning and Unschooling

Betts, George, & Kercher, Jolene (1999). *Autonomous Learner Model: Optimizing Ability*. Autonomous Learner Publications.

Griffith, Mary (1998). *The Unschooling Handbook: How to Use the Whole World as Your Child's Classroom*. Prima Publishing.

Holt, John (1981). *Teach Your Own*. Delacorte Press/Seymour Lawrence.

Holt, John (1967). *How Children Learn*. Pitman Publishing.

Holt, John (1989). *Learning All the Time*. Addison-Wesley.

Llewellyn, Grace (1998). *The Teenage Liberation Handbook: How to Quit School and Get a Real Life and Education*. Lowry House.

Books with an Unschooling Emphasis

Albert, David (1999). *And the Skylark Sings with Me: Adventures in Homeschooling and Community-Based Education*. New Society Publishers.

Leistico, Agnes (1997). *I Learn Better by Teaching Myself*; and, *Still Teaching Ourselves*. Holt Associates.

Moore, Dorothy, & Moore, Raymond (1975). *Better Late than Early: A New Approach to Your Child's Education*. Reader's Digest Press.

Moore, Dorothy, & Moore, Raymond (1979). *School Can Wait*. Brigham Young University Press.

Wallace, Nancy (1983). *Better than School: One Family's Declaration of Independence*. Larson.

Magazines with an Unschooling Emphasis

HELM: Home Education Learning Magazine. A bimonthly print publication focusing on independent learning and self-directed education. www.helmonline.com

Home Education Magazine. Parent recommendation: "Very well written, eclectic home schooling magazine that offers schooling out-of-the-box in most of its articles." www.home-ed-magazine.com

Internet and Web Unschooling Resources

Family unschoolers network   www.unschoolering.org

Unschooling Gifted Children list   www.topica.com/lists/ugc

The Unschooling List FAQ, by Kathy Wentz
http://mc.net/~kwentz/ulfaq.html

Unschooling.com (sponsored by *Home Education Magazine*)
www.unschooling.com

At Home with Unschoolers

Perhaps the best way to understand what unschooling is—and isn't—is to listen to what unschoolers have to say. Following are some parents' thoughts.

Unschooling doesn't mean foregoing all structure and all lessons. It means letting the child learn what he wants to learn when he's ready to learn it. It means providing an atmosphere of enrichment, a house full of books and videos and fascinating stuff to explore. It means taking your children to museums and historical sites, lying on your back at night identifying stars, introducing concepts and authors and ideas, and following up on those things that catch his interest now (while leaving something in his head to draw his interest later).

It's just a different style of teaching—a style that's adapted to the child, instead of the child adapting to the classroom and the school's schedule. All children are most likely to retain material that catches their interest, whether that be handwriting or fractals or butterfly metamorphosis.

I know there are unschoolers who do absolutely nothing to "teach" their children. On the other hand, many of us put a lot of effort into making opportunities available for our children, and even require them to study something they wouldn't choose for themselves, from time to time.

We try to adapt the lessons to the child…. He learned algebra first, and decimals and fractions later—does that matter? No. What matters is that it worked for him, it held his interest enough for him to really get into the subject, and he remembers what he learned.

—Gwen, home school parent

Unschooling doesn't mean foregoing all structure and all lessons. It means letting the child learn what he wants to learn when he's ready to learn it. It means providing an atmosphere of enrichment, a house full of books and videos and fascinating stuff to explore. It means taking your children to museums and historical sites, lying on your back at night identifying stars, introducing concepts and authors and ideas, and following up on those things that catch his interest now (while leaving something in his head to draw his interest later).

—Francis, home school parent

Unschooling has been very effective for us. When we first started, we pulled Lynn from the end of grade three and Sarah from kindergarten. Lynn was rebelling against the school way of doing things. If she was told to do something, she simply wouldn't. She had learned to dislike learning. For her, learning had to come from within or at least be perceived as being a cooperative venture, or it didn't happen. She needed to get excited about learning again. Unschooling was ideal for dealing with this situation.

It took me awhile to catch on, but once I realized how easy it was, we were hooked. I sat the girls down at the kitchen table one day and simply asked them what they'd like to do. They didn't have any answers, so I clarified with, "Well, if you could do anything you wanted to right now, what would it be?" After fantasies of flying to the moon, etc., they started mentioning things they'd always wanted to do but never seemed to have time. I made a list for each of them. Lynn peered out the window and commented, "Gee, it looks like a good day to fly a kite." So our first activity was packing up the kites and heading to the creek to fly kites. I also packed a backpack with a snack, drawing tools, paper, magnifiers, etc. We talked about wind and clouds while we flew the kite and, after a snack, explored the creek with the magnifiers, drew pictures of flowers and bugs, and wrote in journals.

When we came home, Lynn was excited about making her own kite. We made a trip to the library and took out books on making kites. I also went through the children's section for stories about children flying kites, the history of kites, etc. We read the books and made some kites, which we flew the next time we visited the creek. Flying kites was the beginning of many a "field trip" to the creek, and studying the creek in different seasons was the basis of our first year of home schooling.

This kite flying experience led us into many areas of study over the years. Lynn became interested in paper airplanes, which led to an interest in physics through the use of a book called The Gliding Flight. Paper airplanes led to an interest in origami and the Japanese. She has studied Japanese culture and literature over the years and toyed with the language. We initially read a book about a Chinese boy flying a kite and eventually we ended up studying China as well.

We have become more eclectic as the girls have grown. The girls ran out of ideas of things to learn about, so it seemed best to implement some required reading. So far, they've found it interesting and expand from there. They do use some textbooks, but they help choose them. I simply keep an eye on what's required for university entrance—where one child wants to go—and see that it's covered somehow. I let them diverge to do Internet studies whenever they come up with ideas, such as studying linguistics or learning object-oriented programming on a MOO.[15] I am open to their ideas and suggestions, and I encourage them.

—Joan, home school parent

15   What's a MOO? According to the TAGFAM (Families of the Talented & Gifted) website, it is a "text-based virtual reality environment," harder to explain than do. TAGFAM hosts MOO projects for gifted children. To learn more, go to www.tagfam.org or read the book, *MOOniversity: A Student's Guide to Online Learning Environments* by Jan Rune Holmevik and Cynthia Haynes, Allyn & Bacon, 2000.

Families who home school within a religious context have also found success in unschooling. One parent describes her approach as "eclectic, very relaxed, family-centered, God centered, child- and interest-led."

> *My son has many interests of his own, and we let him follow them. We also have certain scheduled activities, but we're very flexible on those. I have a few goals that I gently encourage my son to try based on practical application. I do want him to have more knowledge than I acquired in my schooling, and I'm sure he will. He's off to a good start by simply being allowed to pursue areas of interest at leisure. We vary the way we approach home schooling from day to day, week to week, and month to month.*
>
> —Barbara, home school parent

Barbara recommends *The Joyful Homeschooler* and *The Relaxed Home School: A Family Production*, both by Mary Hood. She also recommends three additional resources for learning about unschooling from a Christian perceptive:

- *Christian Unschooling*, by Teri Brown and Elissa Wahl, Champion Press (2001). www.championpress.com

- *The Science, Art, and Tools of Learning*, by Marilyn Howshall, Lifestyles of Learning Ministries (1994).

- Monthly Christian Home Unschooling e-zine: http://groups.yahoo.com/group/seedling

10 Studying Individual Subjects

Studying each academic subject individually is what most people think of as school; it is the kind of education most of us remember from our childhoods. Many home school families continue to use this model, and many state home schooling laws list subjects to be covered throughout the year, such as writing, reading, math, science, history, and health.

The subject approach to home schooling is comfortable and simplifies record keeping. Because curriculum materials are often designed with this approach in mind, finding resources is simplified. Studying each subject individually also makes it easy to adjust levels of challenge to accommodate a child's areas of strength and weakness. It allows high school level students to easily keep track of pre-college requirements. Even home school families who consider themselves mostly unschoolers (Chapter 9) and those who use classical education theory (Chapter 11) or unit studies (Chapter 12) usually continue to study individual subjects in some way.

A home school schedule can be flexible. There's nothing to prevent a child from spending a full day on math or science or writing; or a family might decide to do math every morning at a certain time but study other subjects in a more unscheduled way. Your child may take a whole week to read a favorite book series and then spend the next week doing kitchen science experiments. To study individual subjects, you do *not* need to break your day into formal classes or 30-minute learning segments. Subjects can be studied according to the amount to be covered—one math lesson a day—or the amount of time the child spends on the subject—an hour of reading per day or two evenings of writing per week.

An exciting opportunity for gifted children whose interests lie beyond the grade-level ceiling of curriculum models is that they can study subjects usually reserved for high school or college, but in a way that is appropriate for their age. An elementary-age child interested in philosophy or world religions or astronomy, for example, can begin to explore these subjects long before they would be formally introduced in the school classroom.

The resources parents choose for the subject areas can be traditional textbooks or non-academic "real life" materials. Science resources, for example, can include not only science texts meant for classroom or home school use, but also trade books, picture books, science magazines, biographies of scientists, cookbooks, user manuals, garage tools, lab materials, etc. The possibilities are endless.

Individualizing Subjects for Individual Children

As you consider how to approach each subject area, keep in mind your child's strengths, interests, and preferred learning style. You may wish to review the section on grade levels in Chapter 8. It is not uncommon for an asynchronous learner to have a wide variance of levels for different subjects. Thus, if an eight-year-old home schooler is working at a third-grade level in reading and a pre-algebra level in math, the parent can accommodate this natural learning pattern without feeling a need to "bring up" the reading to match the child's level in math.

A home school parent of two boys, ages 10 and 12, finds that her children require an individual approach for each subject.

> *I do keep an eye on grade-based curriculum simply to make sure I'm covering the content. But I don't stay within the same grade level for all subjects. I let my children work at the level they are competent in on each subject. For asynchronous children, one of the huge advantages of home schooling is the flexibility to work at many different grade levels, depending upon the subject.*
>
> *One of my children is clearly profoundly gifted in certain subjects but average (at best) in other subjects. Of course, I did not immediately understand this huge discrepancy in ability. I needed an educational assessment from someone familiar with highly gifted children and learning disabilities/differences to clearly pinpoint my child's areas of strength and weakness.*
>
> —Monica, home school parent

Although some parents begin home schooling with a good idea of the levels of challenge their children need and how their children learn best, other parents find an educational assessment of some kind helps them to know where to start and what kinds of resources to look for. An easy, at-home way to get a ballpark idea of what a young child knows in various subjects is to use a CD-ROM test such as the Children's Skills Test Series, by SmarterKids (www.smarterkids.com). This series of four CD-ROMs can be used to assess children through sixth grade. An informal way to assess children's skills and knowledge levels is to do spot checks of workbook series, having your child do selected pages in books designed for specific grades, such as SRA/McGraw-Hill Spectrum Workbook series, available in bookstores and teacher supply stores. Parents can also have their child take end-of-unit tests in textbooks for individual subjects until they reach an appropriate level of challenge. For children who have no barriers to testing well (e.g., text anxiety or learning disabilities), test centers such as Sylvan Learning Centers offer relatively inexpensive achievement tests that provide a breakdown of grade levels for each subject area. Your local school district may also provide testing services for home school families.

Some children will need more detailed or more specialized assessments, especially if the child is highly gifted, is a visual-spatial learner, has text anxiety, or has very uneven abilities. Parents of these children may want to use a center that specializes in testing gifted children or request an assessment from a psychologist familiar with psychological and educational assessment of gifted children. Three testing centers in different parts of the country are the Gifted Development Center in Denver (www.gifteddevelopment.com), the Belin-Blank Center at the University of Iowa (www.uiowa.edu/~belinctr/index.html), and Johns Hopkins University's Center for Talented Youth Diagnostic and Counseling Center in Baltimore (www.jhu.edu/gifted/edplan). These centers offer educational assessments as well as counseling that provide parents of gifted children with information about achievement levels, learning styles, areas of strength and struggle, and suggestions for dealing with particular concerns. Some centers may be able to recommend a test center or assessment specialist in your area.

In addition to different levels of challenge, a child who is home schooled may need a different approach for each subject, such as hands-on work for science, textual learning for history, and a computer course for math. Parents can individualize subjects studied according to their child's interests and needs, not only in terms of level of challenge but also in terms of the way in which the material is presented. A child gifted in math, for example, will need a different approach and curriculum for math from a child whose passion lies in the fine arts and for whom math is more difficult. A talented, young writer will require a different language arts program than a child who resists writing.

One home school parent offers this explanation of how she individualizes subjects for her two children, ages eight and 10:

> *We are traditional in the core topics of language arts and math, but less traditional in history, science, and technology. For math, we use a computer-based distance learning program from Stanford University's Education Program for Gifted Youth (EPGY); for grammar and spelling, we use a mixture of workbooks from Educators Publishing Service (*Wordly Wise 3000, Vocabulary from Classical Roots, Megawords, Rules of the Game*); and for literature, we use* Treasury of Literature *and* Junior Great Books. *We also love the Critical Thinking Press materials such as the* Red Herrings *series, the* History *series, and the* Building Thinking Skills *books and software. For writing, we use Wordsmith.org,* Writing Strands, *personal correspondence, and scripts for competitions such as* First Lego League *and* Destination Imagination. *My son will be enrolled in the distance learning writing tutorials from Johns Hopkins Center for Talented Youth next fall.*
>
> *For history and science, we take a global approach. We use documentaries to introduce topics, then we read aloud from books such as* A History of US, *by Joy Hakim, and supplement with historical fiction. We frequent museums in the Washington, DC area as well as other parts of Virginia. Our science activities were supplemented in the past by a science club we ran for members of the community,*

Resources Mentioned by Margo

Critical Thinking Books & Software
www.criticalthinking.com

Destination Imagination
www.destinationimagination.org

Education Program for Gifted Youth (EPGY)
www-epgy.stanford.edu

Educators Publishing Service
www.epsbooks.com

First Lego League, Lego Mindstorms
www.legomindstorms.com/fll

A History of US, by Joy Hakim, Oxford University Press
www.oup-usa.org/childrens/historyofus/index.html

The JASON Project, A Multimedia Interdisciplinary Science Program for Grades 4-9
www.jasonproject.org

Johns Hopkins Center for Talented Youth, Center for Distance Education
www.jhu.edu/gifted/cde

Junior Great Books, The Great Books Foundation
www.greatbooks.org/programs/junior

NASA Education Resources
http://education.nasa.gov

Treasury of Literature, Harcourt School Publisher
www.harcourt-school.com

Wordsmith.org
www.wordsmith.org

Writing Strands, National Writing Institute
www.writingstrands.com

How to Differentiate Subjects for Quick Learners

> *The biggest challenge for me as a home school parent has been keeping up with my son as he flies through materials. I knew he was gifted when we started, but I had no idea that the pace he would set would be as fast as it is! I'm amazed almost daily by the amount he is learning and the concepts he understands.*
>
> —Casey, home school parent

Quick learners in school may have from one-fourth to three-fourths of their classroom time "left over" as they wait for other children to catch up (Webb, Meckstroth, & Tolan, 1982). It's easy to see how home schooling retrieves that time, either to allow the child to learn more in a particular subject or to pursue other interests. Some home school parents, like Casey, above, find that the speed with which their children learn requires not only a different set of resources, but also a different approach to using them. The techniques of *compacting* and *telescoping* are just two of many differentiation strategies that help parents of quick learners use their resources more effectively and keep up with their children's pace of learning. For additional information about differentiating learning for gifted children, see the books, *Re-forming Gifted Education: Matching the Program to the Child*, by Karen Rogers (Great Potential Press, 2002); *Teaching Gifted Kids in the Regular Classroom: Strategies and Techniques Every Teacher Can Use to Meet the Academic Needs of the Gifted and Talented* (revised and updated edition), by Susan Winebrenner (Free Spirit Publishing, 2000); and *Teaching Young Gifted Children in the Regular Classroom: Identifying, Nurturing, and Challenging Ages 4 to 9*, by Joan Franklin Smutny, Sally Yahnke Walker, and Elizabeth Meckstroth (Free Spirit Publishing, 1997).

Compacting

Compacting allows you to cover material in a shorter amount of time than normally allotted by skipping areas the child already knows or finding ways to do the work more efficiently, then replacing the work with new or more appropriate materials or content (Rogers, 2002). You can begin by pre-testing—by giving the end-of-the-unit test—either formally or informally, *before* the child starts the unit or chapter. Then, assign only the parts of the work the child *doesn't* already know. If you are using a spelling workbook, for example, begin by first giving a written or oral test on the unit spelling words. If the child already knows the words, move on to a unit with unfamiliar words. Pre-testing and subsequent compacting works well for subjects that require specific knowledge, such as math, spelling, grammar, science facts, or history events and dates.

Telescoping

Once you've pre-tested to find an appropriate level of challenge, think of ways to allow your child to cover the material at a pace that will keep learning fun and exciting. For example, if a history curriculum advises home school parents to assign two chapters a week, and the child regularly finishes the chapters in half the time you had expected, allow the child to work at a faster pace, as long as comprehension doesn't suffer. Covering the same amount of material in less time is known as telescoping and is something that quick learners do naturally when they learn on their own, but are prevented from doing when a classroom of students must "stay together." It's not unusual for students who learn quickly to move through two or three grade levels in a specific subject in a single year just because they process material more efficiently or because they are moving quickly through concepts they already know.

Parents of quick learners may also need to use a curriculum resource that covers material more efficiently or that presents material at a higher level. If an eight-year-old is learning third-grade geometry with particular speed, look for a higher-level resource that reviews the easier concepts while introducing more challenging geometry, in effect doing two or more grade levels of work at the same time. If a child is ready for high school level work and finds high school texts simplistic or repetitive, a beginning level college text in the same subject will offer a "review" of high school material that is less repetitious and more thought-provoking, especially for math and the sciences. Browse in used bookstores on college campuses for ideas of the kinds of college texts used in freshman and sophomore courses.

The authors of *Gifted Children at Home: A Practical Guide for Homeschooling Families*, (Baker, Julicher, & Hogan, 1999) advise doing work orally as a way to cover subjects in less time. If your child is doing a math workbook, for example, you might occasionally ask him to tell you the answers to simple drill problems orally. You can write "completed orally" and the date at the top of the page.

Reducing drill work aids efficiency and is a great asset for children who need five practice problems rather than 50. If a child shows she can easily solve the first 10 problems on a page of 30 problems, allow her to skip the rest and move on. If it becomes clear that she needed more practice after all, she can always go back and do some more problems for review. Assign only odd or even problems or every third one. Be aware of resources in all subjects that rely heavily on drill and repetition, such as requiring students to write seven sentences that use a preposition. If your child can write three or four sentences correctly, there is probably no need to do more. Even in the classroom, good teachers do not always assign all of the questions or problems; they select the ones that will benefit students the most.

Parents should keep in mind that the time gained can be used in ways other than moving through a curriculum. Extra time can be used to pursue hobbies or interests that are important to children such as music, art, karate, volunteer work, etc.

Below are some general guidelines for choosing resources and approaches, by subject area, for intense and creative learners. Chapter 15, Home School Resources, contains an even more detailed list of resources listed by subject area. In addition, the Center for Gifted Education, College of William and Mary, offers the "Individual Instruction Plan Menu for the Gifted Child," practical and effective suggestions for individuating education for gifted children, available on-line at http://cfge.wm.edu/Articles/menu.htm.

Language Arts

Language arts is a broad and complex area which includes reading, reading comprehension, written and oral communication, and finally, literature—appreciation, interpretation, and analysis. A child can be an avid reader but have difficulty writing, or be excellent at speech communication but refuse to pick up a book. Home school parents can use a child's strength area—reading, writing, or speaking—as an avenue to the rest of the language arts world.

Gifted readers learn to read early and on their own, usually without direct instruction. It is not uncommon for gifted children to teach themselves to read at age three, four, or five simply by paying attention to the books read aloud to them, the reading cues in everyday life, or TV programs such as *Sesame Street*. As they grow older, children need opportunities to discuss their reading with others and to engage in creative reading, which goes beyond comprehension to analysis of and engagement with the text. In *Some of My Best Friends Are Books: Guiding Gifted Readers from Preschool to High School, 2nd edition* (2002), Judith Wynn Halsted offers advice for adults on how to guide children's reading.

Home school parents may wish to find or start a book discussion group for young readers. Bookstores and libraries often sponsor reading groups for children, and home school groups may offer them as well. Parents can start such a group by approaching a local bookstore, library, or home school group and offering to lead a book discussion group for children. For ideas, see the *The Mother-Daughter Book Club*, by Shireen Dodson, and *More Reading Connections: Bringing Parents, Teachers and Librarians Together*, by Elizabeth Knowles and Martha Smith.

Not all gifted children learn to read at an young age, so if your five-year-old resists reading instruction but is learning in other ways, there is no need to think he "should be reading by now" just because he is gifted. He may simply learn to read a bit later than others his age and will probably catch up quickly when he does learn. Continue to read aloud, and offer plenty of hands-on learning experiences. Parents who think their children may benefit from explicit reading instruction may want to try Educator Publishing Service's reading program, *Explode the Code*.

Gifted children who are reluctant readers may need help in finding ways to enjoy the printed word. Parents can introduce their children to the wide variety of reading genres—fantasy, mystery, detective fiction, science fiction, coming of age stories, classic literature, contemporary fiction, historical fiction, mythology, epics, poetry, plays, short stories, biographies, and autobiographies. Don't forget how-to books, non-fiction books about all topics, magazines, and electronic texts. Large print versions of books and magazines are sometimes more comfortable on the eyes of precocious young readers than small print. To spark an interest in reading and to encourage appreciation for the sound of language, listen to books on tape during long car trips or take the time to read aloud to your children during lunch or rainy afternoons. Above all, keep in mind the long-term goal of helping your children to be lifelong readers. Be sure your children see *you* reading a variety of printed material on a regular basis, both for practical purposes and for pleasure.

Parents are also role models of adults who write both for specific reasons and for pleasure, whether in the form of personal and business letters, e-mail correspondence, poetry, short stories, essays—even grocery lists and notes to family members. A mismatch of intellectual and motor abilities of gifted children often contributes to handwriting difficulties. Wanting the writing to be perfect is also sometimes a factor. When a child struggles with writing or is reluctant to write, it is good for parents to remember that good writing is not the same as neat handwriting. And many gifted children write more easily after learning keyboarding skills.

To encourage and facilitate writing in children ages eight and up, Ralph Fletcher has written an excellent, inexpensive set of paperback books: *A Writer's Notebook: Unlocking the Writer Within You* (1996), *Live Writing: Breathing Life into Your Words* (1999), and *How Writers Work: Finding a Process that Works for You* (2000). Each book offers empowering advice and examples for young writers, such a how to keep a list of favorite words, how to get ideas for what to write, and the importance of *re-reading* in the revising process. For more information as well as tips for young writers and some guidelines for teachers, see Ralph Fletcher's website at www.ralphfletcher.com.

Parents of highly gifted young writers may want to read Jane Piirto's chapter on children with extraordinary writing talent in *Understanding Those Who Create* (1998). Gifted young writers can develop their own writing schedule and begin to submit poems and stories for publication, *if they so choose*. Three good books for young writers ages eight and up are *The Young Writer's Handbook*, by Susan and Stephen Tchudi (1984), *The Young Writer's Guide to Getting Published*, by Kathy Henderson (2001), and *To Be a Writer: A Guide for Young People Who Want to Write and Publish*, by Barbara Seuling (1997).

A good language arts curriculum for any child, regardless of whether the child shows strengths in reading and writing, will integrate aspects of reading, writing, and speaking and will allow students to both capitalize on their strengths and explore less developed areas. It is not difficult for a parent with a strong language arts background to design such a curriculum. Several book and Internet resources offer recommended reading lists. Writing and speaking skills can be honed through real life needs, such as writing letters or e-mail messages, speaking on the phone, giving an informal presentation at a home school or other group meeting, or creating a personal or family website. Parents can encourage children to take responsibility for their own communication needs. If your child missed a community class and would like to ask for a make-up class, have the child write the letter or make the phone call. If your family is planning a vacation, suggest that your children gather brochures and request the necessary information. Even young children can leave notes for family members, order their own meals in a restaurant, and write thank-you cards.

If you'd like to use a comprehensive language arts program, look for one that is both flexible in pace and interesting in content. Some excellent language arts resources for gifted learners are EMC/Paradigm Publishing's *Literature and the Language Arts*; SRA's *Collections for Young Scholars*; Junior Great Books programs;

Write Source's writing programs; and The Center for Gifted Education, College of William and Mary's Language Arts Units for High-Ability Students.

Social Sciences

The broad category of social studies includes history, geography, anthropology, political science and government, psychology, and sociology. Innately multidisciplinary, the field is "a study of systems past and present, human and political" (Clark, 1997). The social sciences provide numerous opportunities for creative learning through problem solving and the quest for meaning and are a natural vehicle for the exploration of diverse cultures and perspectives (Starko, 1995).

A creative approach to social sciences involves a study of both a body of knowledge and how social sciences unearth that body of knowledge. For example, study of American history can include not only what happened and when—dates and names and events—but how we know what happened when. How does the science of archeology inform us about the lives of early American Indians? What can we learn about war from letters and diaries of Revolutionary and Civil War soldiers? How does our perspective of progress change as we consider the Twentieth Century from the point of view of environmentalism? Or information technology?

A creative approach encourages the use of primary sources—first-hand accounts and documents of the period, such as diaries, letters, newspaper articles, treaties, and written agreements or declarations. Even very young children can be encouraged to become historical researchers by studying old family documents and photos and by interviewing grandparents. Jackdaws Primary Sources offers packages of primary source material on a variety of topics, including U.S. history, world history, literature, and science. Critical Thinking Books & Software publish the series *Critical Thinking in United States History* and *Critical Thinking in World History*, which guide children grades six to 12 through the process of historical interpretation. Gifted children, due to their innate perfectionism, tend to be idealistic and even judgmental of others. The multiple perspectives inherent in the study of social sciences help these students learn to be comfortable with a certain amount of ambiguity and to be flexible enough to understand that different viewpoints offer different interpretations and truths.

For the gifted child who naturally seeks meaning, connection, and relevance, home schooling is a wonderful fit. There is time to immerse oneself in the social sciences, spending long hours exploring ancient Egypt or the Middle Ages. Historical fiction such as *The Midwife's Apprentice*, by Karen Cushman, can lead to questions about how medieval children were similar to and different from children of today. The child can make connections between time periods, such as comparing the invention of the printing press with the invention of the Internet, or connections between geographic places, such as discovering what medieval life was like on each continent. Finally, the child can ask questions of relevance to both human history and modern life: What were the events that led up to the medieval period? What effect did medieval society have on the historical eras that followed?

Children who are otherwise reluctant to delve into history, geography, and the social sciences may enjoy resources that build upon their primary interests. The Brown Paper School Books *My Backyard History Book*, by David Weitzman, and *The Book of Where*, by Neill Bell, relate history and geography to the child's immediate time and place. Young children combine play with geography and math when they map their backyard or neighborhood. Students who show little interest in math or science or literature will often do so if the study is tied to history— history of the abacus (math), invention of the steam engine (science), or historical fiction (literature). Science fiction fans can learn about the geographic biomes of alien worlds and the historical reasons for the post-World War II rise in the popularity of science fiction. Family vacations make history come alive when they include visits to historical places or living history museums such as Old Sturbridge Village or Old World Wisconsin. Check with your state's historical society to see what living history museums are available in your area. In addition, children interested in horses may enjoy studying the history of horse breeds and the uses of horses through time. They might learn about medieval history through horses ridden by knights and ladies, geography through horses indigenous to different countries, and social studies through the impact of the horse on the development of the U.S.

Books that combine history with other subjects, such as *Isaac Newton: Discovering Laws that Govern the Universe*, by Michael White, and *How to Count Like a Martian*, by Glory St. John, may interest science and math students. *The Geography Coloring Book*, by Wynn Kapit, and some sharp colored pencils may entice an art-oriented middle school student. Children and adults of all ages can enjoy social studies games such as *Maptitude* or *Take Off!* (Resource Games), *Borderline* (Borderline Games), and *Where In the World?* (Aristoplay). The History Channel, A&E, and PBS all offer television programming in history appropriate for all ages, and your local library probably has a good collection of historical documentaries and biographies on video.

Sometimes an interest in current events can be a route backwards to the past. A current presidential election may lead to questions about previous presidents, previous elections, the history of the Electoral College, and ultimately the historical precedents and inspiration for a democratic government. Such "studies" often come about spontaneously and need only for parents to pay close attention to children's questions, take the questions to the next level, and be willing to do some creative research. Parents who do this promote higher-level thinking and provide a good example of learning for its own sake.

Math

While we may think of the gifted math student as one who breezes through multiplication worksheets and craves long division problems, many children with a talent for math will not necessarily get high grades in math class or even be able to do arithmetic quickly. They will, however, have "an unusually high ability to understand mathematical ideas and to reason mathematically" (Miller, 1990).

The following clues may indicate a child's talent for mathematics:

○ An unusually keen awareness of and intense curiosity about numeric information.

○ An unusual quickness in learning, understanding, and applying mathematical ideas.

- A high ability to think and work abstractly, along with the ability to see mathematical patterns and relationships.

- An unusual ability to think and work with mathematical problems in flexible, creative ways rather than in a stereotypic fashion.

- An unusual ability to transfer learning to new, untaught mathematical situations (Miller, 1990).

Parents who notice these behaviors may be seeing clues that their child is mathematically gifted. Your child is fascinated by the numbers of everyday life; he waits for "lucky times of the day," such as 2:48 or 1:23; he notices, at a very young age, whether his toast is cut in halves or quarters; he applies his understanding of fractions to other situations, such as how to divide his favorite 30-minute video so as to watch half today and half tomorrow. He notices the patterns in the structures of buildings. He asks unusual questions, such as, "Is two plus two ever *not* equal to four?" or "How do I draw a square in four dimensions?"

A math program for such as child should build upon and nurture these innate strengths. The more highly gifted the child is in math, the less the child requires computational drill and cyclical review. Computation certainly has its place in math education, but it need not take center stage. In addition, the program should be extensive in scope and breadth so as to provide a firm foundation for children who wish to pursue mathematical fields in the future (Miller, 1990).

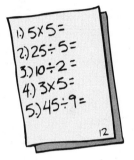

Several books and programs are available that allow for acceleration in math, including workbooks such as Key Curriculum Press' *Key to…*series or *Singapore Math*, specialty programs such as Don Cohen's *Calculus By and For Young People*, and distance learning programs such as EPGY (Education Program for Gifted Youth) from Stanford University. Children who have mastered basic arithmetic computation skills and are strong readers may enjoy the *Math & Music* software program by Wildridge Software, which covers high-level mathematical concepts (grades seven to 12) in a visually appealing, multidisciplinary format.

Children who are profoundly gifted in math often need a program of radical acceleration that allows them to progress to high school and college level material at very young ages. These children are internally driven to learn math at an astounding pace. However, they may not respond well to formal, traditional methods of mathematics instruction, but may prefer methods that allow them to solve problems in intuitive and creative ways (Winner, 1996). If a mathematically precocious child is balking at doing advanced math, parents may wish to try a different approach or several approaches that allow the child to do more experimentation and discovery-based learning.

Parents of children who are already academically accelerated will be wise to be honest with themselves about their feelings and intentions. Do you find yourself needing to tell people that your child is doing eighth-grade math at age nine or that your preschooler can do addition in her head? If so, you may need to back off a bit to test whether your child is truly motivated to progress rapidly through a math curriculum. Will your child enjoy math more and learn more deeply with a more leisurely pace?

A young child may not need to work with high-level math programs or textbooks in order to stay appropriately challenged. Several trade books and software programs, available at most libraries, can challenge and satisfy a gifted learner's desire to learn math. A five- to nine-year-old gifted learner might enjoy books from *The Young Math* series (out of print), published by Thomas Y. Crowell in the 1970s, as a way to explore mathematical ideas such as binary and base five number systems, as well as paper-folding geometry. The Brown Paper School math books (*Math for Smarty Pants*, *The I Hate Mathematics! Book*, and *This Book Is about Time*), written by Marilyn Burns, provide challenging and creative mathematical ideas for children whose reading level is grade four and up in a way that respects the child's development and intellect. The CD-ROM, *The Logical Journey of the Zoombinis*, is a highly visual software program that incorporates advanced logic concepts. And a variety of math games, puzzles, and brainteasers can keep math fun for young students.

Math manipulatives can be purchased or made from everyday materials such as buttons, dice, coins, and playing cards. Children enjoy making their own math board games for the family to play. Assessment is built in to the activity because the game will need to make sense and have rules. Research suggests that regular board and card games played with adults are more effective than either classroom instruction or computer games in helping young children to grasp mathematical ideas. One-on-one spontaneous conversation, questions, and explanations between adult and child seemed to be the important factors (Healy, 1998).

Mathematical conversation and inquiry may be the best way to encourage both creative and rigorous mathematical thought (Lynch & Harris, 2001; Starko, 1995). Parents should talk about mathematical ideas with children and encourage them to ask big questions rather than focus solely on correct and convergent answers to someone else's questions. Suppose your child is learning how to solve an algebraic equation and says, "But I got the answer a different way!" Instead of responding, "But this is the right way," take time to probe further. How did she get the answer? Affirm that there are often several ways to solve a problem. Will her method work for other problems as well?

Another creative way for children to demonstrate knowledge of mathematical ideas is to design their own problems and activities, complete with answer keys. Highly motivated students may even enjoy creating math workbooks for younger siblings or writing their own math newsletter featuring original brainteasers and math word problems.

Finally, keep in mind that some research suggests that it is possible to "overteach" a student in his or her area of strength, and that a change of subject and focus—taking more time to explore art or history, for example—may be a better strategy for the mathematically talented child than an overemphasis on math (Freeman, 1995).

Science

Young children need the opportunity and permission to take chances, make mistakes, and get messy—to borrow the motto of Ms. Frizzle. Playing in the dirt or sand with plastic shovels and other toys, splashing in the bath with kitchen funnels and measuring cups, or helping Mom or Dad cook dinner all promote scientific wonder and interest. Parents can encourage creative, scientific play by resisting the urge to orchestrate a child's experiments and by accepting that a certain amount of mess and uncertainty is necessary to scientific invention. Several high-quality trade books offer suggestions for ways in which parents who don't have a science background can incorporate science into everyday activities. *The Science Chef: 100 Fun Food Experiments and Recipes for Kids* and, *Exploring Matter with TOYS* and other books by Terrific Science Press are good home resources.

For the child who loves to read but resists science, children's literature can open the door to the world of scientific thought and inquiry. In the *Julie of the Wolves* trilogy, by Jean Craighead George, your child will learn about animal communication and the Alaskan tundra. In the *Einstein Anderson, Science Detective* series, by Seymour Simon, children grades four and up will find interesting science mysteries. And *The Science Book*, by Sarah Stein, is a rich source of science information and informal experiments written in a way that both respects and refuses to patronize the potential of young minds.

Creativity is an inherent part of science, "a field in which creative thinking, excitement, and creative achievement form the framework upon which impassioned individuals build innovative new approaches…" (Lynch & Harris, 2001, p 148). Children can learn to appreciate the creativity of science by learning about the lives of scientists—their childhoods, interests, education, and contributions. Many libraries carry Enslow Publishers' *Great Minds of Science* series, biographies of scientists with ideas for hands-on activities, glossaries, chronologies, maps, illustrations, and black and white photographs. The series is appropriate for reading level four and up.

Who is the gifted young scientist? Jane Piirto (1998) writes that young scientists express a sense of wonder about nature and the world by exploring, reading, discussing, or just daydreaming, and that people who later became adult scientists chose activities for play as children that reflected scientific interests, such as observing and collecting insects. These interests can range from gardening and nature collections (botany), to animals and bugs (biology), to playing with building blocks and mechanical gadgets (physics), to kitchen science experiments (chemistry). Parents should encourage children to develop hobbies and interests and then keep an open mind about whether the child's interest is merely exploratory or serious.

Real world problem-based science is an effective approach to science for all children, but especially for children who seek the big picture and personal relevance. The MESA series (Dale Seymour Publications) is a set of science units for grades six to eight that combines pre-algebra with hands-on science for such topics as measuring earthquakes and secret codes. The Center for Gifted Education, The College of William and Mary also offers a series of Problem-Based Science Units for High-Ability Students. Parents who feel comfortable with the subject of science can help children to design their own problem-based science units. What kind of garden design will allow us to grow the most vegetables in a 10' x 10' plot? How can I make compost for the garden? How can I make an environmentally friendly all-purpose cleaning solution? How can I record my findings and communicate them to others?

Fine Arts and Foreign Languages

Children whose gifts lie in the fine arts—visual arts, music, and drama—often have their needs met outside of school through private lessons and ensembles; for them, home schooling offers little change, except the chance to spend more time

in practice or pursuing their passions. Rather than practice violin or clarinet after a full day of school, the home schooled child can choose to concentrate on music first thing in the morning and reserve other learning activities for the afternoon.

Talent in the fine arts is often recognized by parents, but sometimes a child's gift can go undetected, especially if it's in an area with which the parents themselves are not trained. It is also difficult for parents of gifted artists, musicians, or performers to know when encouragement and support slips imperceptibly into coercion and control. Jane Piirto writes that the gifted young artist will pursue art on his own, outside of the art room and apart from artistic assignment, that practice for gifted musicians is joyful rather than drudgery, and that children with dramatic talent will show an intrinsic interest in dramatic activities (Piirto, 1998). A common thread is the degree of interest and drive on the part of the child. No parent can or should try to force talent, any more than a parent can force mathematical genius or precocious reading skills. If you follow the child's lead, you won't go wrong. David Albert writes:

> Lead the horse to water, milk, juice, etc. Let them choose a path. Help remove obstacles in the way of the path. Help them understand what will be necessary to reach their own goals. Find resources and mentors who can help them along their chosen path. Then get out of the way. Above all, love and listen, really listen.[16]

The book *And the Skylark Sings with Me: Adventures in Homeschooling and Community-Based Education* (David Albert, 1999) is a wonderful example for parents whose children show extraordinary gifts in the arts.

What about children who show no obvious artistic or musical talent? For these children, home schooling is a valuable opportunity to explore the arts as a lifetime source of joy and inspiration. Art history, music appreciation, and informal dramatics can be an important and regular part of your curriculum. Make it a habit to listen to a variety of music, attend informal and formal concerts, put out art supplies, go to art exhibits, provide old clothes and props for plays and make-believe, and go to local children's theatre productions.

Music and art are more than academic subject areas. They also provide rich opportunities to address social and emotional issues. By helping children learn how to use music or art to better express moods or explore feelings, we are providing them with lifelong coping skills that may help them later through rough or painful times. For example, after a stressful day, parents can talk with their children about what type of music might be an effective way to help everyone feel calmer. Sometimes the family can listen to music; other times family members may want to play or create their own music. Creating art is a much healthier avenue for emotional release than television, drugs, or alcohol. Parents can use art and music as one way to help children to acknowledge and express feelings of joy, sadness, anger, grief, or anxiety. Encourage children to explore their feelings by drawing or painting, sculpting, working with clay, and listening to music, and let them see you do so yourself.

---

16   Albert, David, personal interview, March 2000.

Home schooling also offers families an enriching opportunity to include foreign language instruction as part their young children's education. Latin is a popular foreign language choice of some home school parents, because it strengthens and facilitates vocabulary development, and because it offers a window to the ancient past. Several Latin programs are available to home school parents, including *Minimus: Starting Out in Latin*, by Barbara Bell and Helen Forte; *Learning Latin through Mythology*, by Jayne I. Hanlin and Beverly E. Lichtenstein; *Cambridge Latin Course*; and *Oxford Latin Course*.

There are several options for helping children learn a modern foreign language, including computer-based programs such as *Rosetta Stone*, audio- and workbook-based programs such as *Power-Glide*, and less expensive tape or book programs such as *Berlitz Kids Language Packs* and _____ in *Ten Minutes a Day*. Some home school families use private tutors or group lessons, or they enroll their children in a class through a school or community program. And a few distance learning programs offer foreign language instruction.

Advantages and Disadvantages of Individual Subject Study for Gifted and Creative Children

Advantages:

+ Is familiar to parents
+ Facilitates record keeping, state compliance, and college entrance requirements
+ Allows students to vary resources and levels according to areas of strength
+ Is easy to differentiate by compacting or telescoping, going deeper or broader
+ Simplifies scheduling
+ Can be combined easily with other subjects and areas of interests

Disadvantages:

- May not hold student's interest
- Does not always encourage interdisciplinary learning
- May neglect areas of study such as fine arts or leadership
- Creativity may be lost if mostly standard curriculum texts are used
- Parent or child may focus too narrowly on grade-based curriculum and progress and neglect delving more deeply into content areas

Key Points

☑ Parents should individualize subjects studied according to the level of challenge, the way in which the material is presented, and their child's interests and needs.

☑ Compacting and telescoping are two of many effective ways that parents can individualize study for gifted children.

☑ Education assessments can help parents know "where to start" and what kinds of resources to look for.

☑ Many gifted children learn to read and write on their own at a young age; other gifted children need help to learn how to read and write fluently.

☑ A good language arts program integrates aspects of reading, writing, and oral communication.

☑ Parents should be models of lifelong readers, writers, and communicators.

☑ The social sciences include history, geography, anthropology, political science and government, psychology, and sociology; these subjects are inherently multi-disciplinary and full of "big picture" ideas.

☑ A creative approach to studying social sciences includes current events, primary sources, multiple perspectives, and meaningful connections across time and disciplines.

☑ Students gifted in math understand and are curious about mathematical ideas and patterns; they do not necessarily excel at computation.

☑ Students with a high aptitude in math may need a program that allows them to move quickly; other math students will require a more leisurely pace.

☑ In addition to textbooks, children can learn math through manipulatives (e.g., dominoes), real life math (e.g., cooking), math fiction, and mathematical conversation and inquiry.

☑ Creative, scientific play and science-related hobbies and collections are good activities for young science students.

☑ Real world problem-based science is particularly effective for gifted learners.

☑ Students talented in and passionate about the fine arts can use the extra time afforded by home schooling to focus on art and music; all home school students can make the arts a regular part of their learning and leisure.

☑ Foreign language instruction can be part of young children's education.

Questions for Reflection

For each subject area to be covered, ask yourself these questions:

1. Is this subject an area of strength for my child?
2. Does my child choose to study this subject on his own initiative?
3. Is this an area of struggle for my child?
4. Does my child avoid this subject?
5. What learning style(s) does my child prefer with this subject?
6. How can I include my child's interest area(s) with this subject?
7. How informed am I about this subject area?
8. What types of resources should I consider using for this subject area?

At Home with Home School Parents

Nina, Home Schooling Several Children

"Ask, 'How can I make this work?'"

The biggest challenges for me have been juggling the diverse needs of my five children ages 14, 12, seven, four, and one—I might be bouncing or nursing a baby or interacting with a toddler who wants attention, while explaining quadratic equations and fervently hoping my pre-schooler is staying constructively occupied. It's tough to keep up on upper-level content (discussing Shakespearean literature, explaining direct and inverse variables, or explaining the War of the Roses) when I'm busy cooking and meeting the needs of the little ones, while still keeping the household running.

We've obviously needed to deal with sibling issues. This is what has worked for us: First, plan your home schooling day so that not everyone needs Mom at once. When I only had two children being home schooled, I wrote each day's assignments on a marker board under that person's name. When assignments were completed, they could be erased. I was careful that each day's schedule, for each elementary-aged boy, contained some things that could be done independently and some things needing parental involvement. If I planned too many things on a given day that needed my involvement, stress would result.

Home schooling three school-aged children while caring for a one-year-old and a four-year-old, I've needed to go to a more structured system than I would otherwise prefer to make sure that everyone's needs are met. Obviously, not everyone can use the computer, piano, or mother's undivided attention at the same time! Now, at the beginning of each school year, I make up a master schedule, taking into account little ones' nap times, optimal work times (math needs to be done in the morning for best results), subjects that can be shared (both my seventh grader and second grader can enjoy participating in my ninth grader's biology experiments, for instance), and activities that are mutually exclusive (two boys cannot read out of the same history book at the same time). Each school age child spends some time working independently, some time contributing to the needs of the family, and some time with Mother's undivided attention. For instance, at 9:30 a.m., my seventh-grade son plays with my one- and four-year-olds, while my ninth-grade son does his math on his own and I have one-on-one learning time with my second-grade daughter. At 10:00, my second-grade daughter takes a break and plays with my four-year-old, while my one-year-old daughter plays independently (hopefully!), my ninth grader is still doing his math, and I do algebra with my 12-year-old. Later, my seventh grader might fix lunch and entertain the 18-month old in her highchair while my 14-year-old son practices piano and I help my seven-year-old daughter with her writing. During my toddler's nap, I can assist my 14-year-old son with his microscope experiment. This kind of teamwork enables us to accomplish much more than if each child does whatever he wants to do when he wants to do it.

As I alluded to earlier, we also combine subjects when possible to streamline preparation and benefit from each other. Last year, when both of my older sons were preparing for the spelling and geography bees, they spent a lot of time quizzing each other. It was an advantage for them to study together. As we're learning Medieval and Renaissance history, they can read many of the same books but do writing assignments individually at their own level.

Once you've decided that home schooling is best for your family, commit to doing the best job you can with your children and family situation. Too often I've seen home schoolers wear themselves out by rethinking and second guessing their decision to home school. This wastes mental and emotional energy. There will be good days and difficult ones, as there will be with any school alternative. Instead, put that energy into problem solving. Ask yourself, "How could I make this work?" and choose to dwell on the positive memories and character qualities that are resulting from your home schooling experience.

Classical Home Schooling

Classical education has recently experienced a surge in popularity among home schoolers. When asked to describe their approach to homeschooling, one-fifth of the families interviewed (through e-mail) for this book mentioned classical education or the book *The Well-Trained Mind: A Guide to Classical Education at Home*, by Jessie Wise and Susan Wise Bauer (1999).

At its simplest level, a classical education is a Great Books education with an emphasis on history, classical languages such as Latin and Greek, formal logic, and composition. At its most complex, it is a detailed and carefully planned study based on the trivium—the grammar, dialectic, and rhetoric stages of education. Classical education is word-based rather than image-based, is history-intensive, stresses analysis and critical thinking, and values self-discipline (Wise & Bauer, 1999).

Much of classical education materials and theory published for home schoolers is Christian-based, but it is possible to approach classical education from a secular viewpoint as well. The emphasis on books, languages, logic, and rhetoric may appeal to students who have strong language arts and critical thinking skills. Study of timelines, ancient history, Latin, and deductive reasoning can be used quite successfully with many gifted learners. If your child is a highly creative or asynchronous learner, classical home schooling, like any other standard educational approach, will need to be adapted to fit his or her preferred learning styles.

The Trivium

Classical education divides learning into three stages, collectively called the trivium:

- *The Grammar Stage:* Emphasis on Facts
- *The Logic or Dialectic Stage:* Emphasis on Reasoning and Argument
- *The Rhetoric Stage:* Emphasis on Communication of Ideas

Specific age ranges for the three parts of the trivium varies. *The Grammar Stage* is traditionally thought to fit ages nine through 11, *The Dialectic Stage* ages 12 through 14, and *The Rhetoric Stage* ages 14 through 16. Some gifted education proponents have modified the ages to better accommodate today's home schoolers, listing *The Grammar Stage* as kindergarten through fourth grade, *The Dialectic Stage* grades five through eight, and the *Rhetoric Stage* grades nine through 12 (Wise & Bauer, 1999).

While classical education might sound like the ideal, rigorous education that gifted children need, it provides little room for creativity or self-expression for young children and does not easily accommodate the asynchronous traits and self-determination of many gifted and creative children, particularly when followed without any flexibility. In *The Well-Trained Mind* (Wise & Bauer, 1999, p. 84), the authors name the grammar stage (roughly grades one through four) the parrot years, and they insist that "Drill—exercises that apply a principle over and over again to a number of different examples—is very necessary for third and fourth graders." They conclude that knowledge of the world should take priority over creative self-expression and that, during the grammar stage, all learning should be parts to whole.

For gifted children, who are by nature divergent thinkers, having to concentrate on rote work and convergent thinking—following the thinking of someone else—may be difficult or impossible. For this reason, parents of especially creative children will need to modify the classical education model when necessary to include side trips, opportunities for self expression, immersion learning, and intuitive learning, taking care to follow the child's lead.

Another potential problem of this model is that strict adherence to the stages of learning assumes that children will move from one stage to the next more or less "on time." But in *Miseducation: Preschoolers at Risk* (1987), David Elkind suggests that gifted learners may enter certain stages several years ahead of average learners. For example, a gifted learner may be ready for logical analysis and creative expression at an age when the classical education model says he should still be concentrating on rote facts. Elkind argues that what intellectually gifted children need is actually a "prolonged period" of self-directed learning and a delay of formal instruction, rather than an early emphasis on following directions and rote learning.

On the other hand, classical education rests on the foundations that all knowledge is interrelated and that during the early years, children should "delve deep," and that we should "Spread knowledge out in front of them, and let them feast" (Wise & Bauer, 1999, p. 54). These principles are well suited to creative home schooling. The challenge is how to tailor a classical education to fit the special needs of gifted and creative children. Following are some ideas.

Making Classical Education Work for Gifted Children

The classical education model offers many advantages for home schoolers—a built-in structure and overriding purpose of education, plenty of resources lists, readily available curriculum materials, and an approach to home schooling that is easily explained and accepted by family and friends. This parent tells why she likes classical education and finds it a good fit for her nine-year-old son:

> We have moved to a classical education after trying various others because there are no grade levels in classical education. There are just great ideas and works of history and literature. It is perfect study for a gifted child because there is no required age for mastery. Everyone, no matter what age, can get something from these works. The classical model for gifted education is different depending on how you use it. We don't do narrative writing, for example, because right now our son is very stubborn about writing.
>
> We have started in the logic stage. He was already there, and the readings were at his level. The beauty of classical education is that there is no wrong way to do it. Each method defines the ages to move to the next level differently. Each curriculum defines what should be studied each year differently.
>
> The classical model is a wonderful model for gifted children. Don't get too wrapped up in one book's philosophy. Read a few books on the subject and then develop a model that will work for your child.
>
> —Valerie, home school parent

As this parent says, if you are thinking of using a classical education model, you need to know that you can't always count on following someone else's detailed plan of what to teach and when to teach it; you will need to make modifications to most classical home schooling guides and curricula.

Another family says they use the classical education approach because it offers "a framework for a well rounded education." They have learned to accommodate the approach to fit their children's asynchronous learning traits.

We are following the basic outline proposed in the book The Well-Trained Mind *for our nine- and 10-year-old girls.*

The nine-year-old is firmly in the grammar stage except for math and spatial skills. Her reading, writing, spelling, and memory work all seem to be following the grammar stage characteristics, and she is into the logic stage with math. She is using EPGY (a distance learning math program through Stanford University) and Singapore Math. She has finished the figural portion of Building Thinking Skills, Book Two *and is fully ready for Book Three, but I am holding off for a bit. We tried some of the* Mind Benders *books last August, and she wasn't quite ready for the logical process.*

Our 10-year-old seems to have been in the logic stage for a couple of years. She has really enjoyed the logic puzzles with Mind Benders *and some other resources that we picked up. She is also doing EPGY for math, as well as using* Singapore Math *and Harold Jacob's* Mathematics: A Human Endeavor. *She reads quite a lot, and we are trying to be more diligent about keeping track of what she reads, and summarizing. She struggles a bit with outlining history. We used a workbook from Remedia Publications about outlining to help in this area. We have also incorporated a laptop computer into our school day because she did not enjoy all the writing. She loves building her timeline. We are working on Ancient Greece right now. We read a piece from Plato's "Last Days of Socrates," and she really understood and enjoyed it. We would never have thought to try this, but another home schooler recommended the activity for a logic-stage child.*

Latin fell by the wayside this year only because we always seem to run out of time in the day. Previously, the children really enjoyed it and did well. We've also done less structured science this year. For now, we are keeping nature journals and doing interest-led science projects instead of following a structured science framework.

The Internet has been a major source of support. Having e-mail support groups has provided a place to exchange ideas and resources and has broadened our scope of possibilities for our children's learning.

—Darlene and Ken, home school parent

The parent examples above illustrate how two different families use classical education with their gifted children. To use classical education with gifted and creative learners, parents can try several strategies.

- Capitalize on the fact that history provides a big picture on which to base interdisciplinary learning. An overview of history from the beginning to the end is one of classical education's greatest strengths. For the child who craves meaning and loves history, this approach offers depth and breadth found in few other curricula. Keep in mind that history can be an emotionally difficult subject for highly sensitive children. The more unpleasant aspects of history and human nature may be better understood, appreciated, and accepted at a later age.

○ Use history as an avenue to other subjects by learning about mathematical ideas and mathematicians from the historical era being studied, science ideas and scientists, literature and writers, philosophers, and ordinary people. Be aware that classical education often stresses history and language arts at the expense of an in-depth and satisfying math and science education. Math and science resources commonly recommended by classical education theorists may not be adequate for gifted and creative children, especially for children who require visual math materials. A good series that explores the science and math of ancient cultures is the *Science of the Past* series, published by Franklin Watts/Grolier. Each book in the series is attractively illustrated with color photos, maps, drawings, charts, and glossaries.

○ Supplement or replace suggested verbal resources with visual material when necessary. CD-ROMs such as Scientific American's *Exploring Ancient Cities*—an interactive exploration of the four ancient cities of Teotihuacan, Pompeii, Petra, and Crete—offer video imagery unavailable in books. Experiment with whether audio-visual material works better with your child as an introduction to an idea, a bridge to new information, or a reinforcement of ideas.

○ Study Latin and other ancient languages in a fun and meaningful way. Connect Latin to mythology, biology, or whatever other interest the child has.

○ Plan to include resources relating to a variety of cultures and viewpoints. Roman and Greek mythology can be used as an entry point to the mythology and cultures of many lands and peoples. *The World Mythology* series, published by Peter Bedrick Books, is a good resource to look for in your library.

○ Allow for creative thinking as an integral part of learning for every age.

○ Realize that a highly gifted child may stray far from the stages of learning outlined by the trivium. Your child may make the connections and notice the relationships indicative of the logic stage years before reaching fourth grade and may be capable of self-expression and synthesis of ideas long before ninth grade. At the same time, the child may be at age level in other skills and interests, so as a parent, be careful to expect neither too much nor too little.

○ When in doubt, follow your child's lead and your own instincts rather than a curriculum's dictates.

Flexibility and adaptability are important if you want to make classical education work for a creative or visual-spatial learner. Anne has learned to follow the lead of her nine-year-old daughter, Denice.

> *When we started home schooling last November, I decided that my role was to be a facilitator. However, my daughter did need a nudge. At that point, I had never heard of* The Well-Trained Mind *but had already decided to start at the beginning. I thought we would start with Paleolithic man and go forward. Denice had other ideas. Her interest was immediately piqued, and we took a major step back to the origins of the universe. She delved into epochs, eras, and ages. She learned about the anthropology and scientific reasoning behind evolution. She discovered the different layers of the earth's crust. Then she was ready to learn about the "Paleolithic dudes." She wrote a newsletter called "Caveman Times," which was four pages long. She would have never written eight little essays of 150-300 words, but writing the newsletter articles was somehow different.*
>
> *She's really enjoying reading and learning about history, art, math, and science as they happened and within the context of how and why they happened. I have to admit I'm learning a lot also. I don't know if we will spend a full year on ancient history. It may be over in three months, but then again, it may be 18 months. We'll see where it leads.*
>
> *We have also added Latin. We're using* Latina Christiana, *which is supposed to be for third- to fifth-grade level and is extremely simple for Denice, so it's not a big deal—20 minutes a week and she gets it. I've been amazed how much she has associated the Latin vocabulary she's learned with everyday English words. The more we do this, the more convinced I am that the classical education approach is our cup of tea.*
>
> —Anne, home school parent

Classical education recommends that students study history from the beginning forward. Anne offers this detailed example, using Sumeria (Ancient Mesopotamia), of how she has adapted the classical education model for her visual-spatial learner and also emphasized interdisciplinary learning by relating other subjects—science, art, math, etc.—to each time period.

The first thing I do is scour the library for documentaries of the particular civilization. These provide a good visual reference to introduce the area we are studying. I also try to find one piece of literature (or more, if available), which I read to her. In this case, we read "The Epic of Gilgamesh." Using Kingfisher's World History *as a base, we then start exploring and reading…*

Science: We discussed simple machines since this was when they were first used.

Math: We got into base 60 (Sumerian number-based), the concept of circles (how early Pi was used), and early units of measurement and their impact on today's system.

Art: We learned about the use of dyes, paints, enamelware, and how the Sumerian art was still religious-based. She carved her name into a red clay slab in cuneiform and made some coil pots.

Poetry: We read the first written poem—by an Arkadian princess.

Archaeology: We explored how scientists date archeological finds.

Civics: We studied Hammurabi's code and its impact on today's laws.

Geography: She drew a map of the region and, in a different color, of today's countries, noting landforms of importance. It starts to take a life of its own.

We have a timeline (on a huge roll of butcher paper) that is added to daily. She gets the graphics off the Internet through clip art searches. We have the timeline divided by continent.

Our final project is to put together a four- to six-page newsletter, which summarizes each area with appropriate graphics (I never thought the scanner would get this much use!).

By the time we're done, she's heard it, seen it, read it, and narrated it. When I read to her, she is practicing "mind-mapping" techniques and early stages of note taking.

—Anne, home school parent

From Sumeria, Anne and her daughter will move onto a study of classical history, medieval history, and so on. Other students might choose a different ancient civilization to focus on, such as Greece or Rome.

Often, but not always, parents who follow a classical education model have a relatively structured schedule, with specific lessons to be covered each day. The structure and discipline of classical education is what attracts many home schoolers, especially families who enjoy and thrive with detailed plans and structure. Parents who have made highly structured, classical home schooling work for their gifted children seem to respect the model's discipline but place the needs of the child first. Followed strictly, most year-by-year classical education guides are not in sync with the gifted child's intellectual needs, but if parents use flexibility and let their child's unique developmental pattern be their guide, classical home schooling can be tailored to the needs of intense and rapid learners.

Ingrid has been home schooling for three and one-half years. She describes her reasons for choosing classical home schooling and the adaptations she has made for her three gifted children:

> *I believe that a classical education produces a well-rounded and disciplined child, moreso than in a less formal home school setting. I follow grade and age guidelines to some extent. I try to give the children an orderly, step-by-step education, but if they complete a step before they "should," I let them move on.*
>
> *I cut out almost all of the repetitive exercises for my children. In writing, for example, if the child understands several grammatical rules and expressions of writing in one day, his writing exercise for that day can incorporate all of this instead of having one exercise for each step.*
>
> *For my oldest son, Lyle, who is 13 and profoundly gifted, we sometimes complete several steps in a day, which consists mainly of my showing him a concept and his already knowing it. He often covers a chapter a day in math. We don't skip chapters. At the elementary grade levels, I think it's important to cover each step thoroughly. Still, the children are flying through the curriculum at an amazing rate. Lyle once covered five grade levels in a year and a half. Sometimes I wonder if the whole grade assessment thing is off. Who ever heard of covering five grades in a year and a half?*
>
> *The best aspect of classical home schooling is the discipline demanded in a classical education. Gifted children sometimes see no point in explaining steps, or in taking time with presentation, or in memorizing a poem word for word. I spend a lot of time on presentation, and I take points off for things like improper headings, no date on the paper, and so on. The most difficult aspect of classical home schooling with gifted children is to balance the focus on self-discipline with the perfectionist tendencies often evident in gifted children.*
>
> —Ingrid, home school parent

Home school parents who use classical education theory may want to read the book *Perfectionism: What's Bad about Being Too Good*, by Miriam Adderholdt-Elliott and Jan Goldberg (1999), for a better understanding of how to encourage an environment that nurtures the pursuit of excellence rather than one that stresses perfection.

Advantages and Disadvantages of Classical Home Schooling for Gifted and Creative Students

Advantages:

+ Emphasis on logic, literature, and languages
+ High level of challenge
+ Comfortable amount of structure for some families
+ Ease of curriculum planning

Disadvantages:

− May inhibit creativity
− May be too much structure for some students and their families
− Risk of overemphasizing perfectionism over love of learning
− May not leave adequate time for student's own interests
− Heavy emphasis on literacy may be frustrating for visual-spatial learners

Key Points

☑ Classical home schooling is a Great Books education with an emphasis on history, classical languages such as Latin and Greek, formal logic, and composition; it is word-based rather than image-based, is history-intensive, stresses analysis and critical thinking, and values self-discipline.

☑ Classical home schooling divides learning into three stages, collectively called the *trivium*—The Grammar Stage (emphasis on facts), The Logic or Dialectic Stage (emphasis on reasoning and argument), and The Rhetoric Stage (emphasis on communication of ideas).

☑ Parents should know that some classical home schooling programs offer little room for creativity or self-expression for young children and do not easily accommodate the asynchronous traits and self-determination of many gifted and creative children, particularly when followed without any flexibility.

☑ Some strengths of classical home schooling are a "big picture" approach to history and an emphasis on language and ideas.

☑ Parents can differentiate classical home schooling for gifted and creative children by incorporating challenging math and science study, visual-spatial and audio-visual learning resources and activities, creative thinking, and multiple perspectives.

☑ Parents who use classical home schooling should follow their child's lead and be flexible in following the trivium.

Classical Home Schooling Resources

Classical Home Schooling

Berquist, Laura (1998). *Designing Your Own Classical Curriculum: A Guide to Catholic Home Schooling.* Ignatius Press

Tapestry of Grace. A Christian classical home schooling curriculum. www.tapestryofgrace.com

Wise, Jessie, & Bauer, Susan Wise (1999). *The Well-Trained Mind: A Guide to Classical Education at Home.* Norton.

Classical Education Theory

Hanson, Victor Davis, & Heath, John (1998). *Who Killed Homer? The Demise of Classical Education and the Recovery of Greek Wisdom.* Free Press. An argument for bringing back classical studies.

Nussbaum, Martha C. (1997). *Cultivating Humanity: A Classical Defense of Reform in Liberal Education.* Harvard University Press. An argument for the inclusion of cultural diversity in a classics curriculum.

Websites

A to Z Home's Cool Classical Christian Education Links
www.gomilpitas.com/homeschooling/methods/Classical.htm

Classical Christian Homeschooling
www.classicalhomeschooling.org

Escondido Tutorial (five-year great books study)
www.gbt.org

Gifted Using Well-Trained Mind E-mail Loop
http://groups.yahoo.com/group/GiftedUsingWTM

Great Books Academy
www.greatbooksacademy.org

Internet Resources for Classics
www.sms-va.com/mdl-indx/internet.htm

ISLAS Classical Academy
www.islas.org

The Well-Trained Mind
www.welltrainedmind.com

The Well-Trained Mind Great Books E-mail Loop
http://groups.yahoo.com/group/TWTM_Great_Books

A Taste of Classical Home Schooling Resources

Bell, Barbara (2000). *Minimum: Starting Out in Latin*. Cambridge University Press.

D'Aulaire, Ingri, & D'Aulaire, Edgar Parin (1986). *D'Aulaire's Norse Gods and Giants*.

D'Aulaire, Ingri, & D'Aulaire, Edgar Parin (1992). *D'Aulaires' Book of Greek Myths*. Picture Yearling.

Hanlin, Jayne I., & Lichtenstein, Beverly E. (1991). *Learning Latin through Mythology*. Cambridge University Press. Thirteen classic myths in both English and illustrated Latin, with vocabulary and writing activities.

Nardo, Don (1998). *Greek and Roman Science*. Lucent Books. Reading level: grades 5-7. Interest level: ages 8 and up.

Science of the Past Series. Franklin Watts/Grolier. Reading level: grades 4-6. Interest level: ages 6 and up (nice for reading aloud).

> *Science in Ancient China*, by George Beshore (1998)
> *Science in Ancient Egypt*, by Geraldine Woods (1998)
> *Science in Ancient Greece*, by Kathlyn Gay (1998)
> *Science in Ancient India*, by Melissa Stewart (1999)
> *Science in Ancient Mesopotamia*, by Carol Moss (1998)
> *Science in Ancient Rome*, by Jacqueline L. Harris (1998)
> *Science in Colonial America*, by Brendan January (1999)
> *Science in Early Islamic Cultures*, by George Beshore (1998)
> *Science in the Renaissance*, by Brendan January (1999)
> *Science of the Early Americas*, by Geraldine Woods (1999)

World Mythology Series. Peter Bedrick Books.

> *Demons, Gods and Holy Men From Indian Myths and Legends*, by Shahrukh Husain (1995)
>
> *Druids, Gods and Heroes From Celtic Mythology*, by Anne Ross (1994)
>
> *Fabled Cities, Prices and Jinn From Arab Myths and Legends*, by Khairat Al-Saleh (1995)
>
> *Gods and Heroes from Viking Mythology*, by Brian Branston (1982)
>
> *Gods and Pharaohs from Egyptian Mythology*, by Geraldine Harris (1992)
>
> *Kings, Gods and Spirits from African Mythology*, by Jan Knappert (1993)
>
> *Spirits, Heroes and Hunters from North American Indian Mythology*, by Marion Wood (1992)
>
> *Warriors, Gods and Spirits from Central and South American Mythology*, by Douglas Gifford (1983)

Resources Mentioned by Classical Home School Families

Building Thinking Skills, Critical Thinking Books & Software
> www.criticalthinking.com

EPGY (Education Program for Gifted Youth)
> www-epgy.stanford.edu

Elementary Algebra, by Harold Jacobs. W. H. Freeman.

The Kingfisher Illustrated History of the World : 40,000 B.C. to Present Day.
> Kingfisher Books.

Latina Christiana. Memoria Press. "Specifically written for the home school
> parent or schoolteacher with no background in Latin." Student books,
> teacher manuals, and pronunciation tapes. Visit www.memoriapress.com
> for on-line sample pages

Mind Benders, Critical Thinking Books & Software
> www.criticalthinking.com

On-line Daily GeoBee Quiz
> www.nationalgeographic.com/geobee

On-line Daily Grammar
> www.dailygrammar.com

On-line SAT Question of the Day
> http://cbweb9p.collegeboard.org/tqod/bin/question.cgi

On-line Word of the Day Sites
> www.m-w.com/cgi-bin/mwwod.pl
> www.wordsmith.org/awad

Remedia Publications
> www.rempub.com

Singapore Math and Singapore Science
> www.singaporemath.com (on-line sample pages)

At Home with Home Schoolers

Denice, Age 9, Grades 4-10

Q: How would you describe a typical day of home schooling?

A: I get up; sometimes I get dressed right away. Every day I do the Geo-Bee, SAT Question of the Day, Grammar Lesson of the Day, and the Word of the Day. I do 10-15 minutes of keyboard practice, alternating days with penmanship. Then we do history for 45 minutes to an hour. I am working out of two math books, Singapore Math *and Harold Jacob's* Elementary Algebra. *I also use* Singapore Science *a couple of days a week. Most days, except when I have music lessons, I practice piano and violin. Once a week I participate in the Youth Symphony, French classes, drama class, and horseback riding lessons.*

Q: How has your home schooling routine changed since you've begun, if at all?

A: The routine hasn't changed, but how we do it has. Last year my mom would read to me and I would dictate a summary for a newsletter we do on each unit. This year I am doing more of the typing and reading myself. We are watching videos/documentaries at the beginning of a unit rather than the middle or end. This really helps to give me a better overview before we start reading and researching. I also discovered that I have better music practice mid-day. This year I am working more independently on science and math also.

Q: What do you like about home schooling?

A: That we can stay in our pajamas all day if we want to. Also that I get done with school three hours early. I can pick what I want to work on and when. Home schooling is fun because you can do things you wouldn't have time to do while in school, for example horseback riding and drama class. Plus I have more free time to just be a kid. When I was in school, all my lessons (French, violin, and piano) were after-school activities. By the time I got home and did my homework, practiced, and ate dinner, it was time to go to bed.

Q: What don't you like about home schooling?

A: Having to be with my mom all day, but she understands how I need to learn. I miss the kids at recess, but not as much as I used to at the beginning.

Q: What does a "good education" mean to you?

A: A good education means you can go as deep as you want to into a subject and not be confined by the school curriculum. I also have time to learn things like French and the Latin/Greek roots of words. It is also more flexible, and sometimes I'll spend the whole day on math and do nothing else.

Q: How would you describe yourself as a learner? What are your learning styles and strengths? How do you learn best?

A: *I learn best by watching documentaries first and then reading about a subject. I also need to be doing something with my hands while listening and watching. I remember more by having my mom read to me while I take notes.*

Q: What are your long-term goals, if any? How are you working to meet them?

A: *To finish a high school curriculum in three years. If I qualify, I would like to go to the [University's] Early Entrance program in three years.*

Q: What advice do you have for other children and young adults who are considering home schooling?

A: *Learn to tolerate your mom. This is much different from loving her. Learn how to manage your time since there are no bells ringing to change subjects. While you are in school, you are told what to think about and when. When you are home schooling, you set the tone and pace. You will get out of it as much effort as you put into it, and on some days, it can be hard to give it your all.*

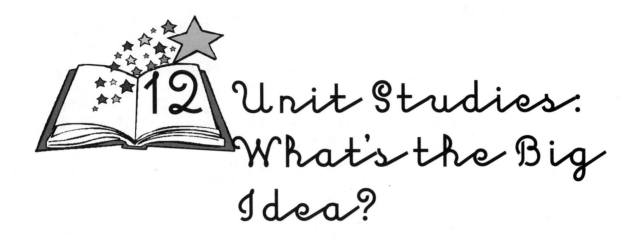

12 Unit Studies: What's the Big Idea?

If I could characterize a single issue that frustrates gifted children, their teachers and their parents, it is this issue of whether the child will do his work. This frustration arises from what I call, "the confusion of pronoun syndrome." I have rarely met gifted children who won't do their work. What they usually resist doing is the teacher's (his or her) work. Gifted children would actually be thrilled to be allowed to use school time to do their work, which I define as learning something they don't already know!

—Susan Winebrenner (2000)

Unit studies or theme studies are popular with home schoolers because they tap into a child's interests and are flexible enough to use with several ages at once. A unit study is simply a collection of learning activities or lessons tied to a single theme or idea. Many children naturally "do" unit studies in their free time—we just call them obsessive interests! An example is the six-year-old who can't learn enough about insects or dinosaurs, or the 12-year-old who lives and breathes the world of computers or science fiction.

Unit studies can last a few hours or several months, depending on the nature of the topic and the extent of the child's interest. In schools, unit studies are sometimes known as thematic units. At their best, unit studies are interdisciplinary—that is, they use the main topic or theme to bring together and offer knowledge from several disciplines or subjects. For example, a 10-year-old who loves horses may study how horses were used in early America (history), where different breeds of horses exist worldwide (geography), how horses have been depicted in literature (language arts), how breeding of race horses leads to fast runners (science), and/or how to calculate the cost of feeding and keeping a horse for a year (math). Thus, an interest in horses leads quite naturally to other subject areas. In this way, thematic units help children see how all things relate. There is history in everything, math in everything, science in everything. Subjects don't stand alone; all disciplines are interrelated.

Several companies publish ready-made thematic unit studies and inter-disciplinary programs on everything from oceans to personality traits. Commercial unit studies often offer ideas for additional resources and activities. Some of these materials are excellent. Wildridge Software's *Math & Music* program, for example, is a multi-disciplinary approach to junior high and high school level math, which incorporates aspects of music, math, science, and history. Many free unit studies are available on the web (see Kathi Kearney's Free Firewood site at www.ignitethefire.com/freefirewood.html). Keep in mind, however, that some commercial and free unit study materials provide only superficial connections between ideas and disciplines, or lack integration of critical and creative thinking skills.

Many home schoolers design their own unit studies to fit their children's specific interests. It's fun—and easy—to make unit studies a family affair.

We used to have family nights when the girls were younger. Once a month, we'd have a night where we'd do different projects and such as a family. We'd pick a theme and work around it. We often did this when we studied certain countries. We'd cook and eat a meal from that country, listen to music, read stories from that culture, watch a travel video, play a game, etc. We planned these nights cooperatively, but I did the bulk of the work in pulling it all together and acting as emcee of the events.

—Joan, home school parent

We do mostly interest-based science. When I notice our daughter getting a stack of books at the library on a certain topic, I will try to find some websites, experiments, science kits, etc., and we study this topic as a family and try to include some field trips so we can actually touch or at least see whatever the topic is. Currently, we are interested in several things, but butterflies are the biggest interest. We started out just reading about them; then we found one of the kits to raise butterflies. We planted a butterfly garden and made a trip to a local zoo to see what it had in its garden. We are now planning a trip to a large botanical garden that has a huge butterfly garden and some interesting educational classes on attracting butterflies.

—Rose, home school parent

For Rose's family, the main topic—butterflies—opened doors to the study of several branches of science—animal habitats, plant pollination, and gardening. Rose and her daughter can now springboard from this main topic to related topics of social studies (geography of migration patterns), math (symmetry and design), literature (poetry about butterflies), and life stages of other insects (entomology).

Big Ideas for Big Thinkers

Unit studies are ideal for a child who exhibits the following learning characteristics:[17]

- O Is easily bored.

- O Prefers democratic decision making.

- O Prefers to learn in his or her own way, especially in reading and math. Sits still only when working on material that is personally interesting.

- O Is frustrated by lack of resources and guidance for exploring his or her own big ideas.

- O Prefers to learn by exploration rather than rote memory or passive listening.

- O May give up and develop lifelong learning blocks if failure is experienced early.

From the perspective of the classroom, many of these characteristics may be viewed by teachers not trained in gifted education as problems needing to be fixed, but such characteristics can actually be a treasure trove of untapped learning potential when the barriers to using them are removed. Ways to capitalize on these characteristics are shown in Table 12.1.

---

17   Adapted from the National Foundation for Gifted and Creative Children at www.nfgcc.org/character.htm.

Table 12.1: Capitalizing on Learning Strengths

Because Gifted/Creative Children…	Big Ideas Unit Studies Allow Them to…
Are intrinsically motivated to learn, prefer personal exploration to authoritarian learning, and prefer do things their own way	Have as much control as possible over what to learn, how to learn, when to learn, and how to record learning; be an active explorer rather than a passive passenger
Are easily bored and can focus best when working on self-chosen tasks	Use their energy according to internal needs and drives, and allow intrinsic interests to regulate challenge and boredom
Crave global connections, perspectives, and significance	Use an area of passion to explore many facets of the world around them
Are easily frustrated by lack of resources and guidance to explore, and to realize their big ideas and questions	Have caring adults as informal mentors who take their big ideas and questions seriously
Like to learn new things, are willing to examine the unusual, and are highly inquisitive	Ask questions about any interest that matters to them, not just those seen as "academic"
See possibilities and relationships others do not see	Follow their natural train of thought, which leads to patterns and new inquiries
Can get lost in pursuing their own thoughts	Have plenty of private learning and thinking time free from outside evaluation and coercion
May give up and develop lifelong learning blocks if they experience early failure	Learn without fear of failure and with the expectation of success; have plenty of private learning and thinking time free from outside evaluation and coercion
Are sensitive and often have intense fears about big life issues	Integrate social and emotional concerns with academic learning; learn in an environment that supports intensity and sensitivity

Parents as Mentors

The Big Ideas for Big Thinkers approach encourages parents to see themselves as *informal mentors* who provide an *environment and relationship conducive to learning*, rather than teachers in the traditional sense. L. S. Vygotsky (1997), an educational psychologist, offers the useful notion of a learner's *Zone of Proximal Development*. In simple terms, this is the difference between what a person is capable of learning on one's own and what the same person is capable of learning with the assistance and guidance of someone else. The job of the home school parent is to provide scaffolding and support so that the child can enter that zone of maximum learning.

For example, if a child asks how the lenses in eyeglasses work and you don't feel qualified to give an adequate answer, you might say, "I'd like to learn more about that myself. Where do you think we could find the answer?" This response helps the child to use the adults around him as facilitators, not authority figures who are bearers of knowledge or facts. After some discussion, you and your child might decide to look in the encyclopedia, read a science book, do experiments with lenses and prisms, or interview an eye-care specialist.

Asking Questions that Matter

Alfie Kohn, in his book *The Schools Our Children Deserve* (1999), argues that education for all students should start with "questions that matter" and that knowing how to ask better questions and pursue the answers is often as important as the answers themselves. The questions that matter to all of us are questions we've come up with ourselves that arise from our own unique needs, circumstances, knowledge, and perspectives.

Questions that matter often demonstrate higher level thinking. Lower level thinking usually is concerned with facts or correct answers. Higher-level thinking is more concerned with ideas and analysis of information or ideas. Classroom instruction is frequently geared toward lower level thinking skills—i.e., acquiring knowledge and facts and *comprehending* them. Learning to spell and knowing what words mean are lower level thinking skills. Knowing dates and events from history and understanding their importance are also lower level thinking skills.

Examples of higher level thinking skills would be analyzing word derivations or evaluating different historical perspectives. Where did this word come from? How is it used in different parts of the world? How sure can we be of the accuracy of different historical perspectives? In history, at what point do we choose to accept the various truths of differing viewpoints? Higher level thinking questions are often open-ended—i.e., there is no single correct answer, but rather different possible answers, depending on your reasons. Questions that matter are usually those that lead to higher level thinking skills.

Gifted students should be encouraged to explore the following higher level thinking skills (Arizona Department of Education, 2001):

- *Analysis*: breaking a whole into its parts to discover their nature, functions, and relationships to other parts, etc.

- *Evaluation*: determining the worth of something, appraising value.

- *Synthesis*: putting together parts or elements to create a complex whole.

- *Problem finding*: following a series of steps to determine objective(s), find facts, identify the underlying problem(s), generate alternative solutions, and select the best solution.

- *Decision making*: describing the issue/problem clearly, generating alternatives, determining criteria for evaluation of alternatives, selecting the best alternative, and supporting choices.

- *Planning*: preparing for a detailed series of steps for accomplishing a task—clear statement of goals, resources needed, step-by-step sequence of activities, methods to detect potential problems, alternative paths to the goal.

- *Deduction*: reasoning from a known principle to an unknown or from a premise to a logical conclusion.

- *Induction*: reasoning from particular facts or individual cases to a generalization.

- *Creative thinking*: generating many, varied, unusual ideas and adding to ideas—fluency, flexibility, originality, and elaboration.

- *Predicting/Forecasting*: Evaluating cause and effect sequences and, based on results, deciding the most likely outcome(s).

Parents and teachers of gifted children can help children ask questions that matter by asking questions that use specific words that trigger higher level thinking skills. Here are some examples (Winebrenner, 1992):

Thinking Category	Trigger Words
Analysis	investigate, classify, categorize, compare, contrast, solve
Evaluation	judge, evaluate, give opinion, viewpoint, prioritize, recommend, critique
Synthesis	compose, design, invent, create, hypothesize, construct, forecast, rearrange parts, imagine

If your child just finished reading the latest popular fantasy novel, instead of asking, "Did you like it?" ask, "How would you *compare* the book with [a book of a similar genre]? How is it similar? For which audience would you *recommend* this book? Why? How did you *imagine* the story would end? Were you able to predict the ending? How well did the author arrange parts of the story?" If you and your child are reading Greek myths, encourage higher level thinking by asking him to *classify* the gods and goddesses according to their origin or purpose, *critique* the usefulness of the myths in helping the people to understand natural phenomena of their world, or *invent* a modern myth that would help explain some aspect of our world today. These kinds of assignments and questions will require your child to analyze, synthesize, or evaluate information he has learned and will lead to a deeper level of understanding.

According to Annemarie Roeper (1992), two important needs of young gifted children are: (1) a global perspective, and (2) exposure to broad, abstract concepts. Commercial unit studies often offer too little substance for gifted and creative learners because they stay in the lower levels of thinking. They focus more on the concrete thinking skills of *knowledge* (gathering facts), *comprehension* (demonstrating understanding of facts), and *application* (making models, drawing pictures) than on the abstract thinking skills of *analysis* (understanding part-to-whole relationships), *evaluation* (forming judgments), and *synthesis* (creating new knowledge). The Big Ideas for Big Thinkers approach lets children move quickly from the local and specific knowledge and application level skills to the global and abstract higher level skills and back again.

Creating a Big Ideas Unit: A Guide for Parents

Your child's role in a Big Ideas for Big Thinkers Unit will be that of an active learner—thinking of questions to research, looking for resources, recording learning, and sharing expertise. The parent's role will be that of *mentor* and *facilitator*. As *mentor*, you will be a model of someone who loves to learn, persists in searching for answers to questions, willingly shares information and expertise, and exhibits a positive attitude toward education and your life's work. As *facilitator*, you will aid your child in getting from where she is, to where she wants to go.

The more you remember these roles, the better the Big Ideas for Big Thinkers approach will work. If you begin to think your role is to *make* your child learn or that your child can develop a love of learning without proper mentoring and assistance, your child may resist the study completely or will be at a loss for guidance and resources.

Primary Roles of Facilitator/Mentor

Assist your child in finding and learning how to find necessary and appropriate resources. If your child is not familiar with your local library, spend a morning simply browsing the stacks, learning how the card catalog works, and finding out what computer and other resources are available. Ask the librarian if your child can get a personal tour, and encourage your child to view the librarian as a source of guidance and information.

Show your child how to use reference materials such as *Literature Connections to World History, K-6: Resources to Enhance and Entice*, by Lynda G. Adamson, or *Adventuring with Books: A Booklist for Pre-K-Grade 6*, by Wendy Sutton, to find books on specific topics. This will take more time and patience on your part (it's much faster just to find them yourself!), but the practice in independent learning and the development of future study skills will be worth it.

Help your child know safe ways to explore and search the Internet. *The Internet Kids and Family Yellow Pages, 2001 Edition*, by Jean Armour Polly, and *Homeschool Your Child for Free: More Than 1,200 Smart, Effective, and Practical Resources for Home Education on the Internet and Beyond*, by Laura Maery Gold and Joan M. Zielinksy, are both excellent guides for home schooling families.

Set the stage for creative and intuitive learning by providing time for daydreaming and by looking for resources that use imagination and "what if" thinking. Think twice before you barge into your child's workspace with questions about what he is learning or what the child has accomplished in a particular time period or day. Give the child plenty of time to find a working rhythm and to share work and ideas on his own timetable.

Abraham Maslow (1971) believed that primary creativeness—the inspirational and inventive aspect of creativity—is the foundation of creative learning. A child exhibits primary creativeness when exploring new ideas, playing with combinations of ideas, and creating for its own sake rather than for evaluation or to produce a product. *Primary creativeness* does not always result in tangible creative products, but that does not lessen its importance. A child is engaging in primary creativeness when she reads a favorite book series over and over in order to internalize characters, situations, and plot. She might draw sketches of what the characters and scenes look like in her mind. Only later might she use this primary creativeness to produce a tangible creation, such as a story she writes herself or a watercolor picture of the characters or a book review that synthesizes all that she learned. Many parents choose home schooling primarily for this benefit—i.e., the flexibility, time, and space necessary for a child to develop skills of creativity and intuition that will make later production meaningful.

Address social and emotional needs through the topic being studied. This is one area that you will need to plan so that the needs are addressed in a natural and unobtrusive way. If your child is dealing with the negative aspects of perfectionism, for example, you don't want this to be an overt part of the unit from his viewpoint. Rather, you can look for ways to integrate his needs with the subject matter without the child's noticing that you are doing so. How can bibliotherapy fit in as part of the unit? Are there opportunities for the child to learn with and from other children? Or to interact with adults who specialize in the subject? Does the topic have global and historical significance? How can you best alert your child to some of these possibilities?

A strategy for bibliotherapy is to sprinkle around the house books that you'd like your child to read. If you have found some good fiction books that deal with friendship, for example, perhaps by browsing the index of Judy Halsted's *Some of My Best Friends are Books: Guiding Gifted Readers from Preschool to High School, 2nd edition* (2002), check them out on *your* library card and read them when your child is watching. Leave them in a place where your child can pick them up. Or you can offer to read a book chapter aloud after lunch or just before bed simply because it's a good book or you are curious to read it. If needed, refer to Halsted's tips for guiding reluctant readers.

Develop and demonstrate a patient and accepting attitude toward your child's education. Nearly every home schooling parent at one time or another becomes panicked that the child isn't learning enough, isn't learning certain things on time, or isn't covering the right material. This is a normal fear, and probably a healthy one, since we want to see our children succeed. We don't want anything we do as a home schooling parent to interfere with their dreams or to preclude their later pursuit of certain vocations or goals.

However, when panic sets in (and it will!), resist the urge to show your anxiety to your child by forcing or rushing into new curriculum or immediately having your child tested extensively. For example, if your family's strength is math and science and you have been happily studying pre-algebra and simple machines with your 10-year-old, you might hear on the radio one day some alarming statistics about geographic illiteracy of American children. You suddenly realize that your child probably doesn't know the names of all 50 states, much less where they are. Rather than rush out to buy worksheets or say, "We'd have to learn this now," take the time to consider the best way to address the concern. You could begin with a game such as *Borderline, USA Edition*, which requires no knowledge of U.S. geography to play, but which develops geographic memory through colorful maps and auditory reinforcement. Or you might look for a jigsaw puzzle of the United States. As the weeks go by, think of ways to include geography in your usual curriculum.

Your child's self-concept as an active learner stays intact, and you will have saved yourself a lot of stress.

Encourage your child to do good work through meaningful activities and self-assessment. When a child has a reason for being accurate and neat, the child is more likely to strive to be accurate and neat. Grades are not a good enough reason for many gifted children (Clark, 1997). What does seem to work is to allow children to choose their own ways to share expertise in ways that are meaningful to them. Encourage them to design their own website, organize a special interest club such as a science fiction club or nature club, or pursue hobbies such as scale model building or coin collecting. All are ways to demonstrate knowledge. While on occasion you may ask your child to fill out a math worksheet or do a spelling test in order to comply with state regulations or to add to the child's portfolio, formal assessments do not have to be the only means of evaluation.

Whenever possible, have the child find ways to evaluate her own work. Provide the child with answer keys, teacher's editions, and other self-checking guides to show the child that she can be trusted with learning (Delisle, 1992). Don't worry if the child resists such strategies at first. In time, the child will see that these can be used as learning tools and that the concept of cheating disappears when learning—rather than grades—is the goal.

An Example of a Big Ideas for Big Thinkers Unit

Because the Big Ideas for Big Thinkers Unit Study approach is tailored to a child's interests and learning styles, it will never be the same twice, even for children in the same family. To get an idea of how you and your children might use this approach, let's look at an example of how a Big Ideas for Big Thinkers Unit is created for an individual child. Following is a sample unit created for a 10- to 12-year-old girl who is a strong reader and craves intellectual challenge and global connections. All resources listed are appropriate for ages 10 and up, reading levels grade five and up. The unit is called **Revolutionary Ideas** and focuses on the events and time period of the American Revolution.

> *You say you want a revolution*
> *Well you know*
> *We all want to change the world*
>
> —John Lennon and Paul McCartney

> *In 1783, the idea of revolution crackled like lightning around the world.*
> *The old ways of government are wrong, thought more and more people.*
> *Rulers have too much power. It is time for a change.*
>
> —from Carol Greene's *Simon Bolivar: South American Liberator*

Phase I. Planning and Packing

Most of us already know that the Eighteenth Century was an important century for the United States. After all, it was the century of our nation's birth. But what else do we know about those 100 years between 1700 and 1800? Was the United States alone in its revolutionary change, or were we just one country in a larger drama of global transformation? What circumstances led to the way? What circumstances made the American Revolution possible? What effect did the revolution have on the rest of the world? What debt do we owe the people of the Eighteenth Century over 200 years later?

These are just some of the questions a student might consider as she explores Revolutionary Ideas. The Eighteenth Century was a time of *revolution*. It was also an age of both *enlightenment* and *reason*, and a period of *restoration*. These are the kinds of big ideas that can guide and give shape to the unit study.

Good unit studies usually begin by exploring what one already knows and then raising questions for possible further investigation. If you don't know much about the topic or historical period being studied, don't worry. The beauty of home schooling is that you are allowed to learn alongside your children. To re-familiarize yourself with the subject or to get an overview, you may want to read an encyclopedia summary or other general resource before starting the unit with your child. One of the advantages of the Big Ideas approach is that you don't need to list learner outcomes or state your child's final destination before your start the unit. You can have in mind some possibilities—for example, to use primary documents to better understand multiple perspectives of the American Revolution—but the entire unit does not have to be mapped out ahead of time.

A Big Ideas for Big Thinkers Unit is an exploration into uncharted territory, much like the Lewis and Clark exploration. Lewis and Clark knew they were starting near St. Louis, that they wanted to follow the Missouri River to its source and then find a water route to the Pacific Ocean. They made careful plans and gathered supplies, but they had to revise their plans many times along the way. Their task was as much to notice details, use their skills of scientific inquiry, take notes, and track their progress as it was to reach their final destination. They didn't know exactly what they would learn until they had finished. As it turned out, they did not reach the Pacific Ocean by water, but had to do some creative problem solving to cross the Rocky Mountains and use both guides and horses to reach their final destination. This approach of improvising as you travel along is very different from the current educational attitude of always needing to have specific learner goals and outcomes—that must not be deviated from—in order for learning to occur.

In fact, a good way to talk with your children about the exploratory approach to learning might be to read about the Lewis and Clark expedition. Some good resources are the chapter "Meriwether and William—or Lewis and Clark" in Joy Hakim's *A History of US, Volume 4: The New Nation: 1789-1850* or the book *Lewis and Clark for Kids: Their Journey of Discovery with 21 Activities*, by Janis Herbert, and the video *"The Trail": Lewis and Clark Expedition*, produced by Robin Williams.

Planning for Social and Emotional Growth. This is a good time for parents to think about what social and emotional issues can be addressed throughout the study. The American Revolution provides many opportunities to explore issues relating to war, death, family, freedom, responsibility, and cultural differences. If your child is highly sensitive and bothered by the idea of war, you may need to read many of the resources together or choose books aimed at a younger audience. Some children will be able to handle reading about tragic events of war better than others. Your knowledge of your child will be your guide.

Many pieces of historical fiction written about this period deal with important emotional issues in sensitive ways. *My Brother Sam Is Dead*, by James Lincoln Collier and Christopher Collier, for example, explores not only the death of a family member but also multiple perspectives on death and war, self-identity, and personal responsibility. *Sarah Bishop*, by Scott O'Dell, is a sensitively written story about a young girl's self-preservation and the meaning of independence. *Jump Ship to Freedom*, by James Collier and Christopher Collier, is the story of a slave who is also the son of a Revolutionary War soldier and addresses issues of freedom, justice, and perseverance. *I'm Deborah Sampson, a Soldier in the War of the Revolution*, by Patricia Clapp, is based on a true story of a young woman who enlists in the Continental Army as a man; it can prompt discussion of gender roles, courage, and personal commitment.

Bibliotherapy, social/emotional growth through books, can include non-fiction as well as fiction. Older students who are ready for a more mature and detailed account of Deborah Sampson may enjoy *America's First Woman Warrior: The Courage of Deborah Sampson*, by Lucy Freeman and Alma Bond. This book discusses all of the challenges Deborah faced as she pretended to be a man so as to fight for freedom, including how she dealt with monthly menstrual periods and how she risked not being inoculated for smallpox so as better to escape detection. Deborah Sampson was an intelligent woman who read John Locke in her spare time and who was largely self-educated. Her story can prompt young modern readers to think about gender roles and what it means to be an intelligent, courageous woman.

Fiction and non-fiction resources provide an introduction to the historical era, perspective on the events offered by the author, the chance to identify with historical figures (real or imagined), and an opportunity to gain insight that the child can apply to her own life and choices. For a list of references for various historical eras, topics, and age levels, see Finding Resources for Big Ideas for Big Thinkers Units, near the end of this chapter.

Phase II. Scouting Expedition: What's Out There?

At the beginning of the unit of study, you will want to pique your child's interest and offer a broad knowledge base from which to springboard to more specific topics later. Give some thought to the best way for your child to get an overview of the topic based on previous knowledge, interests, and learning styles. Is there a certain aspect of the topic in which she is already interested or has some knowledge? Does your child have specific preferred learning styles that will guide the choice of resources? Think about such things as whether your child is comfortable reading independently or would prefer to be read to or to listen to an audio tape, whether she enjoys non-fiction or more fanciful historical fiction, whether she is more interested in interactive software or hands-on field trips, more passive reading or video viewing, and so on.

Here are some common types of resources to consider:

- Books, either print or audio versions
- Videos and television shows
- Software programs
- Field trips
- Games
- Music and art

Ask your child for more ideas.

To begin, look for general resources that give an overview of the topic or resources that approach the topic through the child's specific interest area. Don't start with too much! One or two books, videos, or other resources will be enough for many children. On the other hand, this Scouting Expedition phase of learning can last a long time for some children—weeks or even months—if their interest level is high enough. Let your child determine how long and how far to explore.

Here is a sampling of general resources that a child might find at the local library. Some she will probably read cover to cover; others she may browse through quickly. Notice that these resources include multiple perspectives and a variety of media. General resources should cover a broad range of the human experience. What were the different points of view of British citizens during the Revolutionary War? An African-American slave? A woman or young girl? An American Indian? Books available in your own library will differ from this list, and the needs and interests of your individual student will also affect what resources to include.

Non-Fiction Books

The American Revolution: 1763-1783, by Christopher Collier and James Lincoln Collier, Benchmark Books, 1998. A simple overview.

America's First Woman Warrior: The Courage of Deborah Sampson, by Lucy Freeman and Alma Bond, Paragon House, 1992.

Come All You Brave Soldiers: Blacks in the Revolutionary War, by Clinton Cox, Scholastic, 1999.

From Colonies to Country: 1710-1791, by Joy Hakim, Oxford University Press, 1999. *A History of US* series. An excellent overview of the period for middle school students.

George Washington's World, by Genevieve Foster and Joanna Foster, Beautiful Feet Books, 1940, revised 1997. Newberry Honor Winner.

The Great Declaration: A Book for Young Americans, by Henry Steele Commager, Bobbs-Merrill Co., 1958. This story of the writing of The Declaration of Independence includes numerous primary source letters and reproductions of period art.

Those Remarkable Women of the American Revolution, by Karen Zeinert, Millbrook Press, 1996. Women's roles in the army, as spies, in politics, in the Ladies' Association, and on the home front.

A Young Patriot: The American Revolution as Experienced by One Boy, by Jim Murphy, Clarion Books, 1996. The true story of 15-year-old Joseph Plumb Martin, often told in the boy's own words.

Historical Fiction Books

I'm Deborah Sampson, a Soldier in the War of the Revolution, by Patricia Clapp, Lathrop, Lee and Shepard, 1977.

Jump Ship to Freedom, by James Collier and Christopher Collier, Delacorte Press, 1981.

My Brother Sam Is Dead, by James Lincoln Collier and Christopher Collier, Scholastic Paperbacks, 1989.

Sarah Bishop, by Scott O'Dell, Houghton Mifflin, 1980.

Videos

A&E Biographies. Look for these A&E Home Video titles:
   George III: Mad or Maligned? (1995), 50 minutes
   Paul Revere: The Midnight Rider (1995), 47 minutes
   Thomas Jefferson: Philosopher of Freedom (1995), 50 minutes

Africans in America: Part I: The Terrible Transformation (1607-1861) (1998). WGBH Boston Video, 90 minutes (first of four tapes in a series).

America: Volume 3: Making a Revolution (1988). Ambrose Video Publishing, 52 minutes.

American Experience: George Washington—The Man Who Wouldn't Be King (1992). WGBH Boston Video, 60 minutes.

American Women of Achievement Video Collection: Abigail Adams (1995). Wolfington Productions, 30 minutes.

The Crossing, A&E (2000). 100 minutes.

Founding Fathers, A&E (2000). 200 minutes (four tapes).

Liberty! The American Revolution (1998). PBS Home Video, 360 minutes (three tapes).

U.S. Constitution/Bill of Rights (1999). Goldhil Home Media, 100 minutes (two tapes).

Websites

The History Channel
    www.historychannel.com

Homework Planet's American Revolution Page
    www.educationplanet.com/articles/american_revolution.html

Liberty! The American Revolution
    www.pbs.org/ktca/liberty/index.html

National Museum of American History
    http://americanhistory.si.edu

The Revolutionary War: A Journey Towards Freedom!
    http://library.thinkquest.org/10966

United States History
    www.ushistory.org

Games

The American Revolution Map Game, grades 4-12. Educational Materials Associates. Phone: (888) EMA-GAME. www.emagame.com.

Older children will enjoy using *primary sources* and *opposing viewpoints* as ways to explore multiple perspectives of the period. Primary sources are copies of original letters, diaries, essays, and other documents written during the era being studied. Original literature from the period is also considered primary source material, such as Benjamin Franklin's *Autobiography* or Thomas Paine's *Common Sense*. When a student reads a primary source, she is forced to draw her own conclusions about what it means and its place in historical research and knowledge. Families can purchase packets of primary sources from Jackdaws, or they can search the library for trade books. Volume Eleven of Joy Hakim's *A History of US* series includes several primary source documents.

Opposing viewpoints explore an issue from various sides and perspectives. Sometimes primary sources can provide opposing viewpoints, such the works of both John Locke and Thomas Hobbes. Another source of opposing viewpoints is secondary sources—essays and articles that offer an author's interpretation of the primary sources. Greenhaven Press publishes a series of opposing viewpoints on several topics, including the Revolutionary War and American History. Look for them in your local library.

The use of primary sources and opposing viewpoints helps children develop critical thinking skills and empathy. For example, during a study of World War II, students can include perspectives of Holocaust survivors, such as David Adler's *The Number on My Grandfather's Arm*, or for older students, the intense Holocaust young adult memoir, *I Have Lived a Thousand Years: Growing Up in the Holocaust*, by Livia Bitton-Jackson.

Selected Primary Sources and Opposing Viewpoints

1776: Journals of American Independence, by George Sanderlin, Harper & Row, 1968.

The American Revolution: A U.S. History Jackdaw. Jackdaws Primary Sources. Five broadsheet essays and 18 historical documents. www.jackdaw.com

The American Revolution: Opposing Viewpoints Digests, edited by Don Nardo, Greenhaven Press, 1998. Challenging reading.

The American Revolutionaries: A History in Their Own Words, 1750-1800, edited by Milton Meltzer, Thomas Y. Crowell, 1987.

Critical Thinking in U.S. History Series, by Kevin O'Reilly. Critical Thinking Books & Software. 1990.

A History of US: Sourcebook and Index: Documents that Shaped the American Nation (volume 11), by Joy Hakim, Oxford University Press, 1999.

Primary Source Media On-line: The American Revolution. www.americanjourney.psmedia.com (click on "The American Revolution").

Words that Built a Nation: A Young Person's Collection of Historic American Documents, by Marilyn Miller, Scholastic, 1999.

As students gather information about their topic, parents can encourage them to ask questions to trigger higher level thinking skills. Although parents should not follow curriculum guides and standards in a rigid way that places restraints on children's learning, some curriculum guides and standards can offer ideas for further study and activities. For World or United States history-based unit studies, the National Standards for History is available on-line at www.sscnet.ucla.edu/nchs/standards; it offers ideas for analysis, comparison and contrast, multiple perspectives, and interpretation. For example, United States History Standards include these suggested study topics and activities:

- Analyze political, ideological, religious, and economic origins of the Revolution (grades 5-12).

- Reconstruct the arguments among patriots and loyalists about independence, and draw conclusions about how the decision to declare independence was reached (grades 9-12).

○ Analyze the terms of the Treaty of Paris and how they affected U.S. relations with American Indians and with European powers that held territories in North America (grades 7-12).

Each of these standards goes beyond asking the student to memorize material and instead encourages the student to become a young researcher, to think for herself, and to draw her own conclusions based on evidence and analysis. Parents can rephrase the standards as questions and encourage students to use their preferred learning styles as part of their learning:

○ What were the seeds of the American Revolution in terms of political thought (both in the colonies and Europe), ideology, religion, and economics? What kind of chart, timeline, or other visual organizer would most effectively convey what you learn? (for visual learners).

○ How would you reconstruct a debate between a loyalist and patriot on the issue of independence? Students can stage a mock debate, complete with historically accurate costumes they make themselves (for kinesthetic and auditory learners).

Sometimes, parents will need to break the standards into a series of simpler, more manageable questions:

○ What were the terms of the Treaty of Paris? How did those terms affect the United States' relationship with American Indians? At the time of the treaty, which European countries held land and power in North America? How did the terms affect the United States' relationship with those European countries?

Students' answers to these questions will become a part of their Learning Journal.

Phase III. Charting the Course: The Learning Journal

As children ask questions and pursue answers, they can be encouraged to keep a Learning Journal of their thoughts, questions, activities, and knowledge throughout the unit. The next section, Creating a Big Ideas for Big Thinkers Unit Study: A Guide for Students, offers more details on how to do this. *The Young Learner's Handbook: A Guide to Solving Problems, Mastering Skills, Thinking Creatively*, by Stephen Tchudi, is an excellent resource for helping children learn to become independent learners. Unfortunately, the book is out of print, but look for it in libraries and used book stores.

In the Learning Journal, a student will keep track of books and other resources she's used. She may keep a timeline or write ideas for stories or projects, or she might want to draw sketches and diagrams to help her to understand ideas. The important point is that the Learning Journal is hers to use, not a project to be graded. Children can be encouraged to include visual maps or word maps to list ideas and questions in their journal. The book *Visual Tools for Constructing Knowledge*, by David Hyerle, is an excellent explanation for parents of the importance of visual tools in the learning process.

What a student records in the Learning Journal will later be the seeds of what we normally think of as classroom projects or products. Give your child as much freedom as possible in choosing how to share this knowledge with others. Some children will enjoy writing an essay, poem, or story, or otherwise doing a school-like project; others will see such assignments as yet another attempt to control their learning. Remember that many children, especially visual-spatial learners and children who have chosen not to learn in the classroom, will need to feel success in order to recover their motivation. Creating a diagram or model or putting on a puppet show may bring more success to some students than writing a report.

Phase IV. Becoming an Expert

This is where things get exciting! Once your child has a fairly broad base of knowledge about the general subject, she can springboard to specific areas of interest and expertise. This phase is really just doing what was done before but in a more intense and focused way: What do I know? What more do I want to know? How will I find answers? How will I record and share answers? Students can become expert in several ways—by going more deeply into a topic, spreading wider and becoming more interdisciplinary, and using learning styles to approach the topic in a new way.

Some students will have ideas for learning more deeply about a specific aspect of the American Revolution, such as becoming an expert on George Washington and learning more about his particular role in the war. Other students may want to do a comparison of the American and French Revolutions. Here, again, standards at grade levels higher than the student's age can offer ideas for challenging study, such as the following United States History Standard listed for high school grades:

> *Compare the Declaration of Independence with the French Declaration of the Right of Man and Citizen, and construct an argument evaluating their importance to the spread of constitutional democracies in the 19th and 20th Centuries.*

Or, a student may choose to learn more about the Declaration of Independence, the history of the ideas it contains, and the effect it had on other nations. With either activity, the student is delving more deeply into subjects she encountered in the first part of her study, and the resources she uses will be designed for an older reader or be more detailed. Many 10- to 12-year-old gifted learners can read adult-level material. Documentaries, such as those produced by A&E or PBS, are also good sources of more in-depth study.

Other students will want to make the study more interdisciplinary by focusing more on subjects of interest or strength. Suppose your student loves science. She may want to read *Carl Linneaus: Father of Classification*, by Margaret Jean Anderson, a biography of the man who invented our system of scientific classification of plants and animals in the Eighteenth Century at the same time as our Revolution. She might then become interested in learning the Latin names of animal and plants, which might lead to study of a particular species. Don't worry that she has strayed away from the American Revolution. She has made a connection between Revolutionary ideas in America, and throughout the world, and she may go on to find other Revolutionary thinkers of that century in areas such as music, art, literature, and exploration. In this way, she is studying a theme—Revolutionary Ideas and

Thinkers of the Eighteenth Century—rather than a topic. Her study can be expanded. Bernard Grun's book, *The Timetables of History*, is a valuable resource for making thematic connections within a time period.

Some students will be eager to use their specific learning styles and strengths to explore the unit topic further. If the student enjoys working with her hands, she can use the book *A Sampler View of Colonial Life, with Projects Kids Can Make*, by Mary Cobb, to get ideas for designing and creating her own Colonial-style embroidered sampler, either with floss and fabric or with computer fonts. The project can be made meaningful and challenging by including a study of the importance of American folk art and the geometry of sampler designs. Several American history museums display original works of domestic art and folk art. From this knowledge, she might springboard to a study of other American domestic arts, such as the history of quilting among early American settlers, Southerners, pioneers, American Indians, and African Americans. A PBS website on quilts offers links to Quilt - History Websites (www.pbs.org/americaquilts). Or suppose the student loves music. She may want to study the music of the period using the book *From Sea to Shining Sea: A Treasury of American Folklore and Folk Songs*, by Amy Cohn. She can research the history of "Yankee Doodle" or learn how to play a collection of Revolution-era songs on the piano or violin. She can take her expertise even farther either by learning about the world history of battle songs and war poetry or by doing a study of American poetry using the book *Hand in Hand: An American History through Poetry*, edited by Lee Bennett Hopkins. Or she can compare American music in the Eighteenth Century with music of the same period in different countries. What instruments were common in different countries? What kinds of musical compositions were popular in each country? How does music reflect and shape a nation's culture and ideology?

Any of the expertise possibilities described above would be chosen and directed primarily by the student, with guidance and facilitation from the parent. In this way, the student is learning skills of self-directed learning and planning, skills that are valuable for both higher education and "real life." The student is also learning how to find and accommodate the level of challenge necessary for her to stay interested in the topic—to find her state of "flow" where the work is neither too easy nor too difficult. The student would move on to becoming an expert only after she has gained a firm grasp of the important aspects of the American Revolution, so parents needn't worry that she has strayed off topic. And of course, some students *will* stay with the American Revolution. They are going deeper rather than broader in their study. Parents can always suggest ideas for further study, but for students new to home schooling, it is important that they first be given the chance to follow their own unique line of curiosity.

Phase V. Sharing Expertise

We all like to talk about things that interest us, to share knowledge and explore possibilities. A demonstration of knowledge is much more palatable to children than being asked to prove what they know through tests and assigned projects. What are some of the natural ways that we share what we know? If your child likes computers and knows HTML, she might want to design a web page about the Eighteenth Century with facts, links, and original writing and drawings. If she has artistic interests, she might want to write and illustrate a picture book for young readers. Or she may choose to write a story (historical fiction, mystery, or other genre) or a poem that includes factual details.

Encourage the child to do careful work, but don't overemphasize evaluation. Sometimes how you word a comment or suggestion makes all the difference. "What would be a good way to check spelling?" will be better received than, "You need to fix the spelling before you show that to anyone." With some students who suffer from Performance Syndrome (Amabile, 1989), you may need to wait several weeks or months before making any suggestions at all. Remember, the goal at the beginning of home schooling is to reawaken the child's love of—and purpose for—learning. Any sign from you that what she does might not be good enough may be all that it takes to cause the child to shut down and shut you out of the learning process. Therefore, encourage any ideas the child may have for sharing what she's learned. See how far or how high or how deep in a field her own ideas will take her.

Advantages and Disadvantages of Unit Studies for Gifted and Creative Students

Advantages:
+ Facilitates global, interdisciplinary learning
+ Recognizes the important role of the child's interests
+ Adjusts easily for learning styles, rates of learning, and varied resources
+ Lends itself to higher level thinking skills

Disadvantages:
− Some pre-packaged unit studies offer too little depth or challenge
− May overlook the child's area of strength or weakness
− Can easily be over-orchestrated by parents

 # Key Points

☑ Unit studies are a collection of learning activities and lessons tied to a single theme or topic.

☑ The best unit studies are interdisciplinary—they bring together several subject areas around a theme or topic.

☑ Unit studies fit many of the intellectual, social, and emotional needs of gifted students—preference for self-directed learning, teachers as guides rather than conveyers of information, emphasis on patterns and meaning across disciplines and time periods, and bibliotherapy—using books to grow intellectually, socially, and emotionally.

☑ Unit studies are flexible; they can be used with one or several children; they can be simple or complex—a few days or several weeks or months in length.

☑ Parents can encourage students to ask "questions that matter" throughout the unit study, leading to higher level thinking skills.

☑ Parents can facilitate learning by promoting creative, divergent thought and intuition, addressing affective issues, showing a patient and accepting attitude toward learning, and encouraging work and self-assessment that are relevant to the child.

Creating a Big Ideas for Big Thinkers Unit: A Guide for Students

Note to parents: The next several pages are written for the student, but parents may enjoy reading them as well.

So, you are interested in learning more about X, Y, or Z (you fill in the blank!). One way to learn more about your interest is to create a Unit Study about it. A Unit Study is simply a group of learning activities— books, videos, projects, daydreaming—about one idea or topic. A Big Ideas for Big Thinkers Unit Study allows you to think about all of the important aspects of a topic and also lets you springboard to other interests, times, and places.

A Big Ideas for Big Thinkers Unit can be designed by you, the learner, so you never have to worry that the activities will be silly or won't make sense. Generally, there are five phases or step of study that will help you to create a Big Ideas for Big Thinkers unit that is both interesting and fun. The five steps are:

- ○ Gather Your Ideas and Supplies (Planning and Packing for Your Trip)
- ○ Explore the Big Ideas (The Scouting Expedition)
- ○ Keep a Learning Journal (Charting Your Course)
- ○ Become an Expert (Know Your Facts)
- ○ Share Expertise (Reporting to Others)

Phase I. Gather Your Ideas and Supplies (Planning and Packing for Your Trip)

Start with what you know. What do you already know about the topic? A lot? A little? Here are three ways for you to find out: (1) have a conversation, (2) make a mind map, and (3) make a list. Start with whatever way seems most comfortable for you. This may give you the start you need, or you may want to try the other ways as well.

Have a conversation. Ask your parent or a friend to take some time to have a conversation with you about the topic of your unit study. Sometimes talking about an idea helps us to remember information we have forgotten and to come up with new questions that we want to answer. After the conversation, take some private time to write down on paper some of the things you and your parent or friend said, so that you have a record of them for later. You might ask your parent or friend to take notes while you talk, or you might tape the conversation.

Make a mind map. A mind map is sort of like a conversation with yourself in your own mind. Here's how it works; on a blank piece of paper, write the name of the topic in the middle and draw a circle or oval around the word, like this:

BASEBALL

Next, write other words and phrases that come to mind you think of the topic. Write them anywhere on the page, in no particular order. No answer is wrong, so put down any word that pops into your head. Don't worry about spelling or how your handwriting looks. Draw a circle or oval around each word or phrase just as you did for the main topic word.

When you are finished, hold the paper at arm's length. Can you make any connections between words and ideas? Draw lines to show those connections. You may want to draw a fresh copy of the word map showing the connections you found, like this:

Figure 12.1: Mind Map Example

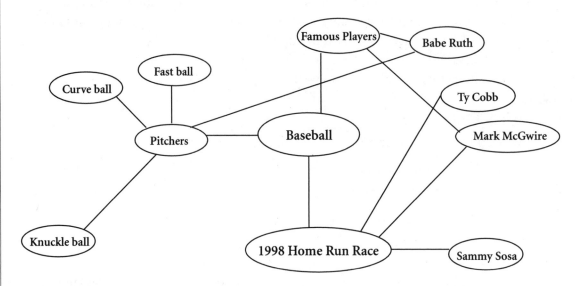

A good idea is to use different colored pencils or pens to indicate different connections.

Make a list. Another way to discover what you already know is to make a list. Use a blank sheet of paper, but this time write the name of the unit at the top. Then list, in no particular order, what you already know about the topic. You can write words and phrases or complete sentences, something like this:

BASEBALL
Babe Ruth is the greatest baseball player ever
Nine players per team
Baseball players make a lot of money
Baseball Hall of Fame
(and so on…)

When you've finished with your list, look for items that are connected in some way, and regroup them or make notations beside them to indicate that they belong together. For example, you might want to circle every item about pitching in red, or a write WS next to all items that relate to the World Series. Also, look for items that may or may not be true, such as "Babe Ruth is the greatest baseball player ever," and put a question mark beside these items.

What if you couldn't think of much to write? That's okay. It might help to have a conversation with a parent or friend to jog your memory. Or you simply may have more questions than answers at this point. That's okay. That's good!

What Do You Want to Know about the Topic? Now that you've explored what you know, you can begin to think about what you want to know. A good place to start is by looking again at your word map or list of what you already know. If you wrote, "curve ball," for example, you might want to learn how curve balls work. If you wrote, "Baseball players make a lot of money," you might want to learn exactly how much money they do make, or what is the average major league salary or who is the highest paid player.

On a blank sheet of paper, write QUESTIONS I WANT TO ANSWER, and write down all of the questions you can think of.

Gathering Supplies. You've gathered your ideas. What supplies will you need? Extra paper? Index cards? Pens and pencils? Many resources will be available at your library, but you may wish to purchase a few items. Will you set a budget for the supplies you'll need? Ask your parent about this.

Phase II. Explore the Big Ideas (The Scouting Expedition)

How will you find the answers to your questions? A good way to begin is by looking for resources—books, videos, and websites, for example—that give an overview of the subject. During this phase of the study, you will immerse yourself in the topic with general resources. General resources are books, videos, games, software, and other learning tools that give a broad overview of the topic. An encyclopedia article about baseball, for example, would cover the basic information. A biography of Babe Ruth, however, would be more specific. Although you will probably learn about some details at this point, you are mostly looking for the big ideas. What do you think is important to know about the topic? Try to look at a variety of resources. Here are some ideas:

- *Books, either print or audio versions.* Are there any books that offer general information about your topic? Check the library's Dewey decimal number for the topic you are studying, write it down and memorize it, or write it on a small piece of paper to keep with your library card. This number will allow you to find library resources about your topic in any library! And don't forget to check the books on tape, or audio books. Audio books are good for long car rides or to listen to in your room.

- *Videos and television shows.* Are there videos or television programs that can help you learn more about the topic? Check your local or cable television listings for the next few weeks to see if any documentaries or other programs will feature the topic you are studying. Check your local library and video store for videos.

- *Software programs.* Are there any software programs that can help you to learn about the topic? Does your library carry them?

- *Field trips.* Are there places you can visit or people you can talk to who will help you learn more about the topic?

- *Games.* Are there any board or card games you can play that relate to the topic? If not, can you think of a way to make such a game?

○ *Music and arts.* Is there any music about the topic you can listen to or learn how to play? Is your topic connected to art in any way? How is the topic depicted in art? Can you use one of the arts— music, drama, or visual arts like painting or sculpture—to explore ideas about the topic or to share what you learn?

During your Scouting Expedition, you are "seeing what's out there," so take as much time as you need. For some students, this may be just a few days. For others, it will be several weeks or longer. Meanwhile, you may want to start listing questions you have along the way and what you are learning in your Learning Journal, which is the next phase of your unit study.

Phase III. Keep a Learning Journal (Charting Your Course)

Throughout your unit study, it is a good idea to keep a Learning Journal—a record of your ideas and questions and your answers to those questions. The format of the Learning Journal is up to you. You can start with the mind map or list you already made; then you can add other notes, drawings, timelines, charts, stories, and poems. The Learning Journal is not to be graded, and it should not be perfect. It is strictly for your own use, to help you to learn, and to allow you to look back on what you have learned. Later, it can also be used as a permanent record of the books you've read and what you've learned about the topic.

A Learning Journal can take several forms:

○ *A spiral-bound notebook.* This is easy to take with you in the car or to the library.

○ *Loose-leaf paper and a three-ring binder or folder.* The advantage of this type of notebook is that you can change the order of the pages.

○ *A sketch book.* This is a good option if you like to include a lot of drawings and doodles with your work.

○ *Large index cards.* Cards aren't really a notebook, but 5" x 8" index cards can be a handy way to record information. You can keep them together in a box designed to hold index cards. If you want to get fancy, you can buy different colors of cards to use for different topics and can make tabs for different topics.

Can you think of other ways to keep a record of your learning? Photographs? Video tapes?

Whatever form of Learning Journal you choose—and you can certainly choose more than one—you should start by putting a title on the cover or front page. You can write it in pen or pencil, or you can use your computer or colored pens to design a fancy title page to glue on the cover of your new notebook or binder. Somewhere near the title or on the first page, write your name and today's date.

What should you include in your Learning Journal? Here are some ideas for various ways to keep track of all of the information you are gathering.

Keep a timeline. At the beginning of the study, make a blank timeline that can be added to throughout you unit. There are a couple of ways to do this. If you are studying the Twentieth Century, for example, you can draw a long line, about 30 inches (tape three pieces of paper together lengthwise), then divide the line into 3-inch segments. Each segment will represent a decade, 10 years, beginning with 1900 through 2000. At the notch of each segment, write the start of the decade, like this:

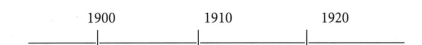

When you learn something that is associated with a date, write it on the timeline. To save space, write the fact below or above the line and then draw a line to the date. Here's another example from a baseball unit:

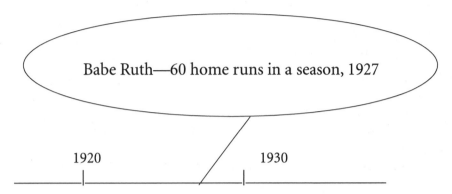

To store the timeline in your notebook, fold it and paperclip it to a page in your notebook. Another way to keep a timeline is to devote one full notebook page to each decade. You could write the years of the decade at the top of the page (for example, 1920-1929), and then record any information pertaining to those years on that page. A sketch book works well for this, especially if you like to draw and add visual aids.

Keep a list of books you read and videos you watch. Reserve one or more pages in your Learning Journal for a list of the books you read during the unit, or use one index card per book. Record the book's title, author, publisher, year of publication, and a sentence or two that summarizes what the book is about. It is also helpful to record how much you liked the book and your reasons for liking or disliking it. You can make up your own rating system. Do the same thing for videos and movies that you see. Eventually, you might want to put together a list of recommended books, videos, and other resources that you can give to friends or publish on a website.

Keep a glossary of important words, their meanings and derivations.

Start a Question and Answer section. As you find the answers to your questions, write the question at the top of a page, then record the answer you've found below it. Eventually, you might want to put all the Q & A's together in a pamphlet, newsletter, or website.

Use pictures, word maps, Venn diagrams, and charts to organize and represent your learning.

Phase IV. Becoming an Expert

This is the really exciting part! After getting a broad base of knowledge about the subject, you can springboard to areas of special interest. What part of the topic do you want to become an expert on? What exciting questions did you have while you were on your scouting expedition? Where do you want to go next?

Some of your springboards will be directly related to the topic, and some will probably go in different directions. Follow whatever path your questions lead you on, and be sure to continue to chart your course in your Learning Journal. (Hint: you might find it interesting to make a mind map that shows the springboards off the main topic.)

In this phase, you are really just doing phases I, II, and III again but in a more intense and focused way: What do I know? What do I want to know? How will I find answers?

Phase V. Sharing Your Expertise

At some point, start thinking about how you can share what you've learned with other people. You might want to share your thoughts and ideas with a family member or friend, a larger group, or even the whole world. Sharing your excitement and interest in the topic with other people not only helps them to know what you've learned, it also helps you to know better what you've learned. Sometimes, explaining an idea to others helps us organize our ideas more clearly in our own heads.

Here are a few ideas for ways to share your expertise. You can probably think of many more.

Make a poster or collage of what you learn. Buy a big poster board and fill it with images and words from your study. You can cut pictures and words from old magazines, use clip art from your computer, draw your own pictures, and write your own headlines.

Write your own story. Write a fictional story about the topic. If you studied a certain period of history, share your knowledge by writing a story about that time period. Put in some facts and real history references to dates or people or events, create fictional characters and situations, and add some original drawings. Use paper and pen or a computer.

Write a newsletter for friends and family. Share your knowledge in a newsletter that you write yourself. Fill it with fun facts, history tidbits, recommended books and websites, and original drawings and cartoons. You can draw your newsletter by hand or use a computer.

Create a web page about the topic. Do you know or want to learn HTML and web design? Use the opportunity to share what you've learned with the world via the World Wide Web. Include interesting facts, a Q&A section, fun clip art, original drawings and writing, and of course, links to some other good sites.

Form an interest group at your local library or home schoolers' group. If you are studying science fiction, for example, see if other children and adults would be interested in meeting regularly to share book experiences, ideas, and projects related to that interest. Science clubs, book clubs, and arts and crafts clubs are other ideas for interest groups.

What other ways can you think of to share expertise?

Summary

That's all there is to it! A Big Ideas for Big Thinkers Unit Study is never really finished, since you will probably continue to learn about the topic for many years, but using the Big Ideas for Big Thinkers approach along with a Learning Journal helps you to organize your learning, enjoy your learning more, and share it with others. If you like baseball, you can start by exploring some of the ideas in the Play Ball! resource guide found next. Or visit your local library to use your own interests and ideas to create a Unit Study of your very own.

Play Ball!
A Big Ideas Unit Resource Guide
(Recommended Ages: 8-12)

Introduction to Play Ball! for Parents

Play Ball! is a Big Ideas for Big Thinkers Unit designed for children who are coming to learning reluctantly, children who may need a break from formal study in order to reawaken their natural love of learning, and most of all, children who love baseball. Because the Big Ideas for Big Thinkers approach is designed around the child's interests, it works particularly well with children who have been labeled underachievers or who appear to be unmotivated. Once you have read the unit, you will be able to plan any unit to fit your child's special interest.

This doesn't mean, however, that your child is taking a break from learning. Far from it! Together, you'll learn about the history of baseball, the science of base-ball, and even the humor of baseball. Your child may choose to apply his knowledge by writing a baseball newsletter, designing his own baseball cards, or sketching a design plan for a new stadium. In the course of doing "nothing but baseball," your child will cover aspects of math, science, history, social studies, and reading.

Nothing prevents you from supplementing this learning with more tradi-tional instruction in certain subjects—spelling or math, for example—but it isn't required. Suggestions for baseball-related math activities are included, and your child can keep a list of baseball vocabulary words to learn. Most of your child's time will be spent learning about what he is intrinsically motivated to learn, which leads to a more meaningful and genuine education. And isn't this the best result of home schooling?

Perhaps most important, learning through Big Ideas for Big Thinkers Units allows inherent individuation of pacing, learning styles, and skill levels. Children can do most of the reading on their own, or you can read aloud to them or use audio books. Visual-spatial learners can immerse themselves in intricacies of stadium diagrams and the designs of team logos, while hands-on learners can construct scale models of stadiums. Books about baseball range from picture books and easy chapter books to intermediate novels or even adult-level works for advanced read-ers. And don't forget conversation! Simple family discussion is sometimes the best way to investigate ideas and opinions.

For this approach to be successful, however, you need to learn *with* your child, to assist in gathering information not in order to home school, but in order to share his interest and to be a model of someone who loves to learn. It won't work if you give the child a pile of books and tell him to "ask questions that matter." Instead, you must ask the questions with him and become genuinely interested in finding the answers. If you sense your child shutting down, it's probably time to back off and give up some more control.

You'll notice that the unit is recommended for ages eight to 12. This simply means that most of the materials and activities are designed with that age range and reading level in mind. It can easily be modified for children a bit younger or older, or for more than one child of varying ages. Some resources are marked as being easier reading (picture books and easy readers), or more difficult reading (young adult).

What about social and emotional development? Baseball offers a "perfect" opportunity to address issues of perfectionism. As Ken Burns says in his documentary film *Baseball*, it is a game where "the men who fail seven times out of ten are considered the game's greatest heroes." Parents and children can talk about what kind of self-confidence and persistence is necessary for a baseball player to continue to play in the continual face of failure. You can look at losing streaks of teams and hitless streaks by some of the great players, or how the 1969 Mets came back from seemingly impossible odds. What might have happened if any of these players or teams had simply given up?

Several works of baseball fiction for children ages nine to 12 deal with social and emotional topics. Two worth mentioning are *Make-Believe Ball Player*, by Alfred Slote, the story of a boy who discovers that make-believe can be used to solve problems, and *Choosing Sides*, by John H. Ritter, an intense book for mature readers about a left-handed son of a preacher who believes that the left side is Satan's side and that baseball is the devil's work.

Baseball also offers a chance to make connections with other times and cultures through a study of the Negro Leagues, the integration of baseball, its relationship to the Civil Rights era, and how baseball has been a unifying force for people from different backgrounds. Some of the more controversial aspects such as player salaries and baseball strikes will provide rich discussion material about complex issues such as fairness, labor, and capitalism.

How long this baseball unit lasts will depend on you and your child. A good plan is to spend an hour or two at a time on the unit. Your child can choose one or two activities and study baseball for a week. Or your child may wish to try them all and study baseball in depth for several months.

Introduction for Students

So, you like baseball! You're in good company. Many famous, intelligent, and creative people have followed our National Pastime. (Why is it called that, anyway?) Nearly every American president in this century has had something to say about baseball. If you want to know what they said, go to the website http://baseball-almanac.com/prz_menu.shtml.

You can approach the topic of baseball from several bases. You can learn about the history of baseball, the science of baseball, and even the humor of baseball. How long will your baseball unit last? It's up to you. A good plan is to spend an hour or two each day on the unit, although you don't have to work on the unit every day. If you really love baseball and choose several of the suggested activities, your study may take several weeks or even months. Whatever you learn, it will not be the end. You can always come back later to learn more.

What is the Dewey decimal number for baseball? _____

Key to Icons

📖 Easy Reading (about grade two and up)

📖📖 Intermediate Reading (about grade four and up)

📖📖📖 Challenging Reading (about grade six and up)

Selected General Baseball Resources:

Books

    Eyewitness: Baseball, by James Kelley and James Buckley, DK Publishing, 2000 (60 pages, 📖📖). If you like lots of colorful photos and drawings, this is a good book for you.

    The First Book of Baseball, by Marty Appel, Crown Publishers, 1988 (96 pages, 📖📖). A very good and easy-to-read introduction to the game, including a section on statistics and keeping score. The book is out of print. Look for it in your library.

    The Story of Baseball, by Lawrence S. Ritter, Beech Tree Books, 1999 (208 pages, 📖📖). This book will take you through the history of the major leagues, from 1848 through the 1998 McGwire/Sosa homerun race. The second half of the book discusses how the game is played (pitching, hitting, etc.).

    The Way Baseball Works, by Dan Gutman, A Byron Preiss/Richard Ballantine Book, 1996 (215 pages, 📖📖). Excellent visual presentation.

Videos

    Baseball: A Film by Ken Burns, PBS Home Video,1994 (9 tapes, 90-120 minutes each). This film is actually nine separate tapes or volumes, each about a different moment or "inning" of baseball history. You can watch them all, perhaps with your family, or choose the time period that most interests you. There is also an audiocassette version read by Ken Burns (Random House Audio) to listen to in the car or in your room.
    First Inning: Our Game, Beginnings to 1900
    Second Inning: 1900 - 1910, Something Like a War
    Third Inning: 1910 - 1920, The Faith of Fifty Million
    Fourth Inning: 1920 - 1930, A National Heirloom
    Fifth Inning: 1930 - 1940, Shadow Ball
    Sixth Inning: 1940 - 1950, The National Pastime
    Seventh Inning: 1950 - 1960, The Capital of Baseball
    Eighth Inning: 1960 - 1970, A Whole New Ballgame
    Ninth Inning: 1970 - Present, Home
    When It Was a Game, HBO Sports, 1991 (57 minutes). Home movie footage taken by baseball fans and the players themselves between 1934 and 1957. If you like this movie, you can also look for *When It Was a Game 2* (1992) and *When It Was a Game 3* (2000).

Baseball Almanac Website. Virtually everything is here.
www.baseball-almanac.com

Major League Baseball Website. Current baseball news and links to your favorite teams' sites.
www.majorleaguebaseball.com

Figure 12.2: Possible Springboards: Jackie Robinson, Architecture, Science and Math

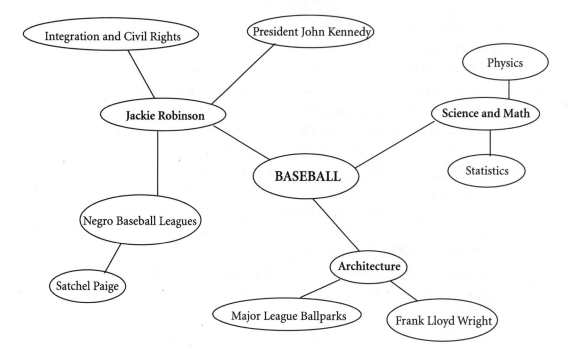

Jackie Robinson

Who was Jackie Robinson? You may already know that he was the first African American player to play in the modern major leagues. Here are some good books and videos to help you learn more (look for them in your library):

Jackie Robinson and the Story of All-Black Baseball, by Jim O'Connor, Random House, 1989 (48 pages, 📖).

The Jackie Robinson Story, MGM/UA Home Video, 1950/1993 (video, 76 minutes).

Jackie's Nine: Jackie Robinson's Values to Live By, by Sharon Robinson, Scholastic, 2001 (108 pages, 📖📖).

A Picture Book of Jackie Robinson, by David Adler, Holiday House, 1997 (32 pages, picture book).

Stealing Home: The Story of Jackie Robinson, by Barry Denenberg, Scholastic, 1997 (116 pages, 📖📖).

The Story of Jackie Robinson, The Bravest Man in Baseball, by Margaret Davidson, Yearling Books, 1988 (92 pages, 📖📖).

Teammates, by Peter Golenbock, Harcourt Brace, 1990 (32 pages, picture book).

Read some historical fiction about Jackie Robinson. Historical fiction uses real historical figures and events combined with fictional settings or with other fictional characters.

In the Year of the Boar and Jackie Robinson, by Bette Bao Lord, Harper-Trophy, 1986 (169 pages, 📖📖). The story of a girl who moves to New York from China in 1947. What does this have to do with Jackie Robinson? Read it and see.

Jackie and Me: A Baseball Card Adventure, by Dan Gutman, Avon, 2000 (160 pages, 📖📖). Joe uses a baseball card to travel back in time to 1947. His skin color has changed, and he meets Jackie Robinson, who helps him to learn about prejudice and the important of self-respect.

Thank You, Jackie Robinson, by Barbara Cohen, Beech Tree Books, 1997 (128 pages, 📖📖). The story of a young "baseball genius" and friendship. Also available as an ABC After School Special on video (45 minutes).

Look at some primary sources about Jackie Robinson. Primary sources are papers, letters and other original items from the time period. A letter written to Jackie Robinson from President Kennedy would be a primary source. A book that talks about the letter would be a secondary source. Primary sources are good because they allow you to understand and interpret a topic without someone else's telling you what to think.

Take a look at the Baseball Hall of Fame Primary Sources Website: http://baseballhalloffame.org/education/index.htm. Here, you can see original documents about Baseball and World War II, Jackie Robinson, Negro Leagues, and Women in Baseball. Click on the Jackie Robinson link. This will take you to a letter from President Kennedy to Jackie Robinson, a photograph of Jackie Robinson in his WWII army uniform, a piece of hate mail, and his obituary. Think about these questions and write your thoughts and subsequent research in your Learning Journal:

○ President Kennedy writes, "You questioned my talk over 16 months ago with the governor of Alabama…." What do you suppose this means? How could you find out more?

○ How many other major league baseball players served in World War II? Did major league baseball continue during this time?

○ How did you feel after reading the hate mail sent to Jackie Robinson? What is the best way to respond to such mail?

○ Jackie Robinson's obituary reads, "He didn't protest on close plays. He ignored the language from opposing dugouts. When he was deliberately tagged on the head with a ball, he didn't scramble to his feet and start fighting." How difficult do you think it was for Jackie Robinson to keep his cool? Why was it important? Is it sometimes difficult for you to keep your cool? How do you handle those situations?

You may wish to use the primary sources to write your own historical fiction story. What would you imagine life would be like if you traveled back in time to meet Jackie Robinson? Write a short description. Use a mixture of historical facts and fantasy.

Learn more about the Negro Baseball Leagues. Here are some good books to look for:

> *Black Diamond: The Story of the Negro Baseball Leagues*, by Pat McKissack and Fredrick McKissack, Scholastic, 1998 (184 pages, 📖📖).
>
> *Leagues Apart: The Men and Times of the Negro Baseball Leagues*, by Lawrence S. Ritter, Morrow Junior Books, 1995 (picture book).
>
> *Satchel Paige*, by Lesa Cline-Ransome, Simon & Schuster, 2000 (picture book).

Baseball and Architecture

Learn about the history of major league ballparks, the building of new parks, the tearing down of old ones, and the controversy involved. Construct a scale model of your hometown ballpark or your favorite ballpark or just of a baseball diamond and field. Imagine how architect Frank Lloyd Wright would have designed a baseball stadium. How could you make a blueprint and scale model of that design?

> **For more information on baseball parks:**
>
> *The Story of America's Classic Ballparks*, Questar Video, 1991 (video, 56 minutes).
>
> *Take Me Out to the Ballpark: An Illustrated Tour of Baseball Parks Past and Present*, by Josh Leventhal, Black Dog and Leventhal, 2000 (book, 128 pages).
>
> **For more information on Frank Lloyd Wright:**
>
> *Frank Lloyd Wright for Kids*, by Kathleen Thorne-Thomsen, Chicago Review Press, 1994 (137 pages, 📖📖).
>
> **For more information on architecture:**
>
> *Architects Make Zigzags*, by Roxie Munro and Diane Maddex, Preservation Press, 1996 (64 pages, alphabet book).
>
> *The Art of Construction: Projects and Principles for Beginning Engineers and Architects*, by Mario G. Salvadori, Chicago Review Press, 1990 (149 pages, 📖📖📖).
>
> *Building Big*, by David Macaulay, Houghton Mifflin, 2000 (192 pages, 📖📖).
>
> *Building Big PBS Video Series*, WGBH Science Unit and Production Group, 2000. Volumes include: *Bridges, Dams, Domes, Skyscrapers, Tunnels* (about an hour each plus activity booklet).
>
> *Draw 50 Buildings and Other Structures*, by Lee J. Ames, Doubleday, 1991 (64 pages, 📖).
>
> *Eyewitness Visual Dictionary of Buildings*, edited by Fiona Courtenay-Thompson, DK Publishing, 1993 (64 pages, 📖📖).
>
> The Great Buildings Collection Website www.greatbuildings.com
>
> *Under Every Roof: A Kid's Style and Field Guide to the Architecture of American Houses*, by Patricia Brown Glenn, Preservation Trust, 1993 (112 pages, 📖📖📖).

The Science and Math of Baseball

There's no science and math in baseball! Or is there? Just check out these books, videos, and websites:

Books

Baseball Math: Grandslam Activities and Projects for Grades 4-8, by Chrisopher Jennison, GoodYearBooks, 1995 (103 pages, 📖📖). Available in many teacher supply stores.

Baseball-istics (The Basic Physics of Baseball), by Robert Froman, Putnam, 1967 (128 pages, 📖📖). If you can find this out-of-print book in your library or used bookstore, you're in for a treat! Written in 1967, the book offers a vision of a World Series game played in the year 2000.

The Magic School Bus Plays Ball: A Book about Forces, by Joanna Cole, Scholastic, 1998 (32 pages, 📖📖).

Mathnet Casebook #1: The Case of the Unnatural, by David D. Connel and Jim Thurman, American Scientific Books for Young Readers, W. H. Freeman, 1993 (62 pages, 📖📖).

Videos

The Case of the Unnatural, A Mathnet Video, Children's Television Workshop Video, 1994 (about an hour).

The Magic School Bus Plays Ball, A Vision Video, 1995/1999 (30 minutes). Forces and motion come into play in this popular Magic School Bus episode.

Websites

Exploratorium's Science of Baseball Website. See if you have the reaction time to hit a 90 m.p.h. fastball, how Babe Ruth's stats would change if he had played from 1980-1997, and how to find the sweet spot on a bat (and the science and math behind all these fun activities). www.exploratorium.edu/baseball

Baseball: The Game and Beyond. Here you can learn the meaning of baseball terms plus why a curveball curves, how an umpire makes the correct call, and how to understand all of the information on a baseball card. (ThinkQuest is a virtual library of websites created by students and teachers for students and teachers.) http://library.thinkquest.org/11902

Baseball…And Math! A site created by elementary school students. http://tqjunior.thinkquest.org/6082/5stm.html

Advanced Reading and Study

The Physics of Baseball, by Robert K. Adair, HarperCollins, 1995 (110 pages, 📖📖📖).

The Science of Hitting, by Ted Williams and John W. Underwood, Simon & Schuster, 1986 (96 pages, 📖📖📖).

More Ideas for Becoming an Expert and Sharing What You Learned

Challenge yourself to learn some new baseball games or techniques, even if you're not the world's greatest player. These books are filled with ideas: *Kirby Puckett's Baseball Games*, buy Kirby Puckett (Workman Publishing, 1996, 112 pages, 📖), and *Baseball Just for Kids: Skills, Strategies and Stories to Make You a Better Ballplayer* by Jerry Kasoff (Grand Slam Press, 1996, 159 pages, 📖📖).

Become an expert on a specific baseball player. Memorize his statistics, years of play, and other interesting facts. Keep a scrapbook or create a web page devoted to your favorite player.

Create your own line of baseball cards featuring your favorite players. Include important stats and career highlights. Use a desktop publishing program to design, format, and print them.

Imagine a world without baseball. Read *How Georgie Radbourn Saved Baseball*, by Larry Johnson and David A. Shannon (Scholastic, 2000, picture book).

Think about how often successful batters miss. A lifetime batting average of .300 (getting a base hit only three out of every 10 times at bat) is considered very good. What kind of an attitude do you think baseball players must have in order to persist without quitting? How can we apply this lesson to our own lives when we feel that we'll never "get it right?"

Investigate the history of the All American Girls Professional Baseball League. Read *A Whole New Ball Game: The Story of the All-American Girls Baseball League*, by Sue Macy (Puffin, 1995, 140 pages, 📖📖) or *Up to the Plate: The All-American Girls Baseball League*, by Margot Fortunato Galt (Lerner Publications, 1995, 96 pages, 📖📖📖).

Compare Japanese baseball and American baseball. Show your findings in a Venn diagram.

Predict what baseball will be like in the year 2050. Write a story as if you were there, or draw a picture of a 2050 ballpark.

Laugh about baseball! Start a collection of baseball jokes. For ideas, read *Play Ball, Amelia Bedelia*, by Peggy Parish (HarperTrophy, 1995; easy reader 📖), *Baseball's Biggest Bloopers: The Games that Got Away*, by Dan Gutman (Puffin, 1995, 📖📖), *Baseball Bloopers: World's Funniest Errors*, by Dan Gutman (Troll, 1998, 📖📖) and *Baseball Jokes and Riddles*, by Matt Christopher and Daniel Vasconcellos (Little Brown and Company, 1996, 📖📖). Listen to "Who's On First?" by Abbot and Costello (transcript and audio available at the Baseball Almanac website). Watch *It's Three Strikes, Charlie Brown* (Kartes Video, 1988, 41 minutes), and read *Big League Peanuts*, by Charles Schultz (Holt, Rinehart and Winston, 1985 160 pages, 📖📖).

Unit Study Resources

Books

Bendt, Valorie (1997). *How to Create Your Own Unit Study.* Common Sense Press.

Bennet, Amanda (1996). *Unit Study Journal* (Unit Study Adventure). Holly Hall Publishers.

Websites

A to Z Home's Cool Unit Studies
www.gomilpitas.com/homeschooling/methods/Units.htm

A to Z Home's Cool Unit Studies—Making Your Own
www.gomilpitas.com/homeschooling/methods/OwnUnits.htm

Planning a History-Based Unit Study
www.geocities.com/Athens/Oracle/4336/unitstudy.html

Finding Resources for a Big Ideas for Big Thinkers Unit

Books

There are several reference books that will help parents and children locate books that address certain topics and needs. Here are a few that you might be able to find at your local library.

Adamson, Lynda (1998). *Literature Connections to American History K-6 and 7-12: Resources to Enhance and Entice* (two volumes). Teacher Ideas Press.

Freeman, Judy (1995). *More Books Kids Will Sit Still For: A Read-Aloud Guide.* Bowker.

Halsted, Judith Wynn (2002). *Some of My Best Friends Are Books: Guiding Gifted Readers from Preschool to High School, 2nd ed.* Great Potential Press (formerly Gifted Psychology Press).

Kobrin, Beverly (1995). *Eyeopeners II: Children's Books to Answer Children's Questions about the World Around Them.* Scholastic.

Lipson, Eden Ross (2000). *The New York Times Parent's Guide to the Best Books for Children.* Three Rivers Press.

Odean, Kathleen (1997). *Great Books for Girls: More than 600 Books to Inspire Today's Girls and Tomorrow's Women.* Ballantine.

Odean, Kathleen (1998). *Great Books for Boys: More than 600 Books for Boys 2 to 14.* Ballantine.

Reed, Arthea J. S. (1994). *Comics to Classics: A Parent's Guide to Books for Teens and Preteens.* Viking Penguin.

Television Programming and Movies

Cable in the Classroom Magazine On-line
www.ciconline.org

PBS Teacher Source
www.pbs.org/teachersource

Teach with Movies Website
www.teachwithmovies.org

Part 3

Your Creative Home School Toolbox

13 Paperwork, Documentation, and Testing

*How we evaluate students' learning can be addressed
only after we've figured out why we want to do so.*

—Alfie Kohn (1999)

L et's assume that by now you've selected a home schooling approach, taken into account your child's interests and learning styles, and considered the numerous and varied resources that are available. The last ingredient in successful home schooling is, for many people, the most difficult, and that is the record keeping. However, maintaining home schooling records gets easier once parents understand *why*, *how*, and *when* document learning.

How will you document your child's learning? Alfie Kohn (1999) suggests we first consider why we're assessing students and keeping records. For most home schoolers, evaluation and record keeping are done for two reasons:

○ To set learning goals, evaluate progress, and document learning.

○ To meet state requirements, or to facilitate entry or re-entry to school or to college.

In the first case, paperwork and assessment serve as tools in the learning process. In the second, records and tests are required by an outside agency, school, or other organization. In either case, home schooling families should consider carefully two questions:

1. **What are all the possible ways to evaluate and document learning?**

    Know your options before you decide. State and college requirements vary tremendously, and there are also many options other than the traditional grade reports and transcripts even for your own personal records. As noted earlier, Barbara Clark (1997) found that grading students' work results in students' completing less work and discourages them from venturing into new, unknown areas of knowledge and study. Thus, grades encourage students to do what is safe, even if it means they will learn less. Instead of traditional report cards and grades, parents can use portfolios, learning logs, student self-evaluation, and narrative progress reports.

2. **What records and assessments will satisfy the requirements and yet interfere the least with the learning process?**

    Although record keeping is important and evaluation can be a useful tool for children's development, home schooling paperwork can easily take on a life of its own. The fun of home schooling will be lost if you spend your time taking notes on what your children are doing minute by minute or administering test after test to prove mastery. Once you know your options, consider doing the minimum paperwork and testing necessary to meet requirements and to satisfy yourself and the members of your family that your child is learning and getting an optimal education. Constant evaluation, especially for creative, gifted, and perfectionistic children, can block learning, especially if it makes the child think more about *how well* he is learning than *what* he's learning. If you use standardized achievement tests as a way to keep track of grade levels, ask yourself whether testing once every two or three years is enough. If you keep a learning log, resist the urge to remind the child to list every single "learning experience" throughout the day. Children who are allowed to learn for the sake of learning, to lose themselves in the task before them, test better on measures of creative thinking and conceptual learning than children who consciously think about grades while they learn (Kohn, 1993).

    By making a decision to *de-emphasize measured achievement* and *emphasize learning*, parents of gifted children can work to prevent what Ellen Winner (1996) calls the "creator parent" syndrome. Creator parents are over-invested and over-involved in their child's success. These parents, rather than follow their children's lead, live their own lives through their child. The child's success becomes *their* success; if the child fails, it is seen as a failure of their own parenting and teaching. By keeping the focus on the child's *learning* rather than the child's *achievements*, parents free the child to pursue his or her own path.

    Some documentation, of course, will be necessary for future admission to high school, to summer gifted and talented programs, or to college. If you think these educational options may be in your child's future, take time to keep a record of specific areas of strength and examples of your child's advanced knowledge, pace of learning, completed curricula, and test results. The book, *Re-Forming Gifted Education: Matching the Program to the Child*, by Karen Rogers (2002), offers interest inventories and advice on how to present proof of ability and an educational plan to school and other officials. Results of Talent Search testing and participation in Talent Search programs are another useful form of documentation to "prove" a child's giftedness or level of achievement.

Records to Satisfy State Requirements

Home schooling laws vary by state. Some states do not require test results or curriculum outlines, while others have a fairly rigorous schedule of testing and curriculum updates. If you live in a state with several requirements, you may feel frustrated by having to submit reading lists and learning objectives or by having your child tested, but you probably won't have to do much additional record keeping. Your state department of education can inform you of current home schooling requirements. Several websites also offer links to information about state home schooling laws, including the Home School Legal Defense Association and *Home Education Magazine*.

- O HSLDA Website: www.hslda.org/laws/default.asp
- O *Home Education Magazine* Website: www.home-ed-magazine.com/lawregs

States that require record keeping may also ask for records of attendance, health and immunization records, curriculum outlines, portfolios, and standardized test scores. Some states have parent associations that assist new home schoolers in getting started and complying with the laws. Most states require parents to fill out a yearly form stating an intent to home school and including basic information—name, address, and the child's age.

If attendance records are required, pay close attention to how attendance is counted—by hours or days. Some states require 875 to 1000 hours of instruction per year (in which case you will record how many hours per day or week your child spends learning). Other states require a specified number of days or months per year. An appointment calendar with plenty of room for each day is helpful to keep track of subjects and hours covered and can be filled out quickly at the end of each day by the child or the parent. Use the space for each day to jot down specific activities, books read, or field trips taken, the subjects covered, and the number of hours spent. A child's learning log can do double duty as an attendance record. If you need to record only days in attendance and no other information, you can simply use a calendar to note days of home schooling minus holidays and sick days.

If you plan to record hours spent home schooling, remember that learning time is more than just sitting at a table with a workbook. A typical school day for an elementary school-age child includes free reading time (reading), singing practice (music), learning softball skills (physical education), planting a school garden (science), playing a geography software program (social studies), and using the newspaper to calculate average weather statistics (math). These hours count in school, and they count in home education, too; they are as much a part of learning and curriculum as reading an assigned book.

A typical day in the life of an eight-year-old home schooler might look like this:

7:00 - 8:00 a.m.	wake up, breakfast, morning routine
8:00 - 9:00	television program about biospheres
9:00 - 9:45	Monopoly® with sister (was the "banker")
9:45 - 10:30	practice piano, followed by making up his own song
11:00 - 12:00	home school open gym
12:30 - 1:00 p.m.	lunch
1:00 - 2:30	free reading (historical fiction)
2:30 - 4:00	make birdhouse with lumber and recycled materials
4:00 - 5:00	play computer math game
5:30 - 6:00	supper
6:30 - 8:00 p.m.	family time
8:15	bedtime

Although this does not seem like a typical school day, it can count as seven and one-half hours of home schooling:

- 1 hour science (television program)
- 1.75 hours math (Monopoly® and computer game)
- .75 hours music (piano practice and improvisation)
- 1 hour physical education (open gym)
- 1.5 hours reading/history
- 1.5 hours woodworking/ecology/art (birdhouse)

Whether or not activities are assigned is not what's important. What matters is whether or not the child is learning. If you're not sure whether an activity counts as learning time, ask yourself these questions:

- Was my child learning or practicing skills?
- Was my child inventing or creating something?
- Was my child demonstrating mastery?
- Was my child applying knowledge in any way?
- Was my child acquiring information by any means?
- Was my child seeking answers or asking questions in order to learn?

Some activities won't fit neatly into traditional subject areas. For example, you and your 10-year-old might have an hour-long discussion of philosophy in which you talk about Plato and Socrates. That counts as learning. Suppose your seven-year-old spends the afternoon at his uncle's auto shop watching the mechanics take apart engines. That also counts as learning. Home schooling allows unusual interests and passions to be a vital part of your child's education, whether or not the topic is a normal part of school curriculum.

If your state requires you to submit curriculum outlines or portfolios, check to see if there is a specific format you must follow or whether you can design your own. Curriculum outlines can range from a simple list of courses covered to a complex outline of goals, objectives, resources, and evaluative measures. Portfolios can keep samples of major projects and learning and can be kept by the child or the parent. If your state requires a detailed curriculum outline and does not provide a template or a sample, Borg Hendrickson's *How to Write a Low Cost/No Cost*

Curriculum for Your Home-School Child (1995) is an excellent resource to get you started. See also the information in the next section, "Keeping Records for Yourself."

Periodic standardized achievement testing is required by some states. You can usually have your child tested by the local school district, but if your child is gifted or has severe learning differences, be sure to ask about testing accommodations made for such children. If the school does not make accommodations for children who learn differently, consider private testing by someone trained to work with gifted students.

Keeping Records for Yourself

There are three types of records you will want to keep for yourself and your child: (1) records that help you set learning goals, (2) records that evaluate progress and assess needs, and (3) records that document learning.

Setting Learning Goals

Some people are more goal-oriented than others. Some spend a lot of time setting goals but don't reach them, while others purposely set fewer goals and accomplish most of them. Learning how to set personal and professional goals and reach them is a valuable study (and life) skill that helps us move forward and fulfill our potential.

In schools, students often have little or no say in setting the learning goals—sometimes called standards, learner outcomes, or learner objectives—set for them in the course of their education. Home schooling offers a valuable opportunity to provide a child with a real say in *what, how,* and *when* she learns. Most children care about their learning when given a chance to have a real say in the matter.

Kathy Wentz, owner of the Internet Unschooling List, reminds home schooling families to take Stephen Covey's advice and "start with the end in mind." Young children are not expected to have a career goal or a long-term educational plan, but they can certainly be asked what they want to know more about a year from now, what skills they would like to perform better, and what new areas of knowledge they want to explore. If a six-year-old says she wants to learn about airplanes, or a 13-year-old wants to submit science fiction stories to magazines, that "end goal" can help refine short-term goals that lead to the bigger goal.

Wayne W. Dyer (1985), author of *What Do You Really Want for Your Children?*, cautions against placing too much emphasis on long-range goals for children and suggests that families instead focus on mutually agreed upon short-term goals. Problems often occur if the long-term goal belongs more to the parents than the child. Asking a child to fulfill a parent's dream career is not the kind of goal setting that helps the child.

What does work is to encourage the child to think about what he wants to do or learn (the goal or outcome) and what steps might be necessary to get there (objectives). If your daughter says she wants to learn to play the piano, it will be much more effective to encourage *her* to think about how she might learn (lessons, a keyboard computer program, self-study), than to schedule practice for her and remove her own sense of responsibility for reaching her goals. She might come up with this plan:

> **Long-Term:** Learn to play the piano
> **Short-Term:** Learn to play songs from my favorite movie
> **Steps to Reach My Goal:**
> 1. Find a teacher and start lessons.
> 2. Practice five days a week after breakfast for 30 minutes.
> 3. Ask Mom to remind me if I haven't practiced.
> 4. Keep a practice chart so I know how many days I've practiced.
> 5. After each lesson, review whether practice time was enough.

Her five steps contain built-in feedback, self-evaluation, and room for change if necessary.

What if the child doesn't follow through? What if the parent's reminders are ignored and the practice chart not used? If the goals are the child's, then the child—and only the child—is responsible for working to meet them—or not. However, since the parent is paying for the lessons, the parent may ask that the child think of another way to pay for the lessons (savings, allowance, chores) or may question the value of lessons that result in no growth. Before taking this step, however, parents should watch the child's practice pattern closely and speak with the instructor. It is possible that the child *is* practicing at other times and just not recording it, or that the level of material is not challenging enough to require consistent practice in order to pass a lesson.

Other goals can be set cooperatively with child and parent, each having input into the goals and steps to reaching the goals. For example, you may both come up with a science goal for the fall months:

Science Learning Goals, Fall 1999

> **Goal:** Learn about insect classification
> **Steps:**
> ❑ Study animal classification.
> ❑ Focus on insect classification.
> ❑ Focus on ant species.
> ❑ Learn about the history of animal classification.
> ❑ Learn to draw ants.
> ❑ Rent video, *A Bug's Life*.
> ❑ Find stories and myths about ants.
> ❑ Find examples of insects outside and sketch them.

The list offers a good mix of long-term and short-term goals for a young child, explores a variety of learning styles, and allows the child a lot of freedom in specific choices. Your child may want to break down some of the goals into further steps:

- ❑ Learn to draw ants.
    - ⭕ Use Mark Kistler's drawing techniques.
    - ⭕ Draw ants with pen and ink.
    - ⭕ Draw three different ant species.
    - ⭕ Draw red ants with watercolors.

Learning goals can be very informal and don't always need to be written down. If you use learning goals as a form of record keeping for home schooling, you might want to list them several times a year, then note which goals are met, changed, or dropped.

If your child needs examples of kinds of things she might like to explore, topic lists for grade or age levels can spark interest and offer guidance. Be wary, however, of thinking that you need to follow a grade-by-grade standards list too closely (review Chapter 8).

Goals and Records for Gifted Learners

When setting goals for gifted learners, parents should try not only to set a faster pace (following the child's lead), but also to offer a broader scope, to take into account that many underlying basic skills are already mastered, to encourage multiple perspectives, and to focus on higher level thinking skills (Van Tassel-Baska, Johnson, & Boyce, 1994). This example of a goal for eighth-grade English from The College of William and Mary's College for Gifted Education illustrates the kinds of learning goals gifted children can be encouraged to consider. Instead of a goal "*to develop understanding of the chronology of American history*," gifted learners might instead "*analyze and interpret key social, cultural, and economic ideas as expressed in literature, poetry, art, and music of America at 20 year intervals.*" The latter goal offers a broader scope of ideas, an interdisciplinary approach, and uses the higher level thinking skills of analysis, synthesis, and evaluation. Students looking at the 1920s would find jazz music, the art of Georgia O'Keeffe, *The Great Gatsby*, and the first appearance of Mickey Mouse. The 1940s would reflect WWII. Students studying the 1960s would discover things related to Civil Rights and peace, with songs by the Beatles; Joan Baez; Peter, Paul and Mary; and poetry and other art by others. How were these different decades similar? Different? How do the arts reflect the differences? How do they help us understand the themes of those decades? What is the purpose of art? These questions ask for analysis and synthesis, and this kind of study will be of more interest than one focused primarily on knowledge and facts.

Agnes Leistico (1990), mother of two gifted learners and author of *I Learn Better by Teaching Myself*, writes that simple observation is the home school parent's most powerful tool for assessing learning and progress toward goals. Wide-scale testing is done in schools because there is no way that a teacher can observe each student closely enough to know what he or she already knows, is learning, and still needs to learn. The home school parent can simply have a conversation with the child to find out if he understands the concept of evaporation or if he needs some historical background for better understanding of a historical novel.

If you use textbooks, you can use chapter tests to pre-test your child for knowledge he already has. Or you can skip the tests except for occasional verbal spot-checking to make sure that nothing important is being missed. Perhaps you may buy some of the readily available worksheet books that contain a year's worth of curriculum, and challenge your child to work through selected portions, making it a game. For a gifted learner with strong language skills, this simple method offers proof to state authorities at the same time that it tests for gaps. If your child struggles with writing, however, the workbook method may not be worth the effort. Various grade-based computer programs contain initial placement tests that help the child to know at what levels to start each of the various games and adventures. These can also be useful for getting a broad view of a child's strengths and weaknesses. Some commercial games test knowledge. If you want to know what your child knows about parts of speech and punctuation, play Madlibs™, a game available at book and teacher supply stores.

Many home school parents do little formal assessment of progress, relying more heavily on informal observation, day-to-day interaction, and subtle modifications. Maria does not keep track of her children's grade level abilities because, as she says, "the child's learning will not speed up or slow down based on my knowing what grade level they are at." She goes on to explain:

> They are where they are, and they need to be allowed to progress at their own natural pace, independent of where others of the same age are on a grade scale. I measure their abilities based on what they were capable of "then" vs. "now." Progress, not competition; learning, not force-feeding, is the goal.
>
> —Maria, home school parent

Another parent uses goal-setting conferences as a way to monitor progress and assess needs.

> We used to hold home school "conferences" at the beginning and end of each week. I'd ask the girls what they wanted to do that week. They'd share their ideas. I'd share my concerns and activities for the week, and we'd come up with a plan. At the end of each week, we would all reassess how things went and discuss how to change things the next week for the better (i.e., more fun).
>
> —Joan, home school parent

Parents might want to make weekly conferences a celebration, where children can share important successes or things they've learned, or hold weekly "breakfast meetings" at a favorite restaurant to plan for the week ahead.

For gifted and highly creative children, encourage adding greater depth, more interdisciplinary connections, or higher level thinking skills instead of "moving on" to the next topic, especially if the child showed great interest in what she was learning. If a child has enjoyed studying insect classification, she can become an expert on a particular insect, such as the Monarch butterfly with its migration to Mexico, or the fruit fly and its use in research. Connections can go further to theories of insects' role in evolution or their place in the food chain. The student can move onto higher level thinking skills by analyzing insect geographic adaptations or evaluating various means for managing insect problems.

Documenting Learning (Or After-the-Fact Record Keeping)

To document learning or keep a cumulative learning record, parents have several options that can be used separately or together and at different times in a child's education:

- A portfolio of your child's work—including written projects, math papers, art work, and photos of projects.

- A learning log—in narrative diary or grid form listing the child's activities.

- A unit study log—listing unit activities, books read, and topics studied.

- Grade reports and transcripts—listing topics studied and level of mastery.

Portfolios

Portfolios are popular with families who home school; they are easy to put together and highly effective for showing a broad range of interests and abilities. Two important ingredients of a strong student portfolio are: (1) a clear idea of what skills and knowledge the portfolio will demonstrate, and (2) student involvement in decisions about what goes into the portfolio.

For example, you might want to keep a writing portfolio to demonstrate the variety of your child's writing, his use of revision, and self-evaluation. The child will know that he should include several different types of writing, different revisions of the same piece, and examples of where he has edited his own writing and has made changes. Photocopies are often best, especially if the child is still working on the original or doesn't want to part with it.

Some families maintain a comprehensive portfolio containing information about all subjects and use an expandable file, sold in office supply stores. This allows inclusion of many sample tests, works of writing, drawings, audio or video cassettes of musical performances or compositions, photographs of science projects or outdoor projects, maps drawn by the child, reading lists, and book reviews. Another inexpensive option is the stackable file box, one for each child per year, in which you place files with the above items. Make a list of the items in the box and glue it on the outside of the cover for easy reference.

A home school parent might keep these following notes and records for a student working above age-based grade level:

- Completed math workbooks, with dates of completion and scores of final tests recorded on the front.

- Print-outs of progress reports from completed lessons of a math CD-ROM program.

- List of biology—or other science—experiments completed and books used.

- Description of Saturday science classes taken through a community enrichment program, including names of instructors, grade level of work, concepts covered, and activities performed (use available course descriptions).

- List of books, short stories, poetry, newspapers, and magazines read throughout the year (with grade level, if available), notes about follow-up activities and topics of discussion, copies of book reviews or book reports written by the student.

- Copies of representative writing by the student, including drafts and finished works, letters, poetry, fiction and non-fiction, self-evaluations, and works in progress (parents uncomfortable with assessment of writing samples can ask another adult with writing skills to provide a critique of the child's writing).

- Photocopy of the cover page of piano books completed, with an audio- or videotape of the child performing.

- Photos or photocopies of art work, both in progress and completed.

- Self-assessment written by the student about what he or she learned during the year.

Scrapbooks

Informal scrapbooks can be the beginning of portfolios and can help organize and record learning activities such as 4-H clubs, Scouts, book groups, camps, classes, and lessons. The scrapbook could include course descriptions from community class brochures, recital programs, photos, personal notes from private instructors, ticket stubs for plays and museum visits, and newspaper and magazine clippings about subjects that are of interest to the child.

Learning Logs

This is another convenient way for families who home school to document their learning. Learning logs can be kept in narrative, grid, or list format for each day or week. Both parents and children can keep them. They can also be called journals or diaries. An easy way for children to begin to keep a learning log is to simply keep a list of the books they read. Sample forms at the end of the chapter offer two ways for a child to remember favorite books. A narrative learning log is a diary-type account of the day's or week's activities. Two examples below show how typical home school days might be recorded in a narrative learning log.

Figure 13.1: Sample Learning Log – Narrative Format
Alice, Age 7

Wednesday, September 1, 2002 (Home School Group Day)

Alice worked with an adult friend who is a science teacher at her home school group. She told him about a biography of Linnaeus she had read, and they discussed the basics of his system of classification. They searched for insects but only caught a moth, which they attempted to classify using field guides. They discussed difference between insects and bugs. Ideas for next week include: classify some ant species, catch and observe more insects, create a "new" insect, and give it a scientific name. Pauline read a story to the children. After lunch, they all swam in the pool until it was time to go home. Reading after supper: George Washington's Socks and DK's Robinson Crusoe.

(Subjects today: Science, Language Arts, Physical Education, Reading)
Total hours: 5

September 2, 2002

After breakfast, Alice began to read a library book about maps, which led to getting out the globe, then a world map and several books about geography. She looked up the entry for Wisconsin in the encyclopedia and found a map that showed how to get from our city to Madison. Using the scale, we found the distance and discussed how long it takes to get there and miles per hour. She also talked about the map in the DK Robinson Crusoe that shows the island, which led to discussion of different kinds of maps and their uses. (geography, language)

Played Yahtzee® (arithmetic)
Time outside looking for insects. (science)
Finished reading George Washington's Socks. (language, history)
We explored several topics in the encyclopedia: ants, home schooling, clothing. In the evening, we read about the first world explorers. Alice finished writing a strategy guide for her invented computer game, printed it, and bound it with tape. She began an insect story about ants. (study skills, history, writing)

(Subjects today: History, Math, Reading, Writing, Language, Science, Study Skills)
Total hours: 6

Following is a daily learning log sheet based on an example from a home school parent. She writes, "My philosophy is: I want a record of every day to keep just in case. Instead of having to write something from scratch every day, I pick what we use most and simply check the boxes." Each family could create sheets unique to their home school approach and curricula. The sheets could be copied and filled out in just a few minutes each evening. Parents could check off activities and subjects studied and note any field trips, materials used, or special concerns or accomplishments. At the end of a month or semester, parents could tally the daily information to form a comprehensive assessment of what was learned.

Figure 13.2: Daily Learning Log

_____/_____/2002-2003

Student Name: _____

❑ Monday ❑ Tuesday ❑ Wednesday ❑ Thursday ❑ Friday ❑ Saturday ❑ Sunday

Number of learning hours completed ❑ 1 ❑ 2 ❑ 3 ❑ 4 ❑ 5 ❑ 6
Outside Activities ❑ ½ hour ❑ 1 hour ❑ 2 hours ❑ 3 hours +

Music

_____ (instrument/voice) ❑ Practice ❑ Lesson ❑ ½ hour ❑ 1 hour +

Language Arts

❑ English ❑ Latin ❑ French _____

Physical Education

❑ Walking ❑ Running ❑ Cycling ❑ Skating ❑ Soccer ❑ Swimming
❑ Other _____

Life Skills

❑ Cooking ❑ Sewing ❑ Cleaning ❑ Pet Care ❑ Craftsmanship ❑ Computer Skills
❑ Other_____

Language Studies

❑ Writing ❑ Penmanship ❑ Journal ❑ Workbook Lessons ❑ Vocabulary List
❑ Other_____

Independent Reading

Book(s) read:_____

Visual Arts

❑ Drawing ❑ Painting ❑ Fabric Arts ❑ Sculpture ❑ Tactile ❑ Crafting ❑ Special Project Photo
attached? ❑ Yes ❑ No ❑ Other_____

Civics and Citizenship (Social Studies)

Community Projects? ❑ Yes ❑ No Project description _____
❑ Self Awareness ❑ Etiquette ❑ Demographics/Geography ❑ Spirituality
❑ Other_____

Mathematics

❏ Cuisenaire Rods ❏ Miquon Studies ❏ Practical Math ❏ Workbook Lessons

Book used/Other:_____

Field Trips and Outside Labs

❏ Planetarium ❏ Museum _____ ❏ Workshop ❏ Nature Study ❏ Gardens
❏ Theatre ❏ Concerts ❏ Festivals ❏ Other_____

Multimedia References Used Today

CDs

❏ Dangerous Creatures ❏ Amazing Animals ❏ Reader Rabbit Kindergarten ❏ Reader Rabbit 2nd Grade ❏ Reader Rabbit Math ❏ Reader Rabbit Reading Journey ❏ Jumpstart Reading ❏ Jumpstart Math ❏ Learning Center Reading ❏ Encarta ❏ Sylvan Test ❏ Explorapedia ❏ Dinosaurs ❏ DK Dinosaur Hunter ❏ Land Before Time ❏ Brain Quest 2nd Grade ❏ Kids Works ❏ Einstein JR's Classroom ❏ Fraction Fireworks ❏ National Geographic Awareness ❏ Kid Phonics

Television

❏ Bear in the Big Blue House ❏ Out of the Box ❏ O'Shea ❏ Crocodile Hunter ❏ Wild Discovery
❏ Amazing Animals ❏ National Geographic ❏ Chris and Martin Series ❏ Bill Nye
❏ Other_____

Games

❏ Geosafari ❏ SET ❏ Uno ❏ Candyland ❏ Card Games ❏ Boggle
❏ Other_____

Concerns/Comments

Child_____

_____

Parent_____

_____

Achievements_____

_____

Special Accomplishment_____

Teacher Signature: _____Student Signature:_____

Still another family keeps a weekly, rather than a daily, learning log for an older child. There is space after each subject area to make notes about specific materials used or topics covered, and the child or parent simply circles the days of the week when the subject was studied. This type of learning log works well for families who don't need to keep track of hours but want a brief record of how often specific subjects are studied.

Table 13.1: Weekly Learning Record and Planner

Name _____ Week of _____

History, Geography	M T W Th F Sa Su
Math	M T W Th F Sa Su
Science: Astronomy, Physics	M T W Th F Sa Su
Science: Biology, Genetics	M T W Th F Sa Su
Writing	M T W Th F Sa Su
Reading	M T W Th F Sa Su
Listening to Oral Reading	M T W Th F Sa Su
Vocabulary from Classical Roots	M T W Th F Sa Su
French	M T W Th F Sa Su
Group Play/Learning	M T W Th F Sa Su
Art and Art Appreciation	M T W Th F Sa Su
Piano	M T W Th F Sa Su
Music Appreciation	M T W Th F Sa Su
Educational Video/Television	M T W Th F Sa Su
Physical Activity/Education	M T W Th F Sa Su
Other/Notes	

Unit Study Journals

If your family uses unit studies, keep an on-going list of materials and resources used, topics introduced, projects undertaken, and insights gained. The Learning Journal described in Chapter 12 offers ways for children to track their own progress. Because unit studies can last several months, a student might have several different unit study journals in progress at any one time.

Grade Reports and Transcripts

There is nothing to stop you from using the kinds of grade reports and transcripts for your child that the schools use. The simplest method is to simply list subjects covered by quarter or semester, with an indication of completion or level of achievement (traditional letter grade, pass/fail grades, or written narrative comments). Here is one parent's version of a report card for her son's first-grade year.

Table 13.2: Home School Report Card

Student: Martin Oslicek   Grade and Age: 1st grade, 6 yrs.

Subject	Quarter			
	1	2	3	4
Language Skills:				
Reading Vocabulary	E	E	E	E
Paragraph Comprehension	E	E	E	E
Spelling	E	E	E	E
Letter/Word Recognition	E	E	E	E
Word Comprehension	E	E	E	E
Usage	E	E	E	E
Mathematics:				
Math Computation	S	E	E	E
Math Problem Solving	E	E	E	E
Science:				
Lab/Research	E	E	E	E
Earth Science	E	E	E	E
Arts:				
Music (Piano)	S	S	S	N
Fine Art (Studio)	E	E	E	E
Voice	E	E	E	E
Citizenship:				
Self-Awareness	E	E	E	E
Neighborhood Geography	E	E	E	E
Physical Education & Health:				
Soccer	E	E	N/A	N/A
Habits of Safety	N	I	S	S
Daily Exercises	S	S	S	E
Practical Life Lessons:				
Etiquette	E	E	E	E
Currency Concepts	S	E	E	E
Homemaking	S	E	E	S
Pet Care	E	E	E	E

CODES: E Excellent S Satisfactory I Improving N Needs Improvement

NOTES: Martin continues to show excellent progress in reading and reads to his younger brother as part of his daily routine. His comprehension and expressive reading are impressive, and he has shown a talent for writing poetry. His artistic talents have expanded to include watercolors. His scientific endeavors now include participation in marine biology through 4-H. His continual love of piano is evident in his practice. He has passed all assessment tests and will proceed to second grade with honors.

Teachers' Signatures: Mirna Oslicek, Vladi Oslicek   Date: 06/30/02

A home school report card can be tailored to reflect specific skills and topics of study for each child. Parents can use letter grades, percentages, or pass/fail or satisfactory/unsatisfactory marks.

Home school students should also be encouraged to evaluate their own work. At the beginning of a unit, if you use grades, discuss with your child what criteria would constitute acceptable and non-acceptable work and progress, as well as what sort of work would earn an A or a B. At the end of the unit, have the child discuss which grade she feels she should get and why. Ask the child to evaluate herself based on each of the criteria discussed earlier. The grade decided upon is less important than the learning gained through this self-evaluation and discussion of how the child sees her work and how the parent sees the work. A final grade should be a merging of the child's evaluation with the parent's. Although this process may seem uncomfortable at first, you will be helping your child to be less dependent on outside evaluations and to pay closer attention to her own learning.

With increasing emphasis these days on standards and assessment, schools now frequently use rubrics, written criteria, to describe what would constitute a math grade of A, B, C, or D or a writing score of 4, 3, 2, or 1 so that the student knows in advance how grades will be assigned. A rubric for paragraph writing, for example, would list the characteristics of each sample grade. An "A" paragraph has a clear topic sentence, shows excellent organization of ideas, shows excellent support for ideas, uses correct spelling and grammar, and shows creativity of thought and presentation. A "B" paragraph has a clear topic sentence but is less organized, shows some support but is not creative, and has one grammatical error. A "C" paragraph has a topic sentence but not matching support sentences, lacks focus, and is even less organized. A "D" paragraph is incomplete, does not stick to one topic but rambles, and has several grammatical and spelling errors. With some sort of written rubric in front of them—whether for math or science or language arts—students can be more involved in their own learning and evaluation. Home school parents can get sample rubrics from their local district or state department of education and can then write their own to suit their own curriculum.

Entering/Re-Entering the School System

What do we do when we've taught them all we can and the only thing left is University...but they're still so young? Fortunately there are some e-mail lists that specifically address this situation which have definitely helped, as others who have gone that route before, successfully, share their experiences. But I still wonder how it will work for us.

—Sam, home school parent

Some home school families enter or re-enter the school system for upper elementary school, junior high school, high school, or at some other point. Other families school at home until their children are prepared to enter college or the work force. Some families begin home schooling during the high school years. Each option presents the student and parents with specific challenges, as well as unique educational advantages. Parents must decide which options best suit the child. The right choice for one child or family might not be the right choice for a similar child of similar ability in another family.

If you think that attending a traditional elementary school or high school is a possibility for your home school student, begin to plan the transition early so that you have the necessary paperwork and coursework in place. It is a good idea to contact the principal, gifted and talented coordinator, and guidance counselor at the school your child may attend to ask how they handle admission of home school students, what records they require, what is required for entry to honors or other programs, and so on. By building a positive relationship with the school personnel ahead of time, you can pave the way for a more successful transition to the classroom for your child.

Many home school students master high school material before high school age. A child whose area of strength is math, for example, may be ready to learn ninth-grade level algebra or high school geometry at age 10 or 12, although other subjects are closer to age level. Parents should begin to think about how to document this learning to avoid their child having to repeat classes he has already completed. Records of curriculum materials used, test papers, and dates of completed course work are much easier to organize if kept from the beginning rather than patched together after the fact. The child may still be asked to take the end-of-the-year algebra exam based on the text used by that high school math department to demonstrate mastery. Or if there is resistance from the school about awarding algebra credit, the parent can suggest the child be allowed to "test out of algebra." Talking to the school early can help determine such options or requirements. Some highly gifted home schooled children have "gone through" an elementary level curriculum in all core subjects before age 13 or 14. Early high school admission is an option for these students. The school may view this choice as a grade skip—omitting one or more years of formal study. The home schooled child has simply been able to work at an individual pace that allowed the child to cover an elementary curriculum in fewer than eight years. Such "rapid progress" or grade telescoping is a particularly good fit for middle school age students who have already begun the abstract and logical thinking required for high school study (Rogers, 2002).

When parents approach a high school about the possibility of early entrance, they can consider whether they will present their child's early entrance as a grade skip or as a continuation of grade telescoping. Karen Rogers, in *Re-Forming Gifted Education*, offers this description of such a candidate (Rogers, 2002):

- Scores above 130 on individual IQ test.
- Scores two or more years above grade level on achievement tests.
- Would be frustrated with the slow pace of regular classroom instruction at grade level.
- Is independent and motivated.
- Prefers fast-paced and challenging learning.
- Enjoys self-directed learning.
- Enjoys working with small groups of children of similar ability.
- Has a wide range of interests.
- Is actively involved in a variety of activities and hobbies.

To make a case for grade skipping, either directly to high school or for entry to any other grade, parents can document how their child exhibits the above characteristics. Documentation can include copies of IQ test and achievement test results, anecdotes that show the child's self-directedness in study, a personal essay in which the child writes about his or her motivation to learn and study, examples of the child's pace of study in specific home-study courses or subject areas, a portfolio of the child's interests, and letters of recommendation from adults who have worked with the child in group settings, especially where the child was younger than other children in the group. If the school is reluctant to accept the above documentation and your child is seeking entry to elementary school, parents can request that the school use the *Iowa Acceleration Scale* (Great Potential Press, formerly Gifted Psychology Press) to help them determine whether their child is a good candidate for grade skipping. For a child who has completed elementary level course work at home, parents can make a case that their child has finished eighth-grade coursework through grade telescoping, shortening the amount of time usually allotted for completion of a specific grade or subject. No grade skip is involved, because no academic year is missed. The book *Re-Forming Gifted Education: Matching the Program to the Child* (Rogers, 2002) can help parents understand grade telescoping so they can explain it to school officials. As with grade skipping, parents will need to document work their child has completed to be ready for ninth grade. Parents can ask the school curriculum coordinator or head teacher for a list of topics covered, or for a curriculum scope and sequence for the grades that their child has completed. Then, parents can use this list to show to what extent the child has met the requirements for each grade level up to the grade of entry.

You might also ask the school principal or admissions director if your child can visit school for a day to get a feel for what a typical school day will be like. Many high schools have special orientation days for visiting eighth-grade students. Call at the beginning of your child's eighth-grade year to ask about possible times to visit.

College

Once your child begins high school level work (at any age), you'll need to be even more diligent about keeping the records for admission to college. Two definitive guides to help home schoolers prepare for college are Cafi Cohen's *And What about College? How Homeschooling Leads to Admissions to the Best Colleges and Universities, second edition,* and *Homeschoolers' College Admissions Handbook: Preparing 12- to 18-Year-Olds for Success in the College of Their Choice.* Cohen suggests that home schooling families begin early to build a "database" consisting of reading lists, learning logs, information about workshops and courses taken, work samples, and other materials that can later be used to form either a portfolio or "home-brewed" transcript. Your student will also need to request letters of recommendation from people who have taught or worked with him.

Many home school students master high-school level material before high-school age. A child whose area of strength is math, for example, may be ready to learn ninth-grade level algebra or high school geometry at age 10 or 12, even though writing skills or other subject areas are closer to age level. Parents should begin to think early about how to document this learning when it occurs to avoid their child having to repeat classes that he or she has already completed. Careful yet succinct records of curriculum materials used, test papers, and dates of completed course work are much easier to keep up from the beginning rather than try to patch together after the fact.

If your child has specific colleges in mind, he can make a project of contacting the schools to see how many home schoolers they admit each year, what their requirements are, and perhaps even the names of current students who were home schooled for your child to interview. This gives your child an important start in feeling a sense of ownership for his decisions regarding higher educational choices and may prevent unforeseen difficulties or anxiety.

Many home schooled children enter college a year or two early. Highly and profoundly gifted children and their families must consider the possibility of much earlier college entrance. Some of these exceptionally gifted home school students are ready and eager to delve into high school course work before middle school age. Such students often progress rapidly through high school level curriculum and have completed their secondary education by age 15 or even younger.

Although parents may think college is the only logical next step for a child who has completed high school level work, there are many other options, including one or more community college classes, internship in a possible career area, a year abroad as an exchange student, self-study of a specific interest, or extensive family travel. One or more of these endeavors may fill the early teen years with as much challenge as a college classroom. Some, such as part-time classes at a local community college or university, may be better suited to a 15-year-old than full-time college life.

Linda, a home school mother of six children, found that delaying early entrance to college was a good choice for her son.

We are very glad we kept our son at home until he was 18 before sending him off to college. We are also very glad that we home schooled him. Home schooling allowed him the freedom to study what he was ready to study, without having to worry about what the school curriculum offered at this age or how he fit in with other students.

Since we home schooled for high school, we didn't have to deal with the social aspects of entering high school as much as we did with entering college. When you begin high school, of course, has a direct effect on when you begin college. Social readiness for university life is a complicated issue. Our son was what I consider a pretty mature young man. He never had the rebellion problems that many teens have. He related well to older students and adults, although he was somewhat shy. So how do you decide when he is ready to "leave the nest" and go on to full-time college? A student entering college early will have to deal with a society of "peers" who are all a few years older. What will they think of him? Will he be a normal part of their social groups, or will he be "the little smart kid" who doesn't really fit in?

As we considered all of these issues, I think we started out with the idea that we should go as fast as we could. By going to college early, he would finish early and have a few years' "jump" on life. Our attitude changed over time. Down the road,

This parent listed the following advantages of home schooling a gifted child until "normal" college age:

O Avoidance of being socially out of sync with older students.
O More freedom for study of special interests.
O More time to mature before leaving home.
O More time to spend with family.

Disadvantages of waiting for college were:

O Absence of like-ability/like-interest learning groups.
O Difficulty meeting high level learning needs.
O Delay in advanced study and career.
O Avoidance of healthy risk-taking, both academically and socially.

In *Re-Forming Gifted Education: Matching the Program to the Child*, Karen Rogers (2002) offers good explanations of several education options, such as early college entrance, grade skipping, moving quickly through curriculum for a specific subject, use of Talent Search Programs, and other enrichment opportunities. She includes research findings on the effectiveness of each option, describes the kind of child who is the best candidate for each option, and advises how to monitor educational choices to ensure that they are working as they should. Rogers recommends that parents consider carefully the pros and cons of early college entrance and other educational decisions for their children.

Some home school families find that early college entrance, part-time or full-time, helps their child learn at an appropriate level of challenge and interest. Loren began home schooling midway through his third grade year and continued until the end of seventh grade. At that point, his mother didn't feel she could teach him fast enough or at the level he needed. "I'm smart," she writes, "but he's very, very smart."

Early college entrance allows Loren to broaden his fields of study, offering him a fuller understanding of some of the careers and disciplines that are future possibilities for him. For other students, like the girl below, early college entrance allows focus on a specific area of strength.

As it turned out, there was little to worry about in terms of her ability to perform on a college level. She was disappointed at the caliber of writing put forth by other students, mostly non-English majors who were taking it as an introduction to writing. But she had a wonderful time getting to know the director of the Kelly Writers' House, an accomplished young poet, and meeting dozens of the visiting poets and novelists who do readings and residencies at the House. Some of her work in that class won honorable mention in the university's annual poetry competition and was published by the student literary magazine, as well as an independent literary magazine recommended by her teacher.

The following semester, she chose a course called, "Women in Twentieth Century Fiction." It was a rigorous class, well taught by a graduate student in the English Department. Students were required to write three drafts of each paper, do a class presentation with a partner, and post a weekly series of comments to the class listserv. She loved it and thrived, but she also worked harder than she's ever had to in her life.

At the end of the semester, emboldened by her 4.0 GPA, we petitioned the university to allow her to take two classes. (The official policy is that very young students take only one.) Our request was approved, and next semester, Kerri will take an upper-level poetry writing course and a linguistics course.

Although she is succeeding and really enjoying her life as a part-time college student, neither we nor Kerri have any plans for her to matriculate early. We want her to have time to enjoy the rest of her childhood and to pursue her many interests at her own pace.

—Maggie, home school parent

Is Kerri a home school high school student taking concurrent college classes, or is she a part-time college student who just happens to be 15? The answer is probably somewhere in between, as her family, like other home school families, seek creative solutions to the needs of atypical learners.

Kerri's story shows how parents can find out about college courses and programs for young students. Parents who do not have an affiliation with a college or university can ask their friends with college-age children for names of professors or college officials who may be willing to talk with them about early entrance options and possible courses. Parents can also ask the director of admissions for more information on policies for early admission.

Some colleges and universities offer full-time early entrance programs for young gifted students. These programs offer support for the transition to higher-level education, as well as a chance for gifted students to learn and interact with a true peer group. The Educational Resource Information Center (ERIC) also offers information. For an updated listing of early entrance college programs, see the ERIC publication "Early Entrance to College" (http://ericec.org/faq/gt-early.html).

Key Points

☑ Home school records are kept to help set learning goals, evaluate progress, document learning, meet state requirements, and gain entry to school, enrichment programs, or college.

☑ Parents can choose the records and assessments that satisfy requirements and which interfere least with the learning process.

☑ By de-emphasizing measured achievement and emphasizing learning, home school parents can prevent becoming over-invested and over-involved in their child's success.

☑ Home school requirements for documentation vary by state.

☑ Children should be involved in setting their own learning goals.

☑ Learning goals for gifted learners should include a broader scope and divergent learning, as well as a faster pace.

☑ Portfolios, learning logs, unit study journals, grade reports, and transcripts are some of the ways to document learning.

☑ In the event that the child re-enters school, home school parents need to have accurate records to document their child's learning. Parents should also think about what grade level is the most appropriate placement.

☑ Home schooled children who plan to attend college have many options: enter college "on time;" use later high school years for exploratory learning, travel, employment, or independent study; enter college "early," either part-time or full-time; and dual enrollment of high school and college simultaneously.

Questions for Reflection

1. What home school records are necessary to meet my state's legal requirements? Which of the following do I need to document: hours, days, weeks, subject areas, academic progress? What kinds of records will most easily fill these requirements?

2. How will we assess needs, set learning goals, and evaluate progress? How can I involve my child in these decisions?

3. How long will we home school? (Note: You may not know—that's okay.) Will I be planning for entry to school or college in the near future? What records will I need to have?

Resources for Home School Teens

Cafi Cohen's Homeschool Teens and College Web Page
www.homeschoolteenscollege.net

Cohen, Cafi (2000). *And What about College? How Homeschooling Leads to Admission to the Best Colleges and Universities*. Holt Associates.

Cohen, Cafi (2000). *Homeschoolers' College Admissions Handbook: Preparing 12- to 18-Year-Olds for Success in the College of Their Choice*. Prima Publishing.

Featherstone, Bonnie, & Reilly, Jill (1990). *College Comes Sooner than You Think! The Essential College Planning Guide for High School Students and Their Families*. Great Potential Press (formerly Gifted Psychology Press). For students and their parents, grades 8-12.

Llewellyn, Grace (1998). *The Teenage Liberation Handbook: How to Quit School and Get a Real Life and Education*. Lowry House.

Sebranek, Pat (1996). *School to Work: A Student Handbook*. Great Source. Workplace communication skills for teens and young adults.

Wright, Avis L., & Olszewski-Kubilius, Paula (1993). *Helping Gifted Children and Their Families Prepare for College: A Handbook Designed to Assist Economically Disadvantaged and First-Generation College Attendees*. The National Research Center on the Gifted and Talented, University of Connecticut.

Sebranek, Pat (1997). *Write for College: A Student Handbook. Great Source.* College communication skills, including writing, documenting, computer research, speech, and vocabulary.

Resources for Record Keeping and Goal Setting

Hendrickson, Borg (1995). *How to Write a Low Cost/No Cost Curriculum for Your Home-School Child*. Mountain Meadow Press. Offers a subject-area breakdown for grades 1-6.

Heuer, Loretta (2000). *The Homeschooler's Guide to Portfolios and Transcripts*. IDG Books.

Juarez, Bernard; Sandra Parks; & Howard Black (2000). *Learning on Purpose: A Self-Management Approach to Study Skills. Critical Thinking Books & Software*. Grades 9-12.

Parks, Sandra, & Black, Howard (1999). *Organizing My Learning. Critical Thinking Books & Software*. Designed for grades 4-8.

Rogers, Karen (2002). *Re-Forming Gifted Education: Matching the Program to the Child*. Great Potential Press (formerly Gifted Psychology Press). Information on assessment and educational planning.

Winebrenner, Susan (1992). *Teaching Gifted Kids in the Regular Classroom*. Free Spirit Publishing. Ideas and forms for self-assessment.

Information about Assessments and Testing for Gifted Children

Belin-Blank Center, University of Iowa
www.uiowa.edu/~belinctr

Center for Talented Youth, Johns Hopkins University
www.jhu.edu/~gifted

The Gifted Development Center
www.gifteddevelopment.com

At Home with Home Schoolers

Lynn, Age 16

On preparing for college: "I like to know 'why' a lot."

Lynn, who lives in Canada, has been a home school student for seven and one-half years. Her mother writes:

> *"I find home schooling easier than classroom education because I don't have to worry so much about the children's psychological health. I also know that their needs are being met, and I am on top of it when they aren't being met. Scheduling is also much easier. The girls get more done in less time at home, leaving large chunks of time free for volunteer work and other activities. The children are less tired and healthier overall. The last benefit alone is worth all the time and money spent home schooling."*

Lynn answers questions about what it's like to be a home schooling teen preparing for college.

Q: How old are you, and what grade are in you in (if applicable)?

A: My age is 16 and I'd be in grade 11 if I were in public school. I add the qualifier to the last part because my age-grade level isn't always the level I work at. I've been told my learning material ranges from grade 10 to university level.

Q: What are your long-term goals, if any? And how are you working to meet them?

A: Right now I'm busy trying to figure out what I want to do in my life. My interests are so eclectic. When I looked at our university's catalog, I wanted to get a BS with double majors in Math and Computing Science and two interdisciplinary minors in Anthropology and Religious Studies! I definitely want to do something in computers, but that's about all I know for sure right now. I'll probably go to university as well.

As for working to meet those goals, I've been ordering university catalogs and inquiring about long-distance courses like crazy. And I've been studying subjects that I'm less than thrilled with because I have to cover them to get into university. I've also been trying to find local jobs and volunteer positions where I have to deal with computers. I'm just getting started installing Linux on my computer. I'm a member of our local Linux user group, and they're very patient with all my questions. I ask questions a lot, about everything.

Q: Why are you home schooling?

A: *School didn't interest me, and I disliked it so much I'd be sick to avoid Social Studies. That was my least favorite subject. It's now one of my favorites. Mom says school gave me a bad attitude. The whole environment just wasn't good for me. We also have methodology differences with public school. I prefer a more individual, tailored approach. Also, I like to know "why" a lot, and my school wasn't good at providing the answers. My school didn't even want me to ask the questions.*

People tell me I'm bright or gifted. I think a large part of it is just that I think for myself. A lot of people cheat themselves by listening to authorities and the establishment and having no interest in knowing how or why those results were reached.

Q: How would you describe a typical day of home schooling? (If you can't describe a typical day, perhaps you could pick a recent day and describe how it went.)

A: *Well...mostly it's the same as what I'll describe below, but sometimes we get bored and go on a field trip.*

Usually I decide to get all of my bookwork over with first. This currently includes some combination of geometry, physics, and biology. Next semester I'm doing chemistry (groan), calculus, and I think more biology. So after I get the science and math done, I usually turn to language arts. This involves essay writing (yuck, I don't like writing essays) and reading literature. Sometimes the prescribed reading is so interesting I'll finish it on my own time for fun.

Examples of things I've read recently are The Glass Menagerie *(a play by Tennessee Williams) and* Kings and Queens *(a book about the Plantagenets of England by Janice Young Brooks). Once I'm done with language arts, I'll do social studies or French. Usually I save piano for after everything else.*

If I can, I'll try to get on the computer at the end of the day. Mom doesn't like us on the computer mid-week. She thinks it distracts us from learning, so during mid-week I use it only for educational purposes.

Q: What outside-the-home activities do you participate in (examples: lessons, play groups, volunteer work, and so on)?

A: *Oh boy, are you in for a list. I currently volunteer at the local free-net (Internet service provider), the city greenhouse (plant care for their display), the TAGMAX MOO (currently rewriting help files), delivering flyers for a local community association, and being assistant webmistress for a website. This winter I hope to start volunteering at the Humane Society and possibly the YMCA. Last year I volunteered at a home school conference, a local arts festival, the university hospital, and was in charge of another web page.*

Now, on to lessons and classes. I take Tae Kwon Do at the local YMCA, piano lessons and drama through the Royal Conservatory of Music, and am doing Driver's Ed through a local public school. I've also been involved in soccer, racquetball, swimming, and gymnastics.

Q: How has your home schooling routine changed since you've begun, if at all?

A: We've become a lot more structured in the high school years, with less hands-on work and more textbooks, less interest-based learning and more catering to curriculum requirements from universities and school boards. I want to go on to university, so it's important that I cover the material they deem necessary as pre-requisites for their courses.

Q: What do you like about home schooling?

A: One-on-one interaction. You can personalize the learning material more. Also, your schedule is far more flexible than a regular school student's, so you have more opportunities to go places and do stuff.

Q: What don't you like about home schooling?

A: You're stuck with your family. Mom can choose to revoke computer privileges if that essay isn't done tonight. A public school teacher doesn't have that kind of authority. Also, just because you've got the sniffles doesn't mean you get the day off! You can still do some bookwork in bed, after all. Also, you see your family for a longer period of time during the day. Depending on parent-child relationships, this can be good or bad.

Q: What does a "good education" mean to you?

A: Actual knowledge, to me, doesn't make up the most important part of a good education. A good education, I think, is one that instills a love of learning in you and encourages you to explore the world around (and inside) you. It doesn't tell you all of the answers; it tells you how to find the answers. It leads you to think for yourself and be independent.

Q: How would you describe yourself as a learner? What are your learning styles and strengths? How do you learn best?

A: I'm a gestalt thinker. That means I like to start with overviews, patterns, and the big picture. Then I move on to the nitty-gritty details, the concrete cases, and examples. I think in terms of the whole first, then the parts.

I'm also a visual learner. I love to read, and I find that a good picture can indeed be worth a thousand words. Of course, a bad picture can confuse the heck out of you, so it goes both ways.

Besides that, I'm a very verbal and mathematical person. Math and writing were my favorite subjects from Kindergarten on. Astrophysics is creeping in there somewhere, too. I loved astronomy when I was younger.

Q: What advice do you have for other children and young adults who are considering or starting home schooling?

A: Well, if you're considering it, the absolute first thing to think about is why you want to do it. Religious reasons? Bad school environment? (It's unbelievable how bad some schools are these days...gangs, violence, everything.) Maybe school isn't "turning your crank?" Whatever you do, don't quit just because school's boring. I've found that oftentimes it's not the material itself that's boring, but how it's presented. For me, at least, who presents the material can influence how I feel about the whole subject matter. A pushy piano teacher turned me off music for five years. For four years after school, I hated French. Finally I gave it another go, but a structured French tutor pretty much squashed my returning interest. I do independent French study anyway.

The second thing to do is research the legal restrictions on home schooling in your area.

Laws very widely from state to state (in the United States) and province to province (in Canada). Other countries will have still different laws.

When you've just started and you are wondering "what do I do?" think about your favorite things to do, your favorite subjects, your interests. Start with those and work other curriculum and learning requirements into them. And most importantly, don't forget that you're a lot freer now! Go for your dreams and (as Miss Frizzle always says): "Take chances! Make mistakes!" It's the only way you learn anything.

14 Special Topics

This chapter explores some common questions asked by home school parents about these topics:

- Profoundly Gifted Children
- Giftedness and ADHD
- Sensory Integration
- Siblings and Learning Styles

Profoundly Gifted Children

Question: How should I home school my extremely precocious (profoundly gifted) young child?

Profoundly gifted children are as different from moderately gifted children as are moderately gifted children from more average children. Profoundly gifted young child will often be able to read and learn at the level of children twice their age. They are learning dynamos, soaking up information as fast as it is presented and spending nearly all of their waking hours asking questions and gaining new knowledge. These are the kinds of children who often skip several grades in school and are ready for college-level material at age 12.

Jon offers insight into his experience with home schooling a young, profoundly gifted child (age five):

> *We don't believe that a public or private school would provide sufficient curriculum accommodations for our profoundly gifted son. It is also his own choice. We offered him several educational options and he chose home schooling without hesitation.*
>
> *We only home school one child. Our daughter is 12 years old and has been going to public school. We offered her home schooling as well because she has tested as exceptionally gifted, but she prefers to keep things as they are. She is in the gifted program at her school in math and language arts and has a lot of extracurricular activities.*

We don't use any purchased curriculum at this point. I am considering using materials in individual subjects later on. But at this point, we can do random studies in many subjects and have fun. I know that he is far ahead of the program in most subjects, so grading him is not that important. We will probably take tests to evaluate his progress annually. Since he is only five, college entrance is not yet on our agenda, so I am not concerned about school grade levels or report cards. Also, our state does not regulate home schoolers and does not have mandatory testing, so we can explore freely.

To home school, you need to have good dictionaries and children's encyclopedias. A good world history atlas, a globe, and basic school supplies are important. A computer is also very important. There are so many excellent resources on the Internet that you can build the whole curriculum on-line. Great educational software is available in reading, math, science, and logic. If your local library loans CD-ROMs, I recommend that you try educational games before you buy them. Your child may be fond of some and dislike others. Some musical instruments are good to have at home. Any old stuff is good for science experiments—empty bottles, cans, pieces of broken toys, plastic bags, pieces of wood, etc. The kitchen is a good source of materials for experiments—baking powder, vinegar, eggs, oil, sugar, salt, etc.

We often take a world history atlas and choose pages at random. We call it travel in space and time. We make up a story about what could have happened with my son's favorite toy in that time and place, then escape successfully to another period. He absolutely loves it. In the last few weeks, we have been doing all lessons with his toys. We build lesson themes around them. For example, his favorite cartoon character travels in space to other planets. The main point is still space exploration, but presence of his toy makes him enjoy the lesson more. A lot of humor is essential. He loves jokes, including silly ones.

We use whatever materials are available and improvise a lot. We make new games and activities. We use the library a lot. He has his own computer with educational software and is doing a lot of independent work with the software programs.

We have always had a great bond with my son, but now it has become even stronger. I am doing something for my child that makes him happy. Yesterday I asked him if he had a wish, and after considering my question, he said "No. I am happy." We maintain a schedule when we study, but now my son is asking me for lessons in the evening and on weekends. He enjoys learning at home, and I believe that he would not be as happy in a regular school setting. He is happy most of the time, in contrast with last year when he was in a private pre-school and was complaining that he didn't like it.

Of course, home schooling takes a lot more effort. It is easier to send your child to school and forget about him until he comes home. But the reward is a happy (and academically advancing) child and a unique bonding between you.

—Jon, home school parent

The profoundly gifted child's insatiable thirst for learning doesn't diminish with age. Throughout the child's education, he will need a pace and breadth of learning that is extremely different from that of age peers and even other gifted children. Profoundly gifted children often need high school level work at age 10 or younger and college level work before their teens. Many of the resources listed throughout this book and in the next chapter work for profoundly gifted children, but parents will need to use them at early than recommended ages and adjust them to accommodate the child's often extreme and uneven development. Full-time home schooling allows many profoundly gifted children to learn at *their* normal pace without restrictions of age, grade, or lags in motor skills or social-emotional development. Part-time home schooling and part-time early high school or college works well for some profoundly gifted children (Chapter 13). See the section "College" in Chapter 13 for more information about early college study.

Giftedness and ADHD

Question: My child never stops moving. How do I know that he's not hyperactive?

Psychomotor superabundance is easily confused with hyperactivity, and ADD or ADHD is a common misdiagnosis of gifted children (Webb, 2001). To understanding the difference, parents need to look at the child's behavior across a variety of circumstances and environments. A truly hyperactive child cannot concentrate comfortably for long periods of time even on projects that interest him; a gifted child with psychomotor intensity (but not ADD or ADHD), on the other hand, can focus easily on tasks that are important to him (Webb & Latimer, 1993). Parents should remind themselves that "tasks that interest them" do not need to be school tasks. For example, gifted children may exhibit ADHD behavior in the classroom but spend hours at home drawing comics or learning about endangered animals or designing a better mousetrap. Those self-chosen tasks are often pursued with great energy and intensity, which should not be confused with hyperactivity.

Of course, gifted children can have ADHD. Parents who wish to pursue professional evaluations need to seek an evaluator who is familiar with the unique characteristics of gifted children. More important than mislabeling your child is to accept the child for who he or she is. Sharon Lind writes:

> *Highly gifted individuals, because of their uniqueness, can fall prey to the public and personal belief that they are not OK. It is vital when discussing OEs [overexcitabilities] that individuals realize that overexcitability [superabundance] is just one more description of who they are, as is being tall, or Asian, or left-handed. Since, OEs are inborn traits, they cannot be unlearned! It is therefore exceedingly important that we accept our overexcitable selves, children, and friends (Lind, 2000, p 47).*

Selected ADHD/Gifted Resources

Born to Explore! The Other Side of ADD. A Clearinghouse for Positive and Alternative Information.
www.borntoexplore.org

Freed, Jeffrey, & Parsons, Laurie (1997). *Right-Brained Children in a Left-Brained World: Unlocking the Potential of Your ADD Child.* Simon & Schuster.

Kaufmann, F.; Kalbfleisch, M. L.; & Castellanos, F. X. (2000). *Attention Deficit Disorders and Gifted Students: What Do We Really Know?* The National Research Center on the Gifted and Talented, University of Connecticut.

Lind, Sharon (May-June 1993). "Are We Mislabeling Overexcitable Children?" *Understanding Our Gifted.*

Lind, Sharon (Fall 2000). "Overexcitabilities and the Highly Gifted." *CAG Communicator.*

Maté, Gabor (1999). *Scattered: How Attention Deficit Disorder Originates and What You Can Do about It.* Dutton.

Webb, James T. (Spring, 2000). "Mis-Diagnosis and Dual Diagnosis of Gifted Children: Gifted and LD, ADHD, OCD, Oppositional Defiant Disorder." *Gifted Education Press Quarterly.*

Webb, James T., & Latimer, Diane (1993). "ADHD and Children Who Are Gifted." ERIC EC Digest #522 1993.
http://ericec.org/digests/e522.htm

Sensory Integration

Question: What can I do at home to promote integration of all of the senses—touch, smell, taste, hearing, sight, and muscle sense?

The book, *Physical Activities for Improving Children's Learning and Behavior,* by Billye Ann Cheatum and Allison A. Hammond (2000), covers in detail issues of sensory motor development and sensory systems, including numerous do-at-home tests to assess sensory integration as well as activities and techniques to use in an informal way with your child. For example, the authors explain that a child who experiences "tactile defensiveness" will avoid situations that are overly stimulating to the tactile (touch) system, such as being rubbed down with a towel after a bath or roughhousing with children on the playground or standing too close to someone in line. For these children, parents will need to understand the reasons behind the child's responses, work to make the child's environment less stimulating (including how other family members act toward the child), and incorporate activities into the child's day that will allow her to better regulate the tactile system. Fun group activities recommended in *Physical Activities for Improving Children's Learning and Behavior* include Centipede Relay, Musical Chairs Pile-On, and Line Tag, which can easily be made part of a home schooling child's physical education.

A parent shares her family's personal experience with sensory integration:

If your child needs Sensory Integration (SI) therapy, then home schooling is ideal. You and your child can incorporate SI activities throughout the day as needed. In a traditional classroom, it is unlikely that your child will be able to bounce or move with freedom when her brain tells her she needs movement.

The path that led us to SI therapy began with the Wechsler Intelligence Scale for Children III (WISC III). We decided to have our six-year-old daughter assessed to decide whether or not to continue home schooling. The assessment indicated a significant variance (two standard deviations) between her Verbal IQ and her Visual Spatial abilities. The assessment specialist recommended that we see a pediatric optometrist for a complete vision evaluation.

The pediatric optometrist concluded that our daughter did have vision problems: she had both nearsightedness and difficulty in getting her eyes to work together. The optometrist's therapy included a rigorous daily exercise regime more suitable for adults than small children. This meant frustrating therapy sessions in which our daughter refused to cooperate. After six months of therapy, an evaluation yielded disappointing results.

We then consulted a different optometrist who recommended SI therapy. Amy has been getting SI therapy one hour per week for three months now and loves it. She is unaware that she is even doing eye exercises during these "play" sessions. The occupational therapist (OT) suggested activities to stimulate the vestibular part of the brain, which she says "wakes up" the vision system. A typical therapy session might start with bouncing, twisting, and bilateral body movements. Amy selects what equipment she wants to play on and they go from there. These activities are then followed by "brain work," as our OT calls it. This may be a game requiring sequencing skills or eye/hand coordination.

We discovered through SI therapy that difficult eye/hand coordination tasks are easier for Amy when she is moving or bouncing. Handwriting has been a struggle for Amy and is an activity that she describes as "hateful." Therefore, we keep writing sessions brief and let her sit on a therapy ball (like a large bouncy ball) during writing. Believe it or not, Amy is able to stay with writing longer and write more legibly when she can move around on the ball as needed.

We also have a playroom in our house which includes equipment to stimulate the vestibular: a standard swing; an inflated inner tube hanging from bungee cords (a swingy, bouncy thing she loves); a mini trampoline; a Dizzy Disc Jr., which is a self-propelled twisty toy; and rings to hang from. All of the equipment was purchased locally at a reasonable cost. We take frequent breaks to the playroom between sedentary activities like reading, writing, and computer time. If the weather is pleasant, we go outside to run and swing. Amy feels better and is more productive with these breaks. I also incorporate bilateral body movements into the day with swimming twice a week and dance lessons. According to our OT, bilateral body movements help to get the eyes working together.

I have seen a positive change in Amy in the last six months. She has taken a new interest in working with her hands, drawing, and crafts. I don't know if it is the result of therapy or just normal growth and development—probably a combination of therapy and everything else going on in her life. I do know this: she is thriving emotionally, physically, and academically in a home school environment where she has lots of choices, from academic subjects to going outside to swing. We're going to keep on home schooling and swinging and bouncing for as long as she wants.

—Margaret, home school parent

Selected Sensory Integration Resources

Cheatum, Billye Ann, & Hammond, Allison A. (2000). *Physical Activities for Improving Children's Learning and Behavior.* Human Kinetics. One of the clearest explanations of sensory systems and motor development, with several suggested activities you can do at home.

Davison, Bev (1998). *Creative Physical Activities and Equipment.* Human Kinetics. All the information you'll need for creating an inexpensive physical education program at home.

Kranowitz, Carol Stock (1998). *The Out of Sync Child: Recognizing and Coping with Sensory Integration Dysfunction.* Perigee.

Songames for Sensory Integration. Bell Curve Records. Twenty-five Songames on cassette or compact disks and a booklet with developmental play activities. Ages 3-8.

Siblings and Learning Styles

Question: I have two children with very different learning styles. How can I support each of them when they require such different approaches?

Home schooling two or more children is nearly always more difficult and time-consuming than home schooling one, and when your children learn in different ways, you'll need to give even more time and thought to how you'll meet their individual learning needs.

Many parents find that time alone with each child is the best way to accommodate learning styles. Arrange your day so that each child has one-on-one time with you while the other children do independent reading or watch a video or have play time. Another strategy is to do unit studies in such a way that each child can choose from different activities and ways of learning; then you can all come together to share what you've discovered and created. One child might choose to read for information, while another might use interactive software programs or do hands-on projects. During your group time, each child gets a chance to explain what and how he or she has learned. This not only allows each child to use individual strengths, it also promotes acceptance of differences and provides practice with attentive and respectful listening.

Here are some examples of how other parents have handled this issue:

With two children home schooling, learning styles play a big role, especially when the two are completely opposite, as in our case. Our older child is calm, very visual, and not strongly verbal in her learning. She prefers to learn independently, have frequent quiet time, and use strong visual material unless her interest level is very high in a given area. Her younger brother is very active, strongly verbal, prefers not to be alone, and can use visual as well as non-visual materials easily. Even watching a TV program together can be a challenge with one wanting to comment and ask questions every 30 seconds and the other preferring quiet and total concentration to the end.

How does this work? We keep the time that we are all working together to a minimum, do lots of compromising, and provide lots of time for each to do their own thing. Just being "around" to monitor problems when we are not doing anything specific seems to be enough at this point. But it did take lots of adjustment for all of us in the beginning, as we needed time to figure each other out to discover and appreciate those differences!

—Kathleen, home school parent

Learning styles have played a large role in our home schooling. The girls learn so differently that it became obvious early on that they could not use the same types of materials with the same degree of success. Lynn learned everything as she read it or was exposed to it. Sarah needed to see it in color and then do it. So we used color writing and action for Sarah. I set out to determine the most efficient way to educate the girls, and that required me to read up on learning styles. We use a multiple intelligences approach, recognizing several ways the girls prefer to access knowledge. We provided as many options as we could to facilitate moving from one approach to another when they needed to. In short, I learned to be flexible but still keep the goal in mind.

—Joan, home school parent

Home School Resources

15

Enjoy the possibilities!

You've learned about giftedness and creativity, common reasons for home schooling gifted children, their unique learning and social-emotional needs, learning styles, and what it takes to be a good home school parent. You've thought about your sabbatical period, curriculum options, the value of self-directed learning, the advantages and disadvantages of several home school approaches, and the most efficient and effective ways to keep home school records. Now comes the fun part—researching and choosing resources. Take your time, order catalogs, try before you buy, check the library, and involve your children in the process. Most importantly, choose resources with *your* child's needs in mind.

The following list of home schooling resources is not meant to be exhaustive. There are certainly books and CD-ROMs and games that may be perfect for your child which are not included on these pages, just as some of the items suggested here may not work for your particular family. However, many of the following resources have been highly recommended by parents who home school gifted and highly creative children, so chances are, you'll find at least many things to explore. For even more ideas for home school resources, look for Mary and Michael Leppert's annual *Homeschooling Almanac*, published by Prima Publishing.

In terms of age and grade recommendations listed with each resource, a grade or age range usually indicates the learning level recommended by the publisher or manufacturer. Use your own knowledge of your child as a guide.

Home Schooling Resources by Subject Area
Study Skills and Personal Growth
Language Arts
History and Social Sciences
Mathematics
Science
Fine Arts
Foreign Languages
On-Site Programs and Distance Learning Programs
Visual-Spatial and Hands-On Learning Resources
Top Parent-Recommended Home School Resources
Resources with Religious and Cultural Perspectives

Note: You'll find publisher, manufacturer, and supplier contact information for items marked with * at the end of the chapter, in the list of "Publishers, Manufacturers, and Suppliers." When books mentioned are out of print, look for them in libraries, used book stores, and on-line resale shops.

Study Skills and Personal Growth

Challenging Projects for Creative Minds, by Phil Schlemmer and Dori Schlemmer, Free Spirit Publishing*, 1999. Self-directed enrichment projects for all grades.

College Transition: A Critical Thinking Approach, by Susan Schapiro and Deborah Marinelli, Houghton Mifflin, 2001. Test taking and goal setting advice, task-management skills, decision-making guidelines. Grades 10-11.

The Gifted Kids' Survival Guide (for ages 10 and under), by Judy Galbraith, Free Spirit Publishing*, 1998.

The Gifted Kids' Survival Guide: A Teen Handbook, by Judy Galbraith and Jim Delisle, Free Spirit Publishing*, 1996. Ages 10 and up.

JumpStart: Ideas to Move Your Mind, by Beatrice J. Elyé, Great Potential Press (formerly Gifted Psychology Press)*, 2000. A guidebook for teens that explains how to use a personal notebook to address issues of organization and time management, creative thinking, social and emotional development, decision making, and self-discovery. High school level and advanced junior high.

The Kid's Guide to Social Action, by Barbara Lewis, Free Spirit Publishing*, 1991. Ages 10 and up.

Mapping Inner Space: Learning and Teaching Mind-Mapping, by Nancy Margulies, Zephyr Press*, 1991. A creative method of recording information and showing relationships between ideas. Grades K-12.

Organizing Thinking, by Sandra Parks, Graphic Organizers, Critical Thinking Books & Software*, 1992. Helps children learn how to develop and use mental maps. Grades 2-8.

Psychology for Kids and Psychology for Kids II, by Jonni Kincher, Free Spirit Publishing*, 1995. Children ages eight and up can learn more about themselves and others. Many self-knowledge tests and experiments.

Too Old for This, Too Young for That! Your Survival Guide for the Middle-School Years, by Harriet S. Mosatche and Karen Unger, Free Spirit Publishing*, 2000. Ages 10 and up.

Write Where You Are: How to Use Writing to Make Sense of Your Life, by Caryn Mirriam-Goldberg, Free Spirit Publishing*, 1999. A guide for teens about how to use writing to make sense of your life. Examples of writing from real teens, advice from published writers, and

numerous resources. Appropriate for advanced writers ages nine and up.

The Young Learner's Handbook, by Stephen Tchudi, Charles Scribners' Sons, 1987. Ages eight and up, or earlier for precocious self-starters.

Language Arts

Textbooks, Curricula, and Activity Books

Aesop's Fables: My Book about Reading, Writing, Thinking (Volumes I-IV), by Dr. Kathryn T. Hegeman, Royal Fireworks Press*, 1998. Language arts enrichment for early reading, writing, and thinking. Reading level grades 2-4.

Ceasar's English: A Vocabulary Foundation for Elementary Scholars, by Michael Thompson and Myriam Thompson, Royal Fireworks Press*, 2000. A vocabulary program for elementary grades that explores the Latin-English-Spanish connection.

Draw…Then Write, by Joy Evans and Jo Ellen Moore, Evan-Moor Educational Publishers*, 2001. A fun activity book for children who love to draw but resist writing. Thirty topics, each with three levels of difficulty: completing sentences, writing sentences, writing paragraphs. Grades 1-3.

Enhancing Writing through Imagery: Using Mental Imagery to Encourage Confidence in Creative Expression, by Karin K. Hess, Royal Fireworks Press*, by Karen Hess. The title says it all. Good for visual thinkers. High school level, but appropriate for precocious younger writers.

Intelligent Learning: Thinking & Writing, by Faith Waters, Margaret MacMullen and John Gade, Royal Fireworks Press*, A three-year writing course. From the publisher: "Particularly successful with students who lack the skills, the confidence, or (as is often the case with accelerated learners) the patience necessary to think through and complete problems and assignments, and for students who 'block' when asked to write." Middle school and junior high.

Junior Great Books Program. The Great Books Foundation. All grades. www.greatbooks.org/programs/junior (on-line reading lists)

Language Arts Units for High-Ability Learners, Center for Gifted Education, The College of William and Mary*. Developed specifically to meet the needs of high-ability learners, the publisher writes that the "goals of these units are to develop students' skills in literary analysis and interpretation, persuasive writing, linguistic competency, and oral communication, as well as to strengthen students' reasoning skills and understanding of the concept of change." Several of William and Mary's language arts units have won the National Association for Gifted Children Award for Outstanding Curriculum. Easily adaptable for home use. Order from Kendall/Hunt Publishing*.

Journeys and Destinations, 1998 (grades 2-3)
Literary Reflections, 1997 (grades 4-5)
Autobiographies, 1998 (grades 5-6)
Persuasion, year (grades 5-7)
The 1940s: A Decade of Change, 1998 (grades 6-10)
Threads of Change in 19th Century American Literature, 1998 (grades 7-11)
Guide to Teaching a Language Arts Curriculum for High-Ability Learners, 1999 (for parents and teachers)

Literature and the Language Arts: Discovering Literature Series, EMC/Paradigm Publishing. An excellent complete language arts series for middle school and high school. Visit www.emcp.com/literature for on-line sample pages.

Literature Guides by Teacher Created Materials, Inc.* These guides, sold in teacher supply stores and some bookstores, offer a variety of activities and viewpoints for several works of children's literature and are available in primary, intermediate, and challenging levels. Rather than use the guides to teach your child, give them to the child to use as self-study aids. www.teachercreated.com

Magic Lens: A Spiral Tour through the Human Ideas of Grammar (Volumes I & II), by Michael Clay Thompson, Royal Fireworks Press*,1995. A comprehensive grammar program for elementary students that incorporates higher level thinking skills and creative thinking. Royal Fireworks Catalog contains sample pages.

Open Court Collections for Young Scholars, SRA/McGraw-Hill*. Encourages independent reading and writing and a love of literature with award-winning fiction and nonfiction, concept-based learning units, integrated science and social studies, and phonemic awareness, phonics, comprehension, and writing. A good program for parents who are uncomfortable with language arts. Elementary grades.

Understanding Great Literature Series from Lucent Books, Greenhaven Press/Lucent Books. Each volume in this series focuses on a single work and explores the author's life, background historical information, plot, character, and themes. Excellent critical reading resource for good readers ages 10 and up. Titles include *Understanding The Catcher in the Rye* (1999), *Understanding Flowers for Algernon* (2000), *Understanding Hamlet* (2001), *Understanding I Am the Cheese* (2000), *Understanding The Outsiders* (2000), *Understanding Romeo and Juliet* (2001), and *Understanding The Yearling* (2000). Available in many libraries.

The Word Within the Word: An Exploration of the Interior of Language for Academically Motivated Students (Volumes I, II, & III), by Michael Clay Thompson, Royal Fireworks Press*. Intensive vocabulary study using higher level

thinking skills of synthesis, divergence, analysis, and evaluation. Royal Fireworks Catalog contains sample pages. High school.

Wordly Wise 3000(2000) (grades 2-12) and *Vocabulary from Classical Roots* (2000) (grades 7-11), Educators Publishing Service*. Parent recommendation for *Wordly Wise*: "Fun workbook format for building vocabulary. My daughter loves doing these independently."

The Write Source Writing (and more) Handbooks (all grades), Great Source*. Popular books include *Writers Express* (2000) (grades 4-6), *Write Source 2000* (1995) (middle school) and *Writers, Inc.* (2000) (high school). The print catalog offers numerous descriptions and examples. Parent recommendation: "*Write Source 2000* is a good, all purpose reference book that is jammed with everything you need to know about writing."

Writing Strands, by Dave Marks, National Writing Institute, 1998. A writing curriculum designed for home schoolers with progressive assignments in the four major writing modes: creative, research and report, explanatory, and persuasive. Parent recommendation: "We use *Writing Strands*. There is nothing I hate more than writing, and my two with visual-spatial tendencies are the same. Or were, I should say! *Writing Strands* has been great for them." All grades. Visit www.writingstrands.com for on-line samples.

Handwriting

*Draw * Write * Now*, by Marie Hablitzel and Kim Stitzer, Barker Creek Publishing, 2000. A daily drawing and handwriting curriculum that integrates handwriting with history, science, social studies, geography, reading, and creative writing. Grades K-6. Visit www.barkercreek.com for an on-line table of contents.

Getty-Dubay Italic Handwriting Series, Third Edition, by Barbara Getty and Inga Dubay, Continuing Education Press, 1996. An italic handwriting series of workbooks for from printing to cursive. Italic handwriting contains no loops and facilitates the transition the cursive. Grades K-6. Visit http://extended.pdx.edu/press/italic/italic.htm for on-line samples.

Handwriting Without Tears, by Janice Z. Olsen, 1998. This unique handwriting program uses a simple vertical form and is geared to children's natural development. Excellent for left-handed children. Visit www.hwtears.com for on-line samples and ordering.

Software and Websites

Carol Hurst's Children's Literature Website
www.carolhurst.com

Destination: Imagination Software, Broderbund Edmark. Students create and write their own stories enhanced with still and animated graphics and sounds. Highly recommended for visual-spatial learners who are resistant to writing. Titles include *Destination: Castle*, *Destination: Neighborhood*, *Destination: Ocean*, *Destination: Rainforest*, and *Destination: Time Trip, USA*. Grades 1-6.

Editor in Chief Software, Critical Thinking Books & Software*. Software encourages an understanding of language rules and facilitates independent learning. Also available in book form. Grade four to adult.

The English Pages Website
www.awl.com/englishpages

LibrarySpot Website
www.libraryspot.com

Merriam-Webster Website
www.m-w.com

Purdue On-Line Writing Lab Website
http://owl.english.purdue.edu

Reading/Language Arts Center Web Page
www.eduplace.com/rdg/index.html

Roget's Thesaurus
www.thesaurus.com

Vocabulary.com
www.vocabulary.com

Magazines

Cicada, Cobblestone Publishing*. Fiction and poetry. Grades eight and up. www.cricketmag.com

Creative Kids Magazine: The National Voice for Kids, Prufrock Press*. Games, art, stories, poetry, and opinions by and for kids. Ages 8-14. www.prufrock.com/mag_ck.html

New Moon, New Moon Publishing. A magazine for girls ages eight and up. www.newmoon.org

Stone Soup, Children's Art Foundation. Original fiction, poetry, and artwork by and for children ages seven and up. www.stonesoup.com

Resources for Parents

Book Links: Connecting Books, Libraries, and Classrooms, American Library Association. A magazine that contains excellent ideas for using books throughout the curriculum, preschool through high school. www.ala.org/BookLinks

Common Ground: Whole Language and Phonics Working Together, by Priscilla L. Vail, Modern Learning Press, 1991. From the author of *The World of the Gifted Child* (1979). For teachers and parents of children grades K-4.

Eyeopeners II: Children's Books to Answer Questions about the World Around Them, by Beverly Kobrin, Scholastic Trade, 1995. An annotated guide to more than 800 non-fiction books, arranged by topic, from preschool through middle school.

From Reader to Writer: Teaching Writing through Classic Children's Books, by Sarah Ellis, Groundwood Books, 2001.

A Guide to Teaching Research Skills and Strategies, by Linda N. Boyce, The College of William and Mary, Center for Gifted Education*, 1997 Grades 4-12.

The Horn Book Magazine. Articles and book reviews about children's and young adult literature. www.hbook.com

The Mailbox Bookbag: The Teacher's Idea Magazine for Children's Literature, The Education Center, Inc. A magazine for teachers of primary and intermediate readers. Thematic unit ideas, new books, "Meet the Author" features, and book reviews. www.themailboxbookbag.com

More Books Kids Will Sit Still For: A Read Aloud Guide, by Judy Freeman, Bowker, 1995. A guide to about 1,400 picture books, poetry books, fiction books, and non-fiction books for grades PreK-6. Indexed by title, author, illustrator, and subject.

Some of My Best Friends Are Books: Guiding Gifted Readers from Preschool to High School, 2nd edition, by Judith Wynn Halsted, Great Potential Press, 2002. Summaries of 300 books for K-12 indexed by title, author, and themes, and categorized by age groups.

The Spelling Connection: Integrated Reading, Writing and Spelling Instruction, by Ronald L. Cramer, Guilford Press, 1998.

What Else Should I Read (Volumes 1 & 2), by Matt Berman, Libraries Unlimited*, 1996. Each section focuses on a popular children's book and offers ideas for "what else" to read based on them. For example, children who like Charlotte's Web will find ideas for over 50 other books about Life on a Farm, Fantasy with Animals, Insects, Funny Stories about Animals, Pigs, Making Sacrifices for Friendship, Sad Stories about Pets, Animals Talking to Humans, Death of a Friend, and Competition with Animals. A good gift for avid readers age eight and up.

History and Social Sciences

Textbooks, Curricula, and Activity Books

African-American History, by Richard Beck, Royal Fireworks Press*, 1994. A rich history from African roots to the present. Twenty-eight lessons. Middle school and high school.

Beautiful Feet Books Literature-Based History Studies, Hewitt Research Foundation, 1999. Study guides and literature packs are reasonably priced and can be used with a variety of ages. Subjects include Early American (primary and intermediate), Early American and World History (junior high), Medieval History, Ancient History, California History, Geography through Literature, History of Science through Literature, History of the Horse through Literature, U.S. and World History from the Civil War to Vietnam, plus timelines and additional resources. www.bfbooks.com

The Book of Where: Or How to Be Naturally Geographic, by Neill Bell, Little, Brown and Company, 1982. Ages seven and up.

Carolrhoda Creative Minds Biography Series, Carolrhoda Books. Well-written and effectively illustrated and formatted, these historical biographies are good for independent reading or reading aloud. Over 60 titles, from Shakespeare to Dr. Seuss. The Women in History series includes biographies of Pearl Buck, Harriet Tubman, Rachel Carson, Phillis Wheatley, Elizabeth Cady Stanton, Eleanor Roosevelt, Dr. Alice Hamilton, and Willa Cather. Teacher guides available. Ages 8-12.

Critical Thinking in United States History Series, Critical Thinking Books & Software*. Children use critical thinking skills to analyze multiple viewpoints of historical events. Historical periods include Colonies to Constitution, New Republic to Civil War, Reconstruction to Progressivism, Spanish-American War to Vietnam War. Grades 7-12.

Critical Thinking in World History Series, Critical Thinking Books & Software*. Higher level thinking skills are used to explore the First Farmers to the Fall of Rome. Grades 6-12.

A History of US (10 volumes), by Joy Hakim, Oxford University Press, 1999. This excellent U.S. history series is written in engaging prose with numerous photographs and illustrations (the revised second edition is in full color). Available in most bookstores. Highly recommended. Grades six and up.

Jackdaws Primary Sources, a division of Golden Owl Publishing. Packets of thematic-based and topic-based primary source material, including reproductions of letters, diaries, telegrams and newspapers, study maps, vocabulary lists, writing activities, and essays. Various topics and themes from American History, Word History, Literature and Humanities, and Science. www.jackdaw.com

Kingfisher Illustrated History of the World, Houghton Mifflin. Parent recommendation: "Very concise overview of history from the beginning. Slated for middle school, but for highly gifted children, it can be used in first grade. We use this as a guide and expand on each section with material from the library and Internet."

Spectrum Geography Workbooks, McGraw-Hill*. High-quality full-color workbooks integrate geography, history, reading, math, and critical and creative thinking. Widely available in bookstores and teacher supply stores. Grades 3-6.

The Usborne Book of World History Dates: Key Events in History, by Jane Chisholm, Scholastic edition, 1998. More than a simple timeline, this resource covers major history themes and events from the last 11,000 years. Over 3,500 dates. Numerous color illustrations, maps, and diagrams. All grades.

The Usborne Geography Encyclopedia, by Carol Varley and Lisa Miles, EDCP, 1994. Excellent visual-based introduction to major geography concepts for ages seven and up. Includes maps, world and nation facts, and a glossary.

What Was It Like in Vietnam? Honest Answers from Those Who Were There, by Linda Calvin and Sandy Strait, Royal Fireworks Press*, 1995. A look at the real Vietnam experience, designed for teens.

You Decide! Applying the Bill of Rights to Real Cases, by George Bundy Smith and Alene Smith, Critical Thinking Books & Software*, 1992. Decide actual Supreme Court cases based on the first eight amendments to the Constitution. Grades 7-12.

Software and Websites

Ancient World 2000+ CD-ROM, Decision Development Corporation. A middle school and high school curriculum covering human prehistory through the fall of the Roman Empire. Compatible with self-pacing and independent study. Order from Kendall/Hunt Publishing*. www.ddc2000.com (on-line samples, including full sample lesson plan)

Ben's Guide to U.S. Government for Kids Website
http://bensguide.gpo.gov/index.html

National Geographic On-line Kids Website
www.nationalgeographic.com/kids/index.html

Outline Maps Website
www.eduplace.com/ss/ssmaps/index.html

Magazines

AppleSeeds, Cobblestone Publishing*. General social studies. Grades 2-4.

California Chronicles, Cobblestone Publishing*. California history. Grades four and up.

Calliope, Cobblestone Publishing*. World history. Grades four and up.

Cobblestone, Cobblestone Publishing*. American history. Grades four and up.

Dig, The Archeology Magazine for Kids, Cobblestone Publishing. Ages seven and up.

Faces, Cobblestone Publishing*. World cultures and geography. Grades four and up.

Footsteps, Cobblestone Publishing*. African American history. Grades four and up.

National Geographic World, National Geographic Society. Ages eight and up.

Resources for Parents

Cooking Up U.S. History: Recipes and Research to Share with Children, second edition, by Suzanne I. Barchers and Patricia C. Marden, Libraries Unlimited*, 1999.

Discovering Geography of North America with Books Kids Love, by Carol J. Fulher, Fulcrum Publishing*, 1998.

Discovering World Geography with Books Kids Love, by Nancy A. Chicola and Eleanor B. English, Fulcrum Publishing*, 1999.

Literature Connections to American History K-6 and 7-12: Resources to Enhance and Entice (two volumes), Teacher Ideas Press*, 1997.

Literature Connections to World History K-6 and 7-12: Resources to Enhance and Entice (two volumes), Teacher Ideas Press*, 1998.

Teaching U.S. History through Children's Literature: Post-World War II, by Wanda J. Miller, Teacher Ideas Press*, 1997.

Through Indian Eyes: The Native Experience in Books for Children, by Beverly Slapin and Doris Seale, American Indian Studies Center, 1998.

U.S. History through Children's Literature: From the Colonial Period to World War II, by Wanda J. Miller, Teacher Ideas Press*, 1997.

Mathematics

Textbooks, Curricula, and Activity Books

Addition the Fun Way Book for Kids: A Picture Method of Learning the Addition Facts (1996) and *Times Tables the Fun Way*, 1996, by Judy Rodriguez, City Creek Press. Colorful cartoons and clever captions provide a hook for memorizing addition and multiplication facts. From the publisher: "A literature-based method of learning the basic facts addresses every learning style. The students visualize the picture, hear the story, and play games to reinforce the facts." From Times Tables the Fun Way: "Remember, when it's 4X4, the fours becomes a 4 by 4 (4 x 4) and you have to be 16 to drive it." www.citycreek.com

A Blueprint for Geometry, by Bill Lombard and Dale Fulton, Dale Seymour Publications, 1997. From the publisher: "In this two to three-week unit, students read and draw floor plans and elevations, figure building costs, and build a scale model. As students solve the problems inherent in building a structure, they learn scale, measurement, and architectural symbols and use their problem-solving skills and creativity. Activities are founded on sound architectural and mathematical concepts. Book includes 17 plans by an architect." Grades 5-8.

Calculus By and For Young People (ages 7, yes 7 and up), by Don Cohen, Don the Mathman, 1989. From Don Cohen: "I work with all ages of students, from 3 to 73 years old, and all ability levels. I feel my materials are not just for gifted children, but all children. The brighter the youngster, the earlier one can begin." Also available by Donald Cohen: *Calculus By and For Young People— Worksheets* (also available on CD-ROM), *Changing Shapes with Matrices, Infinite Series By and For 6 Years Old and Up* (Videotape), *Iteration to Infinite Sequences with 6 to 11 Year Olds* (Videotape), *A Map to Calculus* (poster). www.shout.net/~mathman

Discovering Geometry: An Inductive Approach, second edition, by Michael Serra, Key Curriculum Press*, 1997. This textbook uses a discovery approach to geometry with cartoon-illustrated problems, full-color photos, figures, and artwork. Cooperative learning activities may need to be modified for independent study. Grades 9-12.

Key To… Workbook Series, Key Curriculum Press*. Recommended by several parents of gifted home schoolers, this inexpensive series covers individual math topics. Topics include Algebra, Decimals, Fractions, Geometry, Percents, Measurement, Metric Measurement. Perfect for self-paced independent study. Good for precocious math students. Grades four and up.

A Mathematical Mystery Tour: Higher-Thinking Math Tasks, by Mark Wahl, Zephyr Press*, 1998. Math integrated with art, science, philosophy, history, social studies, and language arts. Grades 5-12.

Mathematical Quilts: No Sewing Required, by Elaine Ellison and Diana Venters, Key Curriculum Press*, 2000. From the publisher: "Written by two mathematics teachers who are also quilters…. Students explore topics ranging from the Pythagorean theorem to Fibonacci sequences, tessellations and tiling, and more. They improve their visualization skills by learning to analyze and compare relationships among shapes." Teacher's notes and solutions included. Supplemental posters ordered separately include Tiling Quilts, Spiral Quilts, Right Triangle Quilts, and Golden Ratio Quilts. Grades 7-12.

Mathematics: A Human Endeavor, by Harold R. Jacobs, W. H. Freeman, 1996. Appropriate for self-paced study, this language arts approach to mathematics is refreshingly well-written and humorous. Student workbook and teacher's guide available. Other math books by Harold R. Jacobs include *Elementary Algebra*, 1998, and *Geometry*, 1998. Parent recommendation: "These books are well-written and entertaining and succeed in engaging an inquisitive child." Middle school and high school. Visit www.whfreeman.com for on-line tables of contents.

Mathematics in Context, Brittanica. Individual units emphasize a problem-based approach to math using contexts with which the student is familiar. Numbers, algebra, geometry, and statistics strands are integrated in every grade. Good for individual study with adult facilitation. Student books and teacher guides. Grades 5-8. Visit www.ebmic.com for on-line sample pages.

MathScape: Seeing and Thinking Mathematically, Creative Publications*, 1998. Funded by the National Science Foundation, the MathScape program uses a learning by doing approach to middle school math. Parents can purchase the entire three-year program or individual units. Grades 6-8.

Math Textbooks, American Guidance Services.* These full-color student textbooks are easy to read (approximately fourth-grade reading level), with clear explanations, -colorful and effective graphics, and self-study aids. While not designed for gifted learners, the books are good to use with young gifted children or visual learners who need interesting and effective integration of visual and verbal information without the demands of a heavy text. Titles include *Basic Math Skills*, *Pre-Algebra*, *Algebra*, *Geometry*, *Consumer Mathematics*, *Lifeskills Math*. Grades 6-12.

Math-U-See, by Steven Demme, Math-U-See Foundation. A multi-sensory, manipulative-based math program for K-12. Parent recommendation: "Having used the *Math-U-SEE* Foundations of Mathematics Student Text and Teacher's Manual last year with my seven-year-old daughter, I would recommend it. The Foundations book covers most of the material to be memorized in math—the addition, multiplication, and 'skip-counting' facts. Subtraction, division, and fractions are a spin-off of these and are covered in the next level text. The publisher says that it covers about three years of math material, however, depending on your child's aptitude, it may be completed in a year or less. The teacher manual is exceptionally thorough." www.mathusee.com

Mental Math Challenges, by Michael L. Lobosco, Tamos Books, 2000. Lots of hands-on math challenges. Ages seven and up.

Miquon Math Materials, Key Curriculum Press*. Economically-priced student workbooks emphasize independent discovery and encourage creative problem solving. Multiplication is introduced early in the program. The non-verbal, pattern-based approach can be used with non-readers. Parents can adjust the amount of hands-on activity to suit the child. Teacher's guide available. Parent recommendation: "I would recommend Miquon math for the K-3 set. It is a concept-based approach to mathematics that takes the child into advanced concepts at a young age. The Cuisenaire rods that are intended to be used with it were appealing to my visual learner. My other daughter enjoyed the challenge of the content of the course." Grades K-3.

Saxon Math Series, Saxon Publishers, Inc. A no-nonsense approach to math used by many home schoolers. Upper grades consist of mostly pencil and paper activities. Parent recommendation: "In grade five we started the Saxon math series. It is very good, but I think the student benefits from supplementing with more 'fun' material. We used activities from Janice van Cleave's *Math for Every Kid* and *Geometry for Every Kid*. We also experimented with origami and codes and ciphers. The girls also read *Do You Wanna Bet?* by J. Cushman and *What Do You Mean by Average?* by E. James and C. Barkin during late elementary years." Grades K-12. Visit www.saxonmath.com for on-line sample pages and placement guide.

Scratch Your Brain Where It Itches: Clever Math Ticklers, by Linda Brumbaugh, Critical Thinking Books & Software*, 1994. Grades 2-8.

Singapore Math Curriculum, Singapore Math, Inc. This math curriculum, used in Singapore classrooms, integrates independent study and teacher facilitation, and it introduces high-level concepts at earlier grades than American texts, with a generous use of graphics. Inexpensive texts and workbooks cover basic concepts with a combination of drill, word problems, and mental calculation. Note that currency used in the exercises is in Singapore dollars and cents, which differ somewhat from American dollars and coins, and measurements are metric. Science curriculum (grades 3-8) is available as well. Parent recommendation: "*Singapore Math/Science* is formatted so that gifted children can teach themselves with very little parent involvement except with experiments. Great for visual-spatial kids." Parent recommendation: "A very good program for all ages. My kids are doing especially well in this because the topics are covered in depth, practiced, and then the course moves on. The review that is built into the program is not the obvious simple problems that were used to teach a topic. The review uses the concepts taught earlier, but the student is expected to apply those concepts to the new problems. Also, the word problems in this series are excellent. The student must really understand the problem and be able to visualize it before he or she can work the answer. The problems do not simply use the only two numbers in the problem and manipulate them for an answer." Grades K-12. Visit www.singaporemath.com for on-line samples and placement guide.

SRA Math Explorations and Applications, SRA/McGraw-Hill*, 1997. This program offers a problem-solving approach to math with early introduction of mathematical concepts such as algebra and geometry and extensive use of games and manipulatives. Grades K-6.

Software and Websites

Consumer Reports On-line for Kids
www.zillions.org

Geometry Blaster CD-ROM, Davidson. High school level geometry software program appropriate for both elementary and high school age children.

Hidden Treasures of Al-Jabar CD-ROM, Sunburst*. This adventure-based program helps students become adept at using mathematical language. By undertaking challenges involving first-year algebra skills, students translate verbal problems and visual situations into symbolic math representations. Grades 7-9.

The Logical Journey of the Zoombinis CD-ROM, Broderbund. Advanced math and logic. From the creators: "Taking cues from children's aesthetics as well as our own, in effect we found the 'game in the math' rather than putting math in a game. And, almost by necessity, the math looks different from how it looks in a classroom." Ages nine and up, but enjoyed by children as young as five.

Parent recommendation: "This is by far one of the most wonderful CD-ROM programs on the market. It progressively gets more difficult as the children master the challenges. Many wonderful thinking problems. *The Logical Journey of the Zoombinis* has been used since my kids were seven, and they still go back to it as a favorite."

Math & Music, Wildridge Software, Inc. From the publisher: "Interdisciplinary educational software for middle school and high school students for use in home school education or public school education. *Math & Music* provides instruction in the basic concepts of mathematics explaining the historical development of mathematics and illustrating the application of mathematical concepts to the understanding of the structure of the musical scale and harmony." An excellent program, well suited to self-directed learning. Good for younger children who have mastered basic arithmetic operations and who are strong readers. Also available from Wildridge Software is *Math & Cosmos* (science and astronomy). Grades 7-12. www.wildridge.com

The Math Forum Student Center Website
http://mathforum.com/students

Math Workshop Deluxe CD-ROM, Broderbund. Young children will find a wide range of skill levels to explore. Ages 6-12.

Natural Math Website
www.naturalmath.com

Mathematical Visualization Resources?[18] (For Middle School and High School)

Beyond the Third Dimension: Geometry, Computer Graphics, and Higher Dimensions, Scientific American Library Series, by Thomas F. Banchoff, W. H. Freeman, 1996. Young adult and above.

Creative Constructions, by Ruben Schadler and Dale Seymour, Creative Publications*, 1974. More than 250 designs for students to make with a straight edge and a compass. Grades 5-12.

Creative Puzzles of the World, by Pieter Van Delft, Key Curriculum Press*, 2001. This four-color book designed for teachers but appropriate for older students to use on their own is an introduction to the history, theory, and craftsmanship behind all types of puzzles and includes 1,000 puzzles to solve and over 1,500 illustrations and drawings.

---

18   From the Department of Mathematics at Cedar Crest College, Allentown, PA. Reprinted by permission.

Exploring Math through Puzzles, Wei Zhang, Key Curriculum Press*,2001. Instructions for making 54 puzzles out of string, beads, and other household items. Kit available with most of the necessary materials. Grades 5-12.

The Factory: Spatial Perception, Mac/Win CD-ROM, Sunburst*. Grades 4-8.

M. C. Escher: Visions of Symmetry, by Doris Schattschneider, W.H. Freeman, 1992. Young adult and above.

Math Space Mission, by Staff of Regional Math Network, Dale Seymour Publications*, 1989. From the publisher: "Students explore our solar system and build a space colony to learn estimation, geometry, and problem solving that involves rounding numbers, estimating, graphing, and investigating ratio and proportion." Grades 7-9.

Mathematics through Paper Folding, by Alton T. Olson, National Council of Teachers of Mathematics, 1975. Elementary through high school.

Non-Euclidean Adventures on the Lénárt Sphere, by István Lénárt, Key Curriculum Press*, 1995. Use with *Key Curriculum Press's Lénárt Sphere Construction Materials: Construction Materials for Another World of Geometry* to explore planar and spherical geometry. Grades six to college.

NOVA: The Shape of Things, Vestron Video, 1985. All ages.

Paper and Scissors: Polygons and More, by Linda Silvey, Loretta Taylor, and Carol Zarny. Dale Seymour Publications*, 1997. Grades 6-12.

Paper Folding for the Mathematics Class, by Donovan A. Johnson, National Council of Teachers of Mathematics, 1995.

The Platonic Solids Video, Key Curriculum Press*. Grades 6-12.

The Stella Octangula Video, Key Curriculum Press*. Grades 6-12.

Symmetry: A Unifying Concept, by Istvan Hargittai, Shelter Communications, 1994. Young adult and above.

Three-Dimensional Symmetry Video, Key Curriculum Press*. Grades 6-12.

Resources for Parents

About Teaching Mathematics: A K-8 Resource, second edition, by Marilyn Burns, Math Solutions Publications*, 2000.

Family Math Books, by Jean Kerr Stanmark, et al. Titles include: *Family Math*, 1996, (grades K-9), *Family Math for Young Children: Comparing* (Equals Series), 1999, (grades PreK – 3), and *Family Math—The Middle School Years: Algebraic Reasoning and Number Sense*, 1999, (grades 5-8). Lawrence Hall of Science, University of California.

Marilyn Burns Talks about Math Teaching Today: Three Audiocassettes for K-8 Teachers: "What's Reform All About?" (60 minutes), "Teaching the Basics" (65 minutes), "Linking Assessment and Instruction" (70 minutes). Purchase from Math Solutions. www.mathsolutions.com

Math: Facing an American Phobia, by Marilyn Burns, Math Solutions Publications*, 1998. A must-read for any home schooling parent who is intimidated by math. All levels.

Math for Humans: Teaching Math through Eight Intelligences, revised edition, by Mark Wahl, Livnlern Press, 1999.

SAMI Website: Science and Math Initiatives. A clearinghouse of resources, funding, and curriculum for rural math and science teachers. An extensive list of math web links. http://sami.lanl.gov

A Visual Approach to Algebra, by Frances Van Dyke, Dale Seymour Publications*, 1998. An approach to teaching algebra that allows students to start with graphic interpretation before moving on to abstract equations. Designed for middle school and high school teachers.

Science

Textbooks, Curricula, and Activity Books

Biotechnology Projects for Young Scientists, by Kenneth G. Rainis and George Nassis, Franklin Watts, 1998. Ages 10 and up.

The Big Beast Book: Dinosaurs and How They Got that Way, by Jerry Booth, Little, Brown and Company, 1988. Ages seven and up.

Blood and Guts: A Working Guide to Your Own Insides, by Linda Allison, Little, Brown and Company, 1976. Ages seven and up.

DK Science Encyclopedia, edited by Susan McKeever, DK Publishing, 1994. An excellent visual introduction to science topics for young curious minds. Good for advanced readers ages six and up.

Environmental Science Units, Royal Fireworks Press*. Titles include "Energy Use and Abuse," "Interdependence in the Natural World," "Endangered Species," "Population Growth and Balance," and "Consumption in a Finite World." Grades 4-7.

Event-Based Science Series, Pearson Learning*. Video media coverage of real events is used to introduce students to science concepts found in everyday life, with lots of hands-on activities and problem solving. Group activities may need to be modified for independent learning. Individual student editions and teacher's guide with video available. Titles include: *Asteroid!, Blight!, Earthquake!, First Flight!, Flood!, Fraud!, Gold Medal!, Gold*

Rush!, Hurricane!, Oil Spill!, Outbreak!, Thrill Ride!, Toxic Leak!, Tornado!, Volcano! Grades 5-9.

How Did We Find Out…? Series, by Isaac Asimov, Walker and Company. This series on the history of scientific discovery is designed for grades 5-8 but is suitable for curious younger children who are good readers. Many titles are *out of print.*

Life Science: All Creatures Great & Small, by Michael J. Spear, Trillium*, 1991. Complete life science text with illustrations, appendices, glossary. Junior high.

The MESA Series, Dale Seymour Publications*. Combines pre-algebra topics with real-life science explorations. Titles include: *Designing Environments, In the Pharmacy, In the Air, In the Wind, Packaging and the Environment, Measuring Earthquakes, Measuring Dinosaurs, Classifying Fingerprints, Investigating Apples,* Secret Codes. Grades 6-8.

Science Units for High-Ability Learners, Center for Gifted Education, The College of William and Mary*. Developed specifically to meet the needs of high-ability learners, these problem-based science units help students to "experience the work of real science in applying data-handling skills, analyzing information, evaluating results, and learning to communicate their understanding to others." Several of William and Mary's science units have won the National Association for Gifted Children Award for Outstanding Curriculum. Easily adaptable for home use. Order from Kendall/Hunt Publishing*.

> *Dust Bowl* (grades 2-3)
> *What a Find!* (grades 3-4)
> *Acid, Acid Everywhere* (grades 4-6)
> *Electricity City* (grades 4-6)
> *The Chesapeake Bay* (grades 6-8)
> *Hot Rods* (grades 6-8)
> *No Quick Fix* (grades 6-8)
> *A Guide to Teaching a Problem-Based Science Curriculum* (for parents and teachers)

Sciencewise! Discovering Scientific Process through Problem Solving, Critical Thinking Books & Software*, 1996. Grades 4-12.

Sports Science Projects: The Physics of Balls in Motion, by Madeline Goodstein, Enslow Publishers, 1999. Middle school.

Thinking Connections: Concept Maps for Life Science, by Frederick Burrgraf, Critical Thinking Books & Software*, 1998. Ages nine and up.

TOPSciences, TOPS Learning Systems. This nonprofit educational publisher is dedicated to making inexpensive, creative, hands-on science and math available everywhere. TOPS hands-on science activity sheets, task cards, and supplies are friendly to home schoolers and cover all branches of science while meeting national content standards. Grades K-12. Visit www.topscience.org for on-line activities and ordering.

What Color Is Newton's Apple?, by Jamie C. Smith, Royal Fireworks Press*, 1998. Physics and chemistry lessons for early childhood learners include higher level thinking skills. Ages 2-8.

Software and Websites

Magic School Bus Software Programs, Microsoft. There are several titles in this popular software series, from dinosaurs to outer space. Good for precocious learners. Ages six and up.

NASA Website
www.nasa.gov

National Science Foundation Website
www.nsf.gov

Science 2000+ CD-ROM, Decision Development Corporation. A complete CD-ROM science curriculum. Good for self-paced study and independent learning. Order from Kendall/Hunt Publishing*. Grades 5-8. Visit www.ddc2000.com for on-line samples, including full sample lesson plan.

Science Education Gateway Website
www.lhs.berkeley.edu/sii

Magazines

Muse, Cobblestone Publishing*. Science and discovery. Grades four and up.

Odyssey, Cobblestone Publishing*. Adventures in science. Highly recommended. Grades four and up.

Science Supply Catalogs

American Science and Surplus
Phone: (847) 982-0870
www.sciplus.com

ScienceKits.com, Inc.
Phone: (301) 294-9729
www.sciencekits.com

Tobin's Lab
Phone: (800) 522-4776
www.tobinlab.com

Tri-Ess Sciences Inc.
Phone: (800) 274-6910
www.tri-esssciences.com

Resources for Parents

AIMS Educational Foundation Website: Activities Integrating Math, Science, and Technology
www.aimsedu.org

American History through Earth Science, by Craig A. Munsart, Teacher Ideas Press*, 1997. Grades 6-12.

Art in Chemistry; Chemistry in Art, by Barbara R. Greenberg and Dianne Patterson, Teacher Ideas Press*, 1998. Grades 7-12.

Curriculum Assessment Guide to Science Materials, by Linda N. Boyce, et al, The College of William and Mary, Center for Gifted Education*, 1993.

From Butterflies to Thunderbolts: Discovering Science with Books Kids Love, by Anthony D. Fredericks, Fulcrum Publishers*, 1997. Grades K-3.

Guide to Key Science Concepts, by Beverly T. Sher, The College of William and Mary, Center for Gifted Education, 1993.

Mudpies to Magnets: A Preschool Science Curriculum, by Robert A Williams, Robert E. Rockwell, and Elizabeth A. Sherwood, Gryphon House, 1987. See also *More Mudpies to Magnets: Science for Young Children* (1991).

Notes from a Scientist: Activities and Resources for Gifted Children: Some Suggestions for Parents, by Beverly T. Sher, The College of William and Mary, Center for Gifted Education*, 1993.

Of Bugs and Beasts: Fact, Folklore, and Activities, by Lauren J. Livo, Glenn McGlathery, and Norma J. Livo, Teacher Ideas Press*, 1995. A wonderful resource for any parent of a child—any age—who loves animals, from bats and buzzards to clams and jellyfish. The authors skillfully present folklore, natural history, and lots of activities, along with special sections on taxonomy and how to take an animal preference survey. The activities integrate a variety of learning styles, creative thinking, and language arts ideas. Highly recommended.

"Planning Science Programs for High-Ability Learners," by Joyce Van Tassel-Baska. ERIC EC Digest #E546. A clearinghouse of resources, funding, and curriculum for rural math and science teachers. An extensive list of science web links. Available on-line at http://ericec.org/digests/e546.htm.

Project 2061 Website: Science Literacy for a Changing Future
www.project2061.org

SAMI Website: Science and Math Initiatives
http://sami.lanl.gov

Science through Children's Literature: An Integrated Approach, by Carol M. Butzow, John W. Butzow and Rhett Kennedy, Teacher Ideas Press*, 2000. Grades K-3. See also *More Science through Children's Literature: An Integrated Approach*, 1998, (grades K-3) and *Intermediate Science through Children's Literature: Over Land and Sea*, 1994, (grades 4-7).

Teaching Physical Science through Children's Literature: 20 Complete Lessons for Elementary Grades, by Susan E. Gertz, Terrific Science Press*, 1996. Grades K-4.

Teaching Science with the Internet: Internet Lesson Plans and Classroom Activities, by Marc Rosner, Classroom Connect, 1997.

Fine Arts

Art Fraud Detective, by Anna Nilsen, Kingfisher, 2001. This book offers hours of fun and learning while studying some of the world's greatest works of art.

Dancing Hearts: Creative Arts with Books Kids Love, by Martha Brade, Fulcrum Publishing*, 1997.

Discovering Great Artists, by MaryAnn F. Kohl and Kim Salga, Bright Ring Publishing, 1997. Over 100 art activities that explore the styles and techniques of famous artists. Ages six and up. Highly recommended.

History of Art for Young People, by H. W. Janson and Anthony F. Janson, Harry N. Abrams, 1992. Ages 10 and up.

Linnea in Monet's Garden, by Christina Bjõrk and Lena Anderson, R&S Books, 1987. Also available on video.

Music Ace and Music Ace II Software, Harmonic Vision.

Sister Wendy's Story of Painting, second enhanced edition, by Wendy Beckett and Patricia Wright, DK Publishing, 2000. Parent recommendation: "Must have...all ages."

Teaching American History with Art Masterpieces, by Bobbi Chertok, Goody Hirschfeld, and Marilyn Rosh, Scholastic Professional Books, 1998. Posters, activities, and background information to explore key events in American history. Grades 4-8.

Teaching Art with Books Kids Love: Teaching Art Appreciation, Elements of Art, and Principles of Design with Award-Winning Children's Books, by Darcie Clark Frohardt, Fulcrum Publishing*, 1999. This excellent book is all you'll need to explore elements of art, principles of design, and artistic styles in early elementary grades.

What Makes a Leonardo a Leonardo?, The Metropolitan Museum of Art, Viking Children's Books, 1994. Other books in the series include books about Cassatt, Degas, Goya, Picasso, Monet, Raphael, Rembrandt, Van Gogh.

The Young Person's Guide to the Orchestra, by Anita Ganeri, Harcourt Brace, 1996. Includes a CD narrated by Ben Kingsley and including Benjamin Britten's original composition as an introduction to orchestral music.

Foreign Languages

10 Minutes a Day Series, by Kristine Kershul, Bilingual Books. Colorful, visual, relatively informal introductions to conversational languages. Available for Chinese, French, German, Hebrew, English, Italian, Japanese, Norwegian, Portuguese, Russian, and Spanish. Carried by most large bookstores. www.bilingualbooks.org

Power-Glide Foreign Language Programs, Provo, UT. Courses on audiocassette or audio CD with student and teacher guides and supplemental CD-ROMs. Available in children's version and adult version (grade five and up). Available for Spanish, French, German, Latin, Japanese, and Russian. From Hal Wallace, Public Relations Manager at Power-Glide Foreign Language Courses: "Our method in general contains a significant element of discovery. We do not provide all the answers. The inquisitive student is encouraged to discover relationships between various elements, and to ask 'Why is this so?' Not having all the answers at hand is frustrating to some, but to the curious, it is a springboard to deeper learning." Visit www.power-glide.com for on-line demos and ordering.

Rosetta Stone Foreign Language Programs, Internet Language Co. On-line and CD-ROM language learning software. Available for Spanish, French, German, English (U.S.), English (U.K.), Dutch, Danish, Portuguese, Italian, Latin, Russian, Polish, Welsh, Hindi, Arabic, Hebrew, Turkish, Chinese, Thai, Japanese, Vietnamese, Korean, Indonesian, and Swahili. Visit www.rosettastone.com for on-line demo and ordering.

On-Site Programs and Distance Learning Programs

Apex Learning. Advanced Placement (AP) and other high school level on-line courses. www.apex.netu.com

Center for Talented Youth, Johns Hopkins University
www.jhu.edu/~gifted

Education Program for Gifted Youth (EPGY), Stanford University. Computer-based, multimedia lectures and on-line and off-line exercises allow students to work at an individual pace, with assistance available from an assigned instructor via phone, e-mail, or virtual classroom. Courses available for math, physics, writing, and computer science. Skill levels K-12. Parent recommendation: "EPGY was there when we needed it. It's not a cure-all, however, and shouldn't be used without supplemental materials and manipulatives. EPGY requires as much parental/teacher involvement as any other math curriculum." www-epgy.stanford.edu

Internet Academy
www.iacademy.org

Kentucky Migrant Technology Project
On-line courses designed to reproduce or complement a full middle- and high-school curriculum. www.migrant.org.

Northwestern University
www.ctd.northwestern.edu

University of Missouri-Columbia High School
http://cdis.missouri.edu

University of Nebraska-Lincoln, Independent High School Study
www.unl.edu/ISHS

Virtual School for the Gifted
www.vsg.edu.au

Visual-Spatial and Hands-On Learning Resources (Toys and Games!)

Hint: Keep a wish list of these items to give to friends and relatives as family gift ideas.

Apples to Apples® (ages 12 to adult) and *Apples to Apples Junior*® (ages 7-11), Out of the Box Publishing*. Match adjectives with common and proper nouns to make the most logical, creative, humorous, or interesting combination in this fast-paced card game. The junior version contains simpler words and fewer popular culture references. Four to 10 players.

Architectural Style Blocks Sets, Mindware. Looking for something different from ordinary building blocks? These maple hardwood block sets come in Japanese, Baroque, Egyptian, Antiquity, and Russian architectural styles. Order from MindWare*.

Artdeck Game, Aristoplay*. A double rummy card game of art masters and masterpieces. All ages.

Bethump'd with Words, Discovery Edition, History Edition, Mamopalire, Inc. Lesson plans available. Grades four to adult, and younger word buffs. www.bethumpd.com

Block Party Alphabet Blocks, Small World Toys*. Sturdy, old-fashioned wooden alphabet blocks with upper- and lower-case letters.

Connections Card Game: Math and Science in Nature, Dale Seymour Publications*. Contains 110 full-color cards which deal with math—geometric shapes, fractals, patterns, etc.—and science. All ages.

Deluxe Visionary, TLI Games*. A boardless board game in which players answer questions about 500 images in five categories. Ages eight and up.

ElementO: A Game Based on the Periodic Table of Elements, Lewis Educational Games*. Ages 10 and up.

Equate, Mindware. A Scrabble®-like game of math equations for ages eight to adult. Order from MindWare*.

Geography Card Games, Resource Games*. *Take Off! The Game that Teaches Geography* (ages six and up), *States of the Union Geography Quiz Game* (ages eight and up), *Maptitude: The Game of Global Proportions* (ages 10 and up), *Take Off!* (ages six and up). *TerraCarta State Playing Cards*.

GeoShapes, Mindware. A board game of geometry, strategy, and risk. Ages eight to adult. Order from MindWare*.

Greek Myths and Legends Cards, Aristoplay.* A simple game of rummy featuring 13 favorite Greek myths and legends. All ages.

It's News to Me!. Complete five assignments using a newspaper while learning about current events and reading skills. Game board, activity book, dice, playing tokens, press passes, and score pad included. Provide your own newspaper! Ages nine to adult. Order from MindWare*.

Lost Art 3-D Puzzles Series, University Games*. Complete famous masterpieces. It's not as easy as it looks. Artists include Michelangelo, Monet, Renoir, Van Gogh. All ages.

Math Card Games, Learning Resources*. *Addition in the Amazon Math Card Game, Subtraction Super Safari Math Card Game, Multiplication Monsters of the Deep Math Card Game, Division Down Under Math Card Game*. Beautiful illustrations and color-coded answers make these games good choices for visual learners. Suitable for any age child who is ready to tackle the arithmetic skill. Hint: Allow children to familiarize themselves with the cards before playing the game.

The Math Kit: A Three-Dimensional Tour through Mathematics, by Ron van der Meer and Bob Gardner, Charles Scribners' Sons, 1994. This hands-on math-kit-in-a-book is a great gift for the mathematically curious ages 6-10.

Mummy Rummy, Gamewright*. This card game of Egyptian treasures takes matching to a new level. All ages. No reading required.

National Geographic Games, University Games*. *National Geographic Pictures of the World Card Game* (ages six and up) and *National Geographic Mystery Voyage Game* (ages eight and up). Use visual clues to guess your destination.

Observation Deck, Mindware. Contains 160 pages of ideas for writing from Pulitzer Prize-winning and best-selling authors, plus 50 flash cards of inspiration. Perfect for any young, serious writer with writer's block. Ages 10 to adult. Order from MindWare*.

The Play's the Thing, Mindware. Choose from four levels of play as you collect scenes from Shakespeare's plays. Ages 12 to adult. Order from MindWare*.

President Cards, Aristoplay*. Each president's official White House portrait and text describing important accomplishments and events while in office. All grades.

Puzzellations, Mindware. Foam pieces for designing tessellations. Ages five and up. Order from MindWare*.

Quiddler, Set Enterprises*. A short word card game in which you arrange your hand into words. Ages eight and up, or as soon as the child can spell simple words.

Roger's Connection. Similar to Zometool (below), but with magnets embedded in the connecting rods. Available in black or a glow-in-the-dark version. Ages seven to adult. www.rogersconnection.com

Rush Hour Traffic Jam Puzzle, Binary Arts*. Sliding block puzzle that strengthens sequential thinking skills. Multiple skill levels. Ages six and up.

SET, The Family Game of Visual Perception, Set Enterprises*. Card game requiring logic and set reasoning. All ages. No reading required. On-line version of SET: www.setgame.com.

Shape by Shape, Binary Arts*. A travel-friendly tangram-like puzzle game. Ages eight and up.

SomeBody Game, Aristoplay*. With levels of play from preschooler to pre-teen, this game of human anatomy explores more that 100 body parts.

TrigO: A Game about Trigonometry, Lewis Educational Games*. Ages eight and up.

United States of America Wooden Map Puzzle and *World Wooden Map Puzzle*, Small World Toys*. Forty-five wooden pieces, 18.5" x 11.75" board, Fun Facts Guide, and clear plastic overlay with state boarders. Ages five and up.

Visual Brainstorms and *Visual Brainstorms 2*, Binary Arts*. A card game of visual brainteasers that can be enjoyed solo or by the whole family. Ages 10 and up.

Wood Blocks (50-piece), Small World Toys*. Classic wooden blocks in a variety of shapes and colors. Ages two and up.

World Geography Activity Cards and Maps and Globes Activity Cards, Evan-Moor Educational Publishing*. Grades 3-6.

Young Architects Building Set, Mindware. Design your own floor plans and 3D models. Templates, model-sizes walls and joint bases, work surface, drafting paper stickers, colored pencils, and instructions included. Ages 10 and up. Order from MindWare*.

Zometool, Zometool, Inc. From the *Duke Gifted Letter*, Fall 2000: "Zometool allows users from age six to adult to construct vectors along 62 directions in space, building anything from simply polygons to complex geometric designs of fivefold symmetries. Zometool teaches the connection between numbers and space—from the simple laws of symmetry and proportion to the complex principles of geometry, trigonometry, and architecture." Ages six to adult. www.zomesystem.com

Top Parent-Recommended Home School Resources

Most of the parents I interviewed offered detailed recommendations for their favorite home school resources. Here is a list of the 20 most frequently recommended books, curriculum publishers, software, and other resources in alphabetical order. Keep in mind that no child or family would use all of these items. As always, use your own knowledge of your child's intellectual needs and learning styles as a guide.

Critical Thinking Books & Software

Publisher of critical thinking products for grades kindergarten through adult level. All subject areas. Highly recommended titles include *Critical Thinking in United States History Series* (grades 7-12), *Critical Thinking in World History Series* (grades 6-12), *You Decide! Applying the Bill of Rights to Real Cases* (grades 7-12), *Editor in Chief* (grammar, grade four through adult), *Revenge of the Riddle Spiders* (logical reasoning, grade two through adult), *Mind Benders* (deductive reasoning, K-12), and *Building Thinking Skills Series* (grade K through adult). Visit www.criticalthinking.com for on-line samples and ordering.

Educators Publishing Service

Publisher of reading, vocabulary, spelling, elementary math, handwriting, and typing workbooks for grades kindergarten through high school, as well as assessment tools and materials on learning differences. Popular choices of home schoolers include *Wordly Wise 3000* (vocabulary, grades 2-12), *Explode the Code* (multi-sensory reading, grades K-4), and *Vocabulary from Classical Roots* (etymology, grades 7-11). Visit www.epsbooks.com for on-line samples and ordering.

EPGY (Education Program for Gifted Youth)

Distance learning programs with computer-based, multimedia lectures available in math, writing, computer science, and physics. Skill levels K-12. To qualify, students must show proof of ability through standardized tests scores or by taking the EPGY Mathematical Aptitude Test. Assigned instructors assist students via phone, electronic mail, and virtual classroom. Students receive both on-line and off-line assignments. Demonstration CD-ROM and on-line application available. www-epgy.stanford.edu

Getty-Dubay Handwriting Program

An italic handwriting series of workbooks for grades K-6. Italic handwriting contains no loops and facilitates the transition from printing to cursive. Visit http://extended.pdx.edu/press/italic/italic.htm for on-line sample pages.

Another popular handwriting program of home school parents with gifted children is Writing Without Tears. www.hwtears.com

Harold Jacobs' Math Books, published by W. H. Freeman

Harold Jacobs has written three math books for the middle school and high school student: *Mathematics: A Human Endeavor, Elementary Algebra,* and *Geometry.* Each book approaches math from a language arts perspective, using real life examples and humor to make math both meaningful and fun. *Mathematics: A Human Endeavor* is appropriate for highly verbal children ages eight and up who crave a deeper appreciation for and leisurely approach to math. Visit www.whfreeman.com for on-line tables of contents and sample pages.

A History of US, by Joy Hakim, Oxford University Press, 1999

This 11-volume U.S. history series includes primary sources and encourages multiple viewpoints without sacrificing historical truth. The second revised edition, published in 1999, includes full-color illustrations. Available in most bookstores and libraries. Reading level: grade six and up. Appropriate for eight years old and up (adults included).

Volume 1: The First Americans, Prehistory to 1600
Volume 2: Making Thirteen Colonies
Volume 3: From Colonies to Country
Volume 4: The New Nation, 1789-1850
Volume 5: Liberty for All?
Volume 6: War, Terrible War
Volume 7: Reconstruction and Reform
Volume 8: An Age of Extremes
Volume 9: War, Peace & All that Jazz
Volume 10: All the People, Post WWII through 1990s
Volume 11: Sourcebook and Index

Internet Resources

While having a computer and Internet connection is not a prerequisite for successful home schooling, computers do make it easier to find resources and add variety. Start with the Hoagies "Home Schooling the Gifted Child"

page: www.hoagiesgifted.com/home_school.htm. Then
bookmark these popular sites:

- The History Channel: www.historychannel.com

- Math Forum Student Center:
  http://mathforum.com/students

- NASA: http://science.nasa.gov

- National Geographic: www.nationalgeographic.com

- National Science Foundation: www.nsf.gov

- Natural Math Website: www.naturalmath.com

- New York Times Learning Network:
  www.nytimes.com/learning/index.html

- Smithsonian Institution: www.si.edu

Key Curriculum Press

Publisher of *Miquon Math* (grades 1-3) and the *Key to...*
series (grades 4-12), as well as many other math materials, including manipulatives and CD-ROMs. *Miquon Math* is recommended for young math students who prefer a concept-based, visual approach to math. All four arithmetic operations and fractions are introduced the first year. Visit www.keypress.com for on-line scope and sequence.

The *Key to...* series includes Algebra, Decimals, Fractions, Geometry, Percents, Measurement, and Metric Measurement. Each workbook set follows the math topic from the simplest level to the complex, covering several grade levels in a single series. Answer keys are easy to use by students for independent study and self-evaluation. An on-line curriculum correlation key allows parents to match specific volumes to students' current needs.

The Logical Journey of the Zoombinis, published by Broderbund

A highly popular software program that allows young children to enjoy challenging logic problems, regardless of the child's reading level. Appropriate for the whole family, but enjoyed especially by ages six through 12. If you are going to buy only one educational CD-ROM, this is the one.

Math Blaster Software, published by Knowledge Adventure (and formerly by Davidson)

Widely available in toy stores, teacher supply stores, software stores, and libraries. These math software programs are available for grades K-6 and use a variety of computer game formats to make math fun.

Many children enjoy the older versions of the Math Blaster software, published by Davidson. Look for these discontinued CD-ROMs in your library or in clearance bins:

Math Blaster 1: In Search of Spot
Math Blaster 2: Secret of the Lost City
Math Blaster Algebra
Math Blaster Geometry

The Number Devil: A Mathematical Adventure, by Hans Magnus Enzensberger, translated by Michael Henry Heim, Henry Holt, 2000

This story of a boy's nightly dream encounters with the Number Devil explores math concepts and principles in a humorous and enchanting way. Mathematically precocious children as young as seven will enjoy hearing or reading this book. Look for it in your library, but you'll probably want a copy of your own to refer to again and again.

PBS

Public television's free, high-quality programming can be a valuable and enjoyable addition to a home school curriculum. Spend some time exploring the PBS Teacher Source web page for programming information, lesson plans and ideas, informative articles, and an e-mail Teacher Previews newsletter: www.pbs.org/teachersource.

In addition to children's programming, many home schooled children enjoy adult programs such as *NOVA*, *The New Americans* and, for older children, selected episodes of *Frontline*. Many of these shows offer free teacher guides either on-line or by mail. www.pbs.org

Public Library

Many home school parents use the library for nearly all of their curriculum needs. In addition to works of literature, you can also use your library for math and science books, biographies, history books, sheet music, video documentaries, foreign language tapes, books on tape, musical CDs, book discussion groups, and research skills. If your library does not already have a Home Schoolers' Book Shelf or program for home schoolers, offer to help your librarian get one started. See Chapter 7 for more ideas.

Right-Brained Children in a Left-Brained World, by Jeffrey Freed and Laurie Parsons, Fireside, 1998

Freed and Parsons describe the learning style of "right-brained" learners and explain how this learning style clashes with traditional classrooms. The book offers much practical advice for living with and teaching children who think in terms of pictures rather than words and who prefer the big picture to details. Contains a section on home schooling and several techniques for helping creative, visual thinkers to learn spelling, reading, math, and writing.

Rosetta Stone Foreign Language Programs

On-line and CD-ROM language learning software. Available for Spanish, French, German, English (U.S.), English (U.K.), Dutch, Danish, Portuguese, Italian, Latin, Russian, Polish, Welsh, Hindi, Arabic, Hebrew, Turkish, Chinese, Thai, Japanese, Vietnamese, Korean, Indonesian, and Swahili. Visit www.rosettastone.com for on-line demo and ordering.

Scholastic Book Clubs

Scholastic books clubs and software clubs are available to home educators, with bonus points for every item purchased and unbeatable prices. There is no sign-up fee or minimum purchase. Home school co-ops may wish to pool their orders and use the bonus points to start a home school reference lending library. www.scholastic.com/bookclubs/index.htm

Singapore Math

This national Singapore math curriculum encourages independent study and includes early introduction of high level concepts. Workbooks with simple colored illustrations are reasonably priced. Singapore Math has been used successfully with many visual-spatial learners. Note that currency is based on the Singapore dollar and coin system, and measurements are metric. Visit www.singaporemath.com for on-line samples and placement guide.

TAGMAX E-mail List

TAGMAX is an e-mail list for parents who are home schooling gifted children. The list is hosted by TAGFAM, Families of the Gifted and Talented. Messages are available in digest form as well as separate delivery. Volume ranges from a handful to several dozen messages daily. www.tagfam.org

The Well-Trained Mind: A Guide to Classical Education at Home, by Jessie Wise and Susan Wise Bauer, W. W. Norton, 1999

This 700+ page book is one of the most popular guides to classical home schooling, but parents who do not follow the classical education curriculum still find value in its extensive resource lists and teaching ideas. For example, the section on fifth-grade biology offers a list of all of the main topics to cover, from cell structures and classification to mammal reproduction and human senses. Parents can use these lists as flexible guides for planning their own home school curriculum. (Note: Parents of gifted and creative children will need to adapt classical home schooling to meet their children's unique needs.)

Writing Strands

Writing Strands is a writing program designed for home schoolers, with skill levels ranging from pre-kindergarten through high school. An on-line scope and sequence chart allows parents to choose the level appropriate for their child. Books on communications and interpersonal relationships, exposition, fiction, and evaluating writing are also available. This program is excellent for parents who are uncomfortable with guiding or evaluating their children's written and oral communication skills. Visit www.writingstrands.com for on-line sample pages and ordering.

Resources With Religious and Cultural Perspectives

Some home school families choose to educate their children at home in order to preserve and nurture the family's religious or cultural beliefs and heritage. Other home school families home school primarily as a way to meet academic, social, and emotional needs, but also include some home school materials that reflect their own religious or cultural viewpoints. Both kinds of families can get valuable ideas and support from other home school groups who share a particular religious faith or cultural background. Here are a few sources of information, materials, and support from a variety of perspectives.

African American

Afrocentric Homeschoolers Association
www.geocities.com/zingha

Freedom Challenge: African American Homeschoolers, by Grace Llewellyn, Lowry House, 1996.

National Black Home Educators Resource Association
www.christianity.com/nbhera

American Indian

Native American Homeschool Association Website
http://expage.com/page/nahomeschool

Catholic

Catholic Heritage Curricula
www.chcweb.com

Catholic Home School Network of America
www.chsna.org

Catholic Homeschool Support Website
www.catholichomeschool.org

Christian (Protestant)

The Elijah Company
www.elijahco.com

Greenleaf Press
www.greenleafpress.com

Sonlight Curriculum, Ltd.
www.sonlight.com

Islamic and Muslim

ArabesQ Services
www.arabesq.com

Palmetto Muslim Homeschool Resource Network
www.geocities.com/pmhrn_2000/PMHRN.html

Jewish

Jewish Home Educator's Network
www.snj.com/jhen

Jewish Home Schoolers Discussion List
www.geocities.com/Athens/Agora/7633/JewishHomeSchoolers.html

Multi-Cultural

A to Z Home's Cool Religion/Cultural Links Web Page
www.gomilpitas.com/homeschooling/religion/religion.htm

The Drinking Gourd Magazine (focus on multicultural home schooling)
P.O. Box 2557
Redmond, WA 98073
Phone: (800) TDG-5487

Minority Homeschool Discussion List
http://groups.yahoo.com/group/minorityhomeschool

Publishers, Manufacturers, and Suppliers

This listing includes all resources from this chapter that were marked with the symbol: *.

American Guidance Service
4201 Woodland Road
Circle Pines, MN 55014-1796
Phone (800) 328-2560
www.agsnet.com

Aristoplay, Ltd.
8122 Main Street
Dexter, MI 48130
Phone: (800) 634-7738
www.aristoplay.com

Binary Arts Corporation
1321 Cameron Street
Alexandria, VA 22314
Phone: (703) 549-4999
www.binaryarts.com

Books on Tape
P.O. Box 7900
Newport Beach, CA 92658
Phone: (800) 88-BOOKS
www.booksontape.com

Center for Gifted Education,
The College of William and Mary
P.O. Box 8795
Williamsburg, VA 23187-8795
Phone: (757) 221-2362
www.wmedu/education/nfgifted.htm

Cobblestone Publishing
30 Grove Street, Suite C
Peterborough, NH 03458
Phone: (800) 821-0115
www.cobblestonepub.com

Creative Publications
Wright Group/McGraw Hill
19201 120th Avenue NE, Suite 100
Bothell, WA 98011-9512
Phone: (800) 523-2371
www.wrightgroup.com

Critical Thinking Books & Software
P.O. Box 448
Pacific Grove, CA 93950-0448
Phone: (800) 458-4849
www.criticalthinking.com

Dale Seymour Publications
4350 Equity Drive
P.O. Box 2649
Columbus, OH 43216-2649
Phone: (800) 526-9907
www.pearsonlearning.com

Educators Publishing Service, Inc.
31 Smith Place
Cambridge, MA 02138-1089
Phone: (800) 435-7728
www.epsbooks.com

ETA/Cuisenaire
500 Greenview Court
Vernon Hills, IL 60061
Phone: (800) 445-5985
www.etacuisenaire.com

Evan-Moor Educational Publishing
18 Lower Ragsdale Drive
Monterey, CA 93940-5746
Phone: (800) 777-4362
www.evan-moor.com

Free Spirit Publishing
217 Fifth Avenue North, Suite 200
Minneapolis, MN 55401-1299
Phone: (800) 735-7323
www.freespirit.com

Gamewright
A Division of Ceaco, Inc.
124 Watertown Street
Watertown, MA 02472
Phone: (617) 924-6006
www.gamewright.com

Gifted Education Press
10201 Yuma Court
P.O. Box 1586
Manassas, VA 20108
Phone: (703) 369-5017
www.giftededpress.com

Great Potential Press (formerly Gifted Psychology Press)
P.O. Box 5057
Scottsdale, AZ 85261
Phone: (877) 954-4200
www.giftedbooks.com

Great Source Education Group
P.O. Box 7050
Wilmington, MA 01887
Phone: (800) 289-4490
www.greatsource.com

Half Price Books
5803 East NW Highway
Dallas, TX 75231
Phone: (800) 883-2114
www.halfpricebooks.com

Kendall/Hunt Publishing Company
4050 Westmark Drive
Dubuque, IA 52002
Phone: (800) 228-0810
www.kendallhunt.com

Key Curriculum Press
1150 65th Street
Emeryville, CA 94608
Phone: (800) 995-MATH
www.keypress.com

Learning Resources, Inc.
380 North Fairway Drive
Vernon Hills, IL 60061
Phone: (847) 573-8400
www.learningresources.com

Lewis Educational Games
Box 727
Goddard, KS 67052
Phone: (800) 557-8777
http://hometown.aol.com/dickwlewis/index.html

Libraries Unlimited
P.O. Box 6633
Englewood, CO 80155-6633
Phone: (800) 237-6124
www.lu.com

MindWare
121 5th Avenue NW
New Brighton, MN 55112
Phone: (800) 999-0398
www.mindwareonline.com

Out of the Box Publishing
P.O. Box 14317
Madison, WI 53714
Phone: (800) 540-2304
www.otb-games.com

Pearson Learning
4350 Equity Drive
P.O. Box 2649
Columbus, OH 43216-2649
Phone: (800) 526-9907
www.pearsonlearning.com

Pieces of Learning
1990 Market Road
Marion, IL 62959
Phone: (800) 729-5137
www.piecesoflearning.com

Prufrock Press
P.O. Box 8813
Waco, TX 76714-8813
Phone: (800) 998-2208
www.prufrock.com

Rainbow Resource Center
Rte. 1, Box 159-A
50 N. 500 East Street
Toulon, IL 61483
Phone: (888) 841-3456
www.rainbowresource.com

Resource Games
P.O. Box 151
Redmond, WA 98053
Phone: (800) 275-8818
www.resourcegames.com

Royal Fireworks Press
First Avenue
P.O. Box 399
Unionville, NY 10988-0399
Phone: (914) 726-4444

Scholastic, Inc.
555 Broadway
New York, NY 10012-3999
Phone: (888) 307-1555
www.scholastic.com

Set Enterprises, Inc.
15402 East Verbena Drive
Fountain Hills, AZ 85268
Phone: (800) 351-7765
www.setgame.com

Small World Toys
5711 Buckingham Parkway
Culver City, CA 90230
Phone: (310) 645-9680
www.smallworldtoys.com

SRA/McGraw Hill
220 East Danieldale Road
DeSoto, TX 75115
Phone: (888) SRA-4543
www.sra4kids.com

Sunburst Technology
101 Castleton Street
Pleasantville, NY 10570
Phone: (800) 321-7511
www.sunburst.com

Teacher Created Materials, Inc.
6421 Industry Way
Westminster, CA 92683
Phone: (800) 858-7339
www.teachercreated.com

Teacher Ideas Press
Libraries Unlimited
P.O. Box 6633
Englewood, CO 80155-6633
Phone: (800) 237-6124
www.lu.com/tips

Terrific Science Press
Miami University Middletown
4200 East University Blvd.
Middletown, OH 45042
Phone: (513) 424-4444
www.terrificscience.org

TLI Games
Gracie Station
P.O. Box 1119
New York, NY 10028
Phone: (800) 604-LINK
www.TLIgames.com

Turn Off the TV
P.O. Box 4162
Bellevue, WA 98009-4162
Phone: (800) 949-8688
www.turnoffthetv.com

University Games
2030 Harrison Street
San Francisco, CA 94110
Phone: (415) 503-1600
www.universitygames.com

Zephyr Press
P.O. Box 66006
Tucson, AZ 85728-6006
Phone: (800) 232-2187
www.zephyrpress.com

Adderholdt-Elliott, M. & Goldberg, J. (1999). *Perfectionism: What's bad about being too good.* Minneapolis, MN: Free Spirit Publishing.

Albert, D. (1999). *And the Skylark sings with me: Adventures in homeschooling and community-based education.* Gabriola Island, D.C.: New Society Publishers.

Amabile, T. (1989). *Growing up creative: Nurturing a lifetime of creativity.* New York: Crown.

Arizona Department of Education (2001). *Education of gifted students in Arizona: A guide to Arizona statutes, services, best practice, and resources.* Phoenix, AZ: Exceptional Student Services, Arizona Department of Education.

Aron, E. N. (1997). *The highly sensitive person: How to thrive when the world overwhelms you.* New York: Broadway Books.

Baker, J., Julicher, K., & Hogan, M. (1999). *Gifted children at home: A practical guide for homeschooling families.* Dover, DE: The Gifted Group Publishing.

Barbe, W. (1985) *Growing up learning: The key to your child's potential.* Washington, DC: Acropolis Books.

Baum, R. (1986). *The home schooling of Andrew Wyeth: A conversation with the artist.* Gifted Children Monthly, 7(5), 1-3, 13.

Betts, G. (1985). *The autonomous learner model for the gifted and talented.* Greeley, CO: Autonomous Learner Publications and Specialists.

Betts, G., & Kercher, J. (1999). *Autonomous learner model: Optimizing ability.* Greeley, CO: Autonomous Learner Publications.

Brostrom, D. (1995) *A guide to homeschooling for librarians.* Fort Atkinson, WI: Highsmith Press.

Cheatum, B. A & Hammond, A. A. (2000). *Physical activities for improving children's learning and behavior: A guide to sensory motor development.* Champaign, IL: Human Kinetics.

Clark, B. (1992). *Growing up gifted: Developing the potential of children at home and at school (4th ed.).* Upper Saddle River, NJ: Merrill/ Prentice Hall.

Clark, B. (1997). *Growing up gifted: Developing the potential of children at home and at school (5th ed.).* Upper Saddle River, NJ: Prentice Hall.

Clark, B. (2002). *Growing up gifted: Developing the potential of children at home and at school (6th ed.).* Upper Saddle River, NJ: Merrill/Prentice Hall.

Cloud, J. & Morse, J. (2001, August 27). *Home sweet school.* Time, 158(8), 46-54

Cohen, L. M. & Gelbrich, J. A. (1999). Early childhood interests: Seeds of adult creativity. In A.S. Fishkin, B. Cramond, & P. Olszewski-Kubilius (Eds.), *Investigating creativity in youth* (pp. 147-177). NJ: Hampton Press.

Csikszentmihalyi, M. (1996). *Creativity: Flow and the psychology of discovery and invention.* New York: HarperCollins Publishers.

Csikszentmihalyi, M. (1990). *Flow: The psychology of optimal experience.* New York: Harper & Row.

Delisle, J. R. (1992). Guiding the social and emotional development of gifted youth: A practical guide for educators and counselors. New York: Longman.

Dixon, J. (1983). *The spatial child*. Springfield, IL: Charles C. Thomas.

Dobson, L. (1998). *The homeschooling book of answers*. Roseville, CA: Prima Publishers.

Dobson, L. (2000). *Homeschoolers' success stories: 15 Adults and 12 young people share the impact that homeschooling has made on their lives*. Roseville, CA: Prima Communications.

Dobson, L. (2001). *The first year of homeschooling your child: Your complete guide to getting off to the right start*. Roseville, CA: Prima Communications.

Dreikurs, R. & Soltz, V. (1992). *Children: The challenge*. New York: Plume.

Drews, E. (1972). *Learning together: How to foster creativity, self-fulfillment, and social awareness in today's students and teachers*. Englewood Cliffs, NJ: Prentice-Hall.

Dunn, R., Dunn, K. & Perrin, J. (1994). *Teaching young children through their individual learning styles: Practical approaches for grades K-12*. Boston: Allyn and Bacon.

Dyer, W. W. (1985). *What do you really want for your children?* New York: Morrow.

Eby, J. & Smutny, J. (1990). *A thoughtful overview of gifted education*. New York: Longman.

Elkind, D. (1988). *The hurried child: Growing up too fast too soon*. Reading, MA: Addison-Wesley.

Elkind, D. (1989). An essential difference. In Noll (Ed.), *Taking sides: Clashing views on controversial educational issues (5th ed.)*, (pp. 197-206). Guilford, CT: Dushkin Publishing Group.

Elkind, D. (1987). *Miseducation: Preschoolers at risk*. New York: Knopf.

Ensign, J. (1997). *Homeschooling gifted students: An introductory guide for parents*. ERIC Document Reproduction Service Digest #E543.

Fern, T. L. (1991). Identifying the gifted child humorist. *Roeper Review*, 14(1), 30-34.

Fletcher, R. (1996). *A writer's notebook: Unlocking the writer within you*. New York: Avon Camelot.

Fletcher, R. (1999). *Live writing: Breathing life into your words*. New York: Avon Camelot

Fletcher, R. (2000). *How writers work: Finding a process that works for you*. New York: Harper Trophy.

Freed, J., & Parsons, L. (1997). *Right-brained children in a left-brained world: Unlocking the potential of your ADD child*. New York: Simon & Schuster.

Freeman, J. (1985). A pedagogy for the gifted. In J. Freeman (Ed.), *The psychology of gifted children: Perspectives on development and education* (pp. 1-22). New York: Wiley.

Gatto, J. T. (1992). *Dumbing us down: The hidden curriculum of compulsory schooling*. Philadelphia: PA: New Society Publishers.

Gleason, J. J. (1991). Developing a humor unit for the gifted. *Gifted Child Today*, 14(1), 60-61.

Griffith, M. (1996) *The homeschooling handbook: How to use the whole world as your child's classroom*. Roseville, CA: Prima Communications.

Griffith, M. (1998). *The unschooling handbook*. Roseville, CA: Prima Communications

Gross, M. (1993). *Exceptionally gifted children*. London: Routledge.

Guterson, D. (1992). *Family matters: Why homeschooling makes sense*. New York: Harcourt Brace Jovanovich.

Hallowell, E. M., & Ratey, J. J. (1995). *Driven to distraction: Recognizing and coping with attention deficit disorder from childhood through adulthood*. New York: Simon & Schuster.

Halsted, J. (2002). *Some of my best friends are books: Guiding gifted readers from preschool to high school (2nd ed.)*. Scottsdale, AZ: Great Potential Press (formerly Gifted Psychology Press).

Healy, J. (1998). *Failure to connect: How computers affect our children's minds—for better and worse*. New York: Simon & Schuster.

Henderson, K. (2001) *The young writer's guide to getting published*. Cincinnati, OH: Writer's Digest.

Hendrickson, B. (1995) *How to write a low cost/no cost curriculum for your home-school child*. Sitka, AK: Mountain Meadow Press

Hollingworth, L. S. (1927). Who are gifted children? *Child Study*, 5(2), 3-5.

Hollingworth, L. S. (1942). *Children above 180 IQ, Stanford-Binet origin and development*. Yonkers, NY: World Book.

Holt, D. G. (1996). Positively humorous: Teaching gifted middle school students to use positive humor to cope with stress. *Gifted Child Today*, 19(1), 18-21, 38-39.

Holt, J. (1983). *How children learn*. New York: Delacorte Press/Seymour Lawrence

Jacobsen, M. (1999a). Arousing the sleeping giant: Giftedness in adult psychotherapy. *Roeper Review*, 22(1), 36+.

Jacobsen, M. (1999b). *Liberating everyday genius: A revolutionary guide for identifying and mastering your exceptional gifts*. New York: Ballantine. (Published in 2000 under the title *The gifted adult: A revolutionary guide for liberating everyday genius*.)

John-Steiner, V. (1997) *Notebooks of the Mind: Explorations of Thinking*. New York: Oxford University Press.

Kearney, K. (1992, September/October). "Homeschooling Highly Gifted Children." *Understanding Our Gifted*, 5(1), 16.

Keirsey, D. (1998). *Please understand me II: Temperament, character, intelligence*. Del Mar, CA: Prometheus Nemesis.

Kerr, B. & Cohn, S. (2001). *Smart boys: Talent, manhood, and the search for meaning*. Scottsdale, AZ: Great Potential Press.

Kohl, H. (1994). *I won't learn from you and other thoughts on maladjustment*. New York: The New Press.

Kohn, A. (1993). *Punished by rewards: The trouble with gold stars, incentive plans, A's, praise, and other bribes*. Boston: Houghton Mifflin.

Kohn, A. (1999). *The schools our children deserve: Moving beyond traditional classrooms and "tougher standards."* Boston: Houghton Mifflin.

Kurcinka, M. (1991). *Raising your spirited child: A guide for parents whose child is more intense, sensitive, perceptive, persistent, energetic*. New York: HarperCollins

Langer, E. (1997). *The power of mindful learning*. Reading, MA: Addison-Wesley.

Leistico, Agnes (1990). *I learn better by teaching myself; and, still teaching ourselves*. New York: Henry Holt & Associates.

Liedloff, (1977). *The continuum concept: In search of happiness lost*. New York: Knopf.

LeShan, E. (1967). *The conspiracy against childhood*. New York: Athenaeum.

LeShan, E. (1974). *What makes me feel this way: Growing up with human emotions*. New York: Macmillan.

Lind, S. (Fall 2000). "Overexcitabilities and the Highly Gifted." *CAG Communicator*. Los Angeles: California Association for the Gifted, 31(4).

Llewellyn, G. (1996). *Freedom challenge: African-American homeschoolers*. Eugene, OR: Lowery House.

Llewyllen, G. (1998). *The teenage liberation handbook: How to quit school and get a real life and education*. Eugene, OR: Lowry House Publishing.

Lovecky, D. (1992a). Exploring social and emotional aspects of giftedness in children. *Roeper Review*, 15(1), 18-25.

Lovecky, D. (1992b). Standing on the shoulders of giants—Part II. *Understanding Our Gifted*, 5(1), 3.

Lovecky, D. (1993). *The quest for meaning: Counseling issues with gifted children and adolescents*. In L. Silverman (Ed.), Counseling the gifted and talented (pp. 29-50). Denver: Love Publishing.

Lowry, C. (1989). *Supporting and Facilitating Self-Directed Learning*. ERIC Document Reproduction Service Digest #E93.

Lynch, M. D., & Harris, C. R. (2001). *Fostering creativity in children, K-8: Theory and practice*. Boston: Allyn & Bacon.

Macmillan, B. (1986). "Home schooling: Is it right for you?"

Marcus, L. (2000). *Author talk: Conversations with Judy Blume…(et al)*. New York: Simon and Schuster Books for Young Readers.

Maslow, A. H. (1971). *The farther reaches of human nature*. New York: Viking.

Masters, D. G. (1996). *Public library services for home schooling*. (ERIC Document Reproduction Service Digest No. ED402936).

Maté, G. (1999). *Scattered: How attention deficit disorder originates and what you can do about it*. New York: Dutton.

Maxwell, E. (1997). "I can do it myself!" Reflections on early self-efficacy. *Roeper Review*, 20(3), 183-187.

Meckstroth, E. (1992) Nurturing resiliency in children: Integrating control and compliance. *Roeper Review*, Volume 14 (3), 166-167.

Miller, R. C. (1990). *Discovering mathematical talent.* ERIC EC Digest E482, ED 321 487.

Monson, J. A. (1994). Getting serious about humor: Using humor with students can lead to creative endeavors. *Gifted Child Today*, 17(5), 14-18, 40-41.

Moore, R. S., & Moore, D. N. (1979). *School can wait.* Provo, UT: Brigham Young University Press.

Morelock, M. J. (1996). On the nature of giftedness and talent: Imposing order on chaos. *Roeper Review*, 19(1), 4+.

NAGC (1998). *Pre-K – grade 12 gifted program standards.* Washington, DC: National Association for Gifted Children.

Piirto, J. (1998). *Understanding those who create (2nd ed.).* Scottsdale, AZ: Great Potential Press (formerly Gifted Psychology Press).

Piirto, J. (1999). *Talented children and adults: Their development and education.* Upper Saddle River, NJ: Merrill.

Reilly, J. (1992). *Mentorship: The essential guide for schools and business.* Scottsdale, AZ: Great Potential Press (formerly Ohio Psychology Press).

Rimm, S. (1997). *Dr. Sylvia Rimm's smart parenting: How to parent so children will learn.* New York: Crown Publishing.

Roeper, A. (1990). *Educating children for life: The modern learning community.* Monroe, TX: Trillium Press.

Roeper, A. (1992). Global awareness and the young child. *Roeper Review*, 15(1), 52.

Roeper, A. (1995). First encounter: A child is born, a self is born. *Roeper Review*, 18(2), 136-137.

Roeper, A. (1996). A personal statement of philosophy of George and Annemarie Roeper. *Roeper Review*, 19(1), 18.

Rogers, K. B. (2002). *Re-Forming gifted education: Matching the program to the child.* Scottsdale, AZ: Great Potential Press (formerly Gifted Psychology Press).

Rohwer, W. D. (1971). Prime time for education: Early childhood or adolescence? *Harvard Educational Review*, 41(3), 316-341.

Ronvik, R. (1993). Re-examining the foundations of giftedness. *Understanding Our Gifted*, 5(6), 1, 8-10.

Roth, M. (2001). Unschooling? School at home? Does it matter? *Home Education Magazine.* May-June 2001, 28.

Rowland, H. S. (1975) *No more school: An American family's experiment in education.* New York: Dutton.

Saunders, J. (1991). *Bringing out the best: A resource guide for parents of young gifted children.* Minneapolis, MN: Free Spirit Publishing.

Seuling, B. (1997). *To be a writer: A guide for young people who want to write and publish.* New York: Twenty-First Century Books.

Shade, R. A. (1996). Humor. *Gifted Child Today*, 22(1), 46+.

Shade, R. A. (1999). *License to laugh: Humor in the classroom.* Englewood, CO: Teacher Ideas Press.

Silverman, L. (1989). Perfectionism. *Understanding Our Gifted.* 1(3), 11.

Silverman, L. (1992). Social development or socialization? *Understanding Our Gifted*, 5(1), 15.

Silverman, L., & Freed, J. (1991). *Strategies for the visual-spatial learner.* Denver, CO: Gifted Development Center.

Silverman, L. (1998). Personality and learning styles of gifted children. In J. Van Tassel-Baska (Ed.), *Excellence in educating gifted and talented learners, 3rd edition* (pp. 29-65). Denver, CO: Love Publishing.

Smutny, J. F., Walker, S. Y, & Meckstroth, E. A. (1997). *Teaching young gifted children in the regular classroom: Identifying, nurturing and challenging Ages 4-9.* Minneapolis, MN: Free Spirit Publishing.

Starko, A. J. (1995). *Creativity in the classroom: Schools of curious delight.* New York: Longman.

Strip, C. (2000). *Helping gifted children soar: A practical guide for parents and teachers.* Scottsdale, AZ: Great Potential Press (formerly Gifted Psychology Press).

Tchudi, S. & Tchudi, S. (1984). *The young writer's handbook.* New York: Scribner.

Terrassier, J. (1985). Dyssynchrony—uneven development. In J. Freeman (Ed.), *The psychology of gifted children: Perspectives on development and education* (pp. 265-274). New York: Wiley.

Tolan, S. (1998). The lemming condition: Moral asynchrony and the isolated self. *Roeper Review*, 20(3), 211+

Torrance, E. P., & Goff, K. (1990). *Fostering academic creativity in gifted students.* ERIC Digest #E484.

Tucker, B. & Hafenstein, N. L. (1997). Psychological intensities in young gifted children. *Gifted Child Quarterly*, 41(3), 66-75.

Vail, P. L. (1979). *The world of the gifted child.* New York: Walker.

Van Tassel-Baska, J., Johnson, D. T., & Boyce, L. N. (1994). *A curriculum framework in language arts for high ability learners K-8.* Williamsburg, VA: College of William and Mary Center for Gifted Education.

Van Tassel-Baska, J. (1997). What matters in curriculum for gifted learners: Reflections on theory, research, and practice. In N. Colangelo and G. Davis (Eds.), *Handbook of gifted education (2nd ed.)* (pp. 126-135). Boston: Allyn and Bacon.

Vitale, B. (1982). *Unicorns are real: A right-brained approach to learning.* Rolling Hills Estates, CA: Jalmar Press.

Vygotsky, L. (1997). *Educational psychology.* Boca Raton, FL: Saint Lucie Press.

Webb, J. T. (1993). Nurturing Social-Emotional Development of Gifted Children. In K. A. Heller, F. J. Monks, & A. H. Passow (Eds.), *International handbook of research and development of giftedness and talent* (pp. 525-538). Oxford, MA: Pergamon Press.

Webb, J. T. (1994). *Nurturing social-emotional development of gifted children.* (ERIC Document Reproduction Service Digest No. E527).

Webb, J. T. (2000a). *Is my child gifted? If so, what can I expect?* VHS Video. Scottsdale, AZ: Great Potential Press (formerly Gifted Psychology Press).

Webb, J. T. (2000b, Spring). *Do Gifted Children Have Special Needs?* VHS Video. Scottsdale, AZ: Great Potential Press (formerly Gifted Psychology Press).

Webb, J. T. (2000c). *Parenting successful children.* VHS Video. Scottsdale, AZ: Great Potential Press (formerly Gifted Psychology Press).

Webb, J. T. (2001, Spring). "Mis-diagnosis and dual diagnosis of gifted children: Gifted and LD, ADHD, OCD, Oppositional Defiant Disorder." *Gifted Education Press Quarterly*, 15(2), 9-13.

Webb, J. T. (2002, Winter). "Cultivating Courage, Creativity and Caring." *Gifted Education Press Quarterly*, 19 (1), 2-8.

Webb, J. T., & DeVries, A. (1998). *Gifted parent groups: The SENG model.* Scottsdale, AZ: Great Potential Press (formerly Gifted Psychology Press).

Webb, J. T. & Kleine, P. (1993). *Assessing Gifted and Talented Children.* In J. L. Culbertson and D. J. Willis (Eds.), Testing young children (pp 383-407). Austin, TX: Pro-ed.

Webb, J. T., & Latimer, D (1993). *ADHD and Children Who Are Gifted.* ERIC EC Digest #522.

Webb, J. T., Meckstroth, E. A. & Tolan, S. S. (1982). *Guiding the gifted child: A practical source for parents and teachers.* Scottsdale, AZ: Great Potential Press (formerly Ohio Psychology Press).

West, T. G. (1997). *In the mind's eye: Visual thinkers, gifted people with dyslexia and other learning difficulties, computer images and the ironies of creativity.* Buffalo, NY: Prometheus Books.

Westphal, C. (2001). *A family year abroad: How to live outside the borders.* Scottsdale, AZ: Great Potential Press.

Whitmore, J. (1980). *Giftedness, conflict, and underachievement.* Boston: Allyn and Bacon.

Willings, D. (1980) *The creatively gifted: Recognizing and developing the creative potential.* Cambridge: Woodhead-Faulkner.

Winebrenner, S. (1992). *Teaching gifted kids in the regular classroom.* Minneapolis, MN: Free Spirit Publishing.

Winebrenner, S. (2000, Spring). What teachers, parents and administrators need to know about gifted students. *Gifted Education Press Quarterly.*

Winner, E. (1996). *Gifted children: Myths and realities.* New York: Basic Books.

Wise, J., & Bauer, S. (1999). *The well-trained mind: A guide to classical education at home.* New York: Norton.

Resource Index by Ability Level and Subject

Multi-Disciplinary

Science

Grades Four–Eight

Critical and Creative Thinking

Fine Arts and Foreign Languages

History and Social Sciences

Life Skills and Study Skills

Literature and Language Arts

Mathematics

Multi-Disciplinary

Science

Grades Nine–Twelve

Critical and Creative Thinking

Fine Arts and Foreign Languages

History and Social Sciences

Index

About the Author

Lisa Rivero, M.A., is a home school parent, writer, and gifted education and home schooling advocate. In her own primary education, Lisa attended a two-room grade school near her family's farm in rural South Dakota, where she learned to count by helping her grandfather keep track of the spring calves. After receiving her B.A. from Marquette University and M.A. from the University of Wisconsin-Milwaukee, Lisa taught college composition and technical composition for several years at the Milwaukee School of Engineering.

Lisa has been actively involved in education for over ten years and gifted education for four years. In addition to her teaching at The Milwaukee School of Engineering, she has taught adults in community center classes, as well as gifted elementary school students. She has served on her local school district's gifted and talented committee, and she edited the district's newsletter for parents of gifted students.

Her gifted education articles have been published in *Parenting for High Potential*, *Gifted Education Press Quarterly*, and the Wisconsin Association for Talented and Gifted newsletter, and her letters to the editor on the behalf of gifted home schoolers have appeared in *The Shepherd Express* and *Home Education Magazine*. Her first book, *Gifted Education Comes Home: A Case for Self-Directed Homeschooling*, was published by Gifted Education Press. Other freelance articles have been published in the *Milwaukee Journal* and *Vegetarian Gourmet*.

Lisa lives in Wisconsin with her husband and home schooled son. She started and leads a book discussion group for home schooled children and their parents, and she is an active member of her local home school community.